Applied Theology 3

'ONE NEW HUMANITY'

The Challenge of AIDS

GW00694487

SPCK International Study Guides

This SPCK series was originally sponsored and subsidized by the Theological Education Fund of the World Council of Churches in response to requests from many different countries. The books are inter-cultural, ecumenical and contextual in approach. They are prepared by and in consultation with theological tutors from all over the world, but have from the outset been as widely used by students and parish groups in the West as by those for whom English may be a second language. The text and pictures are regularly amended to ensure that both scholarship and relevance to contemporary issues are kept up to date. Fully revised editions are marked (R). Titles at a slightly more advanced level are marked (A).

IN PREPARATION

SPCK International Study Guide 33 (Advanced)

Applied Theology 3

'ONE NEW HUMANITY'

The Challenge of AIDS

Anne Bayley

First published in Great Britain 1996
Society for Promoting Christian Knowledge
Holy Trinity Church
Marylebone Road
London NW1 4DU

Unless otherwise stated the Scripture quotations
in this book are from the Revised Standard Version
of the Bible (Ecumenical Edition), copyrighted 1973,
the New Revised Standard Version, copyrighted
1989 by the Division of Christian Education of the
National Council of the Churches of Christ
in the USA, or in the Jerusalem Bible,
copyrighted 1966 by Darton,
Longman & Todd Ltd and
Doubleday and Company Ltd.

British Library Cataloguing-in-Publication Data
A catalogue record for this book is available from the
British Library

ISBN 0 281 04923 8
ISBN 0 281 04946 7 (special edition for Africa,
Asia, S. Pacific and Caribbean)

Typeset by Wilmaset Ltd, Birkenhead, Wirral
Printed in Great Britain by
The University Press, Cambridge

Contents

Illustrations

Author's Preface

Today prophets are more numerous in the United Nations Agencies, and in non-Governmental Organizations throughout the world, than in the Churches. These secular prophets draw attention – sometimes with panic – to overpopulation and critical damage to the physical resources (climate, water, plants, soil) on which human beings depend for survival. They warn that the rapidity of change, and its world-wide scale, threatens not just the well-being of human societies, but their actual survival. Amongst their urgent concerns AIDS is mentioned, but rarely receives the attention it deserves.

I understand the subject matter of theology to be all of reality – from the first beginning of all things to their final end – considered in relation to the mystery of God. I take seriously, therefore, a comment on secular prophets' fears: 'as things at present stand, there seems no chance of bringing off, within the necessary time scale, those comprehensive transformations of heart, and will, and institution, that healing of the world requires' (Nicholas Lash, *Concilium* 1994/6, (20). Lash notes that discussions about the future often end with 'unwarranted expressions of optimism ... The seldom quite explicit dialogue goes like this: "We will make out", "How so?" "Because the alternative is quite unthinkable" '.

The purpose of this book is to attempt to think 'the unthinkable' about AIDS – and then to search for signs of hope, instead of resting in 'unwarranted optimism'. My method will be to ask questions, to encourage readers to explore for themselves the range of questions to which AIDS gives rise. I shall describe how some local answers to specific questions have been developed, and point to strategies which have – in practice – yielded hope. But the most necessary strategy for facing AIDS is, it seems to me, willingness to *live* with questions, and not to be satisfied with premature solutions.

At an international AIDS meeting in 1992, Tom Tuma, a Ugandan priest, spoke of the effects of multiple deaths due to AIDS in his own society. Again and again he used the phrase: 'There is not much time'. He challenged his audience to use the 'reserve store' of human capability and energy to which we (generally) have access in times of emergency. AIDS reminds us that human health is fragile, life is short and uncertain and that large-scale epidemics are serious, even today.

The United Nations (UN) takes the AIDS crisis seriously. In January 1996 the Global Programme on AIDS (which was based in the World Health Organization) will be replaced by a new UN Joint and Co-sponsored Programme on AIDS/HIV, called UNAIDS. This new programme is intended to bring together the AIDS-related activities of no less than six UN agencies: the World Health Organization (WHO), the UN Children's Fund (UNICEF), the UN Development Programme (UNDP), the UN Educational, Scientific and Cultural Organization (UNESCO), the UN Population Fund (UNFPA) and the World Bank. The new head of the Co-sponsored Programme, Dr Peter Piot, will report directly to the UN Secretary General: a sign of the importance of the new Programme – and its subject, AIDS. I hope that the UN's Food and Agriculture Organization (FAO) and the UN Commission for Refugees (UNHCR) will be added to the other six agencies in the near future: FAO recently predicted a reduction in the world's food output as a result of AIDS.

This book attempts to describe, briefly and inadequately, how AIDS affects individual persons and the families and societies to which they belong, drawing attention to factors which influence the speed with which AIDS spreads, and its impact in developing countries. I have been pressed to set out a 'message', a 'grand idea', which summarizes what Christians 'should' be thinking or doing about AIDS. Many workers in the field have attempted to find such a central message, one which would fire the imaginations of peoples and provide a framework for discussion and action. The ideas which have been tried out were small at first and have grown larger.

The smallest concept was 'sexual health', but this idea left out too many important concerns. 'Human rights' was a more comprehensive idea, widening concern to include social and legal consequences of AIDS – but it was still too narrow to take account of economic and industrial effects, especially in developing countries, where the consequences of AIDS are reversing the gains (for example in child survival) which were achieved in the last thirty years. 'AIDS is a development issue' became the larger, yet more comprehensive message. It is still not large enough, in my opinion.

UNICEF, in an annual report on *The State of the World's Children, 1995* (43), pointed to a change in thinking which is gathering momentum all over the world, after starting about forty years ago. For thousands of years most societies have been organized for the benefit of small numbers of people at the top (rulers) rather than for the benefit of the majority (those who are ruled). Revolutions have only succeeded in shifting power from one small set of people to another equally small (and often equally oppressive) set of people, Moreover, despite the contrary evidence of the Gospels, this unbridgeable gap between 'unaccountable rulers and unconsenting ruled' was usually thought of as necessary – and even divinely approved.

Over the last forty years this principle has been challenged, with increasing success and with practical effects, in country after country around the world. Generally the challenges come from small groups of people, not from governments who tend to resist change. 'People-led' movements have grown as education and communication technologies expand, to give everyone a view of the gap between 'haves' and 'have nots' which was less visible in the past. Solidarity in distress and the ideal of 'human rights' have combined to give people more confidence to take a part in managing their own affairs. The scale of managing their own affairs is often limited (at first) to small projects, but thousands of small challenges to the system have had a cumulative effect: 'there is hardly a society in the world today where the idea of a class that is born to rule, an idea defended by moral philosophers and political leaders from Aristotle to Churchill, is accepted as right, normal or in the nature of things.' (UNICEF, *The State of the World's Children 1995*). Moreover, both developed and developing nations begin to see the inescapable *need* to co-operate, to tackle global problems which take no notice of international frontiers. But many international bodies and individuals consider that the struggle for a sustainable way of life has reached a critical stage, because changes in social priorities and practice, which are urgently needed, will be painful and will not produce visible benefits for those people who must make sacrifices. Indeed the long-term benefits will never be 'visible' – except as disasters (such as too-rapid population growth or extension of deserts or failure of crops) – that *could* have happened, but which were avoided by timely effort.

The only 'grand idea' which seems large enough for our situation is the creating of 'one new humanity in place of the two, thus making peace' (Eph. 2.15). Paul, writing to Christians in Ephesus, saw this peace as depending upon the death of Christ: 'For he is our peace; in his flesh he has made both groups into one and has broken down the dividing wall, that is, the hostility between us.' (Eph. 2.14). Caiaphas, who was High Priest in Jerusalem at the time, prophesied that Jesus would die 'for the nation, and not for the nation only, but to gather into one the dispersed children of God.' (John 11.51, 52). Never has it been more necessary for the 'dispersed children of God to be gathered into one' than it is now.

The model for this one new humanity is not any ideal human community, but the mutual indwelling of the Father, Son and Spirit – in the love which led to Jesus's death and procured His resurrection.

I thank the following people who by conversation, comment, hospitality or example have contributed to the making of this book. I remain responsible for all errors and omissions.

Donald Arden, John Austin, Mazuwa Banda, Bernard SSF, Kristina Baker, Michael Banner, Gerald Beauchamp, James Cairns, Ian Campbell, Christopher Conlon, Eularia Chilala, Mike Chirwa,

Patricia Chipipa, Miriam Duggan, Juston Daka, Alison Elliott, Susan Foster, John Gore, Judith Gutiwyo, Alan Haworth, Charlette Harland, John Jellis, Jane Jellis, Katele Kalumba, Pascal Kwapa, Violet Kunda, Michael Kelly, Ernest Katawheire, Mabel Katawheire, Elly Katabira, Agnes Kaddu, Amos Kasibante, Nkandu Luo, Chewe Luo, Graham Leonard, Susan Lucas, Imre Loefler, Maura Lynch, Margaret Malumo, Shirley Mills, Liz Mataka, members of the Matero Womens Group, Christopher Mutsinzi, Mercy Mbewe, Austin Mwale, Stephen Muhindo, Francis Mbaziira, Patricia Ndele, Edward Norman, Brian Zanji Njovu, Benjamin Nkowane, Paul Nunn, Dominic Nicol, Patricia Page, Connie Osborne, Desmond O'Loghlen, Samuel Okware, Anthony Pinching, Katherine Pinching, Rose Sunkutu, Mary Shilalukey-Ngoma, Max Singine, George Solami, Dorothy Sampaya, Danwell Simbeya, Ursula Sharpe, Dinis Sengulane, Ivan Semakula, Robert Schreiter, Sam Tusubira, Verna CHN, Susan White, Kelvin White, Glen Williams, John-Mary Walliggo, Robin Weiss, David Watters, Rose Zulu, Alimuddin Zumla, and finally the Benedictine Community of St Mary's Abbey, West Malling.

Anne Bayley

Editor's Note: The Plan and Use of this Book

Dr Bayley in her Preface has summarized the overall purpose and pattern of this book, highlighting its four Parts. These in turn describe the onset and nature of HIV/AIDS and its medical and social consequences; and consider the significance of AIDS in relation to other present-day crises, some specific problems facing individuals, families and societies in different areas, and finally the theological implications of the pandemic for Churches and Christians in the world as a whole.

It is based largely on the author's own knowledge and experience of working in some of the countries most severely affected by HIV infection and the consequent spread of AIDS, as well as drawing on reports published by WHO, UNICEF and other agencies on the current and likely future global situation.

Like earlier 'practical theology' volumes in the series, this one presents true stories and real-life 'case-studies' of people (here given fictitious names) and communities, distinguished from the rest of the text by a vertical rule at left of the page. These illustrate the many sorts of circumstances confronting pastoral counsellors and 'carers', and give practical guidance for interpreting local needs and finding ways of meeting them.

Study Suggestions

Questions and suggestions for research and discussion (distinguished by an enclosing 'box') appear within and at the ends of certain chapters. These are intended to help readers to check and understand clearly what they have read, and especially to relate the ideas and issues raised to their own experience and situation. The suggestions include questions for study and discussion by groups, which should wherever possible include both men and women, and students of other disciplines besides theology and medicine. AIDS calls for responses from every section of society, and theology related to AIDS needs to be grounded in experience. Readers will find it helpful to make and keep up to date fact and resource files to record the results of local investigations and suggestions.

Bibliography and Further Reading

The Bibliography, Appendix A, p. 311, lists not only the details of books, articles and reports quoted or referred to (identified by bracketed number) in the text, but also those recommended for further reading (likewise indicated by bracketed number) as follow-up to certain chapters.

Definitions and Glossary

The nature of much of the information given necessitates use of 'technical' and other specialist terms, in Part 1 especially where appropriate definitions have been grouped together and distinguished by a rule above and below. They also appear, along with some other words and phrases needing special elucidation, in Appendix B, the Glossary and Abbreviations.

Resources

Details are given in Appendix C, of sources for reliable new information and educational materials about AIDS and AIDS-related issues, with special reference to developing countries, and combined with responsible comment. Some of the organizations listed are able to offer pamphlets, posters etc. free or at subsidized prices.

Bible Versions

The English translations of the Bible quoted are the Revised Standard Version (Ecumenical Edition), the New Revised Standard Version and the Jerusalem Bible.

Index

The combined Index includes proper names of people and places, and the main subjects considered in the book.

Acknowledgements

The illustrations are reproduced by permission of Churchill Livingstone (p. 16); Oxford University Press (for UNICEF, Statistical Tables in *The State of the World's Children*, 1965, p. 18): Scottish AIDS Monitor (p. 33); Dr Afzal Amsary, Medical Illustration Department, University Teaching Hospital, Lusaka (p. 66); The World Health Organization *Global Programme on AIDS* (p. 68); and the author herself.

Grateful thanks for permission to quote extensive material are also due to Faber & Faber Ltd (from T. S. Eliot's *Four Quartets*); New City (from Olivier Clement's *The Roots of Christian Mysticism*); and SCM Press Ltd (from Vincent Donovan's *Christianity Rediscovered*, 1982; C. F. D. Moule's *The Phenomenon of the New Testament*, 1987; and (with Orbis) John V. Taylor's *The Go-Between God*, 1972).

PART 1

WHAT IS AIDS?

CHAPTER 1
Questioning the Questions

'In the noontide of my days I must depart' (Isaiah 38.10)

The words are attributed to Hezekiah, King in Jerusalem at the end of the seventh century BCE, but the thought is familiar to any man or woman who learns that he or she has AIDS. Today the four letters AIDS, standing for 'Acquired Immune Deficiency Syndrome,' (or in French SIDA) are known world-wide.

Yet early in 1982 this acronym did not exist, and AIDS was known by experience to only a few puzzled doctors and a few hundred sick people. Thirteen years later AIDS is viewed with concern by most governments (or should be) and it threatens to delay or prevent essential development in many countries of Africa, Asia and South America.

The World Health Organization (WHO) estimated in December 1994 that around 18 million adults and 1.5 million children throughout the world have been infected with the virus which causes AIDS since the late 1970s, and at least 40 million *will* be infected by the year 2000. Many observers fear that the true number will be much nearer to 110 million. Few HIV-infected people will live out a normal life-span, even though each year thousands of scientists, economists, politicians and people who are personally affected meet to share new knowledge about AIDS.

Why and how has this situation come about, and why is it reasonable to demand special attention for *one* disease, AIDS, amongst the thousands of diseases which afflict human beings?

IMPACT OF AIDS: A PERSONAL STORY
'AIDS is about sex and death together and is loaded with the combined weight of their significance for us', said an anthropologist at a Conference on AIDS in 1988. AIDS is also about a great deal of loss: loss of self-image, health, work, home, status, friends or family, and loss of control of one's destiny – even before a final loss of control in death.

Very few people can 'study' AIDS in a neutral way, without becoming deeply and personally involved, either willingly or unwillingly. I was drawn in before I knew what was happening to me: I remember vividly the final moment of commitment during a visit to Uganda in 1985.

In Lusaka in Zambia, two years earlier, I had watched a change in the behaviour of a disease called Kaposi's sarcoma, which I thought I knew well. In 1983 new patients with this disease were more numerous

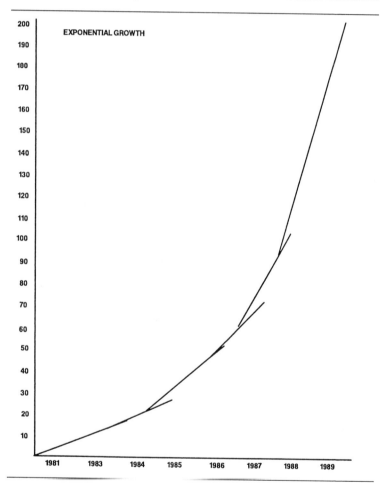

Figure 1. Exponential Growth: Numbers of new patients with HIV-related Kaposi's Sarcoma in a Lusaka clinic 1981 to 1989 (records for 1988 were excluded because incomplete). For explanation of 'exponential' see Glossary.

2

and younger than expected and became sick more rapidly, with signs of disease I had never seen before. They responded to standard treatment at first – but not for long, so that most died in a few months, instead of surviving many years, as in the past. For me, the experience was rather like leaving docile cattle in an enclosure one night and finding they had turned into a herd of buffalo by next morning: I felt fear.

During 1983 to 1985 I plotted numbers of patients with the new form of disease every three months, as doctors in the United States were doing for their new patients with AIDS. I soon noticed, uneasily, that my graph had the same steep slope as theirs. Absolute numbers at this stage were very small: only 13 patients with the new form of Kaposi's sarcoma in 1983, 24 in 1984 and 40 in 1985 – but exponential curves rise alarmingly in ten years.

In 1984 I visited Washington in the USA, where I talked with another doctor who treated people with AIDS; I remember a brief moment when we looked across the room, silently reading fear of the unknown in each others' eyes – before looking away, too disturbed to share our thoughts. In those days few people wanted to listen to our anxieties about exponential curves and I tended to dismiss my hidden concern as an over-dramatic reaction to unusual events.

In May 1985 I visited Kampala in Uganda, to examine medical students at Makerere University. Colleagues asked if I would go with them to Rakai district, where a wasting disease, called 'Slim' by the local people, was responsible for a disturbing number of deaths. Neither traditional nor Western medicine could cure 'Slim' and no-one knew the cause. My friends asked if it could be connected with the new form of Kaposi's sarcoma I had reported from Lusaka.

We travelled to south-west Uganda and spent Saturday afternoon visiting a clinic to see two patients, and a country town where we saw one sick man in a darkened room behind his boarded-up store. As strangers in the town, we were surprised and disturbed to be stopped in the street by a man who asked: 'How can I avoid getting Slim?'

Next morning we went to Masaka hospital, where the medical superintendent had admitted four patients with 'Slim' in one ward. It was the first time I had seen young men and women who looked so prematurely aged; in their weakness, wasting and apathy, they reminded me of photographs of Nazi concentration camp victims in 1945. While my Ugandan colleagues questioned and examined these patients I walked down the ward, idly satisfying my doctor's curiosity about other doctors' work. Very soon I suspected that there were far more than four patients with HIV infection in that ward.

We revised our plans for the day and decided to examine consecutive patients throughout the hospital. One of us walked round the wards looking carefully at every patient – and also at Sunday-morning-visitors at each bedside – feeling each neck for lumps and examining each throat by torch-light. Amongst 109 people examined in this way, we found 29 who had suspicious signs; all these people agreed to have a fuller physical examination and a blood test. All 29 people selected, whether patients or visitors, had signs of HIV infection in their blood.

On my return to Kampala I found it difficult to concentrate on medical students' examinations and it was equally difficult to attend to my ordinary duties when I went back to Lusaka. I could not remove from my imagination the image of the young men and women who were dying of AIDS, and I felt personally involved in the tragedy which lay ahead for a society where one in four young adults already showed signs of HIV infection.

THE NATURE OF AIDS

AIDS is an infectious disease caused by the human immunodeficiency virus (HIV), which is too small to be visible using an ordinary laboratory microscope. HIV is passed from person to person through the exchange of body fluids, which happens most often during a popular activity which is necessary for the survival of the human race: sexual intercourse.

Unlike other diseases which are transmitted in the same way, infection with HIV is not followed in a few days by obvious local signs, such as an ulcer or a discharge from the genital organs. Some people suffer a brief feverish illness soon after infection which suggests malaria or influenza (depending on where they live), but few suspect a sexually-transmitted disease. However, about one week after exposure, anyone infected with HIV becomes infectious to others and remains infectious for the rest of their life.

HIV infection is permanent because normal human defences against disease-producing invaders are ineffective against HIV, at least in the long term and in most people. As natural immunity appears not to develop, some scientists are pessimistic about the benefits which might be expected even if a safe vaccine is developed in the future. Economists and health planners are pessimistic too: they fear that any vaccine would be far too expensive for countries with small health budgets and scattered populations – the very places where AIDS is already common.

HIV infection is the health equivalent of treachery within the defence force of a state. It causes a hidden, slowly progressive breakdown of control of the immune system which should defend the body against invasion by disease-producing organisms. All body systems have large reserves of capacity, so the effects of HIV on the human defence system may not be visible for between two to ten years in adults, though babies usually become ill much sooner. Throughout this period of apparently normal health, infected persons can pass HIV on to others in three ways: by sexual intercourse, whether heterosexual or homosexual; from mother to child during pregnancy or in the early weeks of life; and by blood-to-blood contact – through transfusion, re-use of unsterilized needles by intravenous drug-users or medical staff, or use of unsterile knives or razors in traditional medicine (*scarification**). HIV is *not* passed on by normal social contacts such as sharing meals or shaking hands.

Months to years after the onset of HIV infection, the immune system becomes too inefficient to prevent invasion of the body by certain micro-organisms*. Infections result which can affect any body system: skin, mouth, throat, lungs, gut, brain and other internal organs. At first most illnesses are quite minor and respond well to treatment, but later increasingly serious infections or tumours* occur which threaten life unless well treated. Later still, wasting and weakness, a failing memory and sometimes slowness of thought or confusion show that death is near. Death is usually due to a severe infection which fails to respond to antibiotics*.

EARLY SPREAD OF HIV

In many societies HIV began to spread steadily, but unobserved, in the late 1970s. At first few people had been infected long enough to be visibly ill, and there were no tests to detect infection in apparently fit persons. When tests became available later, stored blood samples showed that infection was very rare in Zaire, Zambia and Uganda prior to 1980 (fewer than 1 in 100 samples were positive) but by 1985, when reliable tests were used for the first time on fresh blood samples in Zambia, 8% of women attending a Lusaka antenatal clinic were HIV-infected.

In 1985 many scientists were still unwilling to accept the unwelcome idea that HIV passes from person to person during normal heterosexual intercourse. It was another two years before the governments of even severely-affected countries were willing to authorize health education to warn their populations that AIDS is both dangerous and sexually transmitted. Two more years passed before enough people were visibly ill (even in the most heavily-affected countries) to persuade their neighbours to believe that AIDS is real – and to begin to change their sexual behaviour. By 1993, therefore, 36% of pregnant women sampled at antenatal clinics in Lusaka were infected with HIV, and similar infection rates are reported from many other African cities.

At this level of infection in a society (for each HIV-infected woman implies the existence of an HIV-infected man) *every* sexually active person is at risk, and the chance of exposure to HIV is high in any sexual relationship which is not strictly monogamous*. In such socie-

5

ties, one out of every three potential partners is likely to be infected, and the risk may be greater: more than 80% of women who sell sex in some countries are HIV-infected.

In the past, sex with more than one partner had some biological advantages: it helped to ensure wide distribution of favourable inherited characteristics and the birth of many children after natural disasters or war had reduced the size of human populations. Now, sex with more than one partner has serious biological disadvantages, for men as well as for women, because it is the principal means by which the AIDS epidemic is maintained and extended. For as long as every infected person passes HIV on to one other man or woman before dying, the epidemic will continue. If each infected individual (on average) passes on the virus to *more* than one other person the epidemic will continue to expand as it has expanded during the last fourteen years. The epidemic will die out only slowly, over at least two generations, when (on average) *not* every infected person passes on the infection to someone else before he or she dies.

CAN AIDS BE TREATED?

There are useful treatments for many of the secondary illnesses which result from the breakdown of immune defences, but all treatments gradually become less effective as the defence system fails. There are no drugs capable of curing the underlying HIV infection, in the sense of eliminating HIV from the body permanently, and it is not likely that this will ever be possible, because of the nature and behaviour of HIV and the failure of the human body to defend itself against this virus.

HIV is too incomplete and too fragile to survive for long outside the body, but it ensures a long-term home for itself by becoming part of the permanent structure of each infected cell. It does this by hijacking cell 'workshops' in which copies of the genetic blueprint* are normally made, and demanding copies of itself instead. The virus then uses a chemical messenger to break into the molecules* which carry genetic information within the nucleus (or control centre) of infected cells, in order to insert these copies of itself. As a result, whenever an infected cell reproduces itself or manufactures chemicals needed for normal cell functions, it is forced to make new copies of HIV too. These new HIV particles are set free to enter uninfected cells in their existing host or to be passed on, through close contact between HIV-infected (cells in semen, vaginal secretions or blood) and the thin skin lining the sexual passages of an uninfected person.

MEDICAL, SOCIAL AND ECONOMIC COSTS OF AIDS

A few drugs have been made which slow down the production of new HIV particles, and thus reduce the rate of damage to the defence system, so prolonging the active lives of infected persons. Drugs do not prevent damage to the defence system indefinitely, however, and though benefits are real there are also side-effects to treatment. The active drugs are so expensive that even rich countries are alarmed at the costs of treating quite small numbers of HIV-infected persons. Where health budgets are small, as in most developing countries, and where nearly a third of urban adults are already infected, the cost of treatment with existing drugs seems to be – and actually is – impossibly high. But the cost of drugs to treat large numbers of chronically ill people is not the only economic or social cost of HIV infection.

The economic and social consequences of AIDS vary remarkably from country to country. Contrasts are so great that well-informed citizens of London or New York cannot imagine the consequences of AIDS in Kampala or Lusaka. Citizens of Dar es Salaam or Harare have equal difficulty in understanding that the situation they recognize with horror in their own homes and streets is *not* the same in every other affected city worldwide. What are the reasons for these large differences?

Many factors influence the impact of AIDS on a particular society, but *three* are of major importance: the *age-structure* of the society concerned, the nature and number of *other problems* experienced by that society, and the main *way or ways in which HIV spreads* from person to person. The first two we shall discuss in ch. 2. At this stage it is enough to point out that the age-structure of a population determines the numbers of sexually-active persons at risk of infection and the average number of orphans who will need care if their parents die prematurely.

Civil war, external debt and structural adjustment programmes, drought and food shortages, refugees, a lowly social status for women, underdeveloped and underfunded health-care systems, unemployment and poverty may not appear to have a direct bearing on the consequences of one particular sexually-transmitted infection. But as I shall show, every one of these factors affects the ways in which AIDS damages and challenges societies.

During the early years of AIDS, in the West, HIV spread from person to person most often through male homosexual acts or needles shared by intravenous drug-users, while in developing countries the most common mode of infection was through heterosexual contact. As a result, the earliest Western epidemic affected mainly men, and became associated with gay communities and drug-users – both groups somewhat separate from the larger societies within which they live, and both already subject to disapproval from their communities. In contrast, in most developing countries, men and women were infected in almost equal numbers in the *general* population, not in semi-closed sub-groups within it.

In every region or society where AIDS appears, the social, cultural, economic and medical factors which influence the spread of HIV and the effects HIV infection has on peoples' lives, are obviously – or subtly – different. Observers need to record and reflect upon these differences as a basis for understanding and responding appropriately to the specific demands made by each local and unique part of the AIDS epidemic. At present there are not enough descriptions of the unique features of AIDS in different societies: as a result, descriptions and predictions in this book can only be provisional. Moreover, the epidemic is still spreading into new areas of the world and its consequences are still developing.

This book attempts to describe and comment upon the impact of AIDS, as a global concern, from the neglected viewpoint of developing countries, rather than from the perspective of privileged Western nations. But I hope to show that the insights and responses of every country faced with AIDS are of interest elsewhere and that creative ideas are worth exporting.

FAMILY CONSEQUENCES OF AIDS IN DEVELOPING COUNTRIES

In countries where HIV is chiefly spread by heterosexual contact, most people are infected early in their sexual lives. As a result, many infected women become seriously ill in their mid-twenties while men fall ill slightly later, at around thirty years. Neither men nor women fulfil their economic or reproductive potential; men die or stop work through illness 20 years before normal retirement age, and male impotence or female infertility stop child-bearing before families are complete.

Both parents often die within a year or two of each other, leaving a family of four or more children aged between four and 15 years. Usually these children are not infected with HIV because they were born before either parent was infected, and HIV is not passed from person to person by shared family life. However, children suffer a great deal during the long illnesses of both parents, and may be feared or avoided because of the way in which their parents died. Although, in the past, extended families cared for orphans in most developing countries, it is unusual for families to be able to cope with the demands of the new situation without help – for several members of the same young-adult generation often die as a consequence of AIDS, leaving several groups of young orphans, all needing support simultaneously. Old people try to carry the burden, but cannot be expected to care efficiently for a dozen or more children, as some Ugandan, Tanzanian and Zambian grandparents are attempting to do in the 1990s – even if this task was not made even more difficult by unemployment, drought and the effects of structural adjustment programmes and world recession.

HISTORICAL PERSPECTIVES

Other epidemics in history caused the deaths of large numbers of people; for example, about one third of the population of Europe probably died from plague (the Black Death) in the fourteenth century. However, these epidemics differed from AIDS in several important respects. First, disease usually started rapidly and suddenly, allowing little time for sick people to pass infection to others before death. Moreover, infected persons were easy to recognize and unable to take part in daily life, so contact with them could be avoided. Secondly, it was unusual for healthy young adults to be the main targets for infection: most often the more vulnerable young children or old people fell ill and died – and they could be replaced, or had already reproduced. Thirdly, natural geographical or cultural barriers limited contacts between separate societies, which helped to ensure that the effects of an epidemic did not extend world-wide: for example, less than a hundred years ago there were no trucks or jumbo-jets to carry infected people from country to country or from continent to continent. Finally, the terminal illness in an epidemic infectious disease was usually brief, so that there was no need to care for chronically sick people for months or years. Eventually such epidemics came to an end so that normal life could go on, even though social circumstances had changed.

No one knows what long-term effects to expect in societies which have to care for many members who are chronically ill, where almost every family is affected, and when those who are actually sick ought be the most vigorous and productive members of society. Moreover, the impact of AIDS is certain to *increase* for at least another twenty years. How will people respond to combined personal, economic and social stresses of uncertain duration? We do not know. Neither do we know what long-term effects to expect in the lives of children who grow up in such abnormal circumstances.

COMMUNITY REACTIONS TO AIDS

Jonathan Mann, the first director of the WHO Global Programme on AIDS (GPA), once said that every person or community goes through three stages of reaction to AIDS: first denial that there *is* a problem, next minimization of the extent of that problem, and finally constructive engagement with it.

But constructive responses develop slowly, as more and more consequences of HIV infection become visible in persons and societies, and as observers and decision-makers allow themselves to see evidence they do not want to see, and to draw from it conclusions which they would prefer not to understand. It was inevitable, for example, that a sexually transmitted infection would be shared between marriage partners, and that if one died, the other might do so later; moreover, if both parents were aged around 30 years when this happened, then young children would be orphaned. Yet few planners allowed themselves to see this consequence at first and as late as 1989 it was thought unnecessary and offensive to talk about 'orphans' in one severely-affected country. Fortunately, Uganda allowed numbers of orphans to be studied from 1989 onwards; by 1991 about 40,000 children had already lost one or both parents in the Rakai district, which has a total population of only 350,000. Not all bereavements were due to AIDS, but this was a common reason.

Similarly, in Lusaka, where both cemeteries were enlarging steadily by 1990, no-one wanted to discuss urgently-needed expansion of mortuary facilities. By 1992 plans for a new mortuary were made at last, but by that time local people regarded the teaching hospital as a transit lounge on the way out of life, and called it, with grim humour, 'Heathrow'.

In 1990 it was still difficult to focus attention on the idea that the numbers of students entering medical, paramedical and nursing training ought to be increased. Yet more staff will be needed in the near future to provide care for more sick people. In addition, when one-third of adults in a city are HIV-infected it is probable that a third of young trainees drawn from that city are HIV-infected too – and they will not give the same long years of service as their uninfected colleagues.

The same line of reasoning applies to other professional and vocational groups: farmers, industrialists, engineers, miners, teachers, police, bankers, civil servants, lawyers, Church leaders – all should expect to lose a quarter to a third of their number, on average twenty years before normal retirement age. For developing nations these losses represent a huge loss of investment in education. For example, university teachers need eight to ten years of tertiary education, yet an HIV-infected lecturer may contribute to academic life for only two or three years before his or her death at 35 years of age.

WOMEN AND AIDS

The AIDS epidemic bears heavily on women in two ways: first, for social and biological reasons, HIV passes more easily from men to women than in the reverse direction. Second, a disproportionate share of the burden of response to AIDS falls upon women.

In most societies men expect to take the initiative and make the choices in sexual relationships and women have no permission or only a limited right to say 'no'. Small girls are expected to be submissive and they learn to be 'carers' long before consciousness of self develops. Later, partly learned but partly innate roles are reinforced by teaching about sexual life which emphasizes a woman's obligation to please men and ignore her own wishes. Young women are vulnerable, therefore, to pressures from sexually-experienced men older than themselves and particularly to middle-aged 'sugar daddies' with money, who search for 'safe' sexual partners amongst virgins. Many girls are expelled from school when pregnant and do not complete their education – and some are infected with HIV in their mid-teens.

Many women do not question their role in society until already heavily involved as wives and mothers. When a woman starts to ask questions, her culture's expectations, the demands of her own children, a labour-intensive economy, low salaries and inadequate housing often combine to ensure that she is economically dependent upon her partner. In these circumstances she may tolerate her husband's sexual infidelity (a technical term, not a moral judgement), through low self-esteem and for practical reasons, although she knows the result of his affairs may be HIV infection for herself and for unborn children.

There can be no 'good' outcome to pregnancy for an HIV-infected woman. If she transmits HIV to her child, unknowingly and unwillingly, then she has to watch that child fall ill, suffer months of misery and in the end die, feeling that she is responsible. But if her child is one of the two-thirds of babies who escape infection, she may feel wretched and guilty in another way when, a few years later, she falls ill herself and worries about what will happen to her children after she dies.

When a marriage or relationship breaks down, many women are left with responsibility for rearing children but without an income. Few women recognize their marketable talents or have the confidence to find and hold employment. Some women find another permanent partner quickly, but others drift or are forced by poverty and lack of hope into selling sex, which is always a marketable commodity. An infected woman who is caught in that way of life spreads HIV as long as she can work, and she and her children are likely to suffer need and neglect when she becomes too ill to attract customers.

There is still some uncertainty about the effect of pregnancy on the rate of breakdown of the immune system, although there is no doubt that for some women progression to serious illness is accelerated. Over a third of babies of HIV-infected African women acquire HIV before or after birth, although in Western countries the risk of infection for the baby appears to be lower. This may reflect a lower risk of passing on HIV during a pregnancy in the early stages of infection, with an increasing risk at a later stage of illness; pregnant women in developing countries are more likely than Western women to have been infected several years ago.

Finally, when anyone is ill, whether the sick person is a parent, child or spouse, women are expected to provide care and rarely challenge this expectation. They merely add a new responsibility to their other tasks of child-care, homemaking, subsistence farming or paid employment, and struggle on for as long as they can, ignoring their own exhaustion or ill-health. In most cultures sick persons are subordinate to healthy people, so to be a sick woman is to be doubly at a disadvantage.

AIDS AND CHURCH LIFE

Church leaders and congregations, like most people, usually deny that there is any problem when they first encounter AIDS. When the impact of HIV infection on society and Church life becomes difficult to ignore, Christians are likely to feel overwhelmed by the situation. At first sight the most difficult questions centre around sexual morality: how should Christians react to government health education programmes which recommend use of condoms and presuppose adulterous relationships, which it was possible to overlook in the past? Should Sunday school and catechism teaching mention AIDS and the ways HIV is spread? How should organizations such as the Family Life movement respond? Sexuality has been a difficult topic for the Church at least since Paul wrote to Christians in Corinth in 57 CE, and it is no less difficult now.

PRACTICAL CARE

Care for HIV-affected families is seen to be a large and growing need. There are more sick persons to visit in their homes, more funerals to conduct and more widows and orphans to care for.

Some sick people are confused, slow to think and speak, and have poor memories for recent events. Family disputes occur over the property of deceased members who did not make a will; there may be no-one willing to organize a funeral or to support orphans and old people. Who is responsible? Both families and medical professionals who care for the sick are exhausted, and so are pastors with an inescapable and enlarging workload. The emergency does not end, and gradually pastors and their people realize that it will not end for at least two generations.

DISCERNMENT

New problems require discernment and the most fundamental question is this: are HIV-infected persons outcasts, or are they still 'people like us'? What if one of 'us Christians' should learn that they have AIDS? What shame! How shall we hide the truth? At present many men and women in affected countries die from tuberculosis or pneumonia, and no-one asks awkward questions. In Britain some priests and religious who are HIV-infected telephone an AIDS chaplain anonymously in the middle of the night, because they urgently need someone to talk to and dare not confide in other clergy or members of their own religious orders.

In every culture some traditional beliefs and practices offer support to HIV-infected people and their families, but other traditions need to be questioned. For example, is it good to continue funeral customs which require many relatives to travel long distances and to be fed for several days by the bereaved family? Could respect for a dead person be shown, and contact with the ancestors maintained – but in less costly ways?

In many cultures people are reluctant to talk about sexual matters, while it is often assumed (without question) that sexual play is a legitimate recreation for men but not for women. Now it is time to question traditions about sexual behaviour.

The place of children in human life needs thought too. Can a woman or a man who has no children, living or dead, be regarded as a whole person? What other role *could* a woman have in society, except to be a mother? Are celibate persons whole human beings – or intrinsically deformed? And should unmarried, divorced or separated persons be expected to abstain from all genital sexual activity? Is it possible for a man's sexual needs to be satisfied by relations with his wife alone or does his health and sanity require that he has other partners? There are many questions which urgently need answers.

LIVING WITH QUESTIONS

Most people expect answers to questions (particularly from a textbook) and become anxious when authors ask questions but provide few answers, especially when readers' hidden presuppositions and prejudices are exposed and questioned too.

Not all the questions posed by AIDS concern practical matters of teaching, discernment or care for the needy. Men and women who are suffering ask urgent and basic questions about the meaning of their lives, whether or not they hold traditional religious beliefs. At first, when a diagnosis of HIV-infection has been heard recently, most people ask: 'Why did this happen to me?' or 'Why should an innocent baby suffer?' or 'Is AIDS a punishment for sexual sins?' Many people, Christian or not, ask: 'Where does evil come from?' or 'How can I believe that God is good if he allows AIDS to exist?' Anger is an almost universal early reaction: anger against a spouse or lover who is blamed as the source of infection, or anger with oneself over behaviour which risked exposure, irrational anger with other people because they are still healthy, and anger with God for the 'way the world is'.

Later, when sickness begins and thinking about death cannot be avoided, both believers and unbelievers ask: 'What *is* death?' and: 'Is there indeed life after death?' People who have no living children ask:

'Who will remember me when I join the ancestors?' and feel guilty because they have broken the chain of life and failed in duty to their families. They may feel great bitterness and mourn for children who died or were never born: 'Am I fully human if I have no children? Why do human beings exist at all? Does their life have any meaning? Where is God in this mess? What kind of a God do we believe in?' Often there seems to be no end to questions.

At any time in the long period between knowledge of HIV infection and death, Christians ask: 'How *can* the gospel be good news for me, if I am HIV-infected?' or 'What is there to hope for when I shall die before I am forty and leave my young family alone?' Many men and women cry out: 'My God, my God, why have you forsaken me?'

QUESTIONING THE QUESTIONS

Perhaps we ask the wrong questions. Perhaps we are mistaken in seeing AIDS only as a problem when we could see it as a gift as well as a problem. In 1987 an unidentified staff member at the Ministry of Health in Lusaka returned a manuscript about AIDS to me, with a note saying: 'Too pessimistic; what is there to hope for?' It was excellent criticism, for deeper reflection did uncover many grounds for hope, which experience has justified.

Experience of AIDS shows again and again that good and bad, hope and despair, triumph and tragedy, defeat and victory are inseparably mixed together, both for HIV-infected persons and for those who care for them. AIDS gives people permission to talk about fundamental questions and to think seriously about whether there *is* a God and what God is like. AIDS forces many affected persons to value life more intensely and to discard trivial concerns which wasted their potential in the past. Some people living with HIV say, with wonder, 'At last I have the chance to become the person I always wanted to be.'

Conferences on AIDS, whether large or small, are a strange experience for participants. At one level scientists and people-living-with-HIV feel distress as they learn about new consequences of the pandemic, or that there is still no vaccine to prevent infection and no safe, inexpensive drug to delay the onset of serious illness. But many delegates also experience a sense of community which they have not known before, in a solidarity with each other which is exhilarating and liberating. Some Christians ask: 'Why is the Church not more like this?'

QUESTIONS WHICH OPEN NEW PATHWAYS

Perhaps we should ask different questions, such as:

1. Does history have direction and a goal? Is God indeed a God of history?

2. What does 'redemption' mean?

3. Is it possible for HIV-infected and uninfected people, carers and cared-for alike, to find redemption from their fears *through*, not in spite of, the AIDS pandemic?

4. What kind of God do we meet in accounts of Jesus's life, death and resurrection, and in the experience of the early Church?

5. Can we know anything about God's final purposes for men and women? How might such knowledge influence our daily lives?

6. Will men and women relate to each other in *new* ways in the coming Kingdom of God which Jesus of Nazareth preached about? If so, should traditional patterns of relationship change to allow the new values of the Kingdom to begin to operate now?

7. Is it possible for HIV-infected persons to live in the light of the resurrection, as well as in the shadow of death?

Study Suggestions

1. Check the meanings of words used in this chapter that are new to you.

2. List your existing resources for information about AIDS. Are these resources likely to be biased in any way?

3. Review the content of this chapter to identify information or ideas which are new to you. Does your own experience provide any evidence to support these new ideas?

4. What kinds of people ought to be invited to join a group of 7 to 10 persons who meet to study the effects of AIDS in your society? Should HIV-infected persons be included?

CHAPTER 2

Population Structure and developing countries

'Be fruitful and multiply, and fill the earth and subdue it' (Gen. 1.28 NRSV).

In any society, the spread of HIV and the impact of AIDS is influenced by the rate at which that society's population has 'multiplied' in the recent past, and the success, or otherwise, of its attempts to 'subdue' the earth. But the question: 'When is the earth filled?' is also important in this (and any) context, because population numbers need to be in a healthy balance with agricultural and other resources, to ensure that everyone has the material, educational and spiritual 'goods' needed for truly *human* life.

POPULATION PILLAR OR POPULATION PYRAMID?

Not all populations have the same age-structure; Figure 2 compares the population 'shape' of a typical industrialized country and that of an

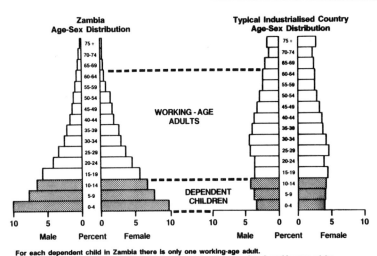

Figure 2. Population Structures: Pyramid and Pillar. Reproduced by courtesy of Churchill Livingstone from *British Medical Bulletin* Vol. 44, 1987.

equally typical developing country. Anyone who travels between Northern and Southern hemispheres sees the truth of this diagram in city streets: in London or New York there are many old people and rather few pregnant women, while in Kampala or Delhi there are few old people and every other woman has a bulge in front – and a child on her back or at her side.

In most developing countries nearly half of the population is under 15 years of age, leading to a high *dependency ratio*, meaning that (on average) every adult has to support one dependent child or old person. But unemployment is very common and unemployed adults are economically dependent too, unless they run small businesses or return to farming. In contrast, in industrialized countries, there are usually two or three working-age adults for each dependent person, in spite of growing numbers of retired people in Western societies.

In a typical developing country, another 45% of the population is in the reproductive and productive age group, between 15 and 45 years of age: this is the age-group most likely to acquire HIV through sexual relationships. Young adults are responsible for dependent children, sick persons and elders, and normally they grow the food and produce the goods or services which everyone needs – so the whole of society suffers if they die prematurely.

The statement: 'every other woman has a bulge in front and a child on her back' seems crude, but it expresses the fact that in many developing countries, on average, each woman has six or seven live births (*total fertility* rate*). A total fertility rate of seven implies that most women will be either pregnant or lactating for about fourteen years of their lives between the ages of 16 and 45.

Figure 3 shows *data* relating to the population of Tanzania in 1992 and 1993, extracted from *The State of the World's Children 1995* (UNICEF) (43). The *birth rate* (number of live babies born per thousand persons in the whole population) exceeded the *death rate* (number of deaths at any age, per thousand people). Therefore the population of Tanzania was increasing at a *growth rate* of 3.4% a year. Other developing countries have had similar population growth rates of 3% or more during the last 20 years, which accounts for the wide base to a typical developing country population *pyramid*.

In most (but not all) industrial countries, birth rates are falling so their population *pillars* widen slightly from a narrow base; in Northern societies infant and child death rates are very low and there are many more adults than children. In contrast, death rates for infants and children are high in developing countries, and their population pyramids continue to shrink during early adult and middle life.

Statistical Tables in the 1990s			
	Tanzania		
	1992/3	1995	
Total population (millions)	28.8		
under 16 yrs (millions)	14.4		
under 5 yrs (millions)	5.7		
life expectancy at birth (yrs)	51		
crude birth rate	48		
crude death rate	15		
crude fertility rate	6.8		
population growth rate	3.4%		
urbanized population	23 %		
access to health care	76 %		
GNP per capita (US $)	110		
% of govt. expenditure (health)	6 %		
% of govt. expenditure (defence)	16 %		

Figure 3. Population data: Tanzania 1992/93.

LIFE EXPECTANCY

Death rates at all ages are high for many reasons. Water supplies may be inadequate and polluted; crops fail due to drought or soil erosion, and even in good years food may be short for a few weeks. In an emergency, medical care may not be available because rural people (80% of the population in many African countries) live long distances from hospitals or clinics and do not have access to transport – and in any case there are few doctors and other health-care workers, even in cities. For example, in 1987 there were over 24,000 people for every qualified doctor in Tanzania, compared with Western ratios of less than a thousand per doctor. Most doctors and nurses in developing countries are concentrated in towns, whereas most people live in rural areas.

Childbirth is commonplace when women have seven children each, but it is still hazardous unless good care is available during pregnancy and delivery. Men die from accidents or violence and children and adults of all ages die more often than their counterparts in industrial countries from dangerous but curable diseases which are either not treated soon enough – or not prevented because vaccination programmes fail, for one of many reasons.

The *gross national product* or *GNP* (the total amount of wealth a country generates each year) is low in many developing countries, thus limiting the amount of money available for health care. In the last decade interest payments on international debt have become an additional burden which has diverted money away from provision of safe water, agricultural development, food production and preventive health care, which are the basic requirements for longer life expectancy.

In planning national budgets for developing countries, education and defence are usually given high priority – even though there may be no obvious threat to national security to justify an army. As a result, preventive and curative health care often has a budget of less than US$5 a year per head of population. This is not much money, and health allocations have been falling, both in absolute *and* real terms since 1985.

All these factors contribute to life expectancies at birth of about 50 years for men and 55 years for women in developing countries – contrasting with life expectancies of 70 years for men and 78 for women in many (not all) industrial countries.

Many misunderstandings between South and North are due to the unexamined assumption that other populations are 'just like ours': otherwise well-informed men and women in both industrial and developing nations just do not know that they live in pillar-shaped or pyramid-shaped societies, and therefore cannot reflect upon the influence such age-structures may have on the consequences of AIDS.

'FILL THE EARTH'

Farmers are familiar with the idea that a given area of land will support only a limited number of cattle: if the optimum number of cows is exceeded then overgrazing soon reduces the quality of the grass and weaker animals will be underfed, while at the same time overcrowding and semi-starvation increase the risk that disease will spread within the herd. Similar principles apply to human groups, but the results of land pressure have been hidden in the past because most expanding populations either travelled away with their herds, or moved to new hunting grounds, or else they fought their neighbours to gain control of additional land. In modern times countries that could not grow enough food solved their problems without violence by importing some of their needs, paying for the imports by exporting raw materials or manufactured goods.

But in the last 20 years populations in many countries have expanded so rapidly that traditional ways of balancing numbers of people against the resources needed to feed them have begun to fail. Birth rates have remained at traditional levels (total fertility rate 7) or have fallen slightly, but despite low investment in health care death rates have fallen very substantially, so that in many developing countries populations have doubled in the last 20 years. This reduction in deaths has been achieved largely through investment in preventive and curative health care, directed mainly towards babies and children, *not* by increasing food supplies, which was the natural way death rates were reduced slowly in the past.

Now, as more children reach adult life, family plots are subdivided between larger numbers of survivors – who in turn try to feed *their* families on even smaller plots, risking loss of quality in both soil and plants, soil erosion, crop diseases and human starvation. This imbalance between a country's population and the agricultural resources needed to feed it is called *demographic entrapment**: a useful shorthand term for a complex and threatening situation. Demographic entrapment is visible already in Rwanda and Malawi and may become a reality in other countries with rapidly expanding populations – unless disease or conflict restores the balance violently.

'SUBDUE THE EARTH'

The concept of a 'Third World' arose in the 1960s when newly-independent nations began to see a role for themselves as a third force in a world dominated by two superpowers: the United States and her allies in the West, and the Soviet Union and satellite communist countries in the East. At that time the first world of the capitalist West and the second world of the communist East confronted each other as opposites in the 'Cold War' – living in fear that the balance of power which allowed an uneasy peace might not be sustainable. Nuclear war was a real possibility, although both sides knew that such a war would have appalling and unpredictable effects in the world, leading to radioactive pollution of water and food chains, and destruction of the infrastructures needed by industrial societies. Such consequences could destroy the present form of civilization and might make it impossible for humankind to survive as a species.

Yet even though neither superpower could 'win' a nuclear conflict, both sides lacked the power or will to act upon this knowledge to reduce tension by (at least partial) disarmament: the Cold War was a fact about the 1960s world with which nations had to live.

Most newly-independent Southern countries, however, were detached from this viewpoint. Such countries faced similar (and similarly huge) tasks of nation-building: in order to feed, educate and improve the health of expanding populations they needed to develop their natural and human resources very rapidly, and to share in the economic life of industrialized countries. To tackle these tasks they needed help from established nations and were impatient with a confrontation between East and West which distracted attention from urgent needs in the South.

New nations accepted technical and economic help from East and from West, but many adopted a policy of non-alignment, refusing to join sides with either party and fearing renewed 'colonial' domination by powers stronger than themselves. Later new nations learned to exploit opportunities to bargain between the superpowers; in time a few countries (chiefly in South East Asia) developed very successful economies but others, especially in Africa, did not fare so well.

DIFFERENCES – AND SIMILARITIES

In 1985 Shiva Naipaul wrote that 'People only look alike when you can't be bothered to look at them closely' and he concluded that 'The promiscuous idea of a Third world does not stand up to close examination'. However, for the limited purpose of exploring the context within which many (mainly Southern) nations have to respond to AIDS, I maintain that similar social and economic circumstances do give 'developing countries' a collective identity which is worth acknowledging – even though it is equally important to recognize (and preserve) their diversity.

The characteristics shared by many developing countries are:
1. Population growth rates of 3% or more per annum
2. Young populations (up to 45% under 15 years of age)
3. Development regarded as the first priority
4. Poverty; low per capita income and Gross National Product
5. An unpredictable income based on export of raw materials with fluctuating prices on international markets
6. A wide gap between 'haves' and 'have-nots' in society
7. Underdeveloped natural resources and lack of technical expertise
8. Underdeveloped educational, medical and social services
9. Self-determination of goals and way of life highly valued
10. A concern to preserve traditional culture and values
11. A policy of political non-alignment
12. International debts with large interest payments.

Not all developing countries share all 12 characteristics: for example, the 'Tiger Cubs' of Asia are not dependent on export of raw materials, and natural resources in some countries are already fully developed or almost exhausted.

RECENT POLITICAL AND ECONOMIC CHANGE

During the last 20 years, nations all over the world fell into debt. Falling prices for primary exports (e.g. copper or cocoa) and rising costs for essential imports (e.g. fuel oil) played a part, combined with inflation. But an important factor was injudicious borrowing for investment, not balanced by countries' ability to earn enough to service debts. Government loans often had low interest rates, but interest on loans from commercial sources rose steeply, and in recently-independent nations the situation was often complicated by other factors: drought, management and supply problems, armed conflict, political instability and migrations of refugees.

Preoccupations have altered too in both North and South. In the North most people have woken up to the reality that 'subduing the earth' has reached a critical point: the Earth Summit in Rio in 1993 heard that 'our children will live through the greatest climate change since civilization began' and that 'this is our last chance to change direction'. Destruction of forests (the earth's 'lungs'), loss of plant and animal species, accumulation of greenhouse gases leading to global warming and massive increases in human populations are the main reasons – for a crisis which affects everyone in the world, wherever they live.

Different parts of the world, however, worry about different aspects of the crisis. Northern nations, which are historically responsible for the increasing pace of environmental damage, are defensive and continue to give priority to economic growth (driven by consumption of goods and services) over measures to preserve a healthy environment. In part, this may be a reaction to their loss of control over resources as they begin to understand the interdependence of North and South. Another reason for defensive over-consumption in the North may be the failure of their political or economic systems to produce the universal wealth and happiness leaders promised in more optimistic days 50 years ago. When Bishop Lesslie Newbigin left India in 1974, people asked him: 'What is the greatest difficulty you face in moving from India to England?' Ten years later he wrote: 'I have always answered: "the disappearance of hope" ' (51). Over the last ten years, hope for anything – other than material goods – is still in the process of 'disappearing'.

In the South poverty and survival are the priorities. Poverty causes continuing damage to natural resources in developing countries which cannot afford to limit primary exports, unless they find alternative sources for foreign exchange. At present Southern nations consume much less, and so contribute much less to pollution of the environment than their Northern neighbours, and do not wish to subsidize a wasteful life-style which they do not share. Their governments are not willing to divert scarce resources to solve problems for which they do not feel responsible, when the measures needed are capital-intensive. In practical terms, Southern nations need more sustainable sources of energy (hydro-electric or solar power to reduce dependence on wood and oil for fuel), clean water to improve health and reduce early deaths, and sustainable development of their land to grow more food. Above all, nations with high population growth rates must decide to limit, voluntarily, the number of children born.

Southern nations urgently need relief from the burden of debts when interest payments drain 'scarce resources of foreign exchange desperately needed to finance essential development'. In the North a movement called 'Jubilee 2000' began in 1990, with the object 'to obtain the remission of unpayable debt; this is both elementary common sense and a proper expression of the desire to help poorer nations'. Supporters of this movement analysed World Debt Tables provided by the World Bank and concluded that debt reduction or forgiveness does not inhibit future private investment (as bankers used to claim) but may attract it: 'Debt reduction, which in the case of nearly all poorer developing countries can only be achieved through some form of debt forgiveness, is "a necessary, but not sufficient condition for future prosperity and for future credit-worthiness for private investment" ' – but only if incompetent borrowers are replaced by sensible managers in recipient governments.

A basis for the idea of debt forgiveness is found in the book of Leviticus in the Old Testament. 'The Lord spoke to Moses on Mount Sinai' to command a 'sabbath rest' for the land of Israel every seven years, and a year of Jubilee every 50 years (Lev. 25.1–12). In the Jubilee year, there were provisions for release from debt for 'your brother'. 'If any who are dependent on you become so impoverished that they sell themselves to you, you shall not make them serve as slaves. They shall remain with you as hired or bound labourers. They shall serve with you until the year of the Jubilee. Then they and their children with them shall be free from your authority, they shall go back to their own family and return to their ancestral property' (Lev. 25.39–41). The interdependence of Northern and Southern nations requires that every human being should now be regarded as 'your brother'.

Nuclear war may be a smaller threat to human society at present than it was in 1970 but the threat, then and now, is at least well-recognized. AIDS, in the long term, also threatens the survival of human societies, for already it hinders development and is responsible for a massive loss of investment in education, health and agriculture. Yet the future impact of HIV infection is usually underestimated. In the Northern hemisphere the possibility of the heterosexual spread of HIV accelerating is too easily dismissed, and the effects of AIDS are perceived to fall only upon small groups of people such as drug-users and homosexuals, who are not well-regarded in wider society. Catastrophic events in the South appear distant because they do not seem relevant to Northern interests, so attention is transient and soon displaced by lesser events at home.

But the impact of AIDS is also underrated in many developing countries, where HIV infection is often disregarded as a factor contributing to underdevelopment or social instability.

NORTH–SOUTH RELATIONSHIPS

Poorer countries need technical assistance and funds for development and have to ask for them. Negotiating from relative poverty not strength, their relations with richer countries are influenced by attitudes which originated when the non-aligned movement was viewed with suspicion, as anti-colonial, by Western powers. In part, suspicions were – and are – due to unrecognized or unacknowledged differences in priorities and values which hinder mutual understanding. In 1961 Nehru said: 'Something we consider a great sin is looked upon . . . as a minor misdemeanour which can be passed by, and something which we consider a minor misdemeanour is perhaps considered a great sin . . . our standards differ.'

Differing standards often conceal *double* standards which allow the rich segments of developing countries to grow richer while their poor people grow even poorer, and Southern criticism of Western expenditure on nuclear weapons has (usually) not been extended to self-criticism of their own defence policies.

In late 1991, for example, UNICEF used figures from the World Bank, the International Monetary Fund (IMF) and other international agencies to estimate that (on average) developing countries allocate 23% of government expenditure to defence and the same proportion, 23%, to health *and* education combined. Servicing of debts requires another 15% of funds, so nearly half of developing country budges are spent on defence and debt: health and education are neglected.

Uneasy relationships between South and North still disturb responses to AIDS, after a bad beginning when early blood tests were thought to show that HIV originated in Africa. The perception that 'all Africans are likely to be HIV-infected' caused much resentment.

Although industrialized nations lead in laboratory and high-technology clinical research aimed at reducing the impact of HIV infection on *individual* persons, affected countries in Africa lead in their understanding of and responses to *community* consequences of AIDS. They have developed strategies for preventive education and community change which are well ahead of Western initiatives – and might like to export successful ideas to uninterested industrialized nations. Furthermore, although more research-results from developing countries now reach international conferences on AIDS, such conferences are dominated (in planning, political agendas, choice of topics and attendance) by the North, while the much larger pandemic in developing countries still has a subordinate place.

SUMMARY

'AIDS is never the only thing people have to worry about.' This chapter has begun to describe the context in which AIDS is encountered in order to focus attention on four key ideas:

1. 'Developing' is an adjective which identifies a group of countries which share common demographic and economic features (rapid growth of young populations, poverty, and underdeveloped resources) – and some priorities.

2. The effects of AIDS on societies in the South will be influenced by their pyramidal population structure, as nearly half their peoples are in the economically productive age group which is most at risk of HIV infection through sexual contact.

3. AIDS threatens the survival of civilizations and deserves more, not less, international attention.

4. The countries of Eastern Europe and the ex-Soviet Union have the population structure of industrial nations, but share many economic and infrastructural problems with developing countries; how the AIDS pandemic will affect them cannot be predicted yet.

For Further Reading see Bibliography, p. 311, (41), (42) and (51).

Study Suggestions

1. Revise and ponder the meaning of words new to you introduced and explained in this chapter (usually identified by italics).

2. Compare basic population data from your own country with the information given about Tanzania, by writing the figures recorded at your last population census in the first blank column in Figure 3. The second blank column awaits the results of your *next* census, which may show changes in population structure (*demographic trends*) in your society. (If you can, visit the Central Statistical Office and ask to see a copy of the last census report).

3. For your own country discuss, as a group:
   (a) Which figures surprise you?
   (b) Which are the expanding or contracting professions in your society? And in industrialized countries?
   (c) Reasons why people have large families in developing countries?
   (d) Reasons for the smaller families in industrialized nations?
   (e) What the women in your group think about the fertility and infant and maternal mortality rates in your country?

(f) What is the life expectancy at birth in your society? If it is low, what are the main reasons?

(g) How may an increased death rate amongst women aged less than 30 years affect population growth rates, in the long term?

(h) What effects an increase in numbers of men dying at age 35 would have on industrial and agricultural productivity?

Note. 1. Most of the questions asked in these exercises will receive 'answers' of some kind in later chapters, but these answers may not apply to the society in which *you* live and work. 2. It cannot be emphasized too strongly that *local* research is needed to learn about your own society and its HIV-related needs, in order to respond effectively to local consequences of AIDS.

It will be helpful to keep brief notes of the answers you, as a group, give to questions asked in group exercises.

CHAPTER 3
Immune Deficiency and HIV

THE ACRONYM AIDS

The letters A I D S (S I D A in French) stand for *acquired immune deficiency syndrome* and refer to a disease which is *acquired*, not present in the ova or sperm of either parent. The primary problem is defective function of the body's defence system (*immune deficiency*), which results in a *syndrome*, or collection of diseases that would normally be prevented by a healthy immune system.

Definitions: *Syndrome** is a term used for a group of *symptoms* (more or less unpleasant sensations reported by a sufferer) and *signs* (abnormalities found during physical examination) which cannot easily be explained by a single diagnosis.

A *diagnosis** labels a disease with a name, as a first step towards understanding and treating it. A diagnosis is made by recognizing a pattern of symptoms and signs which indicates a particular *process*, for example inflammation, occurring in a *named organ or tissue* such as the stomach or skin. Diseases that are rare in normal individuals but which seize the opportunity offered by weakened body defences are called *opportunistic.** People with AIDS suffer repeated opportunistic diseases affecting different parts of their bodies, either simultaneously or in sequence, over a period of years. This pattern is characteristic of an underlying failure of the normal immune (defence) system.

Stories: *Joe* woke one day with an aching pain in the centre of his abdomen. He had no appetite and in the early afternoon he vomited. By this time the central pain in his abdomen had eased but he had a new and sharper pain above his right groin. He went to his local hospital and explained his *symptoms*. A doctor examined him and found that Joe had fever, his pulse was rapid, and there was a tender area in his abdomen where his muscles were in spasm. 'Joe' he said, 'you have *signs* which suggest a *diagnosis* of appendicitis. We should admit you to hospital and take your appendix out today.'

Ngoma trod on a nail at work, swore, and pulled the nail out of his shoe and foot. By evening his foot was swollen and later throbbing pain disturbed his sleep. By morning his foot was more swollen and

27

he had discomfort in his groin on the same side; exploring with his fingers he found some tender lumps. Ngoma went to the clinic where a nurse took his temperature and examined his foot and groin. 'That nail was dirty and has infected your foot' she explained, 'and the infection has travelled up your leg to *lymph nodes** in your groin. Those nodes are swollen and painful because they are trying to stop bacteria from entering your blood. At present you have no fever, so they are doing their work well, but you do need an antibiotic to help your body to fight off the infection.'

THE IMMUNE SYSTEM

From the moment of birth, all animals (and human beings) meet with a great variety of foreign substances, including living organisms, some of which cause disease. But animals are equipped with complex and highly effective *defence systems* which detect and respond to invasion of their bodies by 'foreign' materials, including microscopic* *bacteria* and *fungi*, and sub-microscopic* *viruses* – whether or not these are capable of causing disease.

The *immune system* functions through the co-ordinated activities of very large numbers of potentially mobile cells located mostly in *lymphatic tissue* throughout the body. These cells use the blood stream as a rapid transport system to reach any organ or tissue under attack. Lymphatic tissue consists of localized collections of cells with many different defence roles; 'young' cells have the potential to take on one of several tasks, whereas mature cells are trained and committed to a single function. At each site defence cells are supported on a spongy framework forming a sieve through which tissue fluid circulates to reach thread-like lymphatic vessels, which end in the blood stream. Lymphatic tissue is found in the throat and tonsils, in air passages, in the wall of the gut, and in numerous *lymph** *nodes* in the neck, under arms and in groins, chest and abdominal cavities.

Normally people become aware of their own lymph nodes only when lymphatic tissue is actively defending the body against invasion by disease-producing (*pathogenic**) organisms. For example, the bacteria causing a sore throat provoke a defensive reaction in lymph nodes in the neck, which become temporarily swollen and tender.

THE CAUSE OF AIDS

During 1980 and 1981 doctors in New York recognized unfamiliar but similar signs of serious immune deficiency in several young men. Some of these men had been in sexual contact with each other – which suggested that an *infectious agent* might be responsible for their illnesses. This suspicion strengthened in 1983, when several people who had been transfused with blood or blood products also developed signs of immune deficiency, showing the same basic pattern of illness as the first patients in New York. In the same year (1983) doctors outside the United States reported a new disease, closely resembling descriptions of AIDS, but occurring in citizens of Central and East African countries.

Scientists searched in patients' blood and semen for an infectious agent, which could be *transmitted* (passed from person to person) by blood transfusion or through sexual contact, and which was present both in the United States and in Africa. Their investigations started with viruses which were known already to weaken the immune system, but in 1983 Luc Montagnier and his colleagues at the Pasteur Institute in Paris reported finding a previously unknown virus in the blood of a man with enlarged lymph nodes – who had visited New York. In 1984 Montagnier found the same virus in two brothers with haemophilia*, one of whom later developed AIDS. (Haemophilia is treated by transfusion of blood products.)

Meanwhile on the other side of the Atlantic, Robert Gallo and his colleagues at the National Institutes of Health in Washington isolated a new virus from American patients who had AIDS. Further investigation confirmed that the viruses identified in France and the United States were the same, although known at that time by different names in the two countries. By the end of 1984 a laboratory test was available to detect a specific human protein produced in response to HIV infection in the fluid part of the blood (the *serum**) of infected persons. At this time the virus itself could not be identified directly.

In 1985 international scientists agreed to call the new virus the *human immunodeficiency virus*, using the acronym* HIV. When another virus which also causes immune deficiency was identified in West Africa, the two viruses were distinguished by labelling the commonest HIV 1, and calling the second (less common and found mainly in West Africa), HIV 2.

Definitions: *Fungi* are small organisms consisting of large numbers of similar cells connected together in chains, living in colonies on a suitable food supply such as rotten wood, cheese or animal tissues. Colonies of fungi are visible to the unaided eye, and individual cells can be seen using a laboratory microscope. Fungi provide for themselves strong shells which allow them to survive long periods of hardship away from ideal living conditions. Only a few fungi cause disease in human beings.

Bacteria are single-cell organisms large enough to be visible using a laboratory (light) microscope, but too small to be seen by the unaided eye. There are billions of them in soil, water, and in bodies, chiefly in the cavity of the gut and on the skin. Only a small proportion of bacteria cause disease: the term for the capacity to do so is *pathogenic*. Most bacteria form visible colonies when grown (in culture) in a laboratory.

Viruses are single-cell organisms which are too small to be seen using a light microscope, but can be viewed using special techniques and an electron microscope. Viruses are less robust and less self-sufficient than bacteria so they depend upon the cell machinery of the *host* in which they live for survival. Some can multiply without assistance from their hosts, but others, called *retroviruses**, have to hijack the control mechanisms of host cells in order to reproduce. Viruses are more difficult to grow in laboratories than bacteria, usually surviving only in cultures of living cells: research on viruses is correspondingly difficult and expensive. HIV is a particularly complex retrovirus which has only one known host: human beings.

TRANSMISSION OF HIV

Disease-producing organisms are transmitted from person to person by direct or indirect contacts. Some organisms can survive for long periods outside animal bodies, in air, water, dust or food, and can be transferred by indirect contacts. For example, cholera bacteria are excreted in faeces and only small amounts of stool-contaminated drinking water or uncooked food are needed to infect other people.

Other organisms, including HIV, are too fragile to survive for long outside the body so they can only be transmitted from person to person by *direct* physical contacts which allow for the exchange of body fluids containing infected cells. The only contacts close enough to allow exchange of HIV-containing cells are:

1. Sexual intercourse during which the penis penetrates a body orifice (vagina, rectum or mouth);
2. From mother to unborn child during pregnancy;
3. Transfusion of blood or blood products;
4. Exchange of minute quantities of blood during traditional scarification or medical procedures using unsterile blades or needles, or during intravenous injection of drugs;
5. Through breast-feeding, although this route is rare.

HIV can only enter certain specific cells in the body. These are found in large numbers in blood, semen, and vaginal secretions and also in some internal organs. A few HIV-infected cells are found in milk and saliva.

HIV can enter the human body through obviously damaged skin or directly into the bloodstream through injection, or if infected blood comes into contact with a wound. HIV can also pass through slightly damaged internal membranes such as the lining of the vagina or the *urethra* (the passage through the penis for urine and semen), although the injury to vagina or urethra is usually far too small to be noticeable.

HIV can pass from a man to an uninfected woman, or from a woman to an uninfected man. But there is a 10 to 50 times greater concentration of HIV in semen than in vaginal fluid, and semen comes into contact with a large area of vaginal membrane (compared with the small area of male urethra in contact with female fluids): as a result HIV passes more easily from a man to a woman than in the reverse direction.

Circumcision reduces the risk of a man acquiring HIV, but genital ulcers in either sex increase the risk of HIV transmission. Other factors which influence the likelihood of infection will be discussed later.

Questions.

1. Here is a list of situations in which sexual (genital) contact may take place. Which circumstances *increase* the risk of HIV passing from one partner to the other?

Hasty first intercourse with a frightened teenage girl; one partner has a genital ulcer; rape; the man uses a condom; the woman has a dry vagina (for she is past the menopause); the man's penis penetrates the rectum not the vagina of his partner; sex during menstruation.

2. Here is a list of common activities which may involve physical contact (direct or indirect) with an HIV-infected person. Which of these activities risk transmitting HIV to another person?

Shaking hands; hugging; kissing on the cheek; kissing on the lips; sharing a meal eaten with the hands from a common dish; sitting on the same bench; using the same toilet; using the same bath; sharing one razor; sharing one toothbrush; sharing a cup when the HIV-infected person has a sore lip; sharing a communion chalice; sharing an office or schoolroom; children at play; swimming together; wearing secondhand clothes; changing an infected baby's napkin; changing the sheets on an infected person's bed.

Are there any conditions which would increase or decrease the chance of transmission by any of the activities you have indicated as being 'risky'?

3. What action should a nurse take if she has a cut on one hand, before working in a clinic for HIV-infected persons?

Answers

1. Use of a condom reduces the risk of transmission of HIV, but *all* the other circumstances listed *increase* the likelihood of transmission by sexual intercourse, because there is a chance that the vagina or rectum will be damaged, and ulcers or abrasions make an easy entry-point for HIV.

2. Only *sharing one razor* or *sharing one toothbrush* or *sharing a cup when the HIV-infected person has a sore lip* may result in transmission of HIV between two people. There is risk in changing a baby's napkin or changing bed-sheets *only* if the linen is blood-stained and still wet.

3. The nurse's cut should be covered with an occlusive* adhesive dressing to prevent contact with patients' body fluids.

SEXUAL BEHAVIOUR AND RISK OF HIV TRANSMISSION

A *virgin* is a woman or a man who has never had penetrative sexual intercourse with another person, whether that other person is of the same or the opposite sex. If two young people come together in marriage or a sexual partnership while *both* are still virgins (and when neither has been infected with HIV by a blood transfusion), then their sexual union cannot result in transmission of HIV. For as long as *both* partners continue to have sexual relations *only* with each other, there is no risk of acquiring HIV by the sexual route. The Ugandan slogans: 'Love faithfully' and 'Zero grazing' refer to the safety of mutual faithfulness, and so does the promise 'No sex before marriage and no sex outside marriage' made by members of Zambian Anti-AIDS Clubs.

A relationship restricted to two partners who do not have sexual contact with anyone else is faithful and *monogamous*. A stable *polygamous** marriage is equally safe as a means of avoiding HIV, providing that neither the husband nor any of his wives has sexual relationships outside the marriage.

PARTNERS OUTSIDE MARRIAGE: SEXUAL NETWORKS

As soon as either person in a previously exclusive sexual relationship takes a second sexual partner, there is a risk that HIV will be encountered. The size of this risk depends upon how common HIV infection is in the community to which both people belong, and also the number of other sexual partners which the new partner has at present or has had in the past. It is very important to recognize that in any sexual relationship each partner is in indirect physical contact with every current or past sexual partner of the other person. For example, if a young man pays to sleep with a woman who sells sex, and if she has slept with eight

Figure 4. Sexual networks.

or ten new men every month for five years, then that man (even though *he* may be having sexual relations for the first time) is indirectly in contact with at least six hundred other men, any one of whom may be HIV-infected. He is *also* in indirect contact with all the previous partners of every one of those 600 men: sexual networks soon become very large once a safe pattern of 'One man – one woman, for life' is abandoned. Figure 4 shows how sexual networks (especially in developing countries) expose men and women who have few sexual partners to the risk of encountering HIV through contacts with people who have many partners, such as:

1. Women who sell sex (60 to 85% HIV-infected);
2. Truck drivers (50 to 60%);
3. Defence force personnel (40 to 60%);
4. New patients at clinics for sexually-transmitted diseases (50%).

The figures in brackets refer to common rates of infection with HIV, in these groups, in some affected developing countries.

CONDOMS AND THEIR USE

The risk of transmitting HIV during sexual intercourse can be reduced, although not removed altogether, by using a condom or rubber sheath to cover the penis and so prevent contact between semen and vaginal secretions. A condom is effective and protective only if it is put onto the erect penis before any sexual contact takes place, and only if it remains unbroken throughout the sexual act and is removed and discarded carefully afterwards. Correct use gives greater protection if a sperm and virus-killing jelly (such as Nonoxenol) is smeared onto the surface of the condom before intercourse. But even when used for contraception condoms are not 100% effective, although women are only fertile for 48 hours in each month and sperm are 200 times larger than HIV. Unfortunately, the experiences of couples where only one partner was HIV-infected show that HIV can be passed from one to the other, even when condoms are used carefully for each sexual act. Condoms make intercourse with an infected (or possibly infected) person less risky, but they do *not* make it *safe* – transmission of HIV may still occur. Men control the use of male condoms, and may not listen to women who ask for a condom to be worn during sexual play. Many more sexual acts would be made safer if women could control whether or not a barrier is used; recently a female condom has been designed, but at present such condoms are expensive, obvious to the male partner, and rarely available.

HIV IN COMMUNITIES: EPIDEMIC OR PANDEMIC?

What is an 'average' risk that a new sexual partner will be HIV-infected? This depends on whether a population is rural or urban, near to a main truck route or isolated from transport, and on how recently HIV reached the community concerned.

HIV probably reached Zaire, Rwanda, Zambia and Uganda in the mid-1970s and then began to spread slowly. At first infected people remained well and could not be identified, but five to eight years later (about 1982) they started to suffer from opportunist infections and sought treatment. HIV appears to have reached Kenya and Zimbabwe at a later date, because AIDS-related diseases were not recognized in these countries until three or four years later. HIV reached South Africa and Mozambique later still, which means that even in 1995 these countries have time to limit the spread of HIV by changing common patterns of sexual behaviour. AIDS *epidemics* are described briefly in ch. 7, where I attempt to describe, in general terms, the impact and global extent of *pandemic* HIV-infection.

Definitions: An infectious disease is described as *endemic* when it is constantly present in a community, though affecting only a few people at any one time. The common cold, for example, is 'endemic' in most communities throughout the world.

In some circumstances, due to a change in the aggressiveness (*virulence*) of a bacteria or virus or due to a change in environment (e.g. weather or drought) an infection may begin to pass more often from person to person, until unusual numbers are ill from the same disease, at the same time, in one community. This is referred to as an *epidemic*. The spread of HIV infection in many developing countries is widespread enough to be called an 'epidemic'. Epidemics of some diseases, such as measles or poliomyelitis, can be prevented by vaccinating enough at-risk (susceptible) people to interrupt transfer of the infectious agent from person to person. On the other hand, epidemics of intestinal diseases (e.g. cholera or typhoid) are prevented by changing the environment to provide a clean water supply and hygienic disposal of human excretions.

When one infectious disease occurs in many different countries and spreads easily between them, so that it becomes global in extent, the infection is referred to as *pandemic*. As AIDS is now global in extent, it is rightly described as 'pandemic'.

Cities offer more opportunities than villages for strangers to meet and for casual sexual contacts, so HIV tends to spread more rapidly in towns than in the countryside. Towns are linked to each other and to villages by roads, and most capital cities are linked by airlines. HIV is carried by passengers and drivers from city to city and from city to village; people living alongside main roads are particularly likely to become HIV-infected. To illustrate this, Figure 5 shows proportions of surgical patients who were found to be HIV-infected in selected Zambian hospitals located in rural areas, alongside a main road, in provincial towns and in Lusaka during 1989 and 1990.

HIV-Infected surgical patients in Zambian Hospitals

Rural Hospitals:	Katete	13.8%
	Chikankata	11.7%
	Chilonga	17.4%
Provincial Hospitals:	Mongu	24.2%
	Kasama	25.0%
	Livingstone	25.8%
Main Road Hospital:	Monze	45.8%
Lusaka Teaching Hospital:	in 1989	33.3%
	in 1990	42.2%

The difference between rates of HIV-infection at rural and provincial hospitals was statistically significant (p = 0.0058).

Figure 5. Comparative rates of HIV infection at rural and urban hospitals.

SAMPLING NORMAL POPULATIONS

When information is needed about one characteristic of a group of people the surest way to obtain it is to examine every member – for example, to find out what proportion have normal vision. However, it is impractical and unnecessary to examine every member of a large group such as the population of a whole city, as sufficiently accurate information can usually be obtained by examining a *representative sample*, for example every tenth individual. However, the selected group must be truly representative: if we need information about normal vision it would be wrong to examine only schoolchildren as visual difficulties increase with age. Accurate results would be obtained only if the age structure of the sample was the same as the age structure of the whole population.

It is difficult to sample a population to find out what proportion of persons in it are HIV-infected because many apparently representative groups are either *more* likely or *less* likely than average to be infected. For example, patients attending a clinic for sexually transmitted diseases often have an above-average number of sexual partners and so are more likely to have acquired HIV. Blood donors might appear to be a suitable sample group, but where potential donors know that their blood will be tested for HIV many men or women no longer offer to donate blood, thus reducing the apparent level of infection in their communities. The most satisfactory groups to sample are patients of either sex who are admitted to hospital suddenly for accidental injuries, and women attending ante-natal clinics.

INCREASING INFECTION RATES: INCREASING RISKS

In 1981 less than one in every hundred mothers attending ante-natal clinics in Lusaka was HIV-infected. By 1985 8% of pregnant women sampled were infected and the proportion rose to 25% in 1990 and 36% in 1993. In effect, less than one in every hundred sexual encounters risked HIV transmission in Lusaka during 1981, but twelve years later one in every three casual sexual partners might be HIV-infected. This is broadly true for either sex, because the infection rate in women attending ante-natal clinics implies an equal infection rate in their male partners.

Definitions: *Seropositivity rates**. Tests for signs of infection with HIV will be discussed in more detail in ch. 4. Tests use the pale yellow fluid called *serum* which separates out when clotted blood is allowed to stand for an hour or two in a test tube. *Serology** is a general term for any test done on a sample of serum. When the test result is negative, the sample (or person from whom the sample was taken) is said to be *seronegative*; conversely, when a result is positive, the sample (or person) is said to be *seropositive*. In writing about AIDS, these terms are used loosely to refer to serum samples or people who do not (or do) have signs of HIV infection. Similarly, a *seropositivity rate* refers to the proportion of a group or community who are found to be seropositive when tested. For example, the seropositivity rate amongst pregnant women attending antenatal clinics in Lusaka was 8% in 1985 and 36% in 1993.

So far the basic facts of HIV transmission from person to person have been set out: how can this knowledge be applied to reduce or halt the spread of HIV in communities?

GENERAL STRATEGIES FOR PREVENTION
OF INFECTIOUS DISEASES

In the past strategies used successfully to control infectious disease were:

1. Vaccination to produce individual and community immunity to the causal agent.
2. Changing behaviour to prevent contact between infected and uninfected individuals.
3. Changing the environment to prevent contact between infective agents and susceptible people.
4. Isolation of infectious persons until they are no longer infectious.

With respect to prevention of HIV infection, the last two strategies can be dismissed at once. First, no change in the environment can prevent spread of a virus which can pass from mother to child during pregnancy but which is otherwise transmitted only by deliberate acts leading to close personal contact and exchange of body fluids. Secondly, infected people remain infected permanently, so isolation would have to be continued until death. A few countries have reacted with panic and tried to isolate infected persons to prevent spread of HIV, but most soon realized that this measure is unrealistic as well as inhumane. There is evidence, however, that in some places prisoners and commercial sex workers have been killed because they were found or suspected to be HIV-infected: a warning that extreme fear may lead to an extreme solution – murder.

Only vaccination and behaviour change are left as theoretically possible strategies for preventing transmission of HIV. (52)

VACCINATION AGAINST HIV

In 1995 several 'candidate' vaccines were being tested in laboratories, but so far no vaccine has been shown to prevent HIV infection or licensed for use in human beings. Only if potential vaccines pass stiff safety tests will they even be tried out for usefulness (efficacy) in human volunteers, and such tests will take months or years to complete.

Many scientists are pessimistic about prospects for manufacture of a safe, effective and inexpensive vaccine. The basic reason for pessimism is that immune responses which occur naturally in persons infected with HIV do not eliminate the virus and only delay, but do not prevent, development of fatal disease. Part of the reason for this failure to prevent disease is that HIV alters as it multiplies, until in time it is no longer recognized by the immune system, and so evades destruction. (It is as though customs officials expect illegal drugs to be smuggled through seaports and therefore search ships' passengers and crews but neglect rural borders – while drug dealers change their methods and smuggle drugs in by road.) As vaccines take years to develop and test, it is also possible that yesterday's vaccine will prove ineffective as protection against tomorrow's virus. Moreover, there are enough differences between samples of HIV found in different communities to suggest that a vaccine suitable for one continent might not be as effective in another.

Even if the problems of proving that a vaccine protects against HIV are overcome, many practical questions remain: for example, will people accept vaccination, or will they fail to see themselves as 'at risk' and so refuse to be vaccinated? Or will rumours of complications drive people away? (Some parents refuse whooping cough vaccine for their children through fear – and as a result new epidemics of whooping cough have occurred.) Will a vaccine be too expensive for general use in vulnerable countries where health budgets are already overstretched?

Finally, many countries already have a large reservoir of HIV-infected persons which will persist for decades, so vaccines will have to be capable of protecting people throughout their sexually-active lives, from puberty until old age – during which time HIV itself will change. It will be difficult to produce a succession of new vaccines fast enough to keep pace with HIV.

CHANGING SEXUAL BEHAVIOUR TO AVOID HIV IN-FECTION

This is the most hopeful strategy for preventing spread of HIV to uninfected persons, but the difficulties are great. Sexual conduct is complex social behaviour, partly instinctive and partly learned, governed by strong emotions and influenced by taboos, traditions and religious and cultural beliefs. Sexual behaviour contributes to personal identity and influences social acceptance as an adult in most communities. In chs. 13 and 14 we consider traditional patterns of relationship between men and women which influence sexual behaviour and ways of encouraging 'behaviour change' with the aim of avoiding HIV infection.

Many apparently non-sexual aspects of life in society influence the rate and extent of spread of HIV, as demonstrated by some of the effects of armed conflict on AIDS epidemics.

ARMED CONFLICT AND AIDS

Armed conflict is common in countries where HIV infection is also common. In some places the violence is a sporadic and unpredictable part of a campaign to obtain majority rule or free elections to remove a set of rulers who are out of favour. In other instances, the violence amounts to civil war between different ethnic, religious or political groups, often covertly supported by other countries which seek military or trade advantages. The presence of armed conflict in any country where HIV infection already exists (or may be introduced) complicates spontaneous reactions to the appearance of AIDS and influences deliberate attempts to respond in a constructive way. Depending on the balance between opposing tendencies, the effect of armed conflict may be to delay and slow down spread of HIV, or alternatively, to greatly increase the rate and extent to which HIV spreads.

PROTECTIVE EFFECTS

If prolonged conflict isolates a nation, closes its borders to trade and tourism, discourages travel within the country and concentrates popular attention on survival not procreation, then the overall effects are likely to delay the entry and spread of HIV. Malnutrition, depression and illness decrease sexual desire and capacity, and all three may be consequences of prolonged armed conflict – which act together to discourage sexual adventures and frequent change of partners.

Thirty years of civil war in Mozambique appears to have delayed entry of HIV into the population and discouraged rapid spread of the virus. In 1992 seropositivity rates in pregnant women and in persons attending clinics for sexually transmitted diseases (STDs) were low in Maputo and in most provincial capitals, but higher (about 13%) amongst STD clinic patients in three provinces which share borders with Malawi, Zambia or Zimbabwe, countries where 20% to 20% of urban adults were HIV-infected at that time.

CAN WAR ACCELERATE SPREAD OF HIV?

On the other hand, the effects of war often favour spread of sexually transmitted diseases, including AIDS. A common reaction to fear and abnormal social conditions is a breakdown in normal patterns of behaviour and an increase in sexual freedom. People see that life is short and uncertain and try to escape from their troubles by taking refuge in drink or sex. Even if a man or woman knows the risks of contracting HIV during casual sex (and education-for-prevention is less likely to be effective in war conditions) the risk of AIDS in five years' time seems insignificant compared with the risk of death in battle tomorrow – so the lesser risk is disregarded.

In most countries where they have been investigated, military personnel have a substantially higher HIV-infection rate than the general population, so that women who sell sex to soldiers or who are raped by them have an increased risk of exposure to HIV. In war conditions sexual networks become very extensive and STDs occur more often, but may be poorly treated when medical services are over-stretched: untreated genital ulcers assist the spread of HIV. Sometimes, too, unwilling soldiers or captured civilians are forced to rape as well as to kill as a means of breaking down their normal human inhibitions against violence. During conflict illegal trading across borders may become easier and more attractive – and often seems necessary for survival: trading too, offers opportunities for casual sexual contacts. These factors appear to have played a part in the establishment of HIV infection in south-west Uganda and north-west Tanzania at the time of conflict between these countries in the late 1970s.

ARMED CONFLICT DELAYS CONSTRUCTIVE RESPONSES

In war conditions AIDS seems to be a minor problem: interest, funds and energy are not likely to be 'wasted' on campaigns to alert people to the dangers of casual sex or to persuade them to alter traditional sexual behaviours. Early signs of disease in individuals and communities may be missed, and it is unlikely that blood samples will be systematically tested for evidence of HIV infection, so there will be no serology results to alarm epidemiologists (persons who study the behaviour of epidemics) or health planners. The adverse effects of AIDS on development will be hidden because development is in any case hindered or stopped by war: other problems appear – and may actually be – far more urgent.

But HIV does not go away: HIV spreads unnoticed amongst combat forces, amongst their willing or unwilling sexual partners, to refugees waiting for peace in other countries with higher HIV-infection rates, to conscripted youths and to war-orphans who take to life in the streets of large cities. All these groups need the special attention of military, civil and Church leaders who attempt to rehabilitate their societies (and at the same time to prevent AIDS epidemics) at the end of armed conflict. Returning refugees and unmarried or widowed women with small children to support are particularly likely to act as channels for the spread of HIV into communities previously untouched by infection.

When peace arrives, natural relief at the outcome, together with trade across borders and freedom to travel, lead to conditions which may allow HIV to spread very rapidly in societies that could, at least potentially, have avoided serious AIDS epidemics. What will happen in Mozambique, South Africa and Angola during the next few years?

For Further Reading see Bibliography, p. 311, (44).

Study Suggestions
1. In a *group* of at least four people, plan (in outline) a programme to reduce transmission of HIV in *either* a village, *or* a crowded

suburb of a large city of your own country. Who might decide to obstruct your efforts? Which groups of people within the community particularly need attention? How might you attract their interest and persuade them to listen to your messages? What are the main messages you would try to convey?

2. Again in a group of at least four people, discuss Church involvement in the programme you have planned. If conflicting opinions emerge, can you identify the presuppositions (about the nature of God, or the destiny of human beings or the nature of the Church) which are the foundations for both sets of opinions? Do not attempt, at this stage, to resolve the conflicts!

3. Two modes of transmission for HIV have received very little attention in this chapter but will be discussed further later: what are they? Why has concentration been focused first on heterosexual transmission?

CHAPTER 4
Testing for HIV Infection

HIV-related disease on an epidemic scale is new: the evidence for this statement comes from two sources. First, infection with HIV is very rarely found in stored human blood samples – anywhere – earlier than 1980. Secondly, in the early years of the epidemic infection with HIV was not found in older people who were no longer taking casual sexual partners (but had done so in the past) – and older people did not develop AIDS: the most likely explanation is that HIV was not around in their communities when they were young and more sexually active.

The question: 'Where did HIV come from?' may mean: 'When and where did HIV first cause illness and death?', but more often the questioner intends to ask: 'Where did HIV originate?' The short answer is: no-one knows yet and we may never know the truth.

Several theories for the origin of HIV have been put forward; they are variants on four ideas:

1. HIV has been present for many years, but in such a remote and isolated human community that it was unrecorded until it 'escaped' into wider society in the 1970s – yet there is no evidence to locate that isolated hiding place.

2. Errors (mutations) are common during multiplication of viruses, particularly those, like HIV, which insert DNA* copies of themselves into the genetic blueprint of host cells. Most errors prevent viruses from multiplying altogether; a few do not kill a virus but change its characteristics. Mutation can alter the behaviour of ancestor viruses which were previously harmless to human beings, conferring the capacity (virulence) to cause disease and death.

3. HIV originated in a virus laboratory, by accident or by design, through a 'marriage' between two less harmful viruses.

4. Some chimpanzees (in research laboratories or in the wild) are infected with viruses which resemble HIV 1 and some species of wild monkeys in Africa (but not Asia or Latin America) are infected with viruses which resemble HIV 2; a few viruses can spread from infected animals to humans when both species are in close contact, and HIV may have done so.

At present, there is no evidence to support the first theory – neither is there evidence to falsify it. (Scientific thinking progresses by finding new evidence which contradicts or falsifies a general statement or law, but no law can ever be 'proved' however many examples of its 'rightness' accumulate.)

The mutation theory is *un*likely to explain the origin of HIV – as there are no traces of a harmless ancestor virus in stored human blood prior to the recognition of HIV in samples taken in the 1970s. A change in the virulence of a virus usually allows it to retain the characteristics by which its ancestor was recognized, just as a delinquent son may strongly resemble his law-abiding father in facial features.

Several versions of a theory that HIV was manufactured deliberately in a laboratory (for the purpose of germ warfare or to control growth of populations by killing young adults) are expressed in publications which circulate in Africa as well as in the West. Some pamphlets use the vocabulary of scientific writing and refer to reputable articles in such a way as to suggest that there is substantial scientific evidence to support the 'manufacture' theory. A political motive (on the part of American or Soviet government agencies) is usually expressed or implied.

If true, these would be extremely serious allegations, but the facts offer no basis for the theory. Techniques for growing complex viruses in the laboratory, in such a way as to allow them to combine (whether by deliberate choice or accidentally), did not exist in the past and do not exist now. Finally, the method of manufacture which is assumed (blending of a human virus and a sheep virus) would not work because human and sheep viruses have control systems that are too different to allow for combination.

A variant on the 'laboratory origin' theory is that HIV was carried by polio vaccines grown on an HIV-infected culture of Green monkey kidney cells. But HIV will not grow in cultures of Green monkey kidney cells and many thousands of people in several continents, who received polio vaccine in the 1970s, are not now infected with HIV.

HIV is more likely to have originated in chimpanzees or monkeys than to have been transferred to them from human beings since the AIDS epidemic began, which is very unlikely, given the large numbers of monkeys across sub-saharan Africa which are now infected with viruses similar to HIV 1 or 2. If HIV is distantly related to other primate viruses, it is in the general way that human beings are distantly related to non-human primates such as vervet monkeys. If HIV originated in monkeys it did so long ago but was only transferred to human beings recently – and has 'taken off' as a human–to–human infection since then.

The search for the origin of HIV is driven partly by natural curiosity and partly by the desire to find a person or organization to blame for AIDS. The question 'Where did HIV come from?' may not be answerable; certainly it is more important to concentrate on developing effective responses to the challenges HIV poses now than to search for its origins. We are *all* worthy of blame if we knowingly behave in ways which allow HIV to spread to uninfected people.

TESTING FOR HIV INFECTION

There is no 'test for AIDS' because AIDS is a clinical (bedside) diagnosis made by recognizing one of many patterns of symptoms and signs which identify diseases associated with severe breakdown of immune defences. Many tests have been developed to *detect HIV infection*, and one or more of these is used to support a clinical diagnosis of AIDS.

Tests for HIV infection are of two kinds, direct and indirect. Direct tests identify either the whole virus in a body fluid or tissue or else characteristic components of the virus which are referred to as *antigens**. The whole virus can be grown (cultured) in specialized laboratories, but methods are difficult and costly and cannot be used routinely. Tests to detect components of the virus are less complex, less expensive and already available; kits are being developed to enable HIV antigens to be identified (and their concentrations measured) more easily in future.

Indirect tests identify not HIV itself but proteins manufactured by the immune system of an infected person in response to the presence of HIV in his or her blood and tissues. An immune system responds to invasion of the body by any foreign material (whether disease-producing or not) in both non-specific and specific ways.

Specific responses are of two kinds: the first (*cell-mediated*) response requires a co-ordinated attack by a variety of cells which dissolve, 'eat', immobilize or destroy the invader. The second type of response depends on production of protein messengers (*antibodies*) which are released into the blood and tissues – where they stick onto invading organisms to cause direct damage or to assist in their destruction by defence cells. Antibodies are produced in lymphatic tissue which is located near to the site where the foreign invader entered the body.

Antibody proteins fit the shape of a single component part (antigen) of a foreign invader as uniquely and closely as the right key fits a complicated lock. It is possible to identify an unknown antibody by fitting it onto a known antigen – or conversely to identify an unknown antigen by fitting it onto a known antibody, using a third reagent (often a dye) to show that a specific antibody–antigen reaction has taken place in the test tube.

All laboratory tests have limitations and those which detect antibody to HIV are no exception. Tests may be more (or less) sensitive and more (or less) specific. Often users have to be satisfied with excellent sensitivity but imperfect precision (specificity) – or less sensitivity combined with almost perfect specificity. It is usual to select a test which is appropriate for a particular purpose: for example, to exclude HIV infection before a blood transfusion, an extremely sensitive test is needed to minimize the risk of giving infected blood – and it does not matter if the test is not wholly specific so that it falsely labels as positive one sample which in fact is not infected.

On the other hand, when testing blood from someone who fears HIV infection, it is very important to avoid false positives, and a highly specific test is selected. In practice a single positive test result is checked immediately by a second test (on the same sample) using a different method, and then further tests are carried out on a new blood sample from the worried person, before they are told of a positive result.

Both sensitivity and specificity can be quantified. A *sensitivity* of 99.5% means that 99.5% of people who are genuinely infected will have positive test results. A *specificity* of 99.9% means that 99.9% of persons who are genuinely *not* infected will have negative test results. The probability that a positive result is true is the *positive predictive value* of a test. This numerical value depends partly on the test and partly on the population being tested. In places where very few people are genuinely infected (*low prevalence* areas, e.g. only 100 out of 100,000 persons HIV-infected) false positive results may account for about half of all positive first test results. In contrast, when the prevalence of HIV infection is high (over 10,000 of 100,000 persons infected) almost all positive results are true, and falsely negative results are a more likely error. Many African cities now have such a high prevalence of HIV infection that false positive results are very rare in their clinics.

The initial test for HIV infection is usually a very sensitive *screening** test for antibodies. If the result is positive this is followed by a *supplementary* test which is highly specific, to confirm the accuracy of the screening test.

TESTING FOR HIV INFECTION IN YOUNG BABIES

It is difficult to exclude or confirm HIV infection in babies. A baby is born with an untrained and inexperienced defence system: cells which will develop defence functions or produce antibodies later have not met foreign invaders and have yet to 'learn' how to cope. Normally the process of preparing the immune system for action occurs during the first year of life, with growing efficiency as time passes. During this period a young baby is vulnerable to illness (as every parent knows) but is partly protected from danger by 'borrowed' antibodies from his or her mother. These protective proteins are passed from mother to child across the placenta, and also secreted into the first milk (colostrum) a baby receives when feeding starts – and some antibodies are found in all breast milk. *Passive transfer* of antibodies is one of many benefits of breast feeding, and accounts for the fact that breast-fed babies are less likely to suffer life-threatening infections than bottle-fed children.

HIV antibodies are transferred across the placenta to a child if his or her mother is HIV-infected, together with many other antibodies. For this reason almost every baby with an HIV-infected mother has a positive result if blood is tested for HIV antibodies during the first year of life. This positive test does not mean that the baby is HIV-infected and will become ill later, although a few babies *are* in fact already infected. Passively transferred antibodies from the mother normally disappear from her baby's blood by about a year – and the same is true for HIV antibodies. If, therefore, a baby's blood still gives a positive test for HIV antibodies at 18 months, it means that the child is truly HIV -infected: this is a long time to wait, and it is very difficult for parents to cope with the uncertainty and anxiety they feel during this period.

A positive test for HIV antibodies is potentially dangerous for a baby whose mother is known to be HIV-infected, because poorly-informed health or social workers may assume the test means that 'this child will die soon whatever we do'. There is a serious risk that health workers who think this will fail to give vigorous treatment for curable infections. In 1993 newspaper articles appeared describing AIDS orphans in Tanzania who were HIV-positive, weak and ill when taken into care but who are now fit, developing normally and 'no longer infected'. The conclusion drawn by the writer was that 'AIDS is not a problem in Africa'. In my opinion, the conclusion *should* be that these children were amongst the fortunate two-thirds of babies of HIV-positive mothers who are *not* truly infected, so that (with time) transferred HIV antibodies disappeared naturally from their blood. It was their good fortune that these children were not neglected when ill and malnourished, but received food and treatment for infections which restored normal health. Tuberculosis is particularly dangerous in these circumstances as it easily kills a malnourished baby.

WHEN SHOULD A TEST FOR HIV INFECTION BE DONE?

The only absolute reason for an HIV test is to make sure that blood intended for transfusion is not HIV-infected. In every other circumstance the decision is open to debate. Whether or not a test is done should depend on where the balance lies between 'good' and 'bad' consequences, but in order to decide where this balance lies it is necessary to ask the right questions.

First: 'What use will be made of this test result?' Will it be used, for example, to decide on the best treatment to offer a patient who needs drugs for tuberculosis or who might benefit from an operation? Or will it be used to relieve (or confirm) the fears of a man who had casual sex during a business trip and fears he may be HIV infected? Or will a positive result be used to turn down an application for a scholarship to study overseas? Is the test part of a large survey which is meant to help Ministry of Health planners to forecast the demands for health services in five years time? Is a negative result a requirement for selection for training for a more responsible post?

These examples, which are taken from life, pose ethical questions needing serious thought; for private benefit (or disadvantage) may conflict with public benefit (or disadvantage). It may be 'good' for a theological college to identify an HIV-infected applicant, but it is 'bad' for the applicant if he learns that he is HIV-infected without proper preparation and is dismissed without further care – or even worse, rejected without any explanation at all.

Second: 'Will the result be given to the person tested and if so, how will this be done?' If a test is carried out because a man or woman fears HIV infection, he or she expects to hear the result. But should a test result be imposed upon someone who has not thought about HIV infection, when the test is done to guide treatment decisions? The answer is 'no' – because the right course is to explain beforehand exactly why a test for HIV infection is needed, to obtain *informed consent*. Consent is truly informed when people are told the benefits and disadvantages which may follow from HIV-testing, in language they understand, and have time to think about the decision and ask further questions.

This process is part of *pre-test counselling* which is given by a trained and sympathetic person, who need not be a health professional. As the benefits and disadvantages of tests for HIV infection are so complicated, everyone (including those who are tested voluntarily) ought to be counselled first.

It is equally important that results should be given by a person who is trained to explain the significance of positive and negative tests and to answer questions. This process is called *post-test counselling* and usually requires at least two interviews, because people with a positive result need long-term help while they adjust to the consequences of HIV infection.

PROVIDING TESTING FACILITIES IN COUNTRIES NEWLY AFFECTED BY AIDS

It is desirable to start screening blood intended for transfusion as soon as possible after HIV infection is first detected in a country, because a safe blood supply has a high priority. Next, it is useful to extend testing to allow hospital doctors to confirm suspected HIV infections – because confirmatory tests help doctors to learn to recognize AIDS from signs and symptoms which are unfamiliar when first seen. It is wrong to open clinics where people can be tested for HIV infection at their own request – unless and until *counsellors* have been trained to provide pre and post-test advice and support.

Anyone who is sympathetic but not sentimental, mature, respectful of the dignity of other people and trustworthy with confidential information can be trained as a counsellor: nurses, midwives, clinical officers, doctors, social workers, priests, teachers, personnel officers, youth leaders, nuns, members of women's organizations.

TRAINING FOR COUNSELLORS

In Zambia clinical counsellors were trained from 1987 onwards. The first trainees were health professionals who were already seeing HIV-infected persons in the course of their normal work. Applicants were told that the course would require total commitment of time and energy for two one-week periods in residential workshops, with partial commitment for the intervening four weeks. Trainees were selected in groups from small geographical areas, so that later they would be able to support each other in their new work.

The first residential week provided facts about human sexuality, HIV infection and AIDS, and common reactions to bad news and fear of death. Participants worked together in groups (led by trained facilitators) to explore their own feelings about AIDS and to overcome their discomfort over talking openly about sexual matters. They then returned to their ordinary work, with instructions to talk in specific ways with HIV-infected or affected people, using the training already received.

A month later trainees had a second week of residential training. Some had felt frustrated because supervisors actively prevented them from going anywhere near HIV-affected people, while others had been overwhelmed with requests to talk to unhappy men and women whom no-one else wanted to face! This time there were no hesitations about group work: everyone was only too eager to share his or her experiences, whether of frustration, mistakes, stress or exhilaration at being able to offer help. Everyone learned from everyone else and experienced at first hand the benefits of group support. At the end of the course participants received a certificate from the Ministry of Health confirming their status as trained clinical counsellors, and they returned home to practise their skills and to learn from HIV-infected men and women – who are our most knowledgeable teachers.

Recently trained counsellors helped with the later courses, as group facilitators. The most able men and women received further training to become senior counsellors and trainers of others, ultimately arranging and teaching courses in counselling in their own localities. By 1995, using this 'snowball' process, 1,200 basic clinical counsellors, 90

49

senior counsellors and 27 'key resource persons' had been trained for Zambia (22).

Organizations and institutions which provide materials for use by counsellors are included in the Resources list.

REASONS FOR TESTING FOR HIV INFECTION

At present tests are requested for one or more of the following reasons:
1. to ensure that blood intended for transfusion is safe;
2. when symptoms or signs suggest the possibility of HIV infection, *and* confirmation of the diagnosis is needed for good reasons;
3. before surgery, to guide decision-making and alert the surgical team;
4. at ante-natal clinics, to guide management of pregnancy and labour;
5. after surgery if the surgeon sustained an injury and the patient is at risk (through behaviour) for HIV infection;
6. in order to give early treatments which may prolong life and health, especially when drugs which delay multiplication of HIV are available;
7. to relieve anxiety in people who (justifiably) fear HIV infection as a consequence of risky behaviour;
8. when required by insurance companies or for travel to countries which restrict entry of HIV-infected persons e.g. the USA and Saudi Arabia;
9. anonymously, to study the epidemiology of HIV infection in order to predict needs for care and social services or other resources, or to plan prevention strategies.

PREREQUISITES FOR TESTING

It is wise to distinguish between provision of centres where tests *can* be done on request and active *promotion* of voluntary testing. Results must be recorded accurately, kept confidential and transmitted only to those entitled to hear them – the person tested and the doctor (or other authorized person) who requested the test, obtained informed consent and judged that it would yield more benefits than disadvantages to the patient concerned.

The only exception to these rules relates to tests done to study the spread of HIV infection with a view to planning future provision of care or prevention strategies. Such surveys are controversial in every country where they have been done, because the persons tested do not benefit (or may even suffer harm as a result of testing) and yet have no chance to refuse to take part.

But there is no way to learn (in advance of obvious illness) how many people will need care in the future, and whether or not strategies to reduce spread of HIV are effective.

Results are not given to third parties except on the initiative of the person tested. However, counsellors explain why sexual partners have a right to know test results, so that they can decide whether to seek HIV testing for themselves, and whether or not to end a sexual relationship or to reduce its risks by using condoms.

COMMUNITY WELL-BEING AND TESTING POLICIES

Ian Campbell, who helped develop prevention programmes in Zambia, says" 'Denial does not liberate' and 'Behaviour is influenced by knowledge, but also by care and counselling'. In the experience of many AIDS workers, denial of AIDS is prolonged, and effective responses to it are delayed *until* HIV testing is available in a community. Only then can the slow and uneven process of normalization of HIV infection begin.

CHRISTIAN RESPONSIBILITIES

A basic responsibility for everyone, believer or not, is to learn the facts of HIV transmission and how infection can be avoided. If Church leaders or congregations decide that they need to form a policy about HIV testing, they ought to ask (and answer) some preliminary questions:

1. About *attitudes*: do we regard HIV-infected persons as 'recipients' (who ought to receive our forgiveness or care thankfully!) or do we accept them as brothers and sisters from whom we can learn or receive gifts?

2. Should we try to *influence public opinion* or take part in debates about the morality of HIV testing to establish community infection rates, or obligatory testing (during pregnancy, or for candidates for scholarships or training places)?

3. What *pastoral responsibility* do Church leaders bear towards persons whom they advise or require to have tests for HIV infection?

4. What *advice or support* should Churches offer to people who are considering having a test for HIV, waiting for test results or have just received a positive result – whether or not these people are Church members?

5. What instruction about AIDS and HIV infection ought to be included in the *teaching and nurture* of young people (aged five and older), in marriage preparation classes or marriage encounter groups, or in men's and women's separate organizations?

An unvoiced question relating to HIV tests in Church circles seems to be: 'Should anyone who considers changing his or her state in life be tested first for HIV infection?' For example: 'Should a negative test for HIV be a condition for marriage in church, or training for professional ministry, or entering a religious congregation, or employment?' For senior people a more disturbing question might be: 'Should a negative test result be required during the selection process for a bishop, moderator or religious superior?'

MISUSE OF TESTING

Tests for evidence of HIV infection are often requested for wrong or inadequate reasons, because a positive or negative result is thought to provide indirect information about the behaviour or future of the person tested. For example, an HIV test is sometimes used as a *surrogate* test for future good or ill health or as an indicator of past sexual behaviour. The results rarely yield the information desired.

A test for HIV infection is sometimes thought necessary in order to protect members of the public. In fact only two types of risk exist: HIV transmission or mental incapacity which impairs judgement or skills.

As HIV is not transmitted by close but non-sexual contacts, only sex-workers put their clients at risk of acquiring HIV. In theory blood–to–blood contact between infected surgeons or dentists and their uninfected patients could transmit HIV, but in practice transmission of HIV from a professional person to patients has been demonstrated only once. In contrast, transfer of HIV from a patient to a doctor or nurse has been documented regularly, although not often. The risk appears to be about 0.4% for each exposure (through a sharp injury) to infected blood, but such risks accumulate throughout a working lifetime.

Mental symptoms (usually poor short-term memory and slowness of thought) are common in the late stages of AIDS, especially when treatment with anti-viral drugs is not available, but problems are rare until physical health fails. In occupations where quick responses are needed for public safety direct tests for reaction times are a far more accurate and informative safeguard than testing for HIV infection.

DOES TESTING FOR HIV INFECTION MOTIVATE BEHAVIOUR CHANGE?

Another argument advanced for HIV tests is based on a hope that knowledge of results (positive or negative) will motivate those tested to change their behaviour.

A change in sexual behaviour did take place amongst gay men in the United States during the years 1984 to 1986, but the change occurred before tests for HIV were available and while most gay men opposed the concept of testing. *Peer* pressure, not knowledge of HIV infection, has shown the greatest positive influence on behaviour. In contrast, evidence shows that a negative test result, given to people who know their behaviour is risky, may actually encourage risk-taking to continue.

Behavioural studies suggest that it is not testing itself, but the associated counselling, which leads to sustained behaviour change.

A negative test is valid only for the day when it was done, because people tested may become infected by HIV later, if they behave in ways that are risky. This severely limits the usefulness of a negative test as a predictor of future health, particularly in communities where very high seroprevalence rates (over 25% of young adults infected) increase the risks associated with each and every casual sexual encounter.

CONSEQUENCES OF HIV TEST FOR INDIVIDUALS

A test for HIV infection is never a routine or trivial event. For an adult the *voluntary* decision to have a test requires facing the possibility of having been infected through an accident (blood transfusion or use of an unsterile razor blade), misuse of intravenous drugs, or personal sexual behaviour outside marriage or through the infidelity of a spouse. It also requires the courage to admit this anxiety to the person who arranges the test, and to prepare for the prospect of a positive result after several days of suspense: 'Can I cope with waiting to know the truth?'

Except in the case of blood donors, in many countries the *fact* of having had blood tested for HIV (regardless of the result) is seen as evidence that a risk of infection has existed in the past and will persist into the future. This may make the person tested permanently unacceptable as an applicant for life assurance, health insurance, a mortgage or a loan. Adverse consequences of testing for HIV need careful consideration, and the benefits of knowing about HIV infection at one point in time weighed against long-term disadvantages. Some insurance companies are reconsidering negative attitudes and a few may accept 'risky' clients who are HIV-negative – at higher premiums.

A few persons with negative tests are too anxious to accept the results as true and insist on further tests – but remain unable to believe repeatedly negative results. Some men and women, while waiting for test results, think back over their lives and conclude that the pleasures of casual sexual encounters are not worth the acute fear which they now feel. The advice to 'Love faithfully' may be understood for the first time.

A POSITIVE TEST RESULT

A positive test result is always very bad news, however skilfully and kindly it is given, and often leads to a state of shock similar to the shock felt by anyone hearing that a spouse or child has died suddenly.

Nothing will ever be the same again, for every part of one's life-situation changes instantly and permanently. Every relationship alters and self-image as a living person with a long future is replaced by an image of self as already dying – indeed as almost dead, one with no future. Guilt and anger are common, and in some societies admitting to HIV infection is equivalent to admitting membership of a despised group – unfaithful in marriage, a drug-user, a homosexual or a partner in commercial sex.

Almost at once an HIV-infected person begins to worry about how death will come and to anticipate future losses and rejection by a spouse, family members, employer, friends, Church congregation, pastor and neighbours. Sadly, these fears of rejection are often justified.

So anyone who learns that they are HIV-infected urgently needs support – but may be unable to trust anyone enough to ask for or to accept help. Counsellors discuss this problem during pre-test counselling and suggest that the client chooses, in advance, who to tell the news to first.

ADVANTAGES OF HIV TESTING (AS PERCEIVED BY THIRD PARTIES!)

Here are selected 'benefits', drawn from conversations with Church people, with my own comments:

(a) 'A negative test removes the risk of transmitting HIV to other members of our community or to people encountered during professional ministry.' As HIV transmission requires penetrative sexual intercourse or blood-to-blood contact, there is no risk whatsoever of casual transmission in ordinary community life or during pastoral ministry.

(b) 'A negative test reduces the risk that we shall be responsible for looking after a seriously ill person in a few year's time.' This is true only if the person tested remains uninfected. The statement assumes that community commitment should be limited in advance to 'fair weather' conditions.

(c) 'We cannot afford to invest in training an ordinand or a novice who will not reward that training with many years of service.' This statement assumes that there is a direct relationship between the duration of a ministry and its value, and makes questionable assumptions about the nature of vocation and the role of a community or Church in enabling an aspirant to respond to God's call – a matter to which we shall return.

(d) 'We don't want the sort of person who is HIV-positive in our community or our ministry.' This 'benefit' is unlikely to be explicitly admitted but may well be present, hiding prurient curiosity about the sexual history of an applicant or concern for the ritual purity of a community.

(e) 'If his HIV infection is recognized early our applicant can benefit from specific treatment, which will prolong his active life'. This may be true in the West, but at present most developing countries cannot afford the financial or medical costs of treatment with the active antiviral drugs.

BALANCING ADVANTAGES AND DISADVANTAGES OF TESTING

The meaning of a test for HIV infection rests not with the test itself, but with consequences following upon knowledge of the result: it is the responsibility of everyone involved (the person being tested, counsellors, and any third party) to consider where the balance is likely to lie between advantage and disadvantage in each specific and unique situation.

Potential candidates who refuse to have a test will be lost to the vocation under consideration, yet a negative test result is no guarantee that persons tested will remain uninfected for the rest of their life. Indeed in high-incidence countries a religious vocation may be a liability: nuns are sometimes urged by anxious priests to provide sexual favours because they are thought to be 'safe' partners, a circumstance which may lead directly to HIV infection.

The demand for a negative HIV test as a condition for a scholarship or training place made by a few donor countries may encourage unscrupulous people to set up clinics to provide false tests with consistently 'negative' results. There is indirect evidence that such opportunist clinics do exist in some countries.

Many high-incidence countries do not have enough test kits to test all blood intended for transfusion, or to carry out necessary clinical tests. In these circumstances it is difficult to justify non-essential tests.

THEOLOGICAL ISSUES

A working party on the ethics of AIDS and social policy noted that 'ethical discussions of AIDS policies have tended to focus upon the rights of individuals and less upon the well-being, or common good, of society at large'. Many medical decision-makers base their policies on the explicit assumption that attention to the rights of individuals will generally protect the rights of the communities to which they belong. But is this true?

The working party for 'AIDS and social policy' recorded their conviction that AIDS 'concerns society as a whole and raises crucial issues concerned with the common good. A notion of "common good" is not simply concerned with the will of the majority (as in forms of utilitarianism). It is also concerned with caring for *disadvantaged minorities* ... common good is "common" precisely because it embraces both the good of individuals and the good of different groups, as they contribute to each other and to the well-being of society as a whole' (my italics). In the context of AIDS in Africa and Asia 'disadvantaged minorities' may be very large (most women and hundreds of thousands of orphans) – which increases the complexity and urgency of attempts to balance needs against resources.

RELIGIOUS COMMUNITIES AND PROFESSIONAL MINISTRY

Difficult questions arise for religious communities in a world living with AIDS. How much privacy should members of a religious congregation be expected to yield up to those in authority over them? And what effects does loss of privacy have on a person's capacity for responsibility and spiritual growth? Should people responsible for discerning vocations be influenced by (or even seek to know about) repented sin and its long-term consequences, if forgiveness and grace have effected a change in the candidate's way of life? Do we take metanoia seriously?

Most vocations involve three parties: God, the person called, and a 'significant other' person or group (potential marriage partner, religious community, hierarchy in professional ministry, potential employer). Do both candidate and the 'significant other' bear equal responsibility before God for their complementary responses to a vocation? If not, which party bears the greater responsibility if a truly discerned vocation is not lived out?

Is it important for a community to be ritually 'pure' or is the gospel and historical evidence in favour of the opposite opinion? The creative lives of Mary of Magdala, Mary of Egypt, Augustine of Hippo, Charles de Foucauld, Thomas Merton and numerous less well-known men and women would seem to suggest that past sexual purity is less important to God than it is to pious (and envious?) legalists.

Is mutual commitment between professed religious and community, or between minister and hierarchy limited in advance to fair weather, or is it a 'for better or worse, in sickness and in health' commitment, exactly like that of the marriage relationship? And does an institution or community which requests testing as a condition for entry bear a continuing responsibility for pastoral care of HIV-positive persons so discovered?

Many people experience knowledge of HIV infection as a crisis which leads to radical changes in their self-awareness, priorities and life-styles. Time is seen to be limited; life becomes exceedingly precious, a gift to be lived intensely. In their new circumstances some people may feel (and actually *be*) called to religious life, as a direct consequence of

HIV infection. Perhaps some religious congregations ought to recognize a complementary call to respond to and nurture such HIV-related vocations.

PRACTICAL RESPONSES AND NEW QUESTIONS

1. Some Christians should train as counsellors alongside non-believers.
2. Teaching about transmission of HIV and the consequences of infection, with related sexual issues, should be included in catechism classes, youth work and marriage preparation.
3. Leaflets and books about sexual behaviour, HIV infection and AIDS should be stocked in Church bookshops and sold in Churches.
4. Clergy should show that AIDS can be discussed by mentioning it in appropriate contexts in sermons and conversation.
5. Each congregation might choose two or three lay people to be responsible for learning about local resources which are available to help HIV-infected persons and their families.
6. Clergy should be ready to refer Church members to appropriate secular agencies for help.

The existence of many excellent secular agencies which offer voluntary or professional care to HIV-infected and affected people raises difficult questions for some Church groups, for example:

A. Should Christians collaborate with secular groups, or should they set up their own organizations which duplicate (often less effectively) the efforts of others?

B. Are leaders and laity prepared for the long-term commitments and two-way relationships of giving and receiving which are needed to support HIV-infected or affected people? If we are not ready for this degree of involvement in the lives of others, why do we draw back and what experiences might change our attitudes?

C. Are Christians equipped to offer friendship and (if requested) supportive care and counselling to professional or family carers, even if the carers who need support are not Christians? How do leaders and laity relate to men and women who deny religious belief, or who hold beliefs which are different from our own, when we share responsibility in an AIDS care or counselling service?

D. Should we seek opportunities for ecumenical and inter-faith action, study and prayer *with* as well as *for* people living with HIV? Does our own faith actually commit us to working with others in this way?

E. A reflection group meets in Edinburgh to consider theological questions arising out of the AIDS epidemic in that city. Are similar reflection groups needed in other large cities?

Study Suggestions

1. Why was the meaning of positive tests for HIV in the babies of HIV-infected mothers explained at length? What actions could you, as priest or pastor, take to preserve the lives and health of these vulnerable babies? Why are they vulnerable?

2. P. 57 ended with a list of questions for Christians. Select one which interests you for personal reflection, and note down your thoughts. Discuss your reflections with a group of two or three friends.

3. In pairs, role-play a conversation between a bishop and a prospective ordinand. The bishop explains to the candidate why a test for antibodies to HIV is an essential part of the selection process. Then 'come out of role' and examine, together, the *arguments* each actor put forward to support his own point of view, and the *feelings* (fear, defensiveness, anger?) each person experienced. Change partners and repeat the exercise, taking the opposite role.

4. In a group of four, role-play a conversation between a pastor and a couple who have asked to be married in church. The conversation might start from a question posed by one of the young people: 'Do you think we should have tests for HIV infection before our wedding?' or from the pastor's suspicion that one of the potential partners has had two or three previous sexual partners. The fourth person is an observer who remains silent throughout the conversation, but takes part in discussions when the active participants have shed their roles.

5. Your congregation has decided to set up a club for people who have had a test for HIV infection. How would you plan your first meeting and where would you advertise the existence of your club? Who do you think might attend meetings – during the first year, and later when the club has been open for three years? What opposition would you expect to meet from within the congregation and how would you attempt to deal with this?

6. 'Denial does not liberate ... ' Discuss this statement: do you agree or disagree?

DOES HIV CAUSE AIDS?

Late in 1995 claims are still circulating, in the West and in Africa, that HIV has 'nothing to do with AIDS'. It is alleged that AIDS is not caused by HIV, but attributable to use of drugs (including AZT) in the West, and to malnutrition and the effects of tuberculosis, STDs and other infections in Africa. People who make such claims disregard or reject very strong evidence for the causal link between HIV and death from AIDS. Here is some of that evidence:

1. Malnutrition, malaria, tuberculosis, STDs and other bacterial infections were very common in developing countries long before AIDS appeared, but patterns of illness characteristic of AIDS were unknown in these places until the early 1980s. The earliest cases and deaths from AIDS occurred in the higher socio-economic sections of their societies – amongst people who were well-nourished and previously in better-than-average health, who did not use drugs or engage in male-to-male sex. A new disease appeared: I know, I was there.

2. Many long-term cohort studies of people exposed to HIV have shown, repeatedly and without exception, that *only* HIV-infected persons develop AIDS and die prematurely; HIV-negative persons remain well and have the same death rates as the normal population.

3. Throughout the world, the highly characteristic illnesses of AIDS are preceded by HIV infections, documented five to ten years earlier in the sub-groups (traders, sex-workers, haemophiliacs, drivers) which first suffer from AIDS.

4. In rural Uganda nearly 8,000 persons living in ten neighbouring villages were tested for HIV infection in 1990/91 and their health and survival (or deaths) recorded annually for two years. The overall seroprevalence for HIV was 4.8% for all ages, but 8.2% for adults aged 13 years or more. In two years, 23% of the HIV-infected people had died. During each one-year period the overall risk of an HIV-infected young adult dying was 60 times greater than the risk for non-infected persons in the same age-range. The risk of death for an HIV-infected woman was over twice the risk for an HIV-infected man – which is the basis for fears that, in heavily-affected societies, AIDS will change the normal 1:1 ratio of men to women.

At ages 13–44 years, 90% of deaths were attributable to HIV infection; in contrast, most deaths amongst uninfected persons occurred in those aged 0–4 or over 55 years.

5. The existence of defective immunity or opportunist infections due to causes other than HIV does *not* undermine the evidence that HIV infection is the commonest cause of severe, progressive and finally fatal immune deficiency in the world today.

CHAPTER 5

Medical Consequences and Health Service Responses

HIV infection has serious medical consequences for individuals but, because of the scale of the pandemic, there are serious consequences for health services too, at every level from rural clinic to national teaching hospital and beyond. It is characteristic of HIV-related events that both personal and community consequences remain hidden for years and are difficult to interpret and to accept when they do appear.

First reactions to HIV-related events tend to be disorganized, confused, and driven by denial and fear, whether or not fear is informed by a little knowledge. Later, infected people, health service workers and policy-makers act in ways which are intended to 'put things right'. Some responses are deliberate and informed (within the limits of available information), others are well-meant but ad hoc attempts to deal with urgent situations. Both types of response may have destructive or constructive effects which their originators did not predict or intend and, cumulatively, ad hoc responses may drive policies in directions which no-one has deliberately 'chosen'.

Three confounding factors are of crucial importance for health services. First, the relative speeds of pandemic and response are mismatched: HIV spreads faster and consequences develop faster than any Ministry of Health or government can keep up with – either in terms of gathering and analysing information or through practical responses to new demands. Administrative machinery for making decisions and implementing them is not built for a target which is moving as fast as AIDS.

Next, 'humankind cannot bear very much reality' (17). Every constructive response to AIDS was delayed by months or years because it was so difficult to admit that we are facing a crisis. The battle to recognize crisis is fought within each person as well as within every organization. I remember the split in myself during 1984 and 1985 as I struggled to describe to others what I saw each day in wards and clinics, while part of my mind warned: 'Calm down, you must be interpreting the evidence wrongly, it can't be as bad as you say it is!' Today the situation is not only as bad as I thought it would be as I looked ahead in 1985, but a great deal worse.

Finally, there is a strange mis-match between the priority which we give to 'health' in theory and the resources which we devote to it in practice, both as individuals and as communities. Most people take physical and mental well-being for granted, to the extent of abusing both constantly (by using tobacco or alcohol to excess) – but only until health is lost, when it becomes a 'value' of huge importance. Similarly, government officials state that 'the health of our people is vital to national well-being' while denying health both human and financial resources. The money and political will to develop infrastructures needed to supply safe water, affordable and nutritious food, good housing, sanitation and efficient primary health care are never today's priority. (Instead, a prestigious army appears to be more important than 'health' in many countries, judging from national budget plans.) In 1992 Jonathan Mann pointed out that we do not actually have a global health policy, and that we urgently need to develop one.

We need to know the usual course and consequences of HIV infection in individuals in order to understand the demands AIDS will make on health services – and on the global health policy which we do not yet have.

INDIVIDUALS WITH HIV INFECTION: ONSET

Other sexually transmitted diseases (STDs) cause, within a few days, either a genital ulcer (which may be hidden in women), a discharge, or discomfort during urination. These symptoms have the useful effect of making sexual intercourse less pleasant, so reducing the chance that infection will be transmitted to another person. Unfortunately HIV infection does not cause any local symptoms which inhibit transmission.

However, about 10% of people newly infected with HIV have an acute general illness within two to six weeks of exposure, which seems unrelated to their sexual organs. This illness starts suddenly with fever, sweats, headache, fatigue, aching joints and muscles and loss of appetite; there may be swollen lymph nodes and a skin rash or (rarely) symptoms of disease in the nervous system. The acute illness lasts two to four weeks and then improves spontaneously, but it may be so mild as to pass unnoticed. Western sufferers tend to make a self-diagnosis of influenza, but nearly all are sufficiently ill to consult a doctor; African sufferers often make a self-diagnosis of malaria and take chloroquine, although some consult a doctor because their fever does not improve as quickly as they expect. Other virus infections which are common in the tropics start in a similar way and may be sought or excluded by laboratory investigations.

Although the acute illness improves quickly, many people remain slightly unwell for some months, with persistent swelling of small lymph nodes (especially behind the ears), sweating at night, mild weight loss and lack of energy. Then symptoms disappear and HIV-infected people feel well and energetic, though experienced doctors may still feel their enlarged nodes.

Definitions: With or without an *acute onset illness*, important changes take place in an infected person's blood. Within a few days of infection, proteins (*antigens*) produced by HIV itself appear in the blood, followed later by *antibodies*, which are produced by the infected person in response to the presence of HIV. The tests for infection used in most hospitals detect antibodies, not HIV or its proteins, so usually there is a gap of four weeks to three months after infection occurred before blood tests for antibody become positive. Sometimes this 'window period' last much longer.

If recently-infected people donate blood during the 'window period' when screening tests for HIV give negative results, their infected blood will be transfused – and it will almost certainly transmit HIV to any person who receives it. In cities where new HIV infections are common the chances of this happening are quite high: for this reason it is important to restrict blood transfusions to life-saving situations. An alternative approach would be to reject any blood donor who has sexual intercourse outside a mutually faithful relationship, unless every sexual act is protected by efficient use of a new condom. In most countries such stringent conditions would eliminate many potential donors.

INFECTED BUT WELL

Whether or not an acute onset illness occurred, a period of normal health follows. In adults this usually lasts for several years, although it may be as short as a few months. Most babies remain healthy for a much shorter time, about one year, but may become ill within a few weeks if they were infected early in pregnancy.

During this *latent* period the infected person is infectious, and may learn of their HIV infection if blood is tested in one of the circumstances listed in ch 4; the impact of a test result depends upon whether or not the implications of HIV infection are understood.

A positive test is particularly disturbing if a mother is tested because her child is ill, when the possibility of HIV infection has not entered her mind.

EARLY DISEASE: PRE-AIDS OR THE
AIDS-RELATED COMPLEX

In the mid 1980s HIV-infected patients in African city hospitals were referred from doctor to doctor with gradually thickening files of notes. A typical story included two or three short admissions to an emergency medical ward for cough, fever or diarrhoea, one or two visits to a skin clinic for rashes, several attempts to treat STDs which are usually cured by one course of antibiotics, an abscess (or two) drained in the casualty department, and finally, several weeks in a medical ward for investigation of weight loss or long-lasting fever. The puzzled doctor was faced by a patient – man or woman – around the age of thirty who seemed to have no known disease – but who was clearly seriously ill.

Collectively, the illnesses in the early (outpatient) part of this story are given the label 'pre-AIDS syndrome' or 'AIDS-related complex' (ARC). The serious illness at the end of the story often marks the first recognition of AIDS – the adjective 'full-blown' has no meaning and is best omitted.

At this stage two conditions may occur which are not necessarily related to infections: swelling of lymph nodes all over the body, and easy bruising or bleeding due to a shortage of specific blood cells (platelets) which are needed for clotting. Usually the shortage of platelets is temporary and often no treatment is needed, but unexplained bruises or bleeding from any part of the body in a person who is known to be HIV-infected should be taken seriously and investigated in hospital. Enlargement of lymph nodes is worth a clinic visit too, because some swollen nodes are due to diseases such as tuberculosis (TB), which can be treated effectively, although more often the swelling is due to HIV and cannot be altered by drugs.

The commonest events at this stage are troublesome but not dangerous infections, which begin two or three years before any illness that justifies the label 'AIDS'. Opportunistic infections respond slowly to ordinary treatments and are often cured without admission to hospital, but they increase the workload of already busy clinics. Repeated ill-health reduces productivity at work, disturbs family life and shows that the immune system is critically weak, causing intense anxiety to anyone who knows that they are HIV-infected.

The rate at which immune defences break down depends on a balance between the total amount of virus in body organs, the efficiency of the immune system at the time HIV was acquired and the effects of infections and other stresses encountered later.

In Europe and North America an average time from infection with HIV to the diagnosis of an AIDS-defining illness is nine to ten years, meaning that half of all infected persons remain well for most of ten years. There is growing evidence that the average time from HIV infection to AIDS in developing countries is much shorter, probably about five years. Some strains of HIV may multiply more rapidly than others, and a large initial dose of HIV (e.g. in a transfusion) may allow the virus load to reach a critical level quickly. An immature immune system (in a young baby) or repeated stimulation of immune defences (for example by STDs) may hasten the breakdown of health. The same effect follows from reduced activity in an HIV-infected immune system during normal pregnancy and after accidents or operations. *Malnutrition* is another reason for rapid progression to AIDS; alcohol in excess contributes by reducing the amount of food eaten. Smoking acts indirectly by increasing the frequency of throat and lung infections.

Knowledge about *factors* which accelerate progression to AIDS is useful, because knowledge reduces helplessness and allows HIV-infected people to hope – and to prolong their active lives by changes in life-style. We advise seropositive persons to:

(a) Avoid new sexual partners – and sexually transmitted diseases;
(b) Stop smoking;
(c) Reduce alcohol intake to one beer a day (or its equivalent);
(d) Avoid pregnancy;
(e) Eat more fruit, vegetables and protein foods (groundnuts, fish, eggs, or chicken) using money saved by giving up smoking and heavy drinking;
(f) Obtain early treatment for infections (cough or diarrhoea or rashes);
(g) Avoid skin damage, particularly scarification by traditional healers.

TIME AND HIV INFECTION

Unfortunately time is a factor which has an inescapable influence on breakdown of immune defences due to HIV. The longer the time since HIV infection occurred, the greater the likelihood that immune defences are weak. Specific opportunistic infections, e.g. thrush in the mouth, shingles (herpes zoster) on the skin, warn everyone that immune defences are critically weak, and disappearance of large lymph nodes is another serious warning sign.

Laboratories in referral hospitals may be able to count the absolute numbers of the blood cells which are the primary target for HIV: cells bearing on their surfaces the CD4 molecule which is the 'gate' for entry of HIV into the cell. Soon after HIV enters the body, numbers of CD4 cells in blood begin to fall slowly, but later the rate of loss accelerates and when absolute numbers are very low serious infections occur (because CD4 cells organize and control immune defences in the same way as officers organize and control an army).

ANTI-VIRAL TREATMENTS

Breakdown of the immune system can be delayed by reducing the rate at which HIV multiplies in cells – but at a cost. Several drugs interfere with one stage of HIV production and their use delays, but does not prevent, breakdown of immune defences. Many trials in industrial nations have determined satisfactory doses and shown how often side-effects occur, as well as how long benefit continues. Eventually HIV 'learns' how to avoid each drug, so that it no longer interferes with virus production, and breakdown of immune defences goes ahead. As active drugs are only temporarily effective, it is important to start treatment at the best possible time to achieve maximum benefit – neither too early, nor too late. But there is no agreement, yet, on the best state of HIV-infection at which to begin treatment, especially as all effective drugs have toxic effects. A large study in Europe has shown that starting treatment before signs of illness develop is not necessarily beneficial to persons infected with HIV.

Only three drugs are of some use: zidovudine (AZT), didanosine (ddI), and a related drug, ddC. None of these drugs are generally available in developing countries, partly because serious toxic effects would be difficult to manage in their health systems, but mainly because they are prohibitively expensive in relation to per capita funds for health, and do not cure AIDS but only delay death.

In 1992 the existence of a double standard of care for HIV-infected persons began to trouble the consciences of AIDS workers and people with HIV infection in industrial countries where AZT is used routinely. At present many HIV-infected people in developing nations do not know that such drugs exist.

THE LAST STAGE OF HIV INFECTION: AIDS

Both general and specific signs show that the last stage in breakdown of the immune system has been reached. The *general signs* are shared with many other diseases which are curable so they must never be interpreted as evidence for AIDS in the absence of *specific supporting signs*.

The general signs are unexplained weight loss in excess of 10% of normal adult weight or unexplained failure to gain weight in a baby and unexplained fever or diarrhoea or cough lasting for more than one month in an adult or a child – note that the adjective 'unexplained' recurs.

Several *specific infections or diseases* indicate breakdown of the immune system so certainly that their diagnosis is used as a 'marker' for AIDS (see Figure 6).

Impaired function of the nervous system is very common in HIV-

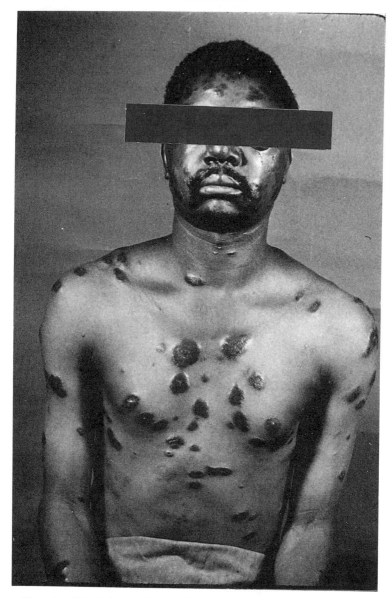

Figure 6. Clinical photograph: signs of Kaposi's Sarcoma.

infected persons in all countries but usually only in the late stages of disease: it is rare (although not impossible) for HIV infection of the brain to cause problems while general physical health remains good.

If the spinal cord and nerves controlling muscle movements are affected a person has difficulty in walking, problems with balance and tremor of the hands. Although some people lose the co-ordination and strength needed to walk, this is rare and only a few need wheelchairs. If the brain is affected a person's memory becomes less reliable, and they think, speak and act more slowly than normal, but usually continue to manage their own affairs competently for some time. Slowness and loss of memory are so common in the final weeks or months of life that it is wise for all HIV-infected people to make a Will, to arrange for care of their children and to put their business affairs in order at an early stage while general health remains good.

In addition to diseases which threaten life directly, persons with AIDS suffer other troublesome problems: skin rashes, repeated attacks of cough or diarrhoea, and thrush or sores in the mouth and on the genitalia. Most infections can be treated successfully (if the right drugs are available), but symptoms disturb sleep and make eating painful or swallowing difficult so contributing to distress, loss of weight and absences from work.

TUBERCULOSIS AND HIV

Tuberculosis was described recently as 'the forgotten plague'. In Europe and North America TB used to flourish in poor living conditions in crowded cities, where it was a common cause of death in all classes of society 150 years ago. At that time the cause was unknown.

After 1882, when Koch identified the tubercle bacillus (TB is used to refer to the tubercle bacillus *and* to the disease which it causes), isolation of patients became a weapon in the fight against infection. TB, unlike HIV, is transmitted from person to person in droplets of fluid from the lungs and air passages (far too small to see), which are sprayed into the air when anyone coughs and breathed in by everyone who is nearby. If such droplets carry TB, infection may result. TB is protected against human defence systems and antibiotics by a waxy covering and it easily 'learns' to resist antibiotics.

During the 1940s trials of anti-TB drugs began, but it was soon found that some TB are naturally resistant to each active drug, so that if only one is used, sensitive bacteria are killed but resistant varieties take over and kill the patient.

The solution was to use three drugs together. If doses were taken absolutely regularly every day, three drugs always cured TB, but if doses were missed occasionally, then TB soon became resistant to treatment, and patients were likely to die. Unfortunately, if they infected other people, *their* disease might not respond to treatment at all, because the infecting TB were already resistant to common drugs. By 1960 there was real hope of eliminating TB worldwide. In developing countries control programmes were set up and two inexpensive but powerful drugs that are taken by mouth, isoniazid (INAH) and thiacetazone, were found to be effective. Babies were vaccinated against TB, even though protection was only partial: most children exposed to TB still became infected but no longer fell ill or died, as TB remained inactive in their bodies, providing that they had normal immune defences.

But about 20 years ago numbers of new cases of TB began to increase in developing countries, in spite of control programmes, although this was not noticed at the time. Ten years later numbers of new cases of TB in New York began to rise too, amongst homeless men.

At first an interaction between TB and HIV was not noticed, because most HIV-infected people in the West had not been exposed to TB in childhood, and in developing countries HIV-infected people did not have enough damage to their immune defences to lose control of 'hidden' TB for several years. Since 1985, however, an alarming increase in new patients with active TB has occurred wherever HIV infection is common, particularly in developing countries. The risk 0of active TB has risen from a life-time risk of 10% for normal people, to a risk of 10% *per year* for persons who are HIV-infected. Moreover, as in the past, irregular treatment fails to cure TB.

In the West there have been several outbreaks of TB which is resistant to *all* active drugs. Because lung TB is very infectious, it is essential to isolate patients with drug-resistant disease from contact with others. In developing countries, too, TB is beginning to resist standard drugs, forcing use of more expensive substitutes. Now a new problem has appeared: severe skin reactions to one drug (thiacetazone) are twenty times more common in HIV-infected patients than in other patients. Thiacetazone has become too dangerous to use.

The World Bank estimates that TB now kills more people, worldwide, than any other bacterial infection, hence this chapter's concentration on global TB in the context of AIDS.

In Zambia the interaction of TB and HIV has been studied since 1988 and control and treatment programmes are being adapted appropriately. Newly diagnosed patients with TB are no longer admitted to hospital but start treatment in clinics. About half of new TB patients in rural areas and 70% in Lusaka are also HIV-infected but, despite this, usually respond well to short courses of more expensive and more effective drugs. The new short treatments are more cost-effective than older drug combinations, which is important in an epidemic situation.

Everyone who understands how TB threatens the health of communities and how easily it spreads has a part to play in preventing it, and should press for TB control programmes to be strengthened at once, in advance of urgent need, particularly in Asia. At the personal level, we must encourage individual TB patients to take their drugs regularly as part of their duty to family and community. If we do so we may have a second chance to save some of the 3 million lives lost each year to TB.

AIDS

The definition of AIDS used in each country is chosen locally by the Ministry of Health and WHO to take account of the commonest opportunistic infections in the region and to make wise use of scarce laboratory resources. Not all definitions require a test for HIV, because the cost of one test may exceed the entire per capita health budget for one year. Similarly, it is not necessary to take tissue for biopsy from most people with Kaposi's sarcoma because disease on the skin or in the mouth can be identified accurately on sight.

The concept 'AIDS' is artificial, as 'AIDS' is only one stage in a continuous process which starts with acquisition of HIV and ends years later with a serious infection or tumour as the immediate cause of death. Some observers of the pandemic think that it would be more logical and useful to divide people into three groups:
  (a) Uninfected.
  (b) Infected but free of symptoms.
  (c) Infected, with symptoms which interfere with work and normal life.
Such a simple classification is not simplistic, because it clarifies objectives for communities and planners by identifying groups of people who make specific demands on health services and society.

It is in everyone's interest to prevent *uninfected persons* from acquiring infection, by helping them to change their behaviour in appropriate ways – permanently.

It is likewise in everyone's interest to keep *well but HIV-infected people* fit and able to fulfil family and social responsibilities for as long as possible. We know that almost everyone who is HIV-infected will make large demands on health services in the future, often for several years, but good health care can be highly cost-effective if it extends productive working life, and equally important, working life as a parent – for whom there is no substitute. Every extra month of normal home life is worthwhile to a potential orphan, and each month of normal work (multiplied by a number equal to 25% of adult workers) contributes to an affected country's economic welfare.

But words such as 'welfare' and 'worthwhile' refer to human values. Here is a difficulty, for providers and users of funds, policy-makers and business men use information expressed in figures to decide how 'needs' will be related to 'resources' and investments balanced against returns and profits. In decision-making, qualitative data tends to be ignored unless it can be translated into quantities, partly because it is perceived as less 'real' than data expressed in figures. Human values are liable to be neglected if they seem likely to impede economic growth, which many countries believe is the road to happiness. Greater fulfilment of human potential does not seem to be seriously considered as an alternative goal. When making money has a higher priority than the welfare of people, Christians have opportunities to challenge the quantitative assumptions and theories on which market economies are based, to attempt to reinstate 'quality' and 'value' as respectable concepts for public use.

All prescriptions for international responses to AIDS should be read from the perspective that plans are for people, and not the reverse. A response to the pandemic succeeds or fails only in so far as it identifies real needs and meets them in a fully human way which respects the dignity of each individual person, however powerless, wasted, confused, inarticulate or unimportant they may be. Although it may be necessary to use the language of the market-place to 'justify' providing care when applying for funds, we should use the language of the gospel in our dealings with each other and introduce its words into the vocabulary of secular meetings whenever we have an opportunity to do so.

UNDOING RECENT DIS-ADVANCES IN MEDICAL CARE

Some techniques of Western medicine have given remarkable results and contributed greatly to human welfare: smallpox no longer exists, birth has been made safer for mother and child, vaccination prevents many infectious diseases, and oral rehydration solution saves babies with diarrhoea. But there have been losses as well as gains in medical care during the last fifty years. Until powerful specific drugs became available, most sick people (anywhere in the world) stayed at home. There they received care from their families and from healers – who treated them as sick persons, not as cases of this or that disease. Healers used drugs which were neither powerful nor certain in their effects as only part of a programme of care which paid attention to the whole situation of the sick person. Physical things mattered – air, warmth, water, special foods, sleep, ointments, particular postures. The emotional, mental and spiritual life of the patient was important too. In some cultures illness was attributed to disordered relationship to God, so that reconciliation with God was necessary; in other cultures disease was attributed to the ill-will of some person who sought revenge for an injury in the past. But whatever the underlying philosophy, healers listened attentively to sick people in order to respond to the whole of their humanity, and sick persons suffered – and either survived or died – surrounded by their families. From about 1945 onwards powerful drugs and complex techniques had the effect of depersonalizing Western medical care. Doctors no longer gave much personal attention or advice because all that was needed for cure was a few injections or pills taken regularly. If cure demanded more complicated treatment, that usually meant admission to hospital amongst strangers who had too much to 'do' to have time to listen to stories of pain or distress, or to 'be there' with a sick person.

As machines and medicines multiplied, care in the home came to be regarded as out-of-date, if not dangerous. In the West home became the wrong place to die, because death was seen as an embarrassing interruption of normal life. In developing countries, too, home is often the wrong place to die, but for different reasons – because it is difficult and expensive to transport a corpse to a mortuary, whereas it is possible (if not exactly easy) to transport a dying person to hospital, there to lie on the floor of an overcrowded emergency ward until he or she is ready to be moved to a shelf in an equally overcrowded mortuary.

AIDS is helping to restore a human face to Western medical care, reinforced by other influences working in the same direction. Doctors who reach the end of their stock of useful drugs must either walk out of the clinic in despair, or else stay and talk to their patients. Talking is difficult, because healers have to admit that they cannot 'cure' (which had become the only acceptable end-point for treatment) and must face their own mortality. But doctors and nurses are slowly learning to meet HIV-infected people (and by extension, most other patients) as human beings who have a life-story, families, fears, hopes and spiritual needs – as well as defective immune systems causing clinical problems, which may have technical solutions.

Sick people are often more comfortable in their own homes than in hospital and those with HIV-impaired immune defences may also be *safer* at home, where they are not exposed to infections carried by other patients in the ward. Medical care at home can be as good as care in hospital if families are lent basic equipment, given drugs, and taught simple nursing methods.

Zambia and Uganda decided several years ago to de-centralize and de-hospitalize care of HIV-infected persons. 'Homecare' developed as a new service in both countries, and the idea has proved adaptable, effective and acceptable in a variety of circumstances – in remote villages separated by miles of dirt track, in high-density urban housing estates, in small country towns, and in élite suburbs. Methods differ in different places. Each locality needs a multidisciplinary team with a mixture of experienced nurses or clinical officers, pastors, drivers, and volunteer listeners, all of whom need training in counselling skills and mutual respect for each other's talents. Homecare, at its best, is not an inferior substitute for hospital treatment (which remains necessary for particular purposes) but supplements hospital and clinic services to make good care more accessible. If care at home becomes a normal part of modern management of other diseases (which is already happening for TB) this advance may be reckoned as a benefit to society from the AIDS pandemic.

ASSESSING NEEDS: COLLECTING FACTS

HIV infection increases the total quantity of illness in a community and alters the qualitative demands upon health services. Not only are more people sick at any one time but their problems tend to respond to treatment less rapidly and complications are more likely. For example, adverse reactions to drugs are more common in HIV-infected people and so are wound infections after routine surgery.

The pattern of demand for health care alters: infections are a more frequent reason for emergency admission and TB clinics enlarge, so reorganization of resources is required in order to benefit as many users as possible.

Planning the wise and humane use of staff, clinics and hospital beds, and seeking additional funds, requires figures and facts, even though human values are important too. Planners need to know how many people in the population are HIV-infected and already ill (and so in need of care now), and how many are infected although still well (but likely to need care later). These figures indicate the demands that AIDS will *add* to the 'normal' needs which health services had to meet before AIDS arrived.

Unfortunately, these calculations are not enough. Health care workers (HCW) have their share of human weaknesses, and they are almost as likely as anyone else to become HIV-infected (in their sexual not their working lives) even though as HCW they are well-informed about AIDS. Numbers of HCW in training ought to be increased, not only to provide more carers to match the increasing number of sick people but also to prepare for premature loss, due to AIDS, of 20% to 30% of all HCW about 25 years *before* their normal retirement age.

Surveys count numbers of seropositive people in order to attempt to answer questions such as:

(a) Should more bankers, miners, farmers, priests, doctors, policemen, teachers or soldiers be trained now and in the future, to ensure enough skilled workers to maintain essential services during the next twenty years?

(b) How will funds be found to pay for more staff and training, and for sickness and other benefits for workers who fall ill in their mid-thirties?

(c) Which groups of people behave in risky ways, and need focused programmes to help them to begin and continue safer patterns of behaviour?

EFFECTS OF HIV INFECTION ON POPULATION STRUCTURE AND GROWTH

During the last two decades, population growth rates in many developing countries have exceeded 3% per annum because numbers of live births have remained well above replacement level, while death rates fell because of better public health and primary care. As HIV-infected women and men die during their peak reproductive years, the average number of children born to each couple is likely to decrease in heavily-affected countries. If family size falls fast enough, and death rates rise (primarily due to AIDS), then population growth will slow down. Is zero population growth, or even depopulation, a real or an illusory possibility?

Mathematicians use demographic data (mostly from developing countries) and computer-operated models to try to answer this question. They produce sets of graphs showing birth and death rates per 100,000 population over several decades, assuming different rates of increase of seropositivity (and different average rates of partner change) within communities.

As a typical developing country has a pyramidal population structure (see p. 16), at any given time about 45% of the population are under 15 years of age – and will soon be producing children themselves. This simple fact gives population growth in the developing world a huge momentum, and accounts for a common opinion that exponential population growth threatens civilization – and even survival of the human species. Will populations continue to enlarge dangerously, or will countries reach a balance between births and deaths, so that their numbers stabilize at manageable levels? Could AIDS so upset the balance between births and deaths that significant areas of the world become depopulated? At present there are no clear answers to these questions.

A recent study imagined a country in which nearly 50% of the *whole* (urban and rural) adult population is HIV-infected by the year 2015. Such a high infection rate would result in a death rate about four times higher than would be expected without AIDS and, by the year 2010, AIDS would cause three times as many deaths as all other causes combined. In this scenario, deaths would exceed births from 2010 onwards, so that population numbers would begin to fall from that date. The authors of this study considered it unlikely (though not impossible) that 50% of adults in a population will ever be HIV-infected, as rural seropositivity levels are still lower than in towns, and because people are likely to learn to avoid risky sexual behaviour.

It is tempting to accept this reassuring conclusion without criticizing the assumptions on which it was based. But it would be safer to examine those assumptions because predictions were presented which do not fit observations that have already been made. This mis-match suggests that the assumptions on which predictions were based are wrong.

A graph is presented which shows predicted increases in seroprevalence rates in a hypothetical at-risk population in which HIV spreads at two different rates, 'expected' and 'higher than expected', starting from a seroprevalence for HIV of 3%. At the end of 25 years the 'expected' rate of spread leads to infection of 18% of the population, while at the 'higher' rate of transmission 25% are infected. If, however, a new curve is added to the graph to show the *actual* increase in seroprevalence already observed amongst women attending an ante-natal clinic in Lusaka (8% in 1985, 24% in 1990 and 36% in 1993), the slope of this additional line is much steeper than the slope of either 'predicted' graph. This discrepancy suggests that assumptions (about numbers of sexual partners, or likelihood of transmission per sexual act, or frequency of partner change) used in the study may not be reliable – unless women attending an ante-natal clinic in Lusaka are more likely than 'average' adults to become infected with HIV. This seems improbable, as similar increases in seropositivity have been observed in other cities. Critical questions ought to be asked.

Another difficulty relates to the effect of AIDS on death rates due to other causes, which are assumed (usually) to remain at pre-pandemic levels. But death rates may rise in high-risk communities for several reasons: because orphans receive less food and less medical care than children with parents, health services are over burdened, or TB becomes more common – or because midwifery is thought to be a hazardous profession, so that fewer midwives train and mothers get less care during pregnancy and labour.

Although we cannot predict the effect AIDS will have on population *growth* with certainty, already we *can* predict large changes in the *structure* of populations, due to selective loss of individuals in two age bands: less than two years, and aged between 25 and 40 years. Loss of young children is tragic for their parents, and their illnesses burden busy clinics and hospitals, but such early deaths do not have direct economic or social effects. On the other hand, the deaths of young adults have direct and indirect effects on the way society functions, which is the subject of ch. 6. Although there were occasions in the past when thousands of adults died over a short space of time in wars or epidemics, usually losses did not continue for decades and they were localized to relatively small geographical areas. There are no good precedents to guide prediction for societies which are living with AIDS.

SUPPLYING NEEDS: ORGANIZATION AND PLANNING

When numbers of HIV-infected persons have been counted and urgent needs identified, the next stage is to choose priorities and examine resources. But someone has to make those choices, and at first there may be no structures ready to tackle a problem on the scale of an AIDS epidemic, even if the will to do so exists.

In the mid 1980s *structures for response* developed in a piecemeal way, hindered by inadequate information about the behaviour of HIV and the behaviour of communities, and by opposition from persons or organizations that were unwilling to admit to the existence of a problem. For example, in Zambia people with AIDS were recognized in clinics during 1983 and thereafter numbers increased rapidly. By 1984 there were reliable tests for HIV in blood, so it became possible to find out what proportion of the population (or sub-groups of it) were already infected and might later develop AIDS. That year a troubled doctor invited a group of overseas epidemiologists to carry out a survey, and when they reached Lusaka in 1985 a meeting was arranged to discuss the project: from this (mainly) medical committee an AIDS Surveillance Committee later developed.

In other countries different events were the occasion for a 'structure' to form, and different structures resulted – with other names (for example, AIDS Control Programme), or a wider membership (more multidisciplinary) or with different objectives. Some Control Programmes soon sub-divided into separate sub-committees for specific purposes, for example, to guide education-for-prevention, or to plan clinical care and protection of blood supplies and hospital staff.

International responses developed in a similarly piecemeal fashion, rather slowly, because at first the scale of the problem seemed small alongside more familiar threats such as malaria or malnutrition. In 1985 Dr Jonathan Mann was appointed by WHO as the director of a Special Programme on AIDS (SPA), set up to co-ordinate research and interventions to reduce spread of HIV in affected countries.

Responses began in collaborating countries with a short-term plan: for example, in Zambia a small team from London visited the country in 1986 to help the Ministry of Health to set up nationwide testing of donated blood for HIV, to reduce the risk of infection through transfusion. Similar short-term projects were done later in other countries.

The next stage was to develop medium-term plans, for a five-year period, to co-ordinate a range of responses to meet needs which were beginning to be identified. The tentative language is deliberate, because many 'needs' (such as care for dependants) were not recognized for several years, and even quite recently AIDS was perceived as primarily a 'medical' problem not as an economic, social, political, philosophical and theological issue. For example, in '*AIDS 1991: a year in review*' (13), 217 pages were given to medical matters and only 48 to social, cultural and political aspects of the pandemic.

Soon WHO enlarged the special programme in Geneva, renaming it the Global Programme on AIDS (GPA), and appointed AIDS Programme Officers in affected countries, to work with counterparts in each Ministry of Health to co-ordinate AIDS projects. Workers caring for HIV-infected and affected people planned detailed projects, emphasizing education to prevent spread of HIV, protection of blood supplies, training for counsellors, provision of gloves, bleach and plastic mortuary bags to protect medical and nursing staff and improvement of STD services. Homecare was accepted, as an experiment, and the prevalence of infection was recorded regularly, to follow the effects of interventions and to watch the progression (or decline) of the epidemic.

In a field where everyone was an explorer and where there were no known landmarks, it was difficult to choose priorities and easy to ignore frightening aspects of the pandemic, such as the possibility that orphans would need care, or that mortuaries might not be large enough to meet demands. When potential donors met with project officers to pledge funds to support the medium-term plan, donor priorities influenced the way projects developed. The reputations, professional interests, negotiating abilities and backstage influence of individual project-leaders also shaped responses. NGOs with overseas offices applied their own international rules, which did not always fit the new situation, and political factors dictated that some projects were accepted and others were not. Even at this early stage, a few national NGOs were set up to try to meet new needs.

Some donor governments pledged uncommitted funds to medium-term plans through WHO or bilateral agreements at government level; others preferred to channel funds through local NGOs, while some donors were directly involved in the day-to-day running of projects. After the first year an external review of progress was carried out, and projects were modified in an attempt to meet newly recognized needs.

IMPLEMENTING PLANS

At first, plans were put into effect through established structures. Blood bank technicians were taught how to test blood for HIV, using newly-imported equipment in existing laboratories. Health education units designed posters which warned a puzzled population to avoid promiscuity, sometimes without explaining what 'promiscuity' means. Seminars were held to enlist the help of Church leaders, and drama groups prepared and performed plays about AIDS in towns and villages. STD clinics distributed condoms and provided education-for-prevention to captive audiences of waiting patients. In clinics, wards and laboratories HCW treated all body fluids as potentially infected and wore plastic gloves more often.

More people attended clinics, especially for TB, and more people were admitted to hospital. Because HIV-infected patients recover more slowly than others from common infections, wards became overcrowded and staff found the frequency of deaths amongst young patients distressing and depressing. Workshops were held to teach the facts of HIV transmission, in order to calm the fears of HCW and to train counsellors. Nurses and clinical officers taught themselves how to care for HIV-infected persons in their homes, and slowly, as their skills and experience grew, they gained confidence and pride in difficult work well done.

AN AIDS 'INDUSTRY'?

In 1985, four years after the first description of AIDS, an international conference was held in Atlanta, USA, to share information about this new disease. By 1988 AIDS was an established medical speciality, with new journals, specialist organizations, a new vocabulary, and proliferating conferences. Is there now an AIDS 'industry' which exploits human misery?

As in most human activities, there are indeed elements of exploitation and opportunities to profit from AIDS. Exploitation is probably more common away from direct contact with HIV-infected people because, face-to-face with suffering, most workers are reminded of their own mortality and drawn into unselfish service. Some carers discover that it is Christ who is asking for care and they become His disciples.

CURING OR HEALING?

There is an old saying that medicine should cure sometimes, relieve symptoms often and comfort always. In recent times, in modern Western medicine, cure (the permanent removal of a disease process) was the accepted goal. Death was not seen as a natural event but as a professional failure, and attention was focused on physical survival. Well-being as wholeness of emotional, spiritual and community life tended to be regarded as an unrealistic goal.

This definition of health as primarily physical well-being is not the viewpoint of the gospel, where physical healing often takes second place to healing of a relationship with God which has been damaged by sin. I use the term 'healing' to refer to wholeness of personal life, with or without physical well-being – but with the reminder that 'wholeness' and 'holiness' are related words in the English language.

The effects of HIV infection on health services and population structure are not the only consequences of the pandemic for society, and to these wider and non-medical consequences we must now turn.

Study Suggestions
1. What effects does HIV infection have on: family size, children's education, father's earning capacity, lives of old people?
2. What is the difference in meaning between 'HIV-infected' and 'HIV-affected?'
3. Why do you think that tuberculosis (TB) was singled out from other infections for more detailed discussion?
4. Do you see any signs in your own community that HIV infection is changing population structure? Do you know of any 'depopulated' villages?
5. Do you see changes in your own local clinic or hospital which might be attributed to the AIDS epidemic? What are those changes? Do they make it easier or more difficult for you and your family to find the medical care you need?

CHAPTER 6
Social Consequences and Responses

During the mid 1980s the impact of AIDS on health and health care was at first denied and later minimized. In exactly the same way, the impact of AIDS on society was at first denied – and is still denied or minimized in some heavily affected countries, even where Ministries of Health are responding constructively to the pandemic. In theory planners recognize that a high incidence of HIV infection hinders achievement of development goals. In practice AIDS still tends to be 'forgotten' or ignored in medium and long-term planning (outside the field of health) because AIDS is thought to have mainly medical consequences, but is not expected to have an impact on economic and political affairs.

The effects of AIDS on social and economic life in developing countries began to be studied, tentatively, in the late 1980s, several years after HIV was first recognized, at a time when 15% – 20% of urban adults in high-incidence areas were already HIV-infected. This chapter offers an overview of observed effects, mixed with speculation about further consequences which are not yet visible – or (if visible) unrecorded, because observers turn a blind eye to frightening evidence: this happened in respect of AIDS orphans in the late 1980s.

As social consequences of AIDS develop, awareness of change and spontaneous reactions to it begin more or less simultaneously, but responses which are intended to 'put things right' take longer to plan. As in the field of health care, reactions and responses to HIV-related social change may have positive or negative results which were neither intended nor predicted.

'SOCIETAL VULNERABILITY' TO HIV AND AIDS

Recently the Harvard-based Global Policy Coalition on AIDS classified the world's countries into those with high, medium or low 'societal vulnerability'* to HIV and AIDS, in order to predict their capability to cope with and respond to the pandemic (*AIDS in the World – a Global Report, 1992*). The methods used imply value judgements about what makes a given society resilient or vulnerable. Not everyone will agree with the factors chosen as indicators of 'vulnerability', which were:

1. Poor access to information (measured by numbers of TVs and radios).

2. Low health expenditure compared to Gross National and Domestic Products.
3. Poor or uneven access to health facilities.
4. High under-five mortality rates (U5MR).
5. A low status for women in society (gender inequality).
6. Weak personal, civil and political liberties.
7. A high ratio of military to health-plus-education expenditures.
8. Poor potential for human development, as measured in terms of years of schooling, life expectancy and per capita income.

Other factors which may be relevant, such as cultural identity, language, tribal structure and religion were not included. There was no attempt to analyse why countries with an apparently high 'societal vulnerability', such as Uganda, have demonstrated a remarkable capacity to cope, despite the additional problems of civil war and inflation.

Worldwide, 57 countries were rated as 'highly vulnerable' by the Policy Coalition, 38 on the African continent. Although the predictive criteria used are debatable, the concept of 'societal vulnerability' is useful if it serves to alert the governments of countries with new epidemics to the need to face up to AIDS early rather than late, because early interventions are most likely to check spread of HIV.

POSITIVE CHANGE

In large cities of high-incidence countries, many people now know that they ought to change their sexual behaviour in order to avoid HIV infection, knowledge expressed mainly as anxiety about casual sexual play but also by an increased sense of responsibility for the consequences of sexual acts. In ch. 13 on 'behaviour change' we consider how communities revise their norms for sexual conduct, and choose and sustain safer behaviours.

In this climate of questioning, the Churches have an opportunity to re-present Christian views of man–woman relationships – but only if they do so within a total view of sexuality which is coherent, consistent, and positive. It will be tragic if this chance is lost because Christians are too frightened to talk about sexuality at all, or deny their views credibility by inconsistent and evasive approaches to the problems of single people, contraception within and outside marriage, marriage breakdown, divorce and remarriage, clerical celibacy, and same-sex relationships. Several of these issues, in so far as they relate to a constructive response to AIDS, are considered in later chapters.

Decisions to change sexual behaviour are made by individuals – but in a social context. It is a matter of experience that changes in norms for sexual behaviour occur most readily in a setting of strong peer support. As we saw, p. 52, spread of HIV between men was reduced dramatically, through behaviour change, in the USA in the 1980s, as individual decisions were supported by a community determination to halt AIDS. At the same time, support groups and care agencies originating mainly within gay communities were set up in the West to help HIV-infected persons to cope with their lives and deaths.

'Communities' is the key word: it appears that only communities can provide the shared values, focus for commitment, sense of purpose and corporate response to adversity which most (not all) men and women need to support their own individual responses. In a later chapter, I suggest that 'communities' have a greater capacity to cope with life's problems than they suspect, although this capacity is often unrecognized and unused. Capacity to cope can be activated and released by a challenge which unites members of a community and focuses their attention on an achievable goal – or a series of goals. The essential changes in attitude and confidence may begin spontaneously within a community, or follow a stimulus (accidental or deliberate) from outside.

AIDS sometimes provides just such a stimulus to an affected community which activates its 'capacity to cope' – not only with AIDS but also with other problems which had previously seemed too large to tackle. At present this is demonstrable mainly for secular communities in developing countries where social changes produced by HIV infection are hard to ignore, but (when tested) it applies also to Church communities.

FAMILY STRUCTURE AND FUNCTION

In the last chapter we concluded that population growth rates are likely to fall as a result of HIV infection but that there is not yet enough evidence to predict whether growth rates of 3% per annum will be replaced by an absolute decline in population size in heavily-affected countries. It is indeed desirable that populations should stabilize at a size which allows everyone to have enough food, education, leisure, and medical care (benefits enjoyed by only a minority at present). But stabilization of populations should happen through a free choice to limit the number of births to replacement level, not through disease and death.

Already it is clear that population *structure* is changing in ways which threaten the stability and functions of families in developing countries, where security in old age, sickness or bereavement traditionally depended on the health and goodwill of an extended family of at least two generations.

The generation of men and women who were born in developing countries between 1940 and 1950 usually produced families of six or seven children, about half of whom survived beyond five years. Many of these children (born after 1960) were infected with HIV in the 1980s and as a result the average family today may be slightly smaller, with a narrower age range than was usual in the past. These contemporary children are fortunate enough (usually) to have grandparents alive to care for them if their parents die, but they are less likely to receive help from aunts or uncles because it is common for several adults in the generation born between 1960 and 1975 to have died of AIDS already. Many of today's grandparents will not have anyone to care for them in old age, because their own children have died already. The extended family network is breaking down: there are not enough aunts and uncles to share in the care of orphaned children and not enough fit adults to care for very old people.

Children born since the AIDS era began (from 1985 onwards) will face difficulties as they enter their own reproductive years, because they may not have parents to provide support and services which were taken for granted in the past. There will be fewer grannies to hand on their skills to new mothers or to care for small children while mothers work, and fewer homes to return to for respite after a failed relationship, or for a roof when homeless, or for care in illness. And if, in the early years of the next century, children born from 1985 onwards begin to contract HIV-infection themselves, there will be fewer grandparents alive to care for *their* orphans, and fewer siblings from the 1985 generation to offer help either. The breakdown of extended families appears likely to become more, not less, serious as the pandemic continues.

The changing structure of families will be reflected in each community, which will no longer have a reservoir of mature, experienced middle-aged men and women to act for it and to defend tradition. There will be fewer people to run small stores, supervise local businesses, attend parent–teacher meetings, become Church elders, teach in Sunday schools, act as local political or social leaders, provide help to young builders of low-cost homes, campaign for improved lighting or water supplies in deprived townships or do any of the hundreds of other tasks for which parents in their forties or fifties are so well-fitted. These effects on community life are visible already in small towns in south-west Uganda.

AGRICULTURE AND INDUSTRY

Of the estimated 19.5 million people already infected with HIV throughout the world, 18 million are adults of working age, so AIDS is certain to have effects in workplaces and on economic life, particularly in developing countries where the majority of HIV-infected people live.

At present, throughout the world, patterns of employment are changing, money is losing value, political and economic systems are being questioned and food and goods are poorly distributed – partly for logistic reasons, and partly because people with very high standards of living are unwilling to give up comforts to which they are accustomed. In developing countries these universal difficulties are made worse by demographic and structural problems mentioned earlier: many children; underdeveloped agricultural and industrial infrastructures; dependence on export of raw materials (crops and minerals) for foreign exchange; a low gross domestic product, and too great a dependence on imported expertise, machinery, and medicines. These problems are compounded now by external debt and loss of control of local monetary and development policies to the International Monetary Fund (IMF) and World Bank (WB) – whose priorities differ from those of the developing country governments they advise.

AIDS interacts with these global and local conditions to increase the difficulty of achieving the only real objective of economic life – which is to provide the goods and services that each man, woman and child needs for health and for the full development of their potential as physical–spiritual persons in community. Dollars, yen, cedis or shillings are not even secondary issues, but rank far below food, ideas and fellowship.

To be specific, AIDS reduces the benefits of investment in training for work and social growth (education), affects the size and stability of the pool of working-age adults (labour), competes for resources to develop agriculture and industry (poverty), and threatens social security (sickness pay and pensions) – as well as other human rights. Finally, AIDS could disturb the political and social stability of heavily-affected societies.

EDUCATION AND TRAINING

At the start of the AIDS epidemic in developing countries there was a direct relationship between years of education and the likelihood of HIV-infection: people with a university or secondary school education were more likely to acquire HIV than people from the same community who had little or no schooling. Probably the contrast was due to differences of opportunity: people with more education had more opportunities for casual sexual acts with several partners than those who travelled less and had less money to 'pay' for sex. As we noted in ch. 1, those who died first from AIDS (and who continue to die, usually soon after reaching their greatest creativity and productivity) were people with special skills, in whose education much time and money had been invested. More skilled people will have to be trained, calling for an increased commitment of resources to education, just when the most vital resource of all – trained people – is in short supply.

Two related responses to the need to increase numbers of skilled people might have particularly positive results: the creation of a 'learning society' and training for greater flexibility at work. Capacity-to-cope, as individuals and in community, is likely to be enhanced when self-esteem and work-satisfaction are increased by developing people's unused potentialities.

A recent critic of the British education system, Sir Douglas Hague, wrote in a newspaper article: 'Our state schools were established to produce clerks (who could write) and bookkeepers (who could calculate). They taught children what to do and how to do it. This is of little use for many of the new jobs. These require innovators. What we need instead is an education system that fosters learning and a new relationship between education and employers.' Sir Douglas saw a close connection between a society's educational 'culture' and the way its workplaces function. He proposed the creation of a 'learning society', encouraging questioning through greater movement between jobs and public and private sectors, and a reduction in specialization in the workplace. He advocated greater sharing of leadership and suggested closing down public bodies that are no longer useful, but instead setting up short-term projects with clearly defined – but limited – tasks.

In practical terms, what would creating 'a learning society' mean? In a developing country responding to AIDS it would require an end to systems of education which limit the kinds of work people can do (as the Bantu Education Act forty years ago limited the employment prospects of black people in South Africa). Pupils would be taught *how* to learn, rather than *what* to learn, and encouraged to ask questions and seek answers through their own efforts. Education would concentrate on acquiring skills for continuing learning, rather than skills applicable to only one job.

Outside schools a variety of people with little or no formal education (mothers, subsistence farmers, traditional birth attendants, grandparents, school leavers, street children and unemployed persons) would be offered more opportunities to learn, through local classes or workshops, drama, or radio – a chance, not just to learn new skills, but to discover the very existence of their own capacity-to-learn. As the surest way to consolidate new skills and attitudes is to pass them on to other people, the pool of 'educators' would be enlarged continuously as those people who had already learned to read, or make concrete blocks, or grow new crops last year were employed to help teach others the same skills next year.

In industry workers would be given a greater part in decision-making and taught not just to do one small task more efficiently, but to tackle a wider range of tasks, so that they would become more flexible, better able to solve problems, and better prepared to take over the work of absent colleagues. As some employers discover, training men and women as peer-educators (to teach their co-workers about HIV and AIDS) has wide implications, because as peer-educators gain confidence and new status they become more capable people: in Christian terms they grow in grace.

THE LABOUR POOL

Worldwide, during the last decade, the proportion of unemployed adults has risen for many reasons: workers are replaced by more 'cost-effective' machines so there are far fewer unskilled jobs; economic recession discourages people from buying non-essential goods and services; the arms trade is shrinking as a result of the collapse of Communism. In developing countries these global effects are felt, and in addition the labour pool is expanded every year by very large numbers of school leavers. Yet opportunities for employment in the formal sector are shrinking, as businesses fail to survive the combined effects of inflation, long supply lines for materials, inability to compete on world markets and diminishing productivity. In many developing countries less than a quarter of the workforce is employed in the former sector of the economy (in Zambia 1994 statistics showed that only 380,000 out of a potential workforce of 3.9 million were in employment); most people work as casual labourers, or subsist as servants, street traders, or by selling beer or sex.

Already high unemployment in developing countries will get worse, as AIDS directly threatens productivity in the formal sector. As survey of industries in Zimbabwe concluded that loss of managers, skilled and semi-skilled workers, the costs and time needed to recruit and train replacements, early retirement on health grounds, higher medical expenses and absenteeism (sickness and funerals) will combine to reduce productivity to such an extent that many companies will not survive. Then thousands of people who are not themselves HIV-infected will suffer the economic and social effects of business failures, alongside their HIV-infected and affected neighbours.

WORK AS A RISK FACTOR FOR HIV-INFECTION

Health care workers, ambulance men, laboratory technicians, police and first-aiders in the workplace may come into contact with HIV-infected blood, although the risks of transmission are very small and can be almost eliminated by following routine infection control measures. Commercial sex workers also face obvious risks, which can be reduced if their clients use condoms correctly.

But far more people in developing countries, in a variety of jobs, are at risk because of the location of their work – or the location of a spouse. Men (and their wives) are at risk if work involves spending time away from home; railway workers, sales representatives, fishermen and long-distance truck drivers are often away from their families for weeks. Truck drivers, in particular, may find no inexpensive accommodation along highways – except in the beds of women who need money. Soldiers are posted abroad for months at a time, teachers and government employees may be transferred away from home while their wives are unable to move too, because family finances depend on the wife's paid work. All too often lonely men away from home seek company and sexual pleasure from girl friends or sex workers, at the risk of HIV-infection for themselves and later their wives.

Migrant workers are part of the culture of central and southern Africa, where men have gone to work in mines or cities since colonial times, leaving their wives behind to work on farms or to tend village plots. In theory the husband sends cash home; in practice the amount left over, after he has paid his own expenses and bought sexual favours from a girl at the beer hall, is often not enough for the family, so that his own wife may be forced to sell sex to find cash for urgent needs, such as school fees or uniforms. The basic human right to live with one's spouse and family while at the same time earning an adequate wage needs to be recognized and supported far more vigorously.

A World Bank report on HIV infection in the context of other sexually transmitted diseases, published in 1990, concluded that one of the most promising ways to fight STDs would be to increase the number of young women in urban centres in Africa and to improve their education. These extra urban women would need jobs: work for women is critically important as a means of reducing the spread of HIV through commercial sex, and increasing women's employment prospects might reduce spread of HIV more rapidly than campaigns to increase use of condoms. A woman who is dependent on selling sex for subsistence survival for herself and her children cannot afford to argue with a man who says: 'I will go to someone else if you want me to use a condom!' But if a woman has another trade she may not need to offer her body for sale at all. One farmer in Zimbabwe grows vegetables in order to provide women with regular employment, so that they are no longer dependent on what their husbands send home from the mines. He also supplies free condoms at the farm shop and the beer hall, so that wives can protect themselves when their husbands do come home.

Labour migration and split families ensure frequent movements of men and women between rural and urban areas, which provide opportunities for HIV to spread in either direction, gradually lessening the initial differences in infection rates between town and country, as changing seroprevalence rates in Zambia and Uganda now show.

FARMING

There is still a relative lack of information about the potential effects of AIDS on agriculture, due to an early perception that 'AIDS is an urban problem' coupled with the uncritical idea that a rural labour pool is inexhaustible. As late as 1991 a reviewer in London found only two papers describing the effects of AIDS on agriculture, from Rwanda and Uganda; the Uganda study was later expanded into a book. In 1992 a description of workplace-based AIDS initiatives added new information about large farms in Zimbabwe.

The majority of farmers in Africa work on a small scale, growing a mixture of food for family use and cash crops for sale in markets or through co-operative organizations. The Rwanda and Uganda studies emphasized the diversity of farming systems and their varying vulnerability to labour loss and to drought – an important factor when farmers lack capital to invest in all-season irrigation. In Uganda (which enjoys a heavier and more evenly distributed rainfall than most African countries) half of the farming systems examined by Barnett and Blaikie were considered 'vulnerable' to breakdown for HIV-affected families. The most vulnerable were systems in dry areas which have only one short rainy season, as these conditions make the greatest demands for seasonal peaks of labour, as well as having the narrowest range of alternative crops. These are precisely the climatic conditions which apply throughout large areas of Tanzania, Zambia, Zimbabwe and Malawi, where maize is the staple crop.

Nuclear families are more vulnerable than extended families, because a single adult illness or death changes the family structure. Widows are less able to call upon other people's labour than male heads of households, and some widows are evicted from land which they need to farm in order to support their children. It appears that it may become necessary to re-create extended families from the remnants of several biological families, especially in rural areas, if farming is to continue to meet community needs. In south-west Uganda this is beginning to happen informally, as the 'guardians' of orphans co-operate with each other to open up new land for cultivation and to build simple homes for orphans who have nowhere to live. A catechist commented: 'fraternal love develops; they help one another'.

Different communities and farming systems will have different needs if they are to survive and support their members. In one village the communal purchase of one piece of labour-saving equipment (for example, a hammer mill to grind maize, a solar-powered irrigation pump, an improved plough drawn by trained oxen) might improve food production; in another, plans made with advice from an agricultural development officer might enable a group of families to make optimal use of their combined labour force of schoolchildren, grandparents and surviving young adults by growing a non-traditional mix of crops. Maintaining cleared land in cultivation, preventing soil erosion (by making drainage ditches, planting trees and building surface stones into retaining walls round steep contours), and keeping children in school ought to be priorities for farming communities.

On family plots shortage of labour is compensated for at first by a shift away from labour-intensive crops – from legumes and cash crops such as tea and coffee, to tubers (cassava, potatoes and sweet potato). Next, the amount of time devoted to tasks and the area of land cultivated are both reduced. At this stage herds of cattle or goats deteriorate if there are not enough children to care for them, and there is a risk that children will be taken out of school to provide more labour.

Barnett and Blaikie, in *AIDS in Africa*, gave a composite account of how AIDS may affect a rural family over a period of years (7).

Example: At the start, their hypothetical family consisted of a man and his wife, with five children aged one to 12 at home, and two sons in their late teens earning cash by trading and fishing away from home. The family cultivated matoke bananas, beans, potatoes, vegetables and coffee as a cash crop, hiring additional labour for the weeding and planting seasons. The older sons died of AIDS, one by one, cutting off the flow of cash, so that the family could no longer afford to hire labour or to buy pesticides. Everyone had to work harder to maintain food production. But by this time the father was ill from AIDS and his wife had to care for him, so the oldest girl was taken out of school to reduce expenses and to help on the farm.

Coffee and banana plants were neglected and other labour-intensive crops were cut back, but more cassava was planted. Two years later the father died and his funeral finished off the family's reserves of cash. By this stage the widow was ill. She took all the children out of school and sent the youngest to live with his grandparents. The coffee plantation was abandoned and the rest of the garden became less productive as weeds and pests took over. After two more years the mother died and the older teenagers tried to earn cash away from home while the younger brothers attempted to cultivate enough bananas, yams, and cassava for survival. Education and human development had been forgotten and the teenagers living away from home risked acquiring HIV themselves while searching for comfort and pleasure, or through sex in exchange for cash.

A PRESCRIPTION FOR SUSTAINABLE AGRICULTURAL DEVELOPMENT?

Care for land, crops, domestic servants and animals was amongst the covenant obligations of ancient Israel. The book of Leviticus (25. 3–7) gave instructions for 'a sabbath of complete rest for the land, a sabbath for the Lord' every seven years, and provided even more detailed prescriptions for a year of jubilee every fifty years. Then the land would rest, land and houses in open country which had been sold during difficult times would be returned to their hereditary owners (though city dwellings 'pass in perpetuity to the purchaser'), bound labourers would be set free, and relationships with neighbours and resident aliens be set right (Lev. 25. 8–55). Deuteronomy chs. 14 and 15 give another version of the same instructions, with more emphasis on the joy and celebration that rest for land and workers makes possible every seven years. In both accounts there is a strong sense of the God-given interdependence of all members of a community, with each other and with the land on which they live, which is held in trust for God 'for the land is mine; with me you are all but aliens and tenants' (Lev. 25. 23,24).

While we consider mobilizing the will to take these ancient ideas seriously, could ways be found to harness the energies of urban Anti-AIDS club members, street kids or unemployed youths to help farming communities, at least during periods of peak labour demand? It would be even more useful to give farming a better image than it has at present, by linking access to land and the chance to build simple homes to instruction in sustainable farming methods, or supervised apprenticeships.

Development schemes which improve the quality of rural life, restore self-esteem, and encourage people to move out of crowded towns are likely to slow down transmission of HIV. This is not just an idealistic dream of mine, but also the opinion of a paper on the economic and demographic impacts of AIDS in sub-saharan Africa, published in *World Development 1990* (47).

FOREIGN EXCHANGE, INVESTMENT AND POVERTY

The interactions between AIDS epidemics, poverty and money supplies are – and will remain – complex. Subtle issues of confidence influence the flow of investment capital into industrial development and the flow of visitors into countries where tourism earns foreign exchange. Countries which depend for foreign exchange on sale of unprocessed crops are often competing with their neighbours for overseas markets, so prices fall as everyone tries to earn more dollars by increasing their own exports, while already narrow profit-margins are threatened by increased labour costs due to AIDS. Other countries rely on mining minerals for a world market where prices are falling as arms production decreases, yet mining is a high-technology industry, dependent on imported equipment and skilled labour, so mines may have to operate at a loss in order to earn at least some foreign currency. Tourism may suffer if potential visitors with a poor understanding of how HIV is transmitted label holiday places 'dangerous'.

In Thailand a family-planning NGO argued that openness about AIDS does not conflict with tourism because efforts to control the spread of HIV ought to reassure tourists. This view is supported by events: Thailand has noticed no reduction in overall numbers of tourists, although the government's openness about AIDS has brought about a change in policy to attract more families and fewer single men. The tourists' image of Thailand is changing and the sex industry there has declined (12). The social and economic consequences of AIDS are not easy to predict. Local research, followed by reasonable interventions – carefully observed – yields more reliable results than speculation.

SICKNESS BENEFIT, LIFE-ASSURANCE AND PENSIONS

Quite apart from AIDS, rising costs threaten profits, development of human and material resources and even the survival of many companies and farms. At present most employers in Zimbabwe are retaining workers who are known or suspected to be HIV-infected, and giving them light duties when they are no longer fit to do their normal work, so that they can die 'in service'. But growing numbers of workers have to be retired on health grounds because there are not enough light jobs to go round. To the direct costs of sickness benefits or company health care, funeral benefit and pensions, and indirect losses from time-off for illness or funerals, employers must add the costs of recruiting and training replacements for those who die. One Health and Safety Officer stated a general opinion: 'We feel that individual workers should not be penalized for this epidemic, because it's not of their making. They should have the right to work, the right to social security, and the right to any other work benefits that are theirs.'(47).

Life assurance is difficult to find in sub-saharan Africa these days. The head of an association of 15 insurances companies in Uganda described AIDS as a 'catastrophe' and added that 'insurance companies do not provide cover for catastrophes'. The largest Ugandan insurance company has abandoned individual policies and concentrates on group insurance. Most insurers who still issue individual policies require HIV testing; for example, in Zimbabwe this is permitted for larger policies. In Malawi, where HIV testing for insurance purposes is prohibited, life assurance for individuals is said to have almost disappeared.

Providers of *medical insurance* and companies which give direct medical care for sickness will not be able to meet the costs of treating thousands of workers and their families for AIDS-related illnesses, without changes in policy.

Pension funds meet with a different set of problems. Members of pension funds receive what they and their employers have contributed to the fund, plus bank interest, but usually only after working for the same company for a minimum length of time. Some pension fund trustees have responded to this situation by introducing policies which discriminate in *favour* of HIV-positive persons, by making larger monthly payments to them – a humane solution which takes account of their shorter life-expectancy.

SOCIAL STABILITY AND NATIONAL IDENTITY

In the societies of developing countries contradictory forces operate: on the one hand traditional loyalties to ancestors, family, clan and tribe still give society a cohesion and warmth which is rare in industrial nations, yet this framework for living is changing rapidly, threatened by many circumstances in addition to AIDS (drift into towns in search of better prospects, economic pressures, shifting values). Many societies now show signs of strain or even potential breakdown. We cannot predict how the balance between the strengths and weaknesses of any given society will work out in advance of its collision with the full impact of AIDS. It *is* possible, however, to look at some of the pressures already operating, to ask how they might develop, or be neutralized by appropriate responses.

The indirect effects of AIDS interlock with and reinforce factors which threaten stability in other ways. It is the complexity and multiplicity of small and large changes, occurring over several years, which may either break societies, or else allow time for them to adapt and learn to cope. Consider health care: recruitment will very probably suffer 'as nursing and medicine become less desirable professions ... it is grim work to care for young adults who are dying and for whom nothing useful can be done' (53). In addition about one quarter of all HCW will be lost to HIV-infection – yet de-centralization of medical care, teaching lay people nursing skills, standardization of treatments and use of Homecare teams for TB management could have positive effects on general health which might partly counterbalance losses due to HIV. Where will the balance lie?

Any city dweller in a developing country knows that unemployment and inflation are linked directly to numbers of burglaries. Worldwide, there is abundant evidence linking alcohol to road accidents and to assaults; crimes of violence also tend to increase wherever poverty, unemployment and hopelessness co-exist. Fatigue, too, may act like a spark in urban situations of deprivation, which resemble piles of dry rubbish, waiting to catch fire. A minor upset can ignite a pile of grievances which might otherwise have been dealt with, slowly, one by one, without an explosion. How will communities cope when large numbers of people are exhausted by nursing sick or confused relatives and at the same time are anxious about their own health? Will exhaustion and living with stress be expressed in more violent behaviour or more drunkenness?

Crime and violence in a community might increase also through fear of (and discrimination against) HIV-infected persons, or due to the direct and indirect effects of AIDS on police and defence forces. A greater turnover of staff in both forces ought to be expected, because surveys show that HIV-infection rates are actually higher than average amongst the police and military men. It follows that, at any given time, a higher than normal proportion of staff are likely to be inexperienced or only partly trained, and recruitment may not keep pace with losses. Moreover, most policemen and soldiers, whether or not HIV-infected themselves, have relatives or friends who are ill. Professional people suffer the ordinary reactions of anxiety, sadness and anger which are common to all carers or families: but preoccupation with private misery may dangerously influence the capacity of police to cope with frustration or conflict at work. There are many contemporary examples, from every continent, of police overreacting to political demonstrations or misjudging their responses to aggressive crowds, 'mistakes' which acted like matches thrown onto piles of dry grass.

Depression is a normal human response to loss. But if losses accumulate and people who suffer repeated bouts of mourning fail to negotiate all the stages which normally lead to acceptance and new life, then depression may become a fixed and pathological, rather than a normal but temporary, reaction to loss. This is particularly likely to happen when unrecognized anger turns inwards against mourners so that they lose self esteem and feel worthless and deserving of misfortune.

People who are depressed eat badly, wake early and cannot go back to sleep again; they lack energy and initiative and have difficulty in making even small decisions. They are often irritable or anxious and incapable of imagining anything at all which could break through their feelings of isolation and deadness to give new life or hope. Sometimes these symptoms are accompanied by feelings of sadness or outbursts of weeping which show plainly what is wrong, but quite often depressed people are not aware of their chronic misery – they just lack energy and cannot get on with life. If enough people in a society are depressed simultaneously, the whole community may become apathetic and fail to do for itself what could be done to improve the quality of life – if only morale were better. There are disturbing signs that the chronic loss of hope and energy characteristic of depression may be occurring already in some societies, where people often make negative statements such as 'we shall all die' or 'we are facing the end of the world'.

A different response to disaster occurred in some places in Europe in the fifteenth century, as plague moved from city to city killing about one-third of the total population. Some people responded with penitence to a disaster which was regarded as a punishment from God, but others expressed their despair through wild parties, at which all sexual restraint was lost and people remained drunk to escape from their fears. A breakdown of normal behaviour is possible in AIDS-affected countries too, although in this less dramatic and long-drawn-out crisis breakdown is likely to be expressed differently. Occasionally even now a person who is aware of being HIV-infected deliberately hunts for new sexual partners with the malicious intention of infecting as many people as possible, although this reaction is extremely rare. A more subtle and dangerous possibility would be spread of an attitude expressed by some young women who have given up trying to avoid HIV, saying either 'who wants to be the only young person left alive?' or 'how can I die without having had a child?'

The maintenance of hope and a sense of purpose to life are critically important if community capacity-to-cope is to survive and grow.

PLACES OF HOPE AND CHANGE

Some effects of AIDS on social and economic life are ambiguous or even positive. In my opinion positive effects usually operate through the release of community capacity-to-cope, which we consider in more detail in ch. 15. The sufferings associated with AIDS have indeed shown a capacity to destroy, but have also demonstrated a potential for building community by breaking through barriers and showing human beings to each other as fragile but beautiful vessels for the loving Spirit of God.

It does not matter that the Spirit is rarely named: He is at work anonymously, 'as if He were effacing himself . . . The Spirit is the hidden God, the inward God, deeper than our greatest depth. He gives life to all things and we breathe Him without being aware of it. He is the breath of God in the breathing of the world, of humanity' (11).

For Further Reading see Bibliography, p. 31, (1), (2) and (53).

Group Study Suggestion
In June 1993 a Zambian newspaper reported: 'Management Systems International has been engaged by the World Bank to try to cushion the effects of the 80,000 job losses expected to

arise from the privatization programme, and the 20% unemployment already present in the formal sector, joined by 150,000 school-
leavers each year. It will . . . provide counselling and training in a bleak situation in which rapid population growth in a sluggish and declining economy is setting the stage for a potentially explosive economic, social and political situation.' Discuss how the consequences of HIV infection may interact with this gloomy scenario, either to increase the likelihood of doom – or in a more positive way.

CHAPTER 7

AIDS in the World

The World Health Organization and the Global Policy Coalition on AIDS (GPCA) estimate that by the year 2000:
1. Between 80% and 90% of all new HIV infections will be transmitted heterosexually;
2. 90% will occur in the developing world; and
3. Over half the people infected will be women.
In 1995 there are no signs that growth of the pandemic is slowing down. Instead, estimates of the number of persons who will be HIV-infected by the year 2000 increase at each revision. The Indian Health Organization, for example, estimates that HIV infections in India may increase from about 1 million in 1993 to 50 million by the end of the decade. If this assessment is correct, then the GPCA prediction that globally about 100 million people will have been HIV-infected by the year 2000 may prove more accurate than WHO's lower forecast of 30 to 40 million. Most HIV-infected people are not ill yet: the main impact of the pandemic is still in the future – even in countries where already hospitals are overburdened, cemeteries are being enlarged and businesses are failing.

Until very recently, no epidemic threatened humankind as a whole because geographic, cultural, climatic and political boundaries limited the spread of infectious agents between continents. These natural checks were reinforced by efficient public health services, set up before development of vaccines and antibiotics allowed peoples and governments to become complacent about contagious diseases. However, about 25 years ago, interest and investment in the study and control of epidemic infections began to decline – because such diseases appeared to be 'conquered'.

During the last 40 years natural barriers to global spread of infections have been weakened by worldwide changes in human populations and behaviours, for example:
(a) The increasing scale of intercontinental travel.
(b) Rapid growth of cities (partly due to rural poverty.
(c) An explosive expansion of the world's population of young people.
(d) The disappearance or modification of cultural and religious barriers which used to limit free social and sexual association between strangers.
Heathrow is the busiest international airport in the world. In 1946 it

95

consisted of a few tents and caravans and was used by less than 64,000 passengers, but in 1993 47.6 million persons passed through Heathrow on their way to over 220 destinations.

This chapter attempts an overview of AIDS in the world in late 1994, based on published estimates of how the pandemic will develop in different regions during the next few years, conversations with experienced observers and my own informed judgement. Both estimates and predictions are based on data which is incomplete, inaccurate (or both) – but all that is available.

Regions are not defined by geography alone, which groups together countries where AIDS has different consequences and elicits different responses (for example Australia and Papua New Guinea) while separating 'Western' nations which *do* have common patterns of transmission and response. I combine geographic, economic and cultural features to identify groups of countries which are similar – at least in the impact of the pandemic on their populations and economies.

TRANSMISSION

The balance between sexual, mother–to–child, and blood–to–blood spread of HIV differs from region to region. In each society the rate at which *HIV spreads* depends on the nature and frequency of acts which are capable of passing the virus from person to person. Sexual spread of HIV is influenced by the size of the most sexually active age group of 15 to 50 years, by economic pressures which draw people into cities or drive women to sell sex, and by geo-socio-political factors (armed conflict, drug-trafficking, political isolation, closed borders, truck routes) which affect the size and pattern of sexual networks. The societies most vulnerable to rapid spread of HIV infection appear to be those where women have a low status and where large differences exist between the lives and opportunities of the richest and poorest members – of either sex.

RESPONSES

Responses to AIDS depend primarily on the 'age' of the local or regional epidemic and whether or not early reactions of denial or minimization are still operating. Everywhere responses are modified by cultural, racial and religious factors which affect progress through denial to constructive engagement with the challenges of AIDS – and which may later cause a positive response to fade away into apathy or despair. In India, for example, there was a long and dangerous delay before public action to limit the spread of HIV began, because the perception that 'we don't behave like that' (and therefore we cannot be at risk) was not challenged until the early 1990s, perhaps for cultural and religious reasons.

Responses are affected, too, by the ethnic composition of a population, the degree of mixing between groups, and whether mixing occurs openly and naturally or modified by historical conflicts (black–white relations in the southern USA or South Africa) or by social disapproval (intravenous drug users, homosexuals). Ethnic mixing may be complicated by differences in status, if one group rules and another is 'expected' to be submissive. Such differences influence the transmission dynamics of HIV within and between groups; for example in South Africa, at present, HIV is spreading in the larger black population mainly by heterosexual and mother–to–child routes, whereas in the white population HIV spreads mainly through homosexual acts and intravenous drug use. In this situation the reactions and responses of black and white people tend to be held apart by mutual misunderstanding of alien behaviour, the remains of ethnic distrust and low self-esteem, cultural pride, and the dissimilar consequences for the two groups. At the present time popular attention in South Africa is focused on political change, not AIDS. Inattention to the presence of HIV does not prevent it from spreading – but instead increases its capacity to do so.

In mixed societies it is essential to include every population group in programmes aiming to achieve AIDS awareness and to persuade people to change their sexual behaviour: but methods and messages must be adapted to the different interests and needs of each group.

IMPACT

The impact of AIDS on any society is related to four variables: the *proportion of the population* who become infected with HIV, the *average age* at which infection occurs, the mean *time-interval* between infection and death from AIDS: and the *interaction* of the local epidemic with other urgent problems. An imbalance between the size of a population and the fertility of the land available to feed it (demographic entrapment), inefficient agricultural systems, under-developed health and education services, armed conflict and poverty seem particularly likely to increase the adverse impact of AIDS, as well as facilitating spread of HIV.

As a basis for action accurate information about each local society needs to be interpreted in a regional context. In respect of any particular society, my tentative framework for thinking about 'AIDS in the world' will be too simple, but the framework will serve its purpose if it draws attention to inequality, poverty, and conflict as factors which shape responses to AIDS and heighten its impact on society.

In theological terms, anything which diminishes the unique dignity of each human person before God, or disregards our dependence on others for survival and development ('you are all one person') tends

97

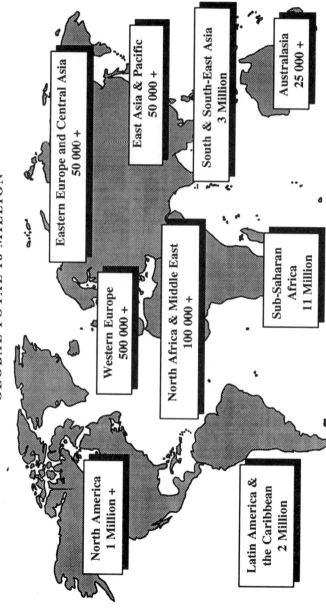

GLOBAL TOTAL 18 MILLION

Eastern Europe and Central Asia
50 000 +

East Asia & Pacific
50 000 +

South & South-East Asia
3 Million

Australasia
25 000 +

Western Europe
500 000 +

North Africa & Middle East
100 000 +

Sub-Saharan
Africa
11 Million

North America
1 Million +

Latin America &
the Caribbean
2 Million

Figure 7.   Estimated distribution of cumulative adult HIV infections from late 1970s/early 1980s to late 1994.

to make responses to AIDS less effective and the impact of the pandemic more devastating.

Definitions: Cumulative *incidence* of HIV refers to the accumulated total number of persons estimated to have been infected with HIV since the start of the pandemic in the late 1970s, and the cumulative *incidence* of AIDS refers to the total number of people who are estimated to have developed an AIDS-defining diagnosis since the pandemic began. But the term incidence is also used to describe the number of new infections with HIV occurring during a *period* of time, usually a year. The *prevalence* of HIV infection refers to the actual numbers (or estimates) of persons infected with HIV at a stated *moment* in time, for example on the day a survey takes place.

Figure 7 shows cumulative incidence of HIV infections in adults, by continent, at the end of 1994. Published figures for the incidence or prevalence of HIV infection or AIDS are always underestimates because infection and disease are recognized less often than they occur, and reported even less frequently. For example, by 31 December 1994, 1,025,073 cases of AIDS had been reported to WHO since the pandemic began, yet WHO estimates that over 4.5 million cases have occurred. Only half these cases of AIDS were reported by developing countries, yet WHO estimates that over 75% originated in the developing world. Therefore our survey of global AIDS starts with the region most affected: subsaharan Africa, and moves next to Asia, where the prevalence of HIV infection is increasing rapidly as I write.

SUBSAHARAN AFRICA

Since much of the detailed information in this book relates to subsaharan Africa, based on my personal experience, the following paragraphs are limited to a summary of the most important features of the pandemic in that region.

At present two thirds of HIV-infected people live in East and Central Africa, where the total population is less than the population of Nigeria. Fifty-five per cent of those infected are women. In some areas men may soon outnumber women by a ratio of 3:2, because women are the more vulnerable sex. By 1992 15 to 20% of female sex-workers were HIV-infected in Nigeria, where rapid expansion of the pandemic is likely if risky behaviours do not change.

Average times from HIV infection to death are shorter than in the

West, perhaps as short as five years, so *increasing* the social and demographic impacts of AIDS. Almost every family is affected by death or sickness, yet stigma and discrimination persist.

Health services are critically overburdened: about one third of surgical patients and two thirds (or more) of medical patients in urban hospitals are HIV-infected, so crowding out people with curable conditions. HIV infection reverses reductions in child mortality achieved in the last 20 years, and over 80% of young adult deaths are HIV-related in worst affected countries.

Many helpful responses have been undertaken by NGOs, WHO, Churches and governments, individually or in collaboration, but constructive action is threatened by the scale of the pandemic, other urgent problems, reduced funding, and community indifference. Huge economic and social losses are inevitable where a third of workers are HIV-infected and early deaths from AIDS halve an average working lifetime. Apathy and loss of hope are the greatest threats to survival, and need the most urgent attention from leaders.

ASIA

At present South Asia, South-east Asia and East Asia and the Pacific hold 2.96 billion (54%) of the world's total population of about 5.5 billion people: six of the world's ten most populous countries (more than 100 million people each) are in Asia. China has the largest population of all, nearly twice the *sum* of the populations of the United States, the Russian Federation, Brazil and Nigeria.

Thirty-four per cent of Asia's population is under 16 years of age. In this huge region HIV infection has spread very rapidly since 1990 so that the impact in Asia may begin to *exceed* the impact in subsaharan Africa by the end of the decade. At present most HIV-infected persons live in India and Thailand, but China is included in this survey because of its vast population.

INDIA

In India the first AIDS patient was recognized in 1986, but between January and November 1992 the number of AIDS cases rose sharply; in the same year a National AIDS Control Organization was set up and media coverage for the pandemic increased. At present, numbers of HIV-infected persons are doubling in just 12 months: this rate of increase is not likely to respond quickly to preventive education. The government's National AIDS Control Organization (NACO) estimated in December 1994 that about 1.5 million Indians are now HIV-infected. Economic and social conditions in India are not encouraging: dense populations, crowded cities, poverty, continuing denial of AIDS, organized prostitution, discrimination against HIV-infected people and prejudices against sex education and condoms – all these conditions unite to favour rapid spread of HIV.

In India modes of transmission are not precisely known because homosexuality and bisexuality are denied and transfused blood and blood products are not regularly tested for HIV. At the end of 1994 NACO estimated that 'promiscuous' heterosexual contact accounted for 43% of infections, blood products for 3%, and intravenous drug use for about 12% – leaving over one-third of infections unexplained.

Homosexuals formed only 0.44% of HIV-positive individuals identified, but it is difficult to admit publicly that some men have sex with men, either as a first choice, or as an alternative when women are not available. At the end of 1992 only one small project was working with men who have sex with men and one other, also small, with truck drivers. Very little is documented about sexual activity in India (except that it occurs frequently!) but bisexual behaviour may be a common but hidden link between homosexual and heterosexual persons, which greatly widens sexual networks.

In Western India Bombay is (at present) the epicentre for spread of HIV through commercial sex. Seroprevalence amongst persons attending an STD clinic in Pune (in the same state), increased from 9% in 1991 to 17% in 1992: a sign that HIV is spreading by the sexual route. So far the State of Maharashtra has reported over a quarter of India's 1,017 cases of AIDS.

India's blood transfusion system relies mainly on paid donors and the government controls only about one-third of blood banks. It was made obligatory to test every bottle of blood for HIV antibodies in March 1989 but diagnostic kits were not distributed until late 1992, and there are not enough to go round. Testing is concentrated in cities – so professional donors move to small towns. Testing methods are capital-intensive and a World Bank loan to combat AIDS was tied to import of test kits from abroad, not to development of simpler tests which could be manufactured locally. In addition to an absolute shortage of testing equipment, there is also a shortage of blood, even though many unnecessary transfusions are done. It seems likely that blood transfusion will remain an important source for HIV infection in India, and will prove more difficult to control than has been the case in Africa.

At present WHO estimates that 65% of HIV-infected persons in India are men, but the greater vulnerability of women to infection will tend to produce almost equal numbers of both sexes within a few years. As HIV infection has been common only since the late 1980s, mother–to–child transmission is not yet visible, but is likely to become important (as in Africa) in the near future.

In India many impacts of AIDS are denied at present. Most educational and preventive work has been directed to sex workers, men who have sex with men, truck drivers and blood donors, not to the general population who remain relatively ignorant about AIDS and unwilling to talk openly about sexual behaviour or HIV. AIDS is still perceived as a narrowly medical problem, a situation which many doctors seem to want to maintain. Orphans are not yet visible or acknowledged as a cause for concern, but it is likely that by the end of the decade many orphans in Asia, as in Africa, will need care and support. There are already many street children in large cities, and their numbers will surely increase.

The economic and demographic impacts of AIDS are likely to resemble those in Africa, but at present their potential scale is rarely admitted. However, the Indian Health Organization predicts that population growth will slow down as mortality rates rise and that traditional coping mechanisms in families and society will be strained and may fail. A disproportionate loss of well-educated people (as in Africa) will result in a younger workforce, and their inexperience, added to absenteeism, may reduce productivity and the volume of exports needed to earn foreign exchange.

In India denial seems to be lasting longer and being more anxiously maintained than was the case ten years ago in Africa or in the West. Added to denial of the reality of AIDS (and of the frequency of sexual activity of all kinds outside marriage), several other factors may hinder constructive responses to the pandemic. Compared with Africa, populations are more dense, cities more numerous and more crowded, and conditions for the poor people who live in them more desperate: HIV spreads faster amongst the urban poor than it does in rural areas.

Next, the technology and infrastructure for essential services in India lies midway between the underdevelopment of Africa and the sophistication of the West, but the greater availability of some form of health care (often unregulated) and of commercial sex (often only too well-regulated by brothel managers) may help HIV to spread even more rapidly than was possible in Africa. It may, for example, be safer to have no blood transfusion than to receive blood contaminated with HIV. As the pandemic develops, health and welfare services in India are likely to prove dangerously fragile and near to breakdown, once their operations are disturbed by AIDS.

Indian society is already divided by the caste system and by deeply-rooted conflicts between Hindus and Muslims, while Christianity is a minority faith. Muslim and Hindu reactions to the threat of AIDS (when it is at last understood) will probably be very different: judgemental with increasing fundamentalism and aggression on the one hand, and resigned and passive on the other. For example, a Muslim leader, speaking at a meeting of the Federation of Asian Catholic

Medical Associations in Bangkok in 1992, divided society into 'sinners' and 'innocent' and regarded control of the pandemic as easy, being simply a matter of following the teachings of the Qur'an.

Religious sanctions which maintain a lowly status for women and allow discrimination against persons who are 'not like us' are likely to delay attempts to deal with gender issues which prevent women from avoiding HIV, and the same sanctions may hinder acceptance of HIV-infected persons as fully human. Women sex workers who become HIV-infected appear to be regarded as expendable and are often replaced with 'clean' girls. Yet infected women may have no other source of income than their bodies when they leave large cities to return home. As in Africa, it is likely that educational efforts to prevent HIV infection will be unsuccessful if not linked to compassionate care for people who are already ill.

Churches are involved in positive responses to AIDS in Asia, and secular NGOs are active too. In late 1992 the Federation of Asian Catholic Medical Associations conference in Bangkok, entitled 'AIDS, life and love', was attended by people from fourteen Asian countries. At that time most participants were not well-informed about AIDS, and considerable denial was reported. Also in 1992, Caritas India held a smaller workshop in Hyderabad, where denial and stigmatization of HIV-infected persons and their families were common reactions (even from health workers); little educational material about AIDS existed and WHO publications were not seen, even by Ministry of Health employees.

Since then a good deal has been achieved through collaboration between the Christian Medical Association of India (CMAI) and the National AIDS Control Organization (NACO). They arranged for 22 Indian doctors to visit Uganda and Zimbabwe in October 1993, and these doctors have since helped to train district-level doctors at 45 sites throughout India in HIV/AIDS diagnosis, management, counselling and reporting. These training courses were short, but several hundred doctors have had some exposure to AIDS-related facts, issues and problems. This initiative shows what can be achieved when governments and NGOs are willing to co-operate, and to learn from people in other countries who are facing similar problems – but with accumulated experience.

THAILAND

By contrast with India, responses to AIDS in Thailand are more open and better developed, as responses built onto experience of family planning programmes begun before HIV arrived. The first HIV infection was reported in 1985, but the epidemic did not expand rapidly until 1988, when seroprevalence amongst intravenous drug users

(IVDUs) rose from 1% to 32–43% in only nine months. Since then IVDU seroprevalence has stabilized at 30–40%. Most IVDUs are male, half have been in prison (where needles are often shared) and although half have heterosexual relations and another 5% are bisexual, few men use condoms.

The second wave of HIV infection in Thailand occurred among female sex workers, beginning in 1989, when a serosurvey showed that 10% of such women in a northern province were becoming infected every month – a rate which fell to 3–5% per month later. Across the whole country the average prevalence of HIV infection amongst brothel-based sex workers rose from 3.5% in June 1989 to 15% in June 1991. Amongst women selling sex to middle and upper-income clients, rates are lower but rising (7% on average in 1993). Prevalence of HIV is highest in northern provinces bordering Myanmar (Burma) and Laos, quite close to southern China. Women sex workers from the northern provinces are over-represented throughout the country and increasing numbers of sex workers come from Burma, Laos or China. These women often cannot understand Thai and therefore do not receive AIDS education. Some HIV-infected women returning to Burma have been murdered: the fate of women returning to China is unknown, but they provide a possible route for HIV to enter that densely populated country.

A census in 1990 suggests that in Thailand there may be one sex worker for every 146 men aged 15 to 44. A national survey of nearly 3,000 Thai men and women found that 65% of men had sexual experience before marriage, and 31% of urban married men continued to have sex outside marriage. Corresponding figures were 1% for unmarried and 1.7% for married women. Unmarried men reported an average of 30 partners but condoms were used by only about one-third of men. Although foreign tourists form only a small proportion of sex workers' clients, Bangkok's reputation as a centre for sex-tourism makes it an important link for spread of HIV within South-East Asia, as well as farther afield. Since 1992 the Thai government has tried to change the image of tourism to promote 'family holidays', but the sex industry continues to thrive and to use under-age children, against the law.

The third wave of HIV infection in Thailand affected heterosexual men who do not use drugs, and was noted first in 1988. Overall HIV prevalence amongst conscripts to the army (selected by lottery) has risen from 0.6% in November 1989 to 4% in May 1993 – but conscripts from the northern provinces had a consistently high HIV prevalence. At present men are more often infected than women; as usual, most are in their 20s.

Buddhism is the commonest religion in Thailand, and its adherents seem to take a positive and humane attitude to AIDS. A Buddhist at the Catholic Medical Association's Conference in Asia in 1992 suggested that religions should play a vital part in changing the way people think.

The Thai Red Cross Society, World Concern International, the Catholic Church, Tear Fund and a Protestant group (ACET) provide education and care for people living with AIDS and for women sex workers. The Thai Red Cross is helping to shape government policies and public attitudes by the non-judgemental and friendly behaviour of workers, their concern for medical confidentiality and the rights of HIV-infected people and their vision of hope. Their programme is described in a Strategies for Hope booklet, *Candles of Hope* (12), which concludes: 'It is only within a climate of hope ... that the threat of AIDS can be confronted and overcome. The Thai Red Cross has not only lit a candle of hope for many thousands of people with HIV and AIDS, but has also translated that hope into practical action.'

CHINA

The first case of AIDS was seen in China in 1985 and up to August 1994 a total of only 40 cases were recorded, some in foreigners. Including these AIDS cases, by August 1994 1,435 HIV-positive persons had been found amongst 3 million people tested. Most of the infections were in the 20 – 39 age group, and most were due to intravenous drug use, centred in one province, Yunnan, which borders Myanmar and Laos. In other provinces the reported HIV seroprevalence is very low, but sexual transmission is increasing and since 1989 the ratio of locals to foreigners had increased.

Sexually transmitted diseases were common in China in the first half of the twentieth century, but had been almost eradicated by 1960. Since the early 1980s, a more liberal policy has developed, and with it, STDs have reappeared. In 1980 a total of 48 cases were reported from the whole country, but in 1990 over 147,000 were recorded; as reports must bear names it is likely that many more cases actually occurred. As usual, the incidence is highest in persons aged 20 to 24 years, and gonorrhoea is the most frequent diagnosis. As condoms give good protection against treatable STDs it can be assumed that most of these patients did not use condoms.

AIDS, too, is a disease which must be reported by name since 1986, and a law for the prevention and control of infectious diseases was adopted in 1989. Although HIV infection is not mentioned, this law prescribes treatment in isolation and directs that 'the public security department may assist medical care institutions in taking measures to enforce treatment in isolation'. Such a law, with the requirement to name patients, may drive HIV-infected persons into hiding and help to spread HIV once it enters the general population – a disaster which may have happened already.

A recent Western visitor to China commented that sexual relations before marriage are said to be uncommon, and that the collective nature of society would seem to make promiscuous relationships difficult. However, members of his party were warned against sex workers in hotels, so commercial sex does exist.

Homosexuality exists in China, too, despite government denials, and a few HIV infections were recorded in gay men. After decades of official intolerance and public ostracism, the proportion of homosexuals is not known, but they may number several million men.

The Director of the Department of Epidemiology Research in Shanghai, writing in January 1995 for the first number of a new journal, *AIDS Analysis Asia* (2), concludes: 'According to the "best case" scenario, by the year 2000 there will be an estimated 55,000 HIV infections and 11,000 AIDS cases. According to the "worst case" scenario, there will be 270,000 HIV infections and 55,000 AIDS cases'. His article began with the statement: 'AIDS is a serious potential threat to the people of China.'

China is the only country in the world which is making a determined effort to reduce its population with an enforced policy of 'one child per family'. As boys are greatly preferred and female babies may be aborted, more boys than girls are being born. It seems likely that a systematic imbalance between the sexes in any society will prove dangerous, once HIV begins to spread, as an excess of men increases the probability that women will have more than one sexual partner. As women are more susceptible to HIV infection, a future AIDS epidemic in China is likely to exacerbate the tendency for men to outnumber women.

LATIN AMERICA AND THE CARIBBEAN

By comparison with subsaharan Africa and Asia, the AIDS epidemic in Latin America is on a smaller scale, but it is still larger than epidemics in North America or Western Europe. In late 1991 the overall cumulative AIDS incidence was 10 persons per 100,000 population, ranging from 63 per 100,000 in certain Caribbean islands, through 40 per 100,000 in Brazil, to 10 or less per 100,000 in Mexico and the rest of South America. In Brazil most AIDS cases are concentrated in Sao Paulo and Rio de Janeiro. The distribution of cases suggests that HIV infection entered the Caribbean islands in the late 1970s and has since spread south, via Sao Paulo and later Rio de Janeiro.

Given the dense populations of cities and countries (Brazil and Mexico together have a population of about 246 million people) HIV could spread easily: in late 1994 about 2 million persons were

HIV-infected. The greatest social and economic impact of the pandemic is yet to come, as annual HIV infections in adults are likely to continue to rise until the late 1990s, and the highest incidence of persons with AIDS will not be reached until the early years of the next century.

HIV spreads in Latin America mainly through intravenous drug use and sexual contact of all kinds, but also through transfused blood and from mother to child; the proportional contribution of each mode is not known. At present about 65% of infected persons are men, but as in Africa and Asia, the greater vulnerability of women and their poor social and educational status may lead to a gradual levelling of infection rates between the sexes. Intravenous drug use has increased tenfold in Brazil over the last decade and bisexual behaviour is common, often combined with commercial sex, so sexual networks may be large, but the influence of the Roman Catholic Church limits the use of condoms. Selling sex is one way of making money to spend on drugs and the two are often linked in large cities. HIV infection is a new hazard which makes the lives of street children even more dangerous – in Brazil such children are numerous already and regarded as vermin to be exterminated, just like rats. Numbers of street children are likely to rise when AIDS orphans are left without support.

Responses are patchy in Latin America, as AIDS competes for attention and funds with campaigns to change oppressive structures or to reduce trafficking in drugs.

There are wide gulfs between rich rulers and poor and powerless citizens living in slums. Society is organized for the benefit of men; women have a low status and little power to make decisions about their own lives. In other regions these social conditions favour spread of HIV – and are likely to have the same effect in Latin America.

In Latin America 'Liberation Theology' supports (mainly Roman Catholic) Basic Christian Communities which challenge oppressive structures and try to increase the capacity-to-cope of poor people. But at present encyclicals which condemn artificial birth control and use of condoms (even to prevent AIDS?) both hinder and reduce the credibility of Church responses to AIDS.

The consequences of AIDS in Latin America may be less severe than in Africa or Asia (although similar in kind) but the impact will exceed the effects to be expected amongst Western nations. Everywhere AIDS interacts with poverty, injustice and unequal opportunities to expose and worsen existing weaknesses in society and to hinder community development.

The recent explosive spread of HIV in India and Thailand is a warning that complacency is dangerous. HIV could at any time begin to spread much more rapidly in Latin America, especially if economic stress forces more men and women to sell sex, or to sell and use intravenous drugs.

EASTERN EUROPE

In Eastern Europe the population structure is similar to that of Western nations, with a narrow base (showing a declining birth rate), a mid-life bulge and a life expectancy at birth of 69 years. In other respects these countries resemble developing nations: many of their citizens are poor and rapidly becoming more needy, infrastructures for health, welfare and education are inadequate, and standards of hygiene and maintenance of equipment are poor. But philosophical and behavioural handicaps may prove even more important than practical obstacles in obstructing responses to AIDS.

For over a thousand years Russia has had authoritarian and sometimes brutal rulers. At the Revolution of 1917 Russia exchanged one form of oppression for another, at least equally autocratic. After 1917 the public influence of the Orthodox Church was weakened by ridicule, persecution and dispersion of Church leaders. Forbidden to teach young people or to take part in public life and cut off from contacts with other Christians, the Orthodox Church survived in hiding, very little influenced by the second Vatican Council, liturgical reform, charismatic renewal, liberation theology, feminism – or any other current of life in contemporary Christianity.

For 70 years citizens feared authority and knew that their daily lives were observed by informers. Threats of death or the labour camps discouraged dissent and enforced passive co-operation with official policies. It was not safe to trust most people, and there was not much to hope for: depression became a way of life. In this atmosphere, organized voluntary responses to distress or injustice could not develop, as they did in the West in the last 50 years.

In Eastern Europe HIV was introduced through contaminated blood into hospitals, and spread by poorly sterilized needles and syringes, and (on a small scale) through sexual contacts with foreigners. In 1987 a huge screening programme began, testing more than 18 million people (6% of the population); only two of 19,000 homosexuals and none of more than 120,000 drug users were HIV-infected, showing that the Russian epidemic began very differently from epidemics in Western Europe and the United States.

In Romania babies and young children were given small quantities of HIV-contaminated imported blood as a 'tonic'; many children were infected and a few passed HIV to their mothers during breast-feeding, an uncommon but effective way for HIV to reach a heterosexual community.

Needle transmission and vertical infection (from a mother infected with HIV by her husband, who had worked in the Congo) both contributed to an outbreak at Elista childrens' hospital, where contaminated equipment led to HIV infection of nearly 40 children – who in turn infected eight of their mothers. At an HIV/AIDS Conference in St Petersburg in early 1992, overseas visitors noticed 'a large sense of guilt in physicians who have been working with AIDS because the problem appears to be ... caused through needles and syringes in hospitals': this perception of medical guilt is almost unique to Eastern Europe.

Numbers of reported HIV infections or persons with AIDS in Eastern Europe remain small in comparison with the sizes of populations, but the figures are likely to be inaccurate, as in developing countries, and for the same reasons: denial that AIDS exists, the severe stigma of HIV infection, lack of testing equipment, difficulty in recognizing AIDS and inadequate laboratory facilities for confirming AIDS-defining diagnoses.

In the new social conditions of the 1990s, HIV is likely to spread more rapidly in Eastern Europe through sexual contacts of all kinds. In the past, homosexuality was denied in Russia and norms for sexual behaviour were repressive, so that the sex industry was small and hidden away from ordinary citizens. In the last decade, Western influences began to change sexual expectations and behaviour, and the pace of change accelerated with the disappearance of Communism. Homosexual acts are now legal and the sex industry approximates to a Western pattern – but inflation and economic reforms have caused poverty, which encourages sex-work for subsistence survival, as in developing countries.

The impact of AIDS and responses to the pandemic may be modified by interaction with other problems, as in Africa and Asia: underdevelopment of health services and industry, the effects of rapid political and economic change, and increasing crime and corruption are the key concerns. Yet, simultaneously, a spiritual revolution is taking place in which millions of people are growing slowly towards responsibility for their own lives – and learning to trust each other in community.

Wherever AIDS appears, signs of hope appear alongside signs of potential disaster, and Russia is no exception. The seeds of hope seem small, but so was the mustard seed in the Gospel. One seed of hope was sown by a group which included members of the Salvation Army, who visited Russia as a technical assistance team in 1992, to talk about the epidemiology of AIDS in other countries, care, counselling and behaviour change, and the usefulness of small groups for support and action. The discussion turned to the nature of the Salvation Army, allowing someone to explain that it is a Christian denomination 'characterized by a sleeves-rolled-up approach ... aimed at the salvation and growth of the whole person'.

At the end a participant commented: 'It is good that the experience of Africa and other countries has been shared in Russia. This has been a good example of how to transfer ideas. Last week two infected people were locked up in Russia – we must overcome this thinking'. Another said: 'Despite all your wide experience you are still willing to see patients'. A Salvation Army member defined mission as 'crossing frontiers in the name of Christ' and added: 'There are many frontiers in Russia, psychological, economic, historic and political, but the spiritual frontier is wide open at present.'

WESTERN INDUSTRIALIZED NATIONS

North America, Western Europe, Australia and white South Africa are geographically separate, but in them HIV shows similar transmission patterns, and AIDS has similar consequences and evokes broadly similar responses.

A severe acquired immunodeficiency syndrome in men was reported first in the USA in June 1981, and appeared in Britain and Europe some time later. At first over 95% of all HIV-infections were in men, and in industrial countries HIV continues to be transmitted most often through homosexual contact or intravenous drug use. In the early years many haemophiliacs were infected by blood products, and blood transfusions infected some women.

From the mid 1980s HIV has been spreading also amongst heterosexuals, through the sexual partners of drug users and the sexual networks of bisexual persons, but explosive spread of HIV (which was feared) has not occurred in the West. This may be due to smaller sexual networks, different sexual practices and fewer genital ulcers, but perhaps 'seeding' of HIV into heterosexual society has not reached a critical level – yet.

However, the proportion of women with AIDS has risen steeply since the epidemic began. In Western Europe the sex ratio amongst HIV-infected adults is 5:1, significantly lower than in North America and Australia. The highest AIDS rates in women are in southern Europe, where injecting drug use is the main risk behaviour. In northern Europe, heterosexual spread is increasingly important, and about half of the women so infected have partners from countries where heterosexual transmission predominates. Over 70% of children with AIDS in Belgium have one parent originating in subsaharan Africa, and a recent commentator noted that in Western Europe 'there are strong interactions between the epidemics in sub-Saharan Africa and Asia ... this trend is likely to continue'.

Except in a few cities (New York, Edinburgh, San Francisco, London and Amsterdam), numbers of HIV-infected persons are very small compared with total populations, and mother-to-child transmission is uncommon, so AIDS has little impact on population structure or economics – except for the economics of health care.

Responses to AIDS are uneven. Most gay men in North America and Europe are articulate and politically active, and they fight for the 'human rights' to respect and effective treatment, while their sense of common identity provides strong support for HIV-infected members.

Outside affected sub-groups, people in the West tend to be complacent and judgemental, as most do not know anyone who is HIV-infected (and do not want to!). Education for prevention assumes that sexual activity is the absolute right of every adult, whether married or single, so that 'safer sex' is the main message, even to adolescents.

Mainstream Churches are actively involved in AIDS care, counselling, advocacy and work with underprivileged minorities, yet there is not much interest in theological issues relating to AIDS, except in the narrow field of same-sex relationships. Many Church members (and their leaders) remain unwilling to talk openly about sexual relationships of all kinds, or about death, and their fears seriously hinder positive responses to AIDS.

For Further Reading see Bibliography, p. 311, (1), (2), (12), (13), (44).

Study Suggestions
1. Is the AIDS pandemic in your country 'young' or well-established? How long ago were the first cases reported to WHO? Do local people deny that AIDS exists, or say 'It is a very small problem'?
2. What political or social factors can you identify in your city or province which may accelerate spread of HIV? What is the commonest way HIV is transmitted?
3. What percentage of HIV-infected persons in your region are male? Has the ratio of infected males to females changed since records began?
4. Do the attitudes and statements of Church leaders influence Church members' sexual behaviour? Do Church statements tend to reduce spread of HIV, have no effect – or actually *increase* spread?
5. How much do you know about your sexual partner(s)' lifestyle(s)? Draw your *own* 'sexual network', in so far as you know it: are question marks needed to indicate uncertainty about your partner's behaviour?

PART 2
AIDS IN A CONTEXT OF CRISIS

CHAPTER 8
Beginning a Theological Response to AIDS

This chapter suggests an approach to two tasks: first, to relate the AIDS pandemic to history and the study of theology, and second, to set AIDS in the context of other present-day challenges to human beings.

THEOLOGY AND HISTORY

'Theology is taught by God, teaches of God and leads to God' wrote Thomas Aquinas (1225–74), but theology, as we know it, is done by human beings within history. Some philosophers, however, have concluded that a supreme Being must be 'outside' history – so that men and women who wish to do theology must escape, first, from the limitations and history of the physical world into a spirit world which is the domain of God. In contrast, Christians and Jews presuppose that God is involved in the physical world and that His self-disclosure is given through the events of history and daily life; this assumption is based on their actual experiences during the last four thousand years.

Like other pastoral or agricultural peoples, Abraham's successors saw a cyclic pattern in their lives: light and dark, winter and summer, times for sowing seeds and times for harvesting crops, birth and death. But superimposed on natural cycles they recognized significant changes, sometimes occurring gradually, sometimes through a catastrophe such as a flood or war or sickness. It seemed to them that such crises, and their own responses to change, gave a direction to history. Life did not remain the same for ever, so the idea arose that it had a purpose and a goal. One Palestinian tribe came to believe that the God of Abraham, Isaac and Jacob acts in history to deliver His people from oppression, and to lead them in warfare – in addition to blessing their fields and flocks, which were the chief roles of the nature gods of other tribes.

It was easy for ancient peoples to make a direct connection between well-being and God's blessing and to regard disaster as a sign of rejection by God, or (at best) as corrective punishment. But during the Exile of the inhabitants of Judea to Babylon in 587 BCE, and after their return to Jerusalem 70 years later, this simple model began to be questioned, and prophets started to speak of a creative or redemptive role for suffering, and to look for special significance in times of national stress. Reading the 'signs of the times' became an important task for theologians and remains important now, whether done in retrospect (for example, seeking new meanings in the Exodus from Egypt) or prospectively, asking 'What is the significance of the AIDS pandemic?' *Theodicy* (justification of God) attempts to make sense of the reality of suffering and evil which everyone experiences, while at the same time maintaining the belief that God creates and loves His people.

A PERSPECTIVE ON HISTORY

History is not composed entirely of crises. Critical periods in the history of a tribe or a people may lead to permanent changes in their way of life, goals and values, but (with time) even dramatic changes are absorbed into 'normal life' by processes of growth and reconciliation, which usually lead into a period of stability. Years, decades or centuries later, another turning point occurs, and the cycle of adaptation and arrival at a new state of stability is repeated. Not all peoples survived the crises which occurred – or which they brought down upon themselves; in an overwhelming crisis a tribe might disappear as a political entity (as the Northern Kingdom disappeared after its conquest in 721 BCE) or a whole civilization (for example the Mayan civilization) might end or be absorbed by a more powerful society.

The choice of a perspective is likely to influence the way in which we interpret events as we attempt to 'read the signs of the times'. Few people think that we are living in a period of stability or engaged in adaptation to a crisis which is now past. Instead, most observers claim that we are living through a major turning-point in human history: a series of events, with a set of human responses to those events, which together threaten the continuing life and values of a tribe or civilization. Historical crises were precipitated by natural disasters (flood, earthquake, disease, famine), or by human action in war or by empire-building to consolidate power over weaker peoples. Other crises resulted from a change in the way people viewed their world (for example, at the Renaissance, Reformation or Enlightenment), or a change in their technologies for living, as happened at the agricultural or industrial revolutions. Some civilizations survived critical challenges, but were changed by their experiences; others were absorbed into competing civilizations or simply disappeared.

AIDS IN CONTEXT

Previous turning-points in history took place in certain physical landscapes, to particular groups of people – cut off from or linked to other groups in specific ways, and events were interpreted in terms of the thought-patterns of their time or of later generations. We may think, from a privileged viewpoint hundreds of years later, that we achieve a deeper and more accurate understanding of the true significance of past events than observers did at the time. However, despite the limitations of an interim viewpoint, we need to interpret our present crises immediately, in a provisional way, in order to choose how to respond. We need an overview of the context in which AIDS must be interpreted: here is one personal view of that context.

1. We live in a global and technological society. No significant segments of the planet remain unknown or unexplored: there are no more blank spaces into which growing tribes can expand. During this century a complex technology for living has developed, mainly in the West, which has spread globally – but very unevenly. Most peoples know about and can envy technologies for growing food or building homes, for medical care, education, transport or communication which far outstrip what is available to them. Communication is critical: there are elaborate means for spreading 'news' (however trivial or significant) worldwide, and equally elaborate ways of hiding information from people who are supposed to have no right to it, even though it concerns their future lives. Very recently, however, computer networks, Internet and fax facilities can by-pass other means of communication, making it far more difficult to 'control' news of atrocities.

Interactions between peoples and economies occur on a scale which would have been unimaginable only fifty years ago. Yet inequalities of possession and opportunity between those who 'have' and those who 'have not' have widened in the last 25 years in both industrialized and developing countries. A successful businessman and an unemployed shanty dweller, living only a mile apart in Nairobi or Lusaka, actually exist in different worlds.

2. The human population has doubled since 1950, which means that more than half of all people alive in 1995 are less than 45 years of age; in the context of the AIDS pandemic these people are in (or will enter within the next 15 years) the most vulnerable age group for acquiring HIV – young adulthood. About two-thirds of young adults live in developing countries, where populations have grown at 2 to 3.5% a year during the last two decades. The United Nations forecasts that the world population in 2050 (within the lifetime of our children) is likely to be 10 to 12.5 billion persons, a further doubling.

3. Knowledge of the physical world, attitudes to human relationships and activities, tools for thinking and personal and community values are changing very rapidly. As a result, people ask new questions but have not yet found new answers. For example:

3 (a). Relationships between women and men are changing, as

people question the patriarchal bias which was normal in most societies until recently. Women with new responsibilities learn to value themselves as independent persons, and in this process may find that they confront men, rather than co-operating with them, so that there is an uneasy, defensive quality to their relationships. Men feel threatened by change, too, and their traditional roles are also being challenged in two other fields: as providers and as defenders. Clearing bush to cultivate gardens and then moving to new land, or hunting antelope for the pot: where does proper use of the environment end and 'exploitation' of natural resources begin? More and more men are unemployed: can they take pride in themselves as 'providers'? Warfare, too, is questioned as a way of resolving disputes or extending territory, as the waste of life and resources caused by war comes to be seen as intolerable. What can a man teach his sons in this time of change? Fatherhood, too, is a changing role.

3 (b). Economic life is in turmoil. Marxism in its Communist form has failed. Capitalism is in difficulties as 'market forces' and human needs are often in conflict. Voluntary socialism could succeed in practice, but only if supported by a common overriding purpose strong enough to persuade millions of people to forego coveted personal benefits for the good of their less fortunate neighbours.

3 (c). There is, however, growing support for the concept that 'small is beautiful' and for the development of 'sustainable societies', from both industrial and developing nations. But practical exploration of these ideas has hardly begun, so we do not know, yet, what kinds of organization, or ways of farming, or factory methods, or political philosophies *would* be sustainable over decades or centuries.

For example, what is the optimal size for a general hospital if it is to function efficiently to meet the human needs of patients and staff? Anyone who has worked in one of the mega-hospitals of East or Central Africa knows that 1,500 to 2,000 beds is too large; staff who have also worked in hospitals with 300 to 600 beds may think (on the basis of experience) that those numbers are right, at least for non-industrial countries.

3 (d). The rights and needs of individuals often conflict with those of the societies to which they belong, and (except in small communities) most people divide their lives into public and private departments, often with different sets of values or ways of relating to others, and even a different personality for private and public roles. Which is the real person? What happens if values or behaviours in the two areas conflict or if the barrier between private and public functions breaks down, at a time of stress? We cannot return to a medieval way of life in isolated self-sufficient societies and we do not wish to do so. It is impossible *not* to be interdependent.

The moral theory which underlies traditional Western ethics assumes co-operation in public life but *uses* competition to encourage enterprise. Competition allows and to some extent favours inequalities between 'haves' and 'have nots', although the size of disparities are reduced by taxes on wealth, which permit some redistribution in favour of the poor. In other words, co-operation reduces socially unacceptable inequalities. Building relationships tends to be seen as a 'private' matter, properly confined to the private part of life.

The twentieth century has seen, on a large scale, both the disintegration which may follow when competitive individuals become detached from communities (as in the West) and the oppression which results when states attempt to impose co-operation by ignoring the rights and privileges of human beings (as in former Communist countries). A creative balance between individuality and community is not easy to achieve or sustain.

THEOLOGICAL PERSPECTIVES

3 (e). We live in a time of confusion about the existence of a transcendent Being. Many people in the West deny the possibility of any reality which cannot be detected and measured by physical means: atheism is a common opinion about the way the world is. Yet there is obvious religious pluralism, and many people who believe in a transcendent Being do so with a passionate intolerance for all other points of view: fundamentalism flourishes in Christianity, Judaism and Islam. When contacts between nations or sects were infrequent it was possible to ignore other systems of belief and the people who held them, but in our interdependent societies interfaith dialogue cannot be avoided, neither can contact with those who hold rigidly to a belief that their own view of reality is complete and totally correct.

People who have very different perspectives cannot easily talk to each other and may give different meanings to the same words. For example, at a UN-sponsored conference about community reactions to HIV-infected persons, some participants used 'faith' to mean: 'We have faith that you have resources within your community to enable you to cope with this distress', while other delegates used 'faith' to refer to their belief in (and relationship to) a personal God, existing outside their communities, who validates their best values.

4. Omnipresent television cameras and reporters hungry for news give people little or no time for reflection before they comment on events or take action. Yet for thousands of years most cultures have valued reflection, solitude, and the wisdom which comes from age, experience and prayer. This is still true for some peoples, especially in the South, who may have to defend their views against implicit Northern claims that traditional values are no longer useful resources for

modern life. 'Values' are devalued: people are urged to grapple with 'real' (physical or political) problems using the methods and concepts of science.

5. But often these approved scientific methods and concepts are derived from a mechanistic understanding of the physical world, even though most contemporary scientists no longer think in mechanical terms, except for limited technical purposes. The newer ways of thinking focus on sub-atomic particles which interact in ways determined partly by necessity or law, and partly by chance – with freedom – so that knowledge of the behaviour of very small particles is imprecise. Moreover, small events start chain reactions which have unpredictable and large consequences. Interrelationship appears to be built into the way the world is at every level, from that of sub-atomic particles right up to the complicated interactions of weather systems or human societies.

The structures of the physical world have a strange relationship to theoretical mathematics – a human activity. Mathematicians see, with awe, that their theoretical calculations reflect physical realities: their theories and proofs, which seem to be a form of imaginative play, yield results which are later verified by physical observations. Mathematicians conclude, provisionally, that their thinking does not create new structures, but discovers truths about the nature of reality. If mathematical knowing gives reliable information about the way things are, then there are grounds for confidence that other, intuitive, forms of human 'knowing' also touch reality, as thinkers have believed in the past.

6. The pace of change is accelerating so rapidly that the period for which reasonable predictions can be made shortens from decade to decade and almost from year to year. Who thought, in 1980, that Communism would be rejected in Eastern Europe and that apartheid would end in South Africa? At the same date most doctors would have dismissed accounts of the start of the AIDS pandemic as science fiction – until they found themselves living science fiction.

7. Finally, this is a suffering world. There are more people alive than have ever been alive before, and each one is capable of suffering. In one century we have experienced global wars; corrupt and sometimes brutal governments in every continent; systematic attempts at genocide; flight of hundreds of thousands of refugees into insecurity or danger; rapid growth of organized crime and terrorism in almost every country; an aggressive trade in addictive drugs; famine, drought, floods and other 'natural' disasters; pandemic AIDS and expansion of cities where life is precarious and degrading for the poor majority.

Behind or compounding external sources of suffering lie fear of, and hatred for, human beings who are 'not our people'. As interdependence and the need to share limited living space become more urgent, at the same time (it seems) differences become more divisive. Diversity and community are not easy to hold together.

Added to external causes for suffering, many people feel an inner separation from their true selves which is expressed through violence, mental illness, alcoholism or drug addiction. City dwellers cannot be materially self-sufficient and often feel powerless to alter intolerable circumstances. If interdependence is not expressed in small friendly communities it becomes almost unbearable, for everyone needs to belong to other people and to know that he or she matters as a person. If populations continue to expand exponentially, the problems of limited living space will become more and more acute.

SUBJECTS OR PARTICIPANTS?

If we view history as a journey of discovery, not as a series of inevitable or predetermined events, then we may be able to improve the outcome of our present turning-point, and we have an obligation to do so.

In my opinion, four sets of problems interact to threaten human societies at this present time.

1. NUCLEAR TECHNOLOGY

Since the feast of the Transfiguration on 6 August 1945 human beings have been capable of destroying each other in vast numbers. Later 'improvements' in technology have greatly increased the range, accuracy and destructive power of nuclear weapons. The effects of such explosions are only partly localized because winds and ocean currents carry radioactive products of the explosion to other continents, where radioactivity persists for decades or centuries in food chains: the blood, bones and ova or sperm of people who eat contaminated crops or domestic animals may be permanently damaged.

Recent agreements to reduce stocks of nuclear weapons appear to lessen the risk of nuclear war. However, the threat will not disappear while any stocks of nuclear weapons exist, or while unstable but charismatic leaders control countries which already have, or may develop, the technical capability to make nuclear weapons. Several trends in the mid 1990s may be increasing the risk of nuclear war once again: political and social instability combined with economic distress in Eastern Europe, the spread of aggressive Islamic fundamentalism, and the 'sickness of war' which is evident in conflicts inspired by ethnic differences. It is truly dangerous to believe that we can or should isolate ourselves permanently from people who are 'not like us'.

The possibly greater risk of serious radioactive contamination from accidents will persist for as long as nuclear reactors are used to generate power – or for any other purpose. The risk will in fact persist for centuries after reactors are abandoned, because nuclear waste takes hundreds of years to become a safe part of the human environment. The history of Chernobyl in 1987 shows how real the risk of accident is, and how a single incident in one reactor has adverse and measurable consequences in more than one continent.

2. GLOBAL ENVIRONMENT

In the 1960s growth of populations and technology reached a critical point at which undesirable changes in the physical world became visible to a few keen observers. At first these prophets found it hard to convince the majority of people that there *was* a problem: the term 'environment' had none of the overtones which it carries today. Anyone who reached adulthood before 1960 remembers a world with more space, fewer people and cars – and no concern at all about global warming, extension of deserts, radiation damage due to thinning of the ozone layer which shields us from the sun, or destruction of critical ecosystems (rain forests, rivers, fertile farm land). In 1976 I watched three rhinos cross a dried water course in the Luangwa valley in Zambia: there are no rhinos left now for any visitor to see.

Human beings, too, could become an endangered species. Some consequences of human misuse of the planet are predictable, and some organizations (but few governments) are acting to reduce damage to the resources on which human beings depend for survival. But the adverse consequences of even a few years of over-use and neglect cannot be undone in a comparably short time: anyone travelling in Africa at intervals over the last 30 years has seen how rapidly desert conditions are extending in countries which were once fertile and full of wildlife.

In 1990 Maurice King wrote that 'a society is demographically trapped if it has exceeded, or is projected to exceed, the carrying capacity of its own ecosystem'. A Kenyan observer commented: 'the trap is set by singling out the child and ensuring survival without first either reducing fertility or increasing food production.' As populations grow, land becomes scarce. The land available is over-used and if crops are inadequate a society must either buy food from someone else, or migrate somewhere else. If it cannot do either, then standards of living fall, people go hungry, and eventually people die.

In the last 50 years new technologies (chemical control of agricultural pests, nuclear power, manipulation of genetic structures) have been introduced, without sufficient understanding of the complex effects which may result. In fact more environmental changes are certain in the next 50 years, because the causative events have already happened. But we do not know enough about biological interactions to predict all or even most of the effects cumulative changes will have on expanding human populations – if populations continue to expand.

3. THE AIDS PANDEMIC

The global impact of AIDS is underestimated by governments, and often ignored in planning, partly because of a limited ability to predict the future effects of AIDS: there are no comparable historical models. Past epidemics were partially contained by geographical or cultural barriers, they affected old people and children more often than young adults, and rarely resulted in disabling illness lasting for several years before death. At the end of 1994 UNICEF's annual report (without mentioning AIDS) reckoned that the effects of poverty, population growth and environmental degradation now *combine* with social and political instability to produce a 'new generation of security threats' (43). AIDS is likely to compound, not reduce, these threats.

4. ALIENATION AND CONSTRAINT: LOSS OF A SPIRITUAL IDENTITY AND TRADITION

A fourth threat to human well-being is less physical and less obvious than the threats described so far, although it influences all our responses, and is in part due to change in the social order. The hidden problem is a loss of nerve or loss of confidence in the frame of reference by which people interpret what happens to them and adapt to new challenges, combined with a profound loss of hope for the future.

The German philosopher Hegel argued in the nineteenth century that the goal of history was freedom in a rationally organized society within which citizens experience neither alienation nor constraint. But in our times experiences of alienation and constraint are the common lot of women and men worldwide, although the particular ways in which they suffer differ according to individual circumstances. Not only do many people feel alienated and constrained in their societies, but often within their own skins too. We are no longer at ease with ourselves.

4 (a). *Fragmentation of knowledge.* The scale of current events differs from the scale of the ideas available to interpret them. The events are very large and very complex, while the sets of ideas (paradigms) to hand as tools for interpretation seem too limited to be of much use – whether those paradigms originate with economists, scientists, historians or politicians. But at present the paradigms used as scaffolding for thought are changing as rapidly as everything else, and paradigms belonging to one discipline are often isolated from contact with those used by other groups of specialists. The content of each 'specialism' is vast and the vocabulary used by its practitioners makes access to its ideas difficult for non-specialists.

Imagine, for a moment, a warehouse holding tools packed in crates or cases labelled 'physics' or 'genetics' or 'economics' or 'communication' or 'politics'. The contents of each separate crate are familiar to the appropriate specialists, and can be used by them at once for their work, but (with a few exceptions) each set of tools is unfamiliar to almost everyone else. However, in this warehouse, even though there are hundreds of labelled boxes of tools and ideas, there are also a large number of uncrated items: these are tools for thought or human experiences which have been left out on the floor. Some rejected tools are concepts and experiences which are dismissed as too old to be useful, others are excluded because they deviate from current assumptions about the nature of reality and are judged to be 'nonsense', while a few tools are rejected because they are a great deal too large to fit into an average box. But two boxes have transparent walls and are surrounded by crowds of eager people sorting through and using the contents: these boxes are labelled 'environmental concerns' and 'AIDS'.

Both subjects are unusual in that they bring together experts in many different disciplines and force them to communicate their ideas to other people in language which non-experts can understand. The urgency of the AIDS pandemic is even encouraging people to re-examine large or discarded tools on the warehouse floor, to see if some ought to be rescued and put to use. The basic ideas of Christian faith are attracting some attention and so are African understandings of human life and community, which differ from the Western perspectives that are regarded (in the industrial world) as normative.

4 (b). *Reason and choice.* In human activities at present there is often a lack of balance between methods and goals, or between short-term gains and long-term losses, or between values which conflict. For example, the short-term benefit of cheap electricity from nuclear reactors was chosen in spite of the long-term problem of disposing of radioactive waste. The same preference for short-term goals (a return to economic growth at any cost) distorts discussion of what needs to be done to reduce atmospheric accumulation of carbon dioxide, which contributes to global warming.

Linear or mathematical reasoning, of a kind which can be simulated by computers, is highly valued, and computer models are used to predict the outcome of many complex activities. In contrast, intuitive or historical understanding tends to be neglected, so that public decision-making is often not influenced by reflection on either the wisdom of contemporary cultures or the insights of previous generations.

4 (c). *Value judgements.* Perhaps the problem is more fundamental – a rejection of 'values' as criteria for making choices. At conferences on AIDS, speakers avoid the term 'drug abuse' because it implies a value judgement, thereby implying that value judgements are in principle wrong, although that, too, is a value judgement. 'Value' may be subjective, influenced by cultural factors and difficult to measure, but can we

afford to abandon the effort to identify and choose between what is 'good' and what is 'better'?

In making choices, reason works with (or against) emotions and with (or against) only partly accessible influences originating in the minds of decision-makers. Perhaps it is this admixture of reason with mysterious forces and feelings, relating to experience, which makes choice between values so frightening.

4 (d). *Powerlessness and violence*. Making choices and acting upon them requires permission and power: the power to assert that 'I have value in myself, and I can recognize and value my own desires'. But city life may make men and women feel and actually *be* so helpless and so lacking in hope that active choice seems impossible. Human beings who lose a sense of their own significance usually lose (with their dignity) permission and power to recognize and to choose their own real needs and desires. Often, it seems, a community's needs can only be defined and chosen over against, and in competition with, the needs of another group whose members are 'not our people'. These other human beings are not necessarily strangers, but they are feared and misunderstood. Daily contacts between 'them' and 'us' are shaped by traditional views and patterns of behaviour which no-one dares to question, often because memories of past injuries are too painful to face.

This combination of powerlessness and alienation from people who are 'not our people' often drives men and women into violent behaviour. In that violence (whether it happens in Kigali or Sarajevo) everyone suffers, 'victims' and 'aggressors' together; there is rarely any reason in the immediate outcome of violence.

4 (e). *Purpose and destiny*? In ordinary circumstances, few people pause to ask 'What are men and women *for*? What is their long term destiny?' But this question soon becomes important in the face of catastrophe, when people recognize that neither they nor their societies have an adequate vision for the future. Escape from catastrophe seems impossible because it requires internal resources which we doubt or deny, or external help which may not exist. In our present climate of thought it is difficult to admit to ignorance or error – and if rescue is ruled out in advance, it seems pointless to repent.

Repentance is not a word or a concept which is familiar to most Western men and women. Repentance implies a willingness to change the direction in which we have been travelling and to take a different path. A major problem is that if we decide to abandon one path there is no consensus about which alternative route offers the best chance of greater well-being. This uncertainty is an expression of *relativism*: the opinion that truth varies from time to time, place to place and person to person, because there is no universal truth which is valid for all peoples, in all places and at all times – or if there is such a universal truth, we cannot know what it is. The conclusion that there is no knowable universal truth can be traced back to abandonment of belief in God as a transcendent point of reference. Western secular thinking generally denies this possibility: 'God, if he did exist, was outside the system of knowing and must be ignored' (28).

Is it possible for human knowledge to go beyond the subjective and cultural conditions which influence it to grasp universally valid truth? And where might truth be found? Is truth revealed to human beings through historical events and through human thinking? If so, how may truth be recognized?

CONCLUSION

From our present perspective the human situation appears precarious on a global scale and the pace of dangerous change is accelerating. AIDS is not a subordinate but a major reason for this precariousness, particularly for the two-thirds of human beings who live in developing (or poor) countries – although what happens in poor countries ultimately affects rich countries too. AIDS tends to expose and worsen pre-existing weaknesses in societies, by aggravating fears of people who are 'different' and sharpening awareness of the gulfs between sick and healthy, carers and patients, rich and poor, righteous and unrighteous, black and white, homosexual and heterosexual, people who do and do not use drugs, monogamous and promiscuous, unbelievers and believers – particularly when several despised characteristics meet in one HIV-infected man or woman.

At the 1992 International conference on AIDS, speaker after speaker used the phrase 'our planet is sick'. Hans Kung insists that human survival depends on finding a new world ethic, and challenges all leaders to search for a minimum of shared ethical principles, on which they can agree. But a 'coalition of believers and unbelievers' needs to seek, too, for the truth which lies behind shared principles. Where do 'shared principles' originate – in ourselves or beyond human society in transcendent Being? And what can we know of the name and nature of that Being?

For Further Reading see Bibliography, p. 311, (26) and (28).

CHAPTER 9
AIDS Challenges Faith and Belief

In ch. 8 I offered a sombre picture of converging crises which threaten human well-being, but also offer new opportunities for humanity. Global AIDS is a major, not a subordinate, contribution to this crisis.

PRELIMINARIES

If Christians are to contribute to the recovery of a framework for response large enough for AIDS, their work should start from a realistic view of their own situation and an appropriate view of their relationship to other people who do not share their faith.

1. Believers share the reactions of fear and denial which are common to everyone, when they first encounter AIDS. In addition, Christians in developing countries usually have to deal with their theological problems while at the same time living with painful personal involvement: most ministers planning another funeral or worrying about the future of a new group of orphans are also worrying about a brother or a daughter or a close friend who is HIV-infected – and about the consequences which will follow for their own families. A detached viewpoint is impossible when one is living with suffering.

2. Christians share limitations of understanding with everyone else. They do not have immediate and privileged knowledge of 'what God is doing' in the AIDS pandemic, or in any other crisis. Christians have to search for meaning and understanding alongside their brothers and sisters of different faiths (or none), and should not pretend otherwise. The Gospels present evidence that Jesus, too, had to search painfully for meaning and understanding in the events of His own life, and He warned us that disciples are not greater than their Master (John 13.16). Christians are part of a suffering humanity which cries out, as did Jesus, 'My God, my God, why have you forsaken me?' (Mark 15.34 NRSV). In the face of AIDS *everyone* has to learn to live with unanswered questions.

3. But responses start in a provisional way long before the questions have been formulated clearly. As Christians share the consequences of AIDS with other human beings who have different beliefs or none, they need not be afraid to share in responses to AIDS already begun by governments, NGOs, and UN agencies. For 'secular' responses start from the assumptions that human beings have value, and that their sufferings matter. These assumptions are part of the faith (or system of beliefs about the meaning of life) which many human beings share, even

though the content of their plural religious faiths differ widely in other respects. This common belief that human beings and their lives matter is a basis for solidarity which demands recognition and celebration: in this respect we *are* already a global family.

4. However, responses to crisis (including those made by large secular organizations and Churches) need to be questioned. All human activities fall under a judgement which is expressed partly by way of the events to which they give rise, and partly through prophetic disagreement from 'insiders' who have a different view of human possibilities, within a framework of shared beliefs. Outside critics approach a situation from another perspective altogether. Everyone, including Christians, may approve or question existing responses to AIDS, but Christians must also expect to find that *their* acts and attitudes, and those of the institutional Church, are being judged too (and often found wanting!) by HIV-infected or affected people.

5. Acts of judgement should apply to acts and attitudes, not to people. The basis of all our thinking about human crises should be that disasters happen to people who share the joys and sorrows which we feel, and share our capacity to give to others as well as to receive from them. We have no reason or authority to treat HIV-infected people as 'them', a class of beings so different from 'us' that we have no obligation to give them the rights and responsibilities of human beings. But as we see constantly, it is difficult and painful to transcend 'us/them' divisions: some Christians and Muslims assume that they have divine permission to regard and treat HIV-infected people as cursed or punished by God. The actions and words of Jesus of Nazareth recorded in the Gospels, and the Christian interpretation of judgement acting in history, suggest that God is not 'over against' but suffering with and in people infected or affected by HIV. Some Londoners wear a lapel badge which states: 'The body of Christ has AIDS'. May we, indeed *should* we, agree with this statement?

6. Finally, we ought to start from where we are, admitting that there are large gaps between Christian ideals and actual behaviour, particularly in relation to sex, fidelity, and attitudes to loss and death. It is also desirable to start from where other people are, not from where we would like them to be. Christians are in general too quick to offer solutions to others' problems, which they have had the audacity to express in their own terms. We need to learn attitudes of humility and openness in order to listen attentively to other people and other points of view. It is essential, too, that we should be practically involved in trying to relieve some consequences of HIV infection, even if that means associating with uncongenial strangers or sharing the negative discrimination which HIV-infected people meet.

From this perspective of being involved, searching for meaning, accepting judgement and starting from where we are, what might Christian experience have to offer to a framework for response to AIDS? I suggest that we do have a good deal to offer:

1. A linear view of history as a story with a direction.
2. A positive interpretation of judgement in history.
3. An optimistic view of the possibilities for human life and of the magnitude of human destiny – based on
4. A particular interpretation of certain historical events, leading to
5. A unique view of the nature of the bond responsible for creating life-enhancing personal or community relationships.
6. Successful (and unsuccessful) experience of building community, by transcending divisions of religious belief, race and culture.
7. Long experience of responding to human mess – violence, guilt, despair, waste and death, combined with
8. Practice in providing communal forms to express universal needs to mourn, celebrate and seek communion with a supreme Being in worship.
9. A faith that God exists and is personal, not impersonal; hospitable not hostile, and involved-with not indifferent to humankind – a faith which is supported by historical and contemporary evidence, although not 'provable' or 'disprovable' in scientific terms.

1. A LINEAR VIEW OF HISTORY

Orthodox Christians have a distinctive view of the history of the universe, which focuses on three events.

First, the universe came into existence, for it had a beginning. Later, amongst the millions of planets in the observable cosmos which show no sign of life, just one planet acquired properties which allowed the development of life. The probability that these special properties occurred by chance alone seems very small. Over millions of years more complex plants and free-moving animals appeared on this planet – earth. Most of these creatures were definitively adapted for life in particular environments. Later still, but at least two million years ago, less specialized animals appeared which had large brains, walked upright, used tools and probably already had simple speech. These were the first human beings: their most striking characteristic was (and is) an enormous capacity to adapt to different circumstances and to alter their environment to suit their needs.

Second, Christians claim that God acted in history two thousand years ago to identify with humankind, by being born as a male child in a small town near Jerusalem. In making this claim they reject a modern distinction which separates 'facts', which are publicly acknowledged, from interpretations, which are regarded as a personal and private matter. Christians view the life, death and being-raised-to-life of Jesus of Nazareth as public facts which require a public explanation.

Christians propose an interpretation of these events which other people are free to examine, test – and accept or reject. But if the claims of Christians are true, then the life of this one man has consequences for every human being, whether or not they are 'interested' in religion. In the context of AIDS, the life and death of Jesus of Nazareth bears directly upon many questions asked by HIV-infected persons and their carers.

Third, Christians expect a future and final turning-point in history which will change fundamentally the form and quality of life in the universe. In contemporary terms, they expect a new level of well-being and consciousness to be established, both in and beyond the human sphere – a change far greater than (but perhaps in a sense analogous to) earlier shifts from organic molecules to living organisms, or from non-human primates to tool and language-using *homo sapiens*. Biblical writers say simply: 'There will be a new heaven and a new earth'.

Within this framework Christians interpret the disasters, triumphs and turning-points of the last two thousand years as stages (or setbacks) in the development of the new humanity which began with the resurrection of Jesus of Nazareth in CE 33 and will reach fulfilment in 'a new heaven and a new earth'. The recognition of AIDS in 1981 is one more event within this developing theme.

There have been many premature attempts to identify past disasters as the start of the long-expected final crisis, though so far all identifications of end-time have been proved wrong. But errors of prediction do not rule out the hypothesis that a final turning-point *will* occur in history, and it is legitimate to take this hypothesis into account when reading the signs of the times in any age, including our own.

Reading the signs of the times is not an activity confined to theologians in universities or to ordained ministers. A good deal of useful work is done by non-theologians in secular terms. Schoolboys in Anti-AIDS clubs or African elders challenging norms for sexual behaviour in their villages may be 'doing theology' without any idea of what they are about.

2. GOD IS BOTH CREATOR AND JUDGE

As origin and creator of all that exists, God may be expected to judge whether or not created beings fulfil the potential they were given. 'Judgement' is often misunderstood to mean total rejection of things or people which do not reach a required standard – as if inadequate objects have to be melted down for reprocessing, or else destroyed. But the biblical understanding of judgement, including that of the Old Testament, is more positive than this. The positive elements become clearer in the New Testament and in developments of doctrine during the last 2,000 years. The early Church identified Christ as the One appointed to judge the lives of all men and women, and rejoiced that He will be a trustworthy and compassionate judge, because He has Himself been through temptation (Heb. 2.17–18; 4.15–16).

The Gospels record, again and again, that Jesus sought out or favoured the outsiders of his own society, sinners who offended moral standards (John 8.3–11), people who were ritually unclean (Mark 5.24–33; Luke 17.11–19) or did not belong to the People of Israel (Luke 7.1–10; Mark 7.24–31), people who had no status or power (Luke 18. 35–43; Mark 2.1–12) and those who had offended against the decrees of God or the prophets. Indeed, Jesus became an outsider, an outcast alongside other outcasts, by dying in a manner which His contemporaries associated strongly with rejection by God: 'accursed is he who hangs on a tree'.

Jesus did indeed judge outcasts, in the sense that He censured actions or characteristics which He saw to be a distortion of what each person was intended to become. This discernment was a necessary start to an offer of healing, or restoration of the capacity to become the whole persons God intended. Often judgement was a three-part act. First, Jesus identified what was wrong and individuals concerned accepted their lack of wholeness and expressed willingness to be changed (discernment). Next, healing or liberation took place, and finally, Jesus gave a command or opportunity to the person healed – in a form which assumed that each hearer had the capacity to obey. Sinners, cripples and lepers were forgiven and healed not for return to a former mode of life, but for a new life with responsibility for proclaiming the good news of God's coming kingdom, and expressing its approach by the quality of their lives (John 8.11; Mark 5.18–20). Judgement offered power to change and restored relationship with God, by restoring the creation-status of human beings as sharers in the image and creativity of God.

3. THERE IS MEANING AND PURPOSE IN HUMAN LIFE

HIV-infected people search for meaning in lives suddenly cut short by disease. Often they experience rejection from families and friends and they long to be convinced that they still belong to the human community. This search for meaning and unconditional acceptance is part of a search for an answer to the more basic question: 'What are human beings for? What is their purpose and destiny?' To this question Christian doctrine gives an answer which is biblical, patristic and affirmed and developed through 2,000 years of controversy: human beings are made for relationship with God and with each other, and they are called to share with God in the continuing creation of the universe, which is not yet fulfilled.

Those purposes are not altered by HIV infection. Everyone, HIV-infected or not, has capacities for relationship and creativity which cannot be lost except by deliberate, repeated and whole-hearted choice. Only individuals who choose to reject God and the needs of other people, who refuse forgiveness and who are determined to destroy themselves (persons whom God loves) will be permitted to do so. For God chooses to limit His own power: He respects the freedom to accept or reject relationship which He has given to each of us. In this freedom human beings are most truly 'made in the image of God'.

When HIV-infected men and women seek meaning for their lives, and make or continue loving and responsible relationships with other people, they become increasingly open to God. This statement is based on repeated observations. The losses and rejections HIV-infected people experience painfully expose the superficial nature of many relationships and the limitations of average creativity: 'I am soon to die and I have done so little; I must die and I have not truly loved anyone.'

Through sorrow and loss many HIV-infected men and women change the direction of their lives, which is the meaning of *metanoia*.

This view of the destiny of human beings presupposes a positive answer to an important question: is 'relationship with God' a relationship which men and women actually want?

4. THEODICY AND CHRISTOLOGY

That depends upon the nature of God: whether or not the general facts of human life and the particular facts of the AIDS pandemic are compatible with the idea that God is loving, as the Gospels claim. Dare Christians call God 'Abba', Father? There is no answer to the mystery of waste and evil and the destructiveness of death except in the life of Jesus of Nazareth, if we are willing to see in Him 'God in human terms' (8).

Jesus was misunderstood and disregarded by His family (John 7.2–10), rejected and condemned by the leaders of His nation (John 11.47–53; Luke 22.54–65) betrayed by one close friend (Mark 14.43–50) and abandoned by others (Mark 26.69–75;) ridiculed, stigmatized, tortured and finally executed in public by a shameful, protracted and brutal method reserved for slaves (Mark 15.16–33). In His fear and agony Jesus was not supported by an unshaken conviction that His death would be worthwhile, or by a sense of the presence of God; on the contrary He was 'greatly distressed and troubled' and longed to escape His fate (Mark 14.32–42): He prayed that, 'if it were possible the hour might pass from him', but also: 'not what I want, but what you want'.

Tradition records that Jesus went beyond His sense of abandonment to commend Himself into His Father's hands as He died (Luke 23.46). 'Why does God allow it?' we cry. Looking at the crucified Christ we can see that, whatever the 'reason', God is not indifferent to our agonies. We do not have a God 'out there', but one intimately close, flesh of our flesh. Christian tradition holds that in the person of Jesus of Nazareth we see, at one and the same time, God the creator of all that is and source of all Being, and also a particular human being, a man who lived in Palestine and died about 1,960 years ago. Halting and permanently incomplete attempts to express (not explain) this view of who Jesus is, constitute the branch of theology known as Christology.

Our understanding of who Jesus is affects the way we interpret the suffering and destruction in our own lives: whether we see disaster as clear evidence for the absence or non-existence of God, or whether we meet darkness and death expecting to find that God shares that darkness with us and has overcome death already.

5. RESURRECTION

The Christian understanding and interpretation of loss and death takes into account what is reported to have happened after Jesus of Nazareth died. The earliest written record dates from about 20 years after the event and is contained in a letter written by Paul to Thessalonian believers. It states 'We believe that Jesus died and rose again, and that it will be the same for those who have died in Jesus: God will bring them with him' (1 Thess. 4.14). In accounts of early preaching attributed to Jesus's followers only a few weeks after His resurrection the phrase 'whom God raised from death' is used repeatedly. The evidence that Jesus was raised from death and the implications of this event for all human beings, should be at the centre of any proclamation Christians make at our turning-point in history.

Several strands of evidence, some circumstantial and others positive, point to an event which 'cannot be confined within historical terms. It transcends history; but for all that, it is rooted in history because it is something to which eye-witness is borne – appeal to eye-witness being an essential part of the early gospel' (29).

The most accessible piece of positive evidence is the coming into existence of the early Church and the continuation of the Church to the present day. Moule states the argument thus: 'there was nothing to discriminate Christians initially from any other Jews of their day except their convictions about Jesus; and it was those which ... ultimately forced them out of Judaism; which means that these convictions were justified or else, if they were not, that the rise and continuance of the Christian Church still await explanation. As a historical phenomenon, the coming into existence of the sect of the

Nazarenes cannot be *explained* (it seems to me) by anything except its distinctive features: and these are due, if not to a huge reality, then to deliberate lying, or to misapprehension; and neither of these latter circumstances seems adequate to account for the facts' (29).

Several features of the Gospel narratives of the resurrection suggest an authentic account of a shockingly unexpected event, rather than a piece of pious fiction. The accounts are brief and convey a sense of disbelief, not credulity. The first witnesses to the empty tomb and to the appearance of Jesus (in all four Gospels) are women, who had no legal standing as witnesses in the male-dominated society of the first century. There is an impressive restraint in the reports of the appearances of Jesus, and no attempt is made to describe the actual moment of resurrection. Instead, the Lord is difficult to recognize or even unrecognized at first, and His body has both normal physical properties and meta-physical features. The few possible adornments to the story (such as the earthquake in Matthew 27.51–54) may be an 'attempt in pictorial language to associate with Jesus within history those eschatological events which really belong beyond history, in the effort to cope with the perplexity involved in his *historical* resurrection. Comparisons with Egyptian stories about Isis or Greek stories about Aesculapius miss the point that these refer to legendary figures of the mythological past, not to a wandering preacher who but yesterday was drawing the crowds' (33). 'No one expected to find a grave empty in the middle of history', wrote John Robinson (35).

Indirect evidence for the resurrection includes the lack of any rumours of Jesus's later death (if He did not die on the cross but was resuscitated and survived for a normal lifetime), an absence of interest in His burial place for several centuries, the Christian choice of the first day of the week rather than the sabbath for worship, and the substantial body of evidence that for early believers death no longer mattered: death had been overcome and life lay on the other side.

Other strands of evidence exist in the ways of speaking about Jesus which began within a few weeks of His death and have persisted until today amongst His followers. In spite of His physical absence from Palestine the early Christians spoke about Jesus as alive, and succeeding generations of believers continue to do so because – in many different forms – this is the conclusion they have been driven to accept, on the basis of their *own* experience. Also, within a few years of Jesus's death there is written evidence for 'the extraordinary conception of the Lord Jesus Christ as a corporate, a more-than-individual personality' (29) into which believers were welcomed. That perception, too, has persisted amongst Christians for two thousand years.

To return to our concern with AIDS: in stating their case for the experience of new life through the death and resurrection of Jesus, Christians find unexpected support in the present-day experiences of HIV-infected people. 'New life' is not just a pious hope for a long-delayed future, but a surprising feature of the actual lives of many HIV-infected people who suffer repeated losses, rage about those losses, mourn, weep, die to a part of themselves, and then find, on the other side of that experience of partial death, new possibilities for creativity or relationship which they could not have imagined earlier. New life, a new humanity, can indeed begin now, even in societies living with AIDS.

6. THE SPIRIT OF GOD AND THE FOLLOWERS OF THE WAY

he next step was a new event which changed a small group of frightened men and women into fearless preachers. As Jews, these people had worshipped God as creator and as the God of Abraham, Moses and the prophets, before meeting the man from Nazareth who referred to God as 'Abba' and who announced His Father's coming kingdom. Jesus's freedom and consistency challenged and frightened the Jews and Romans so deeply that He was removed by a degrading death, which was intended to deter His followers from continuing His 'movement'.

About seven weeks later, Jesus's followers poured out into the street early one morning drunk with the message that: 'this Jesus whom you crucified, God raised from death!' At least, the disciples seemed drunk at first sight, until their audience recognized that these excited people were preaching a coherent message – but in languages which Galilean fishermen did not usually speak. From that time onwards, it was not possible to silence followers of 'the Way' by threats or by the actual deaths of some of their number. These men and women claimed to have received a new experience or gift from God, the arrival of God's Spirit to live in them. Followers of the way repeatedly used two new terms for their relationship to God: they spoke of being themselves 'in Christ', and claimed that the Spirit of God lived 'in' them and guided their attitudes and actions.

7. THREEFOLD EXPERIENCE OF GOD

So followers of the way had three distinct experiences of God: first, as the creator who made a covenant with Abraham, the God who named himself 'I AM WHO I AM' to Moses in Egypt; second, they regarded Jesus as Lord and proclaimed that He was raised from death by God. Finally they recognized the Spirit of Jesus and of the Father living in themselves ever since they acknowledged that 'Jesus is Lord' and received baptism. These three distinct experiences form the basis for the Christian belief in three persons in one God. The doctrine of the Trinity, too, is a part of the Christian proclamation which has direct relevance for human relationships and for communities living with AIDS.

8. A COMMON SPIRITUALITY?

People who are overwhelmed by suffering argue with God and cry out for help spontaneously: 'there are no atheists in wartime trenches'. Men and women who are overwhelmed by joy need to celebrate. Weeping, wailing, rites of passage, prayer, silence, solitude, music, song, dance, laughter and feasting express these poles of human experience. When responses are not private, but shared in communities, then traditions, rituals and worship express a common spirituality. Helping people to develop a spirituality which is capable of expressing their griefs and triumphs in the face of AIDS is an important task for Christians.

Fortunately, the hard facts of the AIDS crisis often force us to abandon attempts to 'control' each other – or God. We need to turn to God, with our difficult questions, directly and bluntly: 'How can God know? *Is* there understanding in the most high?' We *ought* to be silenced by our situation and forced to wait.

A spirituality for societies living with AIDS must be capable of feeling and expressing anger, mourning loss and wasted potentiality, recognizing sin and receiving and proclaiming God's forgiveness for sin. It must be tough enough to grow and endure through decades of distress, for AIDS will not be a short-term problem.

Churches of all traditions need the humility and courage to explore forms of worship and prayer which are unfamiliar to their own communities, and valuable rituals may be found in other faiths which directly express Christian meaning. For example, a North American Indian tribe brings mourning to an end with a ritual which represents each mourner emerging from the cocoon of sorrow as a joyful butterfly, at the command of the Creator – surely a parable of resurrection. Every ritual or tradition was once new, and communities need to find in the spontaneous expressions of their grief or joy new ceremonies to add to the 'traditions'.

9. LIVING IN COMMUNITIES

At the end of the twentieth century a new humanity is coming into being, whether we like it or not. Will it be a new humanity in Christ, or a humanity moving towards self-destruction? After only a few years of confidence in 'progress' and in our 'mastery of the environment', human beings are painfully aware, once more, that physical life is very fragile and our future is insecure.

WHAT IS A COMMUNITY?

'Community' operates at many different levels, starting with the most basic community of one man and one woman in a long-term relationship, and extending to communities of nations. Each level of community-building offers different challenges and possibilities, and each has specific needs for support.

A community is a group of people who co-operate to serve their own interests, basing mutual responsibility and accountability on common values and goals for living. This definition assumes that 'values' come before the attitudes and behaviours which express them, and that shared values and goals are the most important bond between members of a community – especially when those values transcend time and place because they are shared with biological or faith ancestors.

An alternative definition of community is: 'that to which human beings wish to belong'. Human beings depend on others: without a mother's care they cannot survive infancy, and without other people they cannot learn to make adult relationships or sustain normal personalities. Christians see this interdependence of human beings as a reflection of the community of three persons in one God, which is described in the doctrine of the Trinity.

IS COMMUNITY POSSIBLE ACROSS CULTURAL DIFFERENCES?

At a first glance there is little in common between village communities in the Zambezi valley in Zambia, gangs of street kids in Sao Paulo or Maputo, groups of sex workers in Rio de Janeiro, and prisoners in a Puerto Rican jail. Yet each of these groups may have a common concern (the risk of acquiring or transmitting HIV) and common values. 'Care', 'trust' and 'love' are constant values found in all human communities, even when those values are expressed in ways which are culturally specific.

'Values' include community norms for behaviours which preserve harmony and allow people to be accountable to each other, and may include reference to an external authority for support. That external authority may be a political system, an ideology or belief in a creator God. Sometimes norms for behaviour seem to depend upon tradition: 'we have always done it this way'; but often (in modern times) norms are temporary but powerful expressions of fashion – powerful because to ignore peer pressure to conform is to risk exclusion from the community, 'that to which human beings wish to belong'.

Often it does not occur to people that norms *can* be questioned, and that a community might choose to adopt new values and make corresponding changes in attitudes and behaviours. There is unused potential for change in most people which may only be released when suffering drives them to look beyond their own resources for strength.

There appear to be links between suffering and a capacity for transformation, and between capacity to change behaviour and renewed relationships. At an International AIDS Conference in 1992 a woman from New York, who injected heroin from the age of 15 and used drugs for 20 years, spoke of learning that she was HIV-infected while in prison seven years earlier. Her chief concern was for her nine-month-old son and she prayed repeatedly: 'God, please spare my child'. By 1992 she had been free of drugs for three years and was working as an AIDS educator and community organizer in New York. Before a crowd of 12,000 people she said: 'I believe in human ability to change behaviour. I believe in miracles and I believe in God'.

For Further Reading see Bibliography, p. 311, (29).

PART 3
LIVING WITH AIDS

CHAPTER 10
Children and Families

'Our children are our future.' For life on earth this is the most important and basic statement that can be made about children – but children are much more than that. They are proof of fertility, of being fully male or fully female; children represent continuity for a family, linking us to our ancestors and to grandchildren – who will be the ancestors for future generations. At the end of life children mourn our deaths and ensure that we are buried – or cremated – according to custom.

In developing countries children also provide social security, by supporting parents who have no pensions or insurance for sickness. In the past, numerous children gave security (of another kind) when hunting dangerous animals or in battles between rival tribes. In rural life the economic well-being of a family may still depend on having enough children for all the tasks of subsistence farming: 'One to draw water, one to watch over the cattle, one to cut wood, and one to care for the younger children' was a formula I heard from a Kenyan surgeon who was brought up in a village.

Children give status to women. In many cultures a woman who does not bear a child is regarded as a child herself, and more than one baby is needed for feminine 'wealth'. Children are a sign of status for men too, but less essential to the attainment of adulthood: women (providing that they are fertile) are the primary source of male wealth and pride. Finally, adult children may be valued as friends and their accomplishments bring reflected glory (but also the possibility of envy).

CHILDREN'S EXPECTATIONS
Young children cannot express what they expect from their mothers and fathers, and older children rarely do so because they are battling with contrary impulses to rely upon and to reject their parents. All children expect their parents to 'be there for me' – concerned for their safety and well-being, interested in their interests, available with food or a hug or a sympathetic ear or a bicycle or a book or money, according to the need of the moment. This expectation that parents will 'be

there' persists in many people well into adult life, until the demands of their own children open their eyes to the realities of parenthood.

If parents are able to meet this need well enough (perfection is not possible or necessary), then a child develops a basic trust in the goodness of the world which is the natural foundation for trust in God. However, children who are deprived of the fundamental security of a reliable and present parent or parent-substitute, particularly in the first three years of life, are as seriously disabled as children who suffer from malnutrition, and just as likely to show long-term stunting of growth – but of growth in human relationships, not physical stature.

At the end of life expectations are reversed, as ageing parents hope that middle-aged children will be attentively 'present' to their own needs as they approach physical death.

DO CHILDREN HAVE RIGHTS?

All cultures have rituals through which children are accepted into their family and community of origin. Family and community accept responsibility for their care and upbringing and children are given rights, some explicitly recognized, others implicit in tradition but unspoken.

In many countries children have clear rights in law and there are detailed provisions for their welfare at home, in school and at leisure, although some regulations are so defensive that they stifle initiative. Other governments in principle accept responsibility for primary education and for health care, but by default there is no provision for the overall welfare of children in society. This may not be apparent in normal circumstances, but when emergencies arise there is no safety net to ensure that children receive the care they need, despite human failure or malice. For example, some countries do not have inheritance laws to protect children from loss of financial support on the death of a wage-earning parent, or to protect them from exploitation by greedy relatives. AIDS is an emergency which illuminates the inadequacy and injustice of many laws relating to the rights of widows and orphans. Some unwilling societies are being forced to consider, for the first time, the idea that widows and children should *have* rights.

THE CONVENTION ON THE RIGHTS OF THE CHILD

In late 1989 the General Assembly of the United Nations unanimously adopted the Convention on the Rights of the Child. This document was the result of ten years of consultations between governments, UN agencies and over 50 international voluntary agencies. The Convention aims to set universal standards for the defence of children against injustice, neglect and abuse. It provides a comprehensive code stipulating the legal rights of everyone below the age of 18, except where children reach their majority at an earlier age according to national law.

The Convention applies to four areas of children's rights: survival, development, protection and participation in society, with the intention that the 'best interests' of children shall be the guiding principle for all decisions affecting their health, well-being and dignity.

1. *Survival*: Children have a right to life. States must ensure, 'to the maximum possible, the survival and development of the child'. So children have a right to access to health care, including immunizations and curative care, and to adequate standards of living (food, clean water, and a place to live). In addition each child has a right to a name and a nationality.

2. *Development*: All children have a right to education, rest and leisure, and to engage in cultural activities which will provide the chance to develop their potential.

3. *Protection*: The Convention provides for protection for children in a wide and comprehensive range of circumstances. It recognizes the different needs of mentally or physically disabled children, and of refugees and orphans. It seeks to protect children from economic, sexual and other forms of exploitation and from the use or sale of drugs, and sets out rights for children who are in trouble with the law and for times of war or civil disturbance.

4. *Participation*: Each child has a right to freedom of expression and information, and to freedom of thought, conscience and religion. The Convention stipulates that parents (and by implication, guardians too) should give 'due weight' to the views of children when making decisions, in accordance with their age and maturity. Finally, parents are to raise children to be able to play an active part in society at large.

The Convention's provisions became binding in 1990 and have now been ratified by 177 countries, but not by 14. A Committee for the Rights of the Child receives reports from ratifying countries on the steps they are taking to implement the Convention, which is now widely regarded as a universal basis for advocacy on behalf of children.

AGENDA FOR A NEW ORDER

In 1992 UNICEF published ten axioms 'for the new world order that is struggling to be born', based on 40 years' experience of working in over 100 countries 'with some of humanity's greatest problems'.

1. *A new world order should keep the promises of the World Summit for Children* (1990), where goals were agreed for preventing child deaths, halving malnutrition, ending polio and tetanus, ensuring basic education for all children and access to clean water and family planning for all families.

2. *The principle 'children first' should become the accepted ethic of a new world order.* The most critical mental and physical development occurs during the early, vulnerable years of childhood, so children's

needs should have first call on societies' resources, in good times and in bad – a principle which is often ignored both by rich and poor nations.

3. *Improving the health and nutrition of children will help, not hinder, the struggle to slow population growth*, because parents who are confident that their existing children will survive are willing to plan their families.

4. *Market policies should be accompanied by basic investment in people.* Governments should accept responsibility for ensuring that all members of society have adequate food, clean water and safe sanitation, primary health care, family planning services and primary education; these basic investments are essential for humanitarian reasons but equally necessary to sustain economic wellbeing.

5. *Increases in international aid should be based on commitment to meeting minimum human needs.* Aid should be used mainly to improve the lives of poor people, not for prestige projects.

6. *Action on debt, aid, and trade should create an environment in which the people of the developing world can earn a decent living.* Self-sufficiency and independence should be the goals of aid to poor families, but also the goals of aid to poor nations.

7. *Demilitarization in the poor world and falling arms expenditure in the rich world should be linked to increases in aid for development.* The State of the World's Children Report (UNICEF 1992) (42) calculated that the amount spent on the world's military resources exceeds the combined incomes of the poorest half of humanity. But strong counter-pressures hinder full acceptance of disarmament by rich nations (more unemployment, falling standards of living) and by poor nations (relative privilege of military).

8. *The chains of Africa's debt should be struck off.* Subsaharan Africa can pay only about one-third of the interest due on debts, though even this absorbs a quarter of export earnings. For this region the debt burden has increased from about 45% of GNP in 1984 to over 110% of GNP in 1992 (World Bank debt tables).

9. *A new world order should oppose the apartheid of gender as vigorously as it opposes the apartheid of race.* In the developing world women do more work than men but are generally rewarded with less food, less health care, less education and training, fewer rights and less protection in law, and (finally) less leisure.

10. *Responsible planning of births is one of the most effective ways of improving the quality of life on earth – both now and in the future.* Hundreds of thousands of women and millions of children die each year because mothers were either too young or too old to give birth safely, or because too many births occurred too close together in time. According to a UNICEF report (1992), one pregnancy in three is unwanted throughout the world. So if all women had the knowledge,

means and permission from men to decide how many children to bear and when to have them, population growth could fall by about 30%. 'For all of these reasons family planning could bring more benefits to more people at less cost than any other single "technology" now available to the human race' the UNICEF report concludes.

CHILDREN OF GOD AND INHERITORS OF THE KINGDOM OF HEAVEN

Christians may criticize the utilitarian bias in these suggestions for children's welfare, because they are supported by arguments for the cost-effectiveness of 'investing' in children. Although we may want to go beyond a quantitative view, at least our goals for children's welfare should not fall below those of the Convention for the Rights of the Child, as they do (too often) now.

The perspective of the Convention on the Rights of the Child is that of 'life on earth', but the perspective of Christian faith regards life on earth as only a first, brief but important section of the totality of life for which human beings are destined. According to Christian doctrine, human persons are made in the image and likeness of God, for communion with God, so that no possession, achievement or relationship on earth is capable of satisfying us wholly.

CONSEQUENCES OF AIDS FOR CHILDREN

We need to distinguish between children who are *infected* with HIV and a much larger number of children who are *affected* by HIV and AIDS.

Children can be *infected* with HIV during pregnancy or during delivery (perinatal); by transfusion of infected blood, or by an injection or scarification using an unsterilized HIV-contaminated needle. There is also a measurable risk of infection through breast feeding – but the risk is much smaller than the risks of death from diarrhoea or malnutrition for bottle-fed babies in most developing countries, so breast feeding is still safer. Several careful studies in Africa and North America have shown that children are never infected by parents or siblings during normal family or school life. The risk of infection from a seropositive African mother is 30% on average; babies conceived or carried soon after a woman acquires HIV, or when her health is failing, have the greatest risk of becoming HIV-infected themselves.

It is unusual for an HIV-infected child to be ill from birth; most babies appear healthy and grow normally at first, but show signs of disease in the second year of life. Mothers who know that they are HIV-infected are very anxious to be reassured that their babies have escaped infection, but must wait nearly two years for reassurance based on standard laboratory tests.

Infants of HIV-infected women are born with antibodies to HIV in their blood, which were transferred across the placenta from maternal blood, along with useful antibodies to other infectious diseases. For this reason, screening tests for HIV-infection (which detect antibodies) are positive at birth and remain so for about nine months; then tests become negative as uninfected babies lose this maternal antibody. At about the same time, children who truly *are* infected with HIV begin to produce their own antibodies, which will be found on re-testing their blood at 18 months. By this age many such children show other signs of infection, such as failure to gain weight, unexplained fever or frequent diarrhoea.

FAMILY REACTIONS

The pastoral care of an HIV-infected child requires the pastoral care of an entire family. A miserable baby who fails to grow and is often ill strains the resources of any parent, but if the illness is known to be fatal and carries the stigma and blame attached to AIDS, then the parents' sadness and guilt may prevent rejoicing: 'How *can* we delight in this child who is going to die?' Yet such parents often make great, self-sacrificial efforts to express their love and to give their child the best possible life.

The difficulties are greatest when neither parent was aware that either was infected until their child's blood was tested for HIV. Then there are complex and very painful feelings to admit and to live with: the shock of learning that HIV infection is permanent and incurable (seen at first as an immediate death sentence); guilt and anger directed at partner or self over behaviour which has allowed infection to occur, with hurt and anger if sexual infidelity was not suspected earlier. Later, parents experience the long-drawn-out pain and guilt of watching a son or daughter suffer and die, followed by emptiness and a sense of failure, especially if they have no living children – like Mercy and Francis.

Story: *Mercy* and *Francis* married, knowing that Mercy was HIV-infected, during the third month of her pregnancy. They were delighted when their son was born apparently healthy, but at six months he died of AIDS-related pneumonia. Gently, I warned Mercy that it would be better not to attempt another pregnancy because the same tragedy was likely to happen again, and her fragile health would probably break down. She did not come to the clinic for a time, then returned when she was four months pregnant. 'I know you warned me not to try for another baby,' she said, 'but I was so lonely for my son!' Mercy lost weight and strength and at seven months she delivered a dead baby. We wept together in the ward and all I could find to say was: 'I don't believe that God wastes anything, and certainly not a child who is loved as much as your baby.' Mercy survived to leave hospital, but died herself a few weeks later.

There are times when pastors or counsellors must be willing to stay silent and feel helpless as they do the one thing that is necessary – which is to be there, to stay with a distressed person.

PASTORAL CARE

However, priests and pastors can and should reflect upon their experiences and plan the elements of care for HIV-affected families. Their pastoral needs are most easily summarized in the form of questions, although it is not always necessary to answer every question.

1. *The parents*: Do both parents know of the diagnosis and that the child will not survive long? The mother is likely to be told the diagnosis first: when and how can she share this knowledge with the child's father? Have either or both parents been counselled and tested for HIV themselves? Is one or other parent already suffering ill-health? Is either partner shocked and distressed by newly-disclosed sexual infidelity on the part of the other? Is one partner angry with the other? Are they living together or apart? Have they received counselling about their sexual relationship and the risks of further pregnancies, with appropriate contraceptive advice? Is reconciliation between the partners needed? Are the parents in a stable relationship which they would like to make permanent and to have blessed? Is marriage in church possible and appropriate? Do they receive support from their own parents or siblings?

2. *The infected child*: Is the child receiving good medical care, including immunizations, to minimize suffering? Has the child been accepted by parents and family, and are his/her emotional needs being met? Do the parents ask for baptism for their child? Does the mother need practical help with the burdens of caring, particularly if she is sick herself? Do the family have enough water, food, soap, bedding and clothing? What support is needed, as the child approaches death, to prepare the parents for bereavement? Who should make pastoral visits, how often and for what purposes? When would it be appropriate to offer the sacrament of anointing or other ministries of healing?

3. *The other children*: How many are there and are they in good health? Has their sibling's illness affected their well-being, and if so, in what ways? Are these ill-effects recognized by the parents and is it possible to correct them? When will it be appropriate to prepare the other children for the death of an infected baby? Do the older children suspect that their parents are ill and, if so, how much of the truth should

they be told? When and by whom (remembering that uncertainty and fear may be more difficult to bear than bad news)? Who will look after surviving children when the parents die (as they will)? Are the older children being expected to take on caring tasks which are beyond their strength? Are any children in trouble at school, or with the law, on account of the distress in the family – or for any other reason?

4. *Money, housing and legal matters*: Is there a wage-earner? Is housing tied to work and where will the family go and how will they eat if employment (and housing) are lost due to illness? Is it possible to improve the family's standard of living by finding work for one or more unemployed persons? Do the family need advice about using money more efficiently? Have the parents made a Will? Has a guardian for the children been appointed? Does the potential widow know how to achieve her rights and will she need protection from greedy relatives?

5. *Community support*: Are the family welcomed into the Church community or stigmatized and rejected 'because they have sinned'? Are the family receiving all the help which is available locally from government, NGOs, and volunteer groups? Are neighbours supportive or rejecting? Are family members honoured for their endurance, compassion and faith? Is their endurance and faith seen as a gift to the community, as well as a grace for themselves?

This list of questions applies to most HIV-affected families, whatever way their distress comes to light. To write out a list like this demonstrates the complexity and number of possible problems, although it is encouraging to remember that not all apply to every family, and that these problems are spread out over months or years and may be less formidable in practice than they appear in theory. Moreover, not all problems are the direct concern of a Church community, although their range should be known to the pastor. The basic challenge to Christians is to express, through actions and 'presence', the attentive loving care God offers to each child, each man and each woman.

A FAMILY IN DISTRESS: BECOMING ORPHANS

Story: *John* was 38 years old, married with four children. He lived in Lusaka, but was studying overseas in 1987, when he began to have severe headaches and consulted a doctor. Many tests were done, and one showed antibody to HIV in John's blood; the results were explained to him and he returned to Zambia. By 1988 he had a chronic cough and felt tired, and later his wife *Irene* developed the same symptoms. After investigations both started treatment for tuberculosis (TB) and after six months Irene was able to return to her work as a sales manager. John's health continued to fail; he would be able to work one week, and then the next he would be in bed. John's employers were understanding and allowed him to work whenever he was fit, and his wife and children were very caring. The children knew only that their father had TB; as he remained cheerful and was nursed at home, they hoped he would soon be well again. At this time there were no problems over food or transport because Irene had a good job and drove a car, and there were few effects on the children, although they were miserable when John was too weak to leave his bedroom.

The problems started as John was hospitalized when Irene was seven months pregnant. John's elder brother and three sisters consulted a witch-finder on the Copperbelt and came to the hospital ward in Lusaka. There they accused Irene of bewitching her husband, showered her with insults and chased her from the bedside. These relatives told Irene they would kill her if she was found at home and she was made to hand over her car keys to John's brother. She pleaded with him to let her stay by John, but the brother pushed away nurses who tried to come to Irene's rescue.

Irene spent the night at her sister's house and returned to the hospital next day to find that her husband's family still rejected her: she was accused of bringing harmful 'medicines' to John and was told never to set foot in the hospital again. She left and never returned. At home the children stopped going to school; food was short and the older children feared to find their father 'gone' if they left the house. The eldest boy, Ben, aged 12, tried to make life more normal for the younger children, but that was difficult with the house full of strangers – for John's parents, and his three sisters and three brothers had come to stay.

John died after two weeks in hospital. His wife was not allowed at the funeral house and she did not attend his burial. Immediately after the burial all their household goods were auctioned at a dealer's rooms in Lusaka. The children were taken by relatives, each to a different home, but Ben refused to go and stayed on in Lusaka with a friend of his father.

Irene delivered a baby boy two months after her husband's death, but the child died at nine months and none of her husband's relatives attended the funeral. At present the other children are back with Irene because relatives could not cope with school fees. She lives in a company flat and is still working, although her health is failing. Irene's chief worry is: who will look after the children when she dies?

This story is told almost entirely in the unemotional language used by the counsellor who wrote it down. If it is painful to read, how much more painful must it be to live such a story? It is not unique or even unusual; in cities such experiences are often hidden behind the everyday sight of a manager at his or her desk – tired perhaps, but working.

CONTINUING LOSS AND STRESS

John's family was richer than many affected families, but is otherwise close to the average family discovered by a survey done in Zambia during 1990/1991 by Haworth and his colleagues (22). They studied 116 families, 61% living in towns and 39% in rural areas; 30% were (or had been before the death of the only parent) one-parent families. The average number of dependent children was four, and the overall mean age was 10.8 years; the mean ages of youngest and oldest children were 5.1 and 13.5 years, respectively, but 25% were 15 years of age or older. Both parents had already died in 11% of families but few of the surviving parents were still healthy. Nearly a quarter of children had to care for a sick parent, and in 24% of families the last child had died, too.

The survey showed that, as in John's family, stress for the children began long before they were orphaned, and that the process of becoming an orphan was traumatic. In around 10% of families the mother was accused of responsibility for her husband's death (as Irene was) and maltreated by her deceased husband's relatives. In 29% of cases, property (often held jointly by husband and wife) was taken by the husband's relatives as their 'right'. Several harrowing accounts of widowhood show that seizure of property usually happens within a few days of death, while the widow is too upset to seek legal protection, even if the law of her country allows this. Economic problems followed in 91% of rural and 84% of urban families and food was short in 60% of households. Nearly half of all families reported moving to poorer housing and 17% lost access to electricity or piped water.

In spite of education campaigns designed to reduce stigmatization, 24% of families reported experiencing it. Schooling was affected in several ways: 86% of children had inadequate funds for uniforms, books or transport, and 42% expected to have to stop schooling; many of those who continued reported that their schoolwork had suffered because of irregular attendance or preoccupation with misery at home.

Where there is a vigorous AIDS education campaign in schools, older children will understand only too well the nature and meaning of a diagnosis of AIDS. Adolescents, at a critical time when they are coming to terms with their own sexuality, learn (in tragic circumstances) that their parents are infected with a sexually transmitted disease. Often adolescent girls become unpaid servants in relatives' families, deprived of freedom, status and schooling as well as parents. Some girls in this situation may also suffer sexual harassment.

The term 'extended family' refers to grandparents, siblings of the parents and the older siblings of young children. Aunts and uncles usually have large families of their own and are reluctant to take on more children, especially unproductive and demanding adolescents. Nevertheless, uncles or aunts took over care of orphans in 22% of 90 families for which information was available, but grandparents had the burden of care in 53%. It is a great burden, as grandparents were often dependents themselves, until their adult children died. A Ugandan survey showed that, there too, grandparents (like Grace) are most often responsible for orphans.

Story: *Grace* is a widow, living in a village in the Rakai district of Uganda. She had nine children but seven have died of AIDS. She started by caring for three orphaned grandchildren and later an older grand-daughter, who was dying of AIDS, was brought to her for nursing. Grace may be fortunate, for some grandparents are struggling to care for 16 or even 25 orphans.

FURTHER LOSSES; BEING AN ORPHAN

There is confusion about the use of the term 'orphan'. UNICEF identifies an orphan as a child whose mother has died, WHO agrees but adds 'or both parents', while a study done in Uganda counted children who had lost 'one or both parents' – which is the definition I use. We need standard definitions and agreed terminology for single-parent families.

Some groups working with orphans use 'single orphan' to refer to a child who has lost one parent, others to a child who has lost both parents, for whom the alternative term 'double orphan' may be used. Other groups reserve 'double orphan' for children who lose substitute carers when they, too, die – usually from AIDS.

When the second natural parent dies the family unit seems likely to break up. A few relatives can afford to take into account the trauma of separating brothers and sisters, and will arrange to care for them together in one home, sharing expenses with other adults. Often this optimum arrangement is not possible and children are divided amongst several families, sometimes living hundreds of miles apart so that contact between siblings is impossible, and children are separated from friends, school and familiar surroundings too. How do these arrangements affect childrens' development?

HUMAN GROWTH AND THE GROWTH OF FAITH

The normal stages of physical, neurological, and emotional development are closely linked to a child's capacity to meet society's expectations (socialization) and to learn at school (formal education). But human growth is linked to the growth of faith, and influences the ways in which faith is expressed and lived (30), so it is useful to sum-marize important developmental needs and to draw attention to possi-ble consequences of loss of parents at different stages of childhood. At present there are few formal studies of bereavement in children.

Few babies lose their parents to AIDS, but some *pre-school children* aged four to seven do so. At this age children's understanding of such loss is limited and they react with confusion and great anxiety: their primary need is for a new and sympathetic person who will 'be there' for them, with whom strong bonds of attachment can form, and who will provide continuity of good care. A stable home environment and the continued presence of other children will help them to adapt to their loss, but older siblings may need to be shielded from too much responsibility for small children.

At this stage children are experiencing many things for the first time, with the vivid impact of newness and wonder, aided by an active ima-gination. However, their limited ability to think prevents them from creating order out of a chaos of images, where real and fantasy objects exist side by side. Their world is episodic, not patterned like a story, and it revolves around themselves. Their social awareness is limited to the family; any adult is a potential authority figure. Faith, like everything else, imitates what adults do, but may be fed richly by symbols. At this age symbols *are* what they represent, and the symbols of liturgy and devotion are 'understood' at a deep and intuitive level to which adults return only after a long pilgrimage. 'Young children who are excluded from ritual and sacrament because "they don't yet understand" may be being cut off from a vital form of nourishment' (30). Images of God seem likely to be non-anthropomorphic, at this stage, but more re-search in different cultures is needed. Adults may be startled by the maturity of thoughts about the nature of God or the world recalled from childhood, or observed in their own children.

Growth in faith at this (or any other) stage of life presupposes a capacity for trust, or faith in the basic reliability and goodness of the world and God. It is this essential element of trust that is most likely to be lost by a child who loses parents but does not soon find loving and reliable substitutes. Loss of trust leads to withdrawal from people, who are perceived as untrustworthy, so that it becomes more and more difficult to form relationships which might later restore a sense of trust. As trust has been betrayed, although a vision of how the world *should* be remains, anger is a common but unrecognized re-action. So is depression, which expresses a conviction that loss (of any kind) was appropriate because 'I am worthless' and 'I do not deserve anything better'. God, too, is perceived as untrustworthy and uninter-ested in the one who suffers loss; it usually seems too dangerous to be angry with God, but anger may be felt very strongly.

EARLY SCHOOL YEARS

Children at primary school, who have not reached puberty, are exploring their world and have different physical and emotional needs. A reliable person with whom to form bonds remains important, to provide a secure base to return to after adventures. They need permission to *be* children, and must be protected from excessive or premature responsibility, while they receive consistent discipline, combined with genuine interest in their interests and attainments. At this stage children are learning to think, to link cause and effect and to distinguish between objective reality and private fantasy: 'the world is becoming predictable and losing its enchantment'. They delight in stories, through which they gain a sense of their own identity and begin to learn the stories of the communities to which they belong – including the stories of the Christian Church. Belonging to a group is intensely important to them, and through such belonging their social horizons widen and their sense of self is strengthened.

Children are not yet capable of self-criticism or abstract reflection, so they can only 'tell stories *in* life, not *about* life'. Although they can imagine what it is like to be someone (rather like themselves) in a story, they cannot enter, yet, into the experience of another person in an empathetic way, so there is a danger that stories may form prejudices. 'If people are to develop beyond this stage, the master-stories on offer must be open-ended enough to allow a future escape.'

At this age symbols are seen in a concrete way, because all thinking is concrete, and images of God are likely to be anthropomorphic.* Moral thinking, which now influences decisions, tends to be based on mutual fairness and immediate justice. If just, reliable and loving parents (or parent substitutes) are not available, children have no models around which to form a picture of 'God'. Moreover, when life has treated them with great injustice, by removing the persons on whom they so much depended, they can be forgiven for thinking that fairness and justice are not a necessary basis for their own ethical decisions.

INTO ADOLESCENCE

In societies where only one-third of children progress from primary into secondary schools, the next stage may be *transition to secondary schooling or adaptation to being 'out of school'*. Either process is likely to be complicated by the nearly simultaneous arrival of puberty and the need to come to terms with sexuality and a new image of self. Children who fail to achieve places in secondary schools are often unable to find further training or employment either, so that already they are burdened with a sense of failure, and feel anger and resentment at the injustice of having no prospects of independence or of a role in society.

In most developing countries diversion of funds to pay interest on external debts has had the effect of reducing investment in developing agricultural or industrial resources which could, in turn, have created productive work.

Whatever their educational circumstances, adolescents need continued but unobtrusive support, and freedom to explore new possibilities in the company of their peers; they have a huge need for peer approval and will go to great lengths to win this. They need initiation into the world of work (if it can be found) and into adult social and sexual roles, and at the same time to be protected from sexual exploitation or abuse, and from premature commitment to a long-term relationship or parenthood.

Adults (especially parents or their substitutes) usually find it difficult to acknowledge that adolescents are sexual beings with impulses which are as strong as, and certainly less well-known, than their own sexual drives. Adults also tend to ignore or devalue the ideas and opinions of adolescents – who therefore keep their real concerns for talk with their peers. If adults dared to listen to their children the gap between generations might turn out to be narrower than most people suppose.

Young people at this stage think abstractly and reflectively and their relationships are very important. Adolescents build up a world-view and a faith, influenced by people they respect, but unaware (usually) that they are trying to hold together very diverse values and beliefs. As a result, often their true beliefs and values are partly hidden from their own knowledge. Youth is a time for conforming faith, which swims with the tide, usually of peer influence. Moral thinking, too, tends to be based on 'what is expected' or on keeping rules.

Later, tensions between diverse influences force young adults to ask further questions. Such questioning is likely to begin when a young person leaves home, or if people on whom they have relied are lost through death. An important consequence of the AIDS pandemic is that it forces the pace of human growth, so that stages of the journey which would normally take several years and occur at a particular point in the life cycle, have to be compressed into a few months at too early an age. Certainly this is true for the acceptance of death as something which will happen 'even to me', but it may also be true for growth out of conforming faith into a more reflective and chosen system of beliefs and values.

ENTERING ADULT LIFE

Most societies provide for the emotional and material support of children into *early adult life*, preparing them for marriage and for the difficulties of its first years, and helping after the birth of the first child. For example, in traditional Zambian society newly married couples are closely supervised by older relatives, who instruct both partners in the detail of their behaviour to each other; when the first child is born the new mother has an older woman at hand to teach her how to care for her baby. Only when the second child is born are the couple reckoned to have 'graduated' and to be ready for life on their own.

Leaving home, emotionally as well as physically, is an important watershed in the lives of most people. They begin to take responsibility for their beliefs and acts in a new way, choosing how to live and which authorities to accept, even when situations of poverty, disability or traditional culture limit the choices available. The expectations of a traditional culture may press heavily upon young people who have acquired a wider world-view through education or travel, and who want to admit new values into their own system of belief.

Leaving home and becoming autonomous is a process which can (and probably should) take several years. If the pace is forced because 'home' no longer exists – through death of parents, loss of dwelling place, and separation from siblings and friends – then growth may occur more rapidly than usual at a much younger age, or it may be stunted or destroyed. There are real risks that values and beliefs associated with a way of life which has (seemingly) rejected a bereaved child will, in their turn, be rejected.

Whether or not the passage from conforming faith to chosen faith is negotiated safely, there will be a period of suffering and disorientation resulting from that transition itself, over and above suffering related to the events which precipitated it. 'Growing up in faith always involves a loss of (an old) faith, and a time out in the wilderness before the new way of faith can be entered upon' (30).

Young orphans are more likely to attract the care they need than orphaned adolescents. Similarly, it is clear that children who have lost both parents need a home, but it is easy to ignore their needs during several years of anxiety, misery, and diminishing prospects at school, which precede those actual deaths. Churches need to attend closely to their responsibilities towards pre-orphans and adolescents.

CHRISTIAN RESPONSIBILITIES TOWARDS YOUNG PEOPLE

Three interrelated and interdependent responsibilities exist:
1. Physical, emotional and spiritual care of pre-orphans and actual orphans;
2. Detailed instruction about how HIV is transmitted before children become sexually active, together with teaching about the meaning and conduct of man/woman relationships;
3. Integration of children into communities (when values and norms in society are changing) – and initiation into the Kingdom of God, which transcends temporal, spatial and cultural barriers.

AIDS is a new and global problem. The consequences for families which we have summarized will be roughly similar wherever hetero-sexual spread of HIV is common, but there will be differences in detail, due to cultural and political differences and the effects of additional problems such as civil war or corruption. Problems must be recognized and (to some extent) analysed before appropriate responses can be made.

FINDING DIRECTIONS FOR WORK WITH AND FOR YOUNG PEOPLE

We cannot yet offer tried and documented 'solutions' to problems concerning the day-to-day care of children and their integration into communities. Everyone is learning, the existence of AIDS orphans in Africa was only admitted in the late 1980s, and their numbers and needs are unknown in many affected countries. However, a few guiding principles seem to be emerging from experience in Uganda, Tanzania and Zambia.

No attempt to count orphans or to assess their needs will succeed until the community concerned recognizes that it has more orphans than usual. The first step is to create or strengthen *awareness of the presence of orphans*. This may happen spontaneously when teachers talk with relatives about children who are absent from school or doing badly, only to learn that there is a common reason for these failures: actual or impending bereavement. Or health care and social workers may help to promote concern by calling a meeting of community leaders to discuss the needs of neglected children they have seen in the courts or in hospital.

The next step is to generate or strengthen a conviction that this is *our* concern, and, moreover, we *can* do something about it. So long as a community thinks that it is someone else's job to look after orphans, no constructive action is likely. But the difficulty is only how to begin; once a good start has been made in one city or country town, the contagion of good ideas and the enthusiasm of people who have discovered their own power-to-act usually ensures that concerned groups multiply.

Healthy *groups form spontaneously* in communities, not as a direct result of the efforts of outsiders who dictate aims and methods. At this stage in the pandemic there is no 'best' way of organizing a working group, and local circumstances should mould the way it develops. A group led by a retired civil servant, composed of professional people with cars who live in a low density suburb, will be very different from a group led by a primary school teacher, whose members are unemployed or manual workers living in a township which has no electricity, no sanitation and poorly maintained standpipes and roads. Yet both

Figure 8.   A family in Uganda.

groups should have the same basic aim: to care for orphans in *their* community, in ways appropriate to *their* circumstances.

An *extended family* is the most important resource for the care of orphans. Orphans themselves are an unrecognized and undervalued resource for their own care, and ought to be involved in making and implementing plans. Professional workers with the greatest experience (in south-western Uganda) say that it is very rare for a child to be totally without relatives, at least at present. (The situation may change in the next generation when many children will not have any grandparents.) There are few orphanages in Africa, and those which do exist are mostly designed for babies whose mothers died in childbirth, and intended only for the first year or two of life, after which weaned children normally return to their families. Some attempts to set up AIDS orphanages have been disastrous; the inmates were poorly fed, dirty, overcrowded, cut off from their communities and treated badly through unjustified fear of infection, or the stigma still associated with HIV. When orphanages are closed, orphans nearly always turn out to have relatives who are able to take responsibility for them.

The best policy, on present experience, is to *support orphans within the family unit* which is providing care already, in whatever ways are necessary to sustain care indefinitely. Each family unit has different needs: a robust, sensible but unemployed 20-year-old may be quite capable of rearing younger siblings – if given training, helped to find work and rooms large enough for the family, helped with advice about money, discipline, and schooling, and (above all) given self-respect and sensitive appreciation for the task taken on. A fit but tired grandmother, living in a tiny hut in a village, may be able to care for four or five school-age children if a better home is built for her by the community, the family's material needs (water, food, school fees, bedding) are provided, and she has friendly but respectful support from a village elder or schoolteacher, who can help with discipline and deal with problems that are too great for her strength.

Caring for orphans is a team or *community activity*, not an individual task, and it should *involve the children* who are receiving care. The repetition of this statement is deliberate, because it is so important. For example, in the Rakai district of Uganda groups of orphans are expected to contribute towards their own food supply by growing cassava which is drought-resistant, reasonably nutritious, stored in the ground, and not too labour-intensive. *Seed-money* is needed too, quite literally for the purchase of seeds for growing food or cash crops, but also for training and for equipment – such as pots and a stove for a woman who will sell cooked food in a market.

CO-ORDINATING CARE

Definitions: Most *resources for caring should come from within a local community*. To define terms: a *guardian* is a person (grandparent, uncle, older sibling) who provides day-to-day care for one or more orphans; a *caretaker* (Zambia) or *community worker* (Uganda) is a volunteer who provides long-term support and help to one or more family groups, each in the care of a guardian; a *local co-ordinator* is a person who leads and oversees the activities of caretakers, usually and properly receiving expenses and a small allowance in recognition of the effort and responsibility involved.

At each level *training* can and should be provided through local workshops, for which funds will be needed. Roles may alter with circumstances: for example, guardians may become caretakers if their direct responsibilities to orphans lessen; a caretaker may become a guardian if a relative dies, and drop his or her work for other families. In Rakai district, in Uganda, local co-ordinators are elected from among community workers (CW) who have given two years' service. The organization is linked to diocesan and parish structures and each co-ordinator supervises 20 or so volunteer CW.

Senior co-ordinators or *directors of community workers* have regional responsibilities, and may be government officials, Church leaders, or on the staff of an NGO. They should be well-paid, full-time professionals, probably with a background in social work. The director needs integrity (and warmth), status and respect in the community, efficient transport for travel in the district, stamina, a spontaneous interest in people, empathy with children and adolescents, a good memory for faces and a record system which is consistently used.

Experience in both Uganda and Zambia shows that caretakers can be recruited locally as volunteers and that their enthusiasm can be maintained by pride in achievement – and appreciation from good leaders. But they need also *the support and resources of a larger community and to see themselves as part of a larger whole*: for Christians this 'larger community' should be the universal Church, 'hidden with Christ in God', but expressed through the pastoral care of the local Church community.

In principle *funds for the care of orphans should be generated within each community*, although external funds or advice may be needed as 'seed resources' to start income-generating projects and for training workshops. The *teamwork and consultation needed to care for orphans can strengthen communities* and improve their ability to co-operate over other matters. In Uganda this by-product of caring is noted and fostered by co-ordinators, who told me that 'guardians chat together, they share responsibilities, they become more creative and a spirit of fraternal love develops'.

Orphans may experience rejection or discrimination in a negative sense from their communities, and so learn to see themselves as worthless, disabled, or unfortunate. But there is evidence from Uganda that these consequences are not inevitable; *orphans may learn to consider themselves fortunate or even privileged*, if their experiences of care are good and if they receive respect and hope for the future.

Regional and national co-ordination of work with orphans is required for many reasons. At national level, provisions for orphans must be weighed against other priorities and children need advocates for their rights and needs when policies are decided. Second, minimum standards for care should be maintained and policies for intervention established, at least at national level, and perhaps regionally. Third, the content of training programmes should be agreed, and interchange of community workers or co-ordinators for training workshops is beneficial. Community workers, in particular, gain confidence and competence if they have the chance to pass on their attitudes and skills to less experienced people. Finally, a multidisciplinary *central organization* is needed to maintain *national records* as a basis for long-term planning; to initiate basic and operational research and to see that important results reach those who might benefit from them; to apply for external funds when needed; to co-ordinate the work of regional directors of community workers and to represent their country at international policy-making conferences.

Efforts to improve the lot of children should not be restricted to those orphaned by AIDS but *open to all children* (or families) in need, to avoid creating resentment in those whose difficulties arise from another cause, and to acknowledge that *children in general should have priority in the allocation of national and community resources.*

These principles were derived from successful community and Church projects in Zambia and Uganda and can be illustrated by describing some of their work.

In *south-western Uganda*, a rural area where thousands of young men and women have died and seroprevalence of HIV is estimated to be increasing at about 3% per annum, the Roman Catholic Church has set up integrated Homecare and Orphan Care projects, with some external funding. At the diocesan level the Chief Catechist has overall responsibility, the Project Director is an expatriate religious sister and there are Ugandan directors for the two branches of the scheme. Each parish has a co-ordinator for orphans to supervise the work of about 20 community volunteers, who were trained in local workshops. All orphans are registered and their needs assessed, as a basis for decisions about who will receive support and what that support will be. Guardians may be loaned land and given seeds to enable them to grow crops for food and cash. Every effort is made to keep children living in family homes so that they do not lose their title to family land, and they are expected to help to support themselves. If the family home is inadequate it is repaired or replaced; the project built over 80 houses in 1991, using local labour and materials, usually mud and wattle walls and a thatched roof. Headmasters are asked to be tolerant of delays over school fees, for in some schools up to half the pupils are orphans.

The Director of Community Workers had an impressive knowledge of his area as we travelled through it. He said that registration of new orphans rose from 500 in 1989 to 4,600 by early September of 1992. As we drove along a remote road, he said: 'All the houses on this road have orphans in them . . . in this one four brothers died leaving orphans . . . there a lady keeps 12 orphans and we help with 9 of them . . . so many, all the houses on this road'. On either side, there were banana plantations by small homesteads, and under the bananas we saw four or five concrete grave slabs near each house.

In Zambia, in 1992, organizations were less structured and numbers of identified orphans fewer than in Uganda. In Lusaka I met the head-master of a Church secondary school. He was appointed in 1990 and soon heard about a group meeting to discuss the problems of children orphaned by AIDS. He joined this group and used the school minibus to encourage fellow teachers to attend meetings with him. As they soon outnumbered other members, they shifted meetings to their own school and people from the township joined them. Senior secondary school pupils carried out a simple enumeration study in the township and the committee were dismayed at the number of orphans found. They evolved a system of 'caretakers': responsible people who under-take to watch over and help one or more distressed families, with the general aim of helping them to be self-sufficient and able to care for orphans indefinitely. The headmaster produced a thick file of corre-spondence relating to their activities and told me proudly about two success stories.

Stories: 1. The committee heard of a 22-year old woman, *Joyce*, who was living with 10 children in a tiny room – the headmaster indi-cated space equivalent to one quarter of his average-sized office. They were three months in arrears with rent. Joyce had been mar-ried and one of the children was hers, but she was sent away by her husband when her nine siblings arrived, expecting to be looked after by their oldest sister, after both parents died of AIDS within one year. No-one was in work and there was one single bed and not much food. An 18 year-old girl was losing weight and coughing: she was investigated and treated for tuberculosis.

The committee paid off the arrears of rent and found a two-bed-roomed house which they rented for the family. They made a grant equivalent to $250 to Joyce to start up a business in a city market, where she now sells maize porridge. The headmaster told me with rueful pride that 'she now earns more than I do!' At least she earns enough to pay the rent, feed her large family and buy the shoes and other necessities for the younger children to go to school. Her sister, now well, has a baby of her own and stays at home to do the domes-tic work. Joyce takes a great pride in her independence and the com-mittee have learned from this experiment to make self-sufficiency their general policy.

2. *Moses* was 13 years old and lived in a small house close to George's school, but he was a pupil in a secondary school on the other side of the city, over three miles away. He walked to school because both his parents had died of AIDS within one year, and he

had six younger sisters and brothers, who he was trying to look after; the youngest was two years old. There was no money for bus fares. The headmaster and his wife assessed the situation. There were three adult relatives – an old woman who was herself dependent, a woman with too many children of her own to take on any more, and an uncle who was very keen to gain control of the house and to earn rent from it, but not at all keen to support his nephews and nieces.

The headmaster arranged for Moses to be transferred to his own secondary school and he started visiting the family at home. It was possible to move the two youngest children to the care of a distant relative in Kitwe, and lodgers were found for one room in the house, to bring in an income. The committee finds more money for food, clothes and other necessities and the headmaster and his wife act as surrogate parents. Gradually Moses is gaining confidence and (to the headmaster's delight) he is also doing well in his studies.

Obviously all these activities cost money: fortunately the inhabitants of the township recognize that this money must come from within their community. 'When the donors have gone home we shall still be here' a woman told me. She is a member of a group of about 50 women who have undertaken to raise this money. One long-term plan is to bake buns and cakes for sale, for which they intend to use solar power, with advice from a priest who knows about simple solar baking technology. They began by holding a fund-raising tea-party, a function designed to give their plans publicity, to enlist influential support (they asked the First Lady to come and she did so), and to generate money immediately for orphans' expenses – but also for starting more ambitious long-term projects. Their next (medium-term) plan is to open a nursery school, which will have two functions: to raise money through fees, and to fill a real local need. The bakery is a long-term plan.

There is a happy integration of fund-raising with projects which satisfy social needs – as well as building community solidarity and competence. Individually these women have many burdens: they look after a mean of seven children each (range 2 to 13), a few have formal employment, others were working at road-building which is paid for with food provided by the World Food Programme, and a few sell sex occasionally to make ends meet. Most women were critical of their husbands, who do not give them enough money to feed their families – because they spend too much on beer and women at one or other of over 200 bars in the township. When I asked the women if they could talk with their husbands about these problems, I was told, with angry humour, that their men rarely come home until they are 'too drunk to talk about anything!' 'Some men have hard hearts like a stone; women are their things to use, like a Biro pen.'

In these circumstances the existence of a group of women with a common unselfish purpose has immense significance. It provides mutual support, develops self-respect, and gives women an exhilarating experience of their own power-to-be and of their capacity to alter their situations. The group has a by-product, for it draws together women of several different denominations, so encouraging ecumenical links at a local level. The women talked with a freedom and enthusiasm I had not dared to hope for. When I asked, anxiously: 'Do you remember to have fun together, too?' I was answered by a lively song; it was abundantly clear that they *do* have fun together.

But the status of women, income-generating projects and the building of community capacity-to-cope will be considered in more detail in chp. 15.

For Further Reading see Bibliography, p. 311 (22), (30) and (42).

Group Study Suggestion Obtain a copy of the latest annual UNICEF report on *The State of the World's Children* and read and think about one chapter each, then discuss what you have learnt. How does the situation for children in your own country match up to the goals for 2000 which were agreed at the 1990 World Summit for Children? What can Church leaders (yourselves, soon) do to change public opinion and mobilize local action for children's welfare? Are there one or two 'do-able' projects which could make a difference for children where you live?

CHAPTER 11
Vulnerable people

'What do you think? If a man has a hundred sheep, and one of them has gone astray, does he not leave the ninety-nine on the mountains and go in search of the one that went astray? And if he finds it, truly I say to you, he rejoices over it *more* than over the ninety-nine that never went astray. So it is not the will of my Father who is in heaven that one of these little ones should perish.' (Matt. 18. 12–14, RSV)

There could hardly be a clearer statement of the value to the Father of each individual human person. Many of Jesus of Nazareth's parables represent unimportant, uncongenial or even 'lost' members of His society as guests who are invited – even compelled – to be guests at feasts given by earthly rulers. In this way Jesus identified outsiders as essential guests at the banquet which will inaugurate the kingdom of His Father. Jesus's practice strongly reinforced His stories, for again and again the Gospels describe Him seeking out or welcoming people who were on the edges of His own society, in order to offer them table-fellowship or healing. Jesus stopped to listen to a blind beggar (Mark 10. 46–52), He accepted invitations to meals in the homes of a leper (Matt. 26.6) and a tax-collector (Luke 19. 1–10), He allowed a woman who was ritually unclean through illness to approach and touch Him (Mark 5. 25–33) and He welcomed and defended a woman who gate-crashed a dinner party to make an emotional demonstration: 'weeping, she began to wet his feet with her tears, and wiped them with the hair of her head, and kissed his feet and anointed them with the ointment' (Luke 7.37–38, RSV). There are enough examples in the Gospels of this disturbing and embarrassing behaviour to allow us to conclude that Jesus intended to challenge His contemporaries' view of who is acceptable to God.

There is a message for contemporary Christians in the very fact that the Gospels include so many parables and actions which turn normal standards of propriety or wisdom upside down. This emphasis suggests that the early Church understood reversal of human standards as an essential sign of the Kingdom of God begun in Jesus Christ.

Twentieth-century societies are willing or eager to label a wide variety of people as dangerous 'outsiders'. In the context of AIDS we are concerned only to identify groups of people who may act as reservoirs or routes for HIV transmission, thus increasing the speed with which the virus spreads, and to ask how we ought to regard them. As stated earlier, it is actual *behaviour*, rather than membership of an 'at-risk' group, which is important, although it is unwise to ignore clear links between shared circumstances and individual behaviour.

I choose to describe people who may act as rapid routes for spread of HIV as 'vulnerable' for two reasons: first, because their circumstances and behaviour interact to increase the risk that each one will *acquire* HIV. Secondly, their circumstances and behaviour often expose such people to discrimination even before HIV infection occurs, and greatly increase the likelihood of rejection by society and exclusion from care, once the disadvantage of AIDS is added to their other handicaps.

Vulnerable people who are rather likely to acquire HIV tend to have less freedom to choose how to behave than other people, because they are poor, lack education or status or employment, and suffer from low self-esteem and low societal esteem. Risk-taking behaviour often interlocks with difficult circumstances because it appears to be the only way to obtain money for subsistence survival or to win much-needed approval from peers. Jonathan Mann emphasizes that AIDS finds out the weaknesses in our societies: it certainly identifies people whose choices are limited because their circumstances are limited.

Who are these people whom society may regard as dangerous, but the Gospels ask us to accept as fellow-guests at God's banquet, while hinting that they may even take precedence over respectable citizens? In the context of AIDS they are: street children, women, (in particular women who sell sex), men who have sex with men, intravenous drug users, refugees and prisoners. Such people arouse our hostility partly because they are 'different', but fear of difference may be mixed with guilt (because these groups exist), or envy (because their members seem to enjoy a freedom we lack). Half-attraction is balanced by half-repulsion: we shrink from identifying with vulnerable persons when their circumstances are too harsh to imagine as applying to ourselves, or if their sexuality exposes doubts about our own orientation.

Over and above the discomfort which most people feel about 'others' who are numerous (women and refugees), evoke guilt (street children) or challenge family values (men who have sex with men), many Christians experience conflict between a desire to reduce spread of HIV and their distrust of specific methods for achieving this aim. Some Christians (not all) fear that if intravenous drug use is made safer, through schemes which provide sterile needles in exchange for used needles, then drug use will increase. Similarly, some Christians oppose free or low-cost condoms *not* because condoms only provide imperfect protection from HIV, but through fear that making condoms easily available will increase the number of sexual acts which take place outside marriage and encourage contraception within marriage.

Faced with these dilemmas, there is a crucial question to ask: 'Is it right to oppose measures which reduce the risk of HIV infection associated with risky behaviours, in order to demonstrate a (Christian?) desire to reduce the number of acts which go against Christian values?

For some people it appears to be more important to show their disapproval of certain acts than to protect the health and lives of men and women who will (in any case) behave in dangerous ways. The basic issue is whether we ought to accept people as they are, in their actual situations of risk and show concern *there* – or instead demand abandonment of behaviours which *we* judge to be immoral or undesirable, as a pre-condition for concern. Does Christian faith present us with a primary demand to save lives by preventing HIV infection because people are infinitely valued by God, whether or not we happen to approve of their behaviour? Are acts and habits of secondary importance, compared with persons?

In respect of each possible risk-reducing intervention, however, it is wise to weigh the risk (of encouraging more unsafe acts) against the benefit of increasing the safety of individual acts, if the relative sizes of 'risk' and 'benefit' are known. For example, if a certain measure produces a substantial reduction in the risk of HIV infection for each unsafe act, there would have to be a large increase in the number of unsafe acts to outweigh hoped-for benefits – and the criterion would be an 'unsafe' not an 'immoral' act, in the context of this book.

In practice, increasing the safety of unsafe behaviours does not usually result in a greater number of unsafe acts, but has the reverse effect, as many studies now show. For example, increased availability of condoms in workplaces in Zimbabwe appears to have decreased, not increased, the numbers of extra-marital partners most workers have. Similarly, several projects have shown that training an unemployed woman as a peer-educator may be the first step towards increasing her self-confidence and helping her to earn enough to be able to give up selling sex altogether.

Many Christians find it difficult to admit that marginal people may be the agents of creative change in communities. Gospel and patristic evidence *requires* us to see vulnerable men and women as persons who are infinitely valuable to God, but we are invited to take the further step of admitting that these outsiders may be valuable to *us*, as they have new things to teach us about sexuality and death – if we are humble enough to receive from them.

STREET CHILDREN

Street children are defined as children 'for whom the street has become their real home, and who lack adult protection and supervision'. Street children are difficult to count, because they are constantly on the move and sleep in hidden places – under parked lorries, in derelict buildings, in sewers or near rubbish tips which they pick over for useful scraps. They are most numerous in Latin America, but growing numbers are found in many developing countries, and to a lesser extent in industrialized societies, surviving (or dying) mainly in large cities. At best, street children are seen as a nuisance because they beg or hang around public places or pick pockets; at worst they are regarded as vermin or criminals who deserve to be eliminated because they threaten community security. Street children are murdered in some large cities, and evidence suggests that police may turn a blind eye to these killings or even take part in them.

Children on the streets cluster in gangs or groups for self-protection and mutual comfort, scratching a living from odd jobs ('watching' cars for shoppers, cleaning shoes, selling single cigarettes), begging, picking pockets, thieving, picking over rubbish tips, selling sex, and pushing drugs. They get what little comfort they can from sniffing petrol or glue – which may lead on to addiction to valium, mandrax, crack or heroin (according to availability). Older children may seek comfort through sex with each other. Some groups of youngsters gang up against people more fortunate than themselves, or fight rival gangs over territory or facilities – such as a municipal rubbish dump. Street kids are likely to be malnourished or to starve; they are exposed to all the diseases associated with poverty and poor or crowded living conditions – malaria, dysentery, pneumonia, meningitis, tuberculosis and AIDS and, whenever sick, they are much less likely than family-based children to receive adequate medical care. In some societies they become non-persons and are denied access to health and social services because they do not qualify for registration cards as they cannot give an address.

In these circumstances, some children graduate from petty theft to major crime, or learn to rely on violence; others are sold or drift into sexual slavery or join adult gangs pushing drugs. It is hard to escape from street life, and after a time children probably lose the desire to do so. It is likely that street children are essentially lost to the societies in which they hide, but remarkably little is known about their fates.

The *causal* background to life on the streets differs from country to country. In the industrialized West many children are running away from distress at home: physical, sexual or emotional abuse, neglect, or a sense of being unwanted by step-parents, or trouble with school or police. In developing countries some children sleep at home, but spend all day on the streets because of violence at home, while others have no homes to run from because they are orphans, or unwanted in families which are too large because contraception is banned or not available.

In whatever way children arrive on the streets, they are at risk of

HIV infection, yet they are unlikely to learn how to protect themselves from anti-AIDS education programmes which are aimed at the general population through schools (they do not go to school) or through the media (many cannot read and newspapers are for sleeping on, not reading) and they do not identify with posters aimed at sexually active adults. Street kids need specific anti-AIDS programmes with an approach and materials designed to identify with their actual situations.

First, it is necessary to win street kids' confidence and to show them why AIDS is important and that HIV infection is not inevitable. Whether at risk through sexual activity or drug use (both common on the streets, especially in Latin America), children can avoid HIV infection if they know how to protect themselves.

In the short term many strategies have been used to reduce the immediate risks of HIV infection: informal discussions in places where children congregate, cartoons, drama, songs, specially designed comic books, supplies of free condoms and instruction in how to use them, and introductions to needle exchange schemes for established drug users. But a great deal more than emergency care is needed – in particular measures to fore-warn and fore-arm children before they reach life on the streets, and, secondly, for those already established in street culture, a chance to rejoin normal society.

In Puerto Rico, in 1991, the San Juan AIDS Institute began to teach pre-school children how to avoid AIDS, through educational programmes in Capital City, where many youngsters are multiple drug users or drug dealers by the time they reach adolescence. The ideas and methods used in this project could be adapted for other countries, to fore-warn and fore-arm small children against the risks of street life, while they are still living with their families.

Pre-school children aged three to five, attending community centres in Capital City, were taught through play using clowns, dolls, a puppet show and drama that AIDS is a deadly disease which can be transmitted through drug abuse. Children were also taught how to prevent sexual abuse (using dolls) and to accept classmates who may be HIV-infected, because HIV is not spread by everyday classroom contacts. The long-term success of such a programme is not known, but it has been shown already that such instruction interests children, and that it is not impossible to explain AIDS to the very young.

For children who are already established in street culture, patient long-term help is needed. Potential helpers have to start by learning about the actual backgrounds and needs of children who live on the streets (or in the sewers) of *their* city, before ways to offer help and friendship can be identified. Clubs or drop-in centres providing primary health care, including condoms and immunizations, a shelter from rain, supplies of used clothing, showers and laundry facilities are attractive starting points. Training in street survival (how to run a street stall without falling foul of police or municipal regulations!) or literacy classes or training in skills needed to join small-scale industries in their locality may appeal to some street kids. Adult leaders have to be tough, secure enough in their own sexuality to recognize and ignore seduction, imaginative and good-humoured to withstand many rejections and yet to go on working. Sometimes it is necessary, quite literally, to go out into the market place to 'compel them to come in' (Luke 14:23) because only that degree of commitment convinces rejected children that they do really matter to someone.

The most successful approaches to street children are broad-based programmes which accept gangs as units of 'community' and work slowly, humbly and informally, willing at first to reach out through fun rather than care – which may be viewed with suspicion by its intended objects. In Lusaka, for instance, a Rastafarian worker cycles round making friends, listening, answering street kids' questions, and singing songs with them. Clowns and impromptu entertainment have always been part of street life.

In the end, street kids need new homes and a new life in the community, but at present their concerns are under-represented at AIDS conferences and in the planning and funding of national anti-AIDS programmes – and so are the children themselves. Most children are not on the street through their own fault or at their own wish, and ought to have the same rights and opportunities as other children. Street kids, too, are potential parents and citizens, and they are lost sheep that the shepherds of Christ's flock are bound to search for, as God does. When lost sheep are found, Jesus promises that there will be rejoicing in heaven as well as on earth.

WOMEN WHO SELL SEX

The general vulnerability of *all* women to HIV infection and its consequences has been described already. The sub-group of women who sell sex are an important route for HIV transmission because of their place in sexual networks, which link men and women who have never met and never *will* meet face-to-face. Women who sell sex are not just transmitters of HIV, but can reduce spread of the virus: they are the only people who can identify and reach men who *buy* sex.

Women who sell sex are not a homogeneous group.* In a few cities it is relatively easy to contact them and offer services, such as medical care, and to teach them how to protect themselves from HIV. In other cities and in rural areas women who sell sex are difficult to identify and locate. Sex is sold at a variety of levels: to tourists and wealthy citizens in hotels or through 'personal services' agencies; in the middle market through contacts in bars or inexpensive hotels, and through advertisements in newspapers or telephone booths. Even men who have little money to spend can buy sex in bars, beer halls or streets.

Women doing sex work in all these varied situations need to know how to protect themselves from HIV infection – but different approaches will be needed to provide that knowledge. Most national AIDS programmes are well aware of this, and already work at the first-aid level. 'First-aid' projects aim to make women aware of the risks attached to their work, to improve their access to health care, and to provide free condoms. Most health workers now recognize that it is not enough to provide condoms; it is essential to empower women to demand that clients use them, by providing assertiveness training and opportunities to practise non-threatening replies to responses from clients. Rather fewer agencies recognize a parallel responsibility to alter the prevailing culture in male society, by encouraging men to feel that 'real men' care enough for their own and their wives' health to use condoms. *Both* parties in the commercial transaction need knowledge and motivation to change their sexual behaviour.

Clients seeking commercial sex may do so openly in 'red light' districts in some cities, but for the most part clients are anonymous and difficult for anti-AIDS education programmes to reach at the face-to-face level which is most likely to change sexual behaviour. Only their commercial partners have the opportunity to shock men who buy sex into recognizing the risks they take with their own health, and the health of their wives and future children. A sex-worker can say – in the words of a Ugandan comic book: 'no glove; no love!' In the comic quoted the shocked client ran home to his pregnant wife and adolescent son, greatly disturbed by the possible consequences of his past behaviour and terrified at the prospect of 'taking an AIDS test'.

Health planners who hope that women who sell sex will play their part in the fight against AIDS need to understand that women do sex-work in a buyer's market. Women are expected to be passive providers of pleasure to clients who are physically stronger than they are, already sexually aroused and unaccustomed to having their wants denied or even delayed.

A woman who sells sex often urgently needs money, and she is likely to have experienced violence in the past. She may have been lured into sex-work through deception, or sold into it by families who see no other way to avoid starvation. Such a woman has low self-esteem, no-one to defend her from aggressive clients, and little support in the outside world, where – if the nature of her work is known – she is likely to meet with condemnation and hostility from a self-righteous society. She may, or may not, receive support from other women engaged in the same work. She is less likely than most women to have access to good health care, but more likely to suffer repeated STDs. When she is ill (through HIV infection or for other reasons) she is also less likely to be in effective contact with parents or other relatives who are willing to nurse her and care for her children. Where sex-work is well-organized, as in south-east Asia, a woman worker is likely to be at the mercy of commercially-minded and possibly brutal owners of sex-houses, lacking both the means and the confidence to escape from slavery.

In summary, women who sell sex have many disadvantages and few resources; they need to be offered respect, imaginative understanding of their situation, justice and alternative opportunities to make a living by fellow-citizens, whether Christian or not.

Clients who *buy* sex need imaginative understanding too, for some seek temporary acceptance of their value as men, rather than sexual pleasure. Particularly in the West, some men feel emasculated by wives who repeatedly find fault with their behaviour, lack interest in their interests, and no longer (it seems) pay attention to them as persons. In these circumstances, a man may go to a professional sex-worker for attention from a woman who makes him feel that he is still a fine fellow, even if it is only for an hour or two. Sex-workers have another, rarely regarded role, for most cultures ignore the sexual needs of men and women who are too odd in appearance or capabilities to have much chance of a normal marriage. Disabled persons have always been amongst the clients of men or women who sell sex: for both partners, a sexual meeting of this nature which enacts acceptance and gives a measure of self-respect may go beyond commerce and become a hidden sign of God's love.

As in every field of response to the AIDS pandemic, planners need local knowledge of the circumstances surrounding sex-for-sale in order to act appropriately. Only a few agencies, notably the Society for Women and AIDS in Africa (SWAA) and some industries and commercial farms in Zimbabwe, have taken the further step of making opportunities for women to leave sex-work altogether. Some groups in Zimbabwe, have grasped the suitability of women who sell sex for training as peer-educators, which empowers women to find alternative work by restoring their self-esteem and raising their status in society. SWAA and small Christian communities in Kampala also offer women training for tailoring or other trades to enable them to set up small businesses to support themselves and their children. In this field, and in projects to provide care for sick women and long-term care for their orphans, Churches should have much to offer.

Story: *Loveness* when four months pregnant, attended a clinic in Lusaka for treatment of Kaposi's sarcoma. She was tested for HIV, found to be infected, and counselled about the meaning of a positive result and the implications for her health and behaviour. Loveness told staff that she had two children already, but did not volunteer any other information about her circumstances. At first her health improved with treatment, but soon she was covered once more with dark spots which most people in Zambian towns identify as a sign of AIDS. She returned to the clinic and asked for her pregnancy to be terminated. The doctor told her that at six months termination is not allowed by law. A week later Loveness returned, to renew her demands for termination, on the grounds that 'I can't work any longer – and how can I feed my children?' Her skin spots, added to her advancing pregnancy, made her unattractive to clients, and she hoped that removing one impediment would enable her to go on working. She had no relatives or friends in Lusaka, and had lost touch with her parents, who lived hundreds of miles away. The doctor, too, was distressed by this situation, but did not know of any group, Christian or otherwise, which could offer help. Loveness went away and survived a back-street abortion – but only for a few weeks. I do not know what happened to her children.

On one occasion Jesus of Nazareth was asked his opinion about a woman who had been caught in the act of adultery. The question was asked, as a test, by a group of Pharisees who wanted to use His answer against Him. At first Jesus gave no answer, then He said: 'If there is one of you who has not sinned, let him be the first to throw a stone at her.' He bent down, and wrote on the ground with His finger. One by one the accusers went away, until Jesus was left alone with the woman, who remained standing there. Jesus looked up and said: 'Woman, where are they? Has no one condemned you?' 'No one sir,' she replied. 'Neither do I condemn you' said Jesus, 'go away, and don't sin any more.' (John 8. 1–11, JB). The challenge to Churches is not only to refrain from condemning women who sell sex – following the Lord's lead, but also to make it truly possible for such women to go away and 'not to sin any more'.

MEN WHO HAVE SEX WITH MEN

Men who have sex with men are a heterogeneous* group too. Some men have a *homosexual orientation*, meaning that they feel sexual attraction only towards their own sex and not towards women. In the West such men dislike the term 'homosexual' and prefer to call themselves 'gay'. During the last 30 years many Western gay men have ceased to be secretive about their preferences and have 'come out' (into the open), although a hidden gay culture is much older. Confident pride in same-sex preferences, and the promotion of gay partnerships as morally and socially equivalent to marriage, *is* new. Lesbian relationships between women are not relevant to this book, as they are uncommon in developing countries, and sexual contacts between women rarely if ever transmit HIV.

Unfortunately, the same is not true about sexual contacts between men who seek physical and emotional satisfaction, by penetration of the partner's anus and ejaculation into his rectum (anal sex), or by ejaculation into the partner's mouth (oral sex or fellatio). Anal intercourse is the most efficient way there is of transmitting HIV sexually from one person to another, because the lining of the anal canal and rectum is thinner than that of the vagina, and easily damaged during sexual intercourse. Anal sex is very risky, whether the partners are both men, or a man and a woman using anal sex as a means of birth control. The risk is reduced, but not eliminated, by careful use of a new condom for each act of penetration. The risk associated with oral sex is probably slightly smaller than the risk of transmitting HIV during normal vaginal sex, unless the receptive partner happens to have ulcers in his or her mouth. In some cultures oral sex is practised also between men and women, regularly or occasionally.

Careful enquiries have shown that the frequency of homosexual orientation and behaviour appears to vary from country to country. Amongst the indigenous populations of developing countries, homosexual orientation as a life-long preference is less common than in the West (though even there, less than 5% of males are thought to be wholly gay), and long-term gay partnerships are almost unknown. The reason for these differences between populations is not known, although recent evidence suggests a genetic basis.

Same-sex acts and relationships show the same variety, in respect of number, quality and meaning, as heterosexual acts and relationships, ranging from exploitation and violence at one end of the scale to loving fidelity at the other. For example, in the course of a single year, one gay man may have hundreds of casual sexual contacts with different partners picked up in gay bars, or by purchase of sexual favours from male sex-workers (known as 'rent boys'). This kind of behaviour helped to spread HIV rapidly in the 1970s in the United States, but has become less common in the West in the last ten years, as one gay community after another altered its norms for sexual conduct to avoid HIV. This change was achieved using strategies for behaviour change outlined in a later chapter, which apply to homosexuals as well as to heterosexuals.

Many radical gay men reject the model of marriage for their own partnerships, but others choose to be faithfully monogamous, and to care for each other 'for better, for worse, in sickness and health, until death us do part'.

Some men and a few women are *bi-sexual* in orientation, meaning that they are attracted both to women and to men, so that at different times they seek sexual partners of either sex. Men who are bisexual make hidden links between homosexual groups and the general heterosexual population in countries where homosexuality is common, and they are particularly important vectors for HIV in countries, such as India, where homosexual behaviour is quite widespread but difficult to acknowledge because it offends family values.

Bisexual *behaviour* is not always the consequence of bisexual *orientation*, for it is often a temporary second-best source of sexual pleasure when women are not available. In some developing countries, for example India, social systems discourage or prevent exploratory relationships – or even friendships – forming between young people of opposite sexes, with the result that men with heterosexual inclinations may have sex with other men, as a temporary way of finding physical satisfaction while waiting for a chance to marry. Bisexual behaviour without bisexual orientation also interlocks with poverty and unemployment in some large cities, especially in Latin America. In these places young men who cannot get training for work or who have low wages, sell sex for subsistence survival or to save money in order to marry their girl-friends later.

In all these circumstances, genital acts between partners of the same sex (which do not express personal relationship) occur not just for financial and sexual reasons but also partly as a result of other deprivations. Casual same-sex acts are most likely to occur between heterosexual men who are deprived of freedom in prison, or who do not have jobs, influence, status, adequate living conditions, respect for themselves or prospects for a better future: both men and women lose confidence and capacity for personal relationships when their social and spiritual circumstances seem unchangeable and hopeless.

Before considering how Christians might respond to circumstances which dehumanize sexual behaviour, we need to examine two aspects of same-sex relationships which have been ignored so far: the theological–ethical position of Christians in regard to homosexual orientation and its expressions, and the development and stability of sexual orientation.

At present scientists and sociologists do not agree on the reasons for sexual orientation, in either direction, although most societies have traditionally regarded homosexuality as a diversion away from normal sexual development. Different theories explain sexual orientation in terms of biological or psychological factors, or as the result of social learning, or by a combination of all three acting together. Most theories do not attempt to explain why there are large variations in the incidence of male homosexual orientation between different cultures and countries – perhaps because the makers of theories do not want to know that such variations exist. The suggestion that genetic factors may play a part is too recent for informed comment.

Despite the absence of an agreed theory for the development of sexual orientation, several useful statements appear to be generally accepted, which are worth quoting because they have ethical relevance:

1. Basic sexual orientation is relatively fixed by ages five to seven, before a growing child is capable of deliberate choice.

2. Most people are neither exclusively heterosexual nor exclusively homosexual, but have a marked tendency towards one or other end of a scale of orientation.

3. A short period of homosexual attraction is a common stage in the sexual development of adolescent males and females, who later pass on to heterosexual orientation. Whether sexual abuse can interrupt or divert normal progression through this stage is uncertain but abuse usually affects behaviour rather than orientation.

4. Efforts to reorientate adult sexual preferences may alter some behaviours, but do not usually have lasting effects on feelings, or sexual desires and fantasies.

5. Predominantly homosexual orientation is not associated with detectable clinical pathology; when gay or lesbian persons have behavioural or psychological problems it is likely that these result from social oppression, as they are similar to problems experienced by other socially oppressed groups.

Although homosexuality has existed in all known cultures throughout history there have been no consistent patterns of cultural and religious response. Homosexuality tends to be more hidden and less well tolerated in societies which are under pressure to reproduce in order to survive.

In one culture or another homosexuality has been in turn tolerated, approved, ignored, penalized, criminalized, institutionalized, or even affirmed as a means of contact with the gods. In the Judeo-Christian tradition homosexuality has been denied consistently as a permissible orientation, but only inconsistently persecuted, at least until the middle ages. Negative attitudes and behaviours towards homosexual people were accepted in community tradition, but supported by remarkably few biblical statements, and some texts can be interpreted in more than one way.

No sayings attributed to Jesus of Nazareth have any direct relevance. The biblical tradition rests on two accounts of the complementarity of men and women at creation (Gen. 1 and 2, which are widely separated in time and have different sources), and on six other texts which either appear to, or actually do, make negative statements about same-sex genital acts. However, some biblical scholars question the relevance of these texts to *all* homosexual relationships, as the focus of attention is not always on homosexuality as such, but rather on social injustice and hostility to strangers (Gen. 19), condemnation of pagan cults (Lev. 18.22 and 20.13), homosexual lust when persons choose to act contrary to their 'natural' inclinations (Rom. 1.26–27) and homosexual exploitation of children (1 Cor. 6.9–10; 1 Tim. 1.9–10). At present Christian theological–ethical positions on homosexual orientation and its genital expressions lie along a four-point scale, ranging from severe rejection to relaxed approval. The first position rejects homosexual orientation and behaviour as wrong, not only for Christians but for everyone, and therefore its supporters feel justified in taking a punitive attitude towards *all* gay or lesbian persons. Their theory and practice is based, at least overtly, on contextual and literal interpretations of the Biblical evidence, but it is often strongly influenced by cultural stereotypes about gay people, and may hide fears about their own sexuality (and its orientation) which are deeply disturbing to advocates of the *rejecting-punitive* position.

A less aggressive stance is taken by rather more Christians, who condemn homosexual acts as unnatural, idolatrous and contrary to God's creative will, but who make a practical distinction between act and orientation. This position has been described as *rejecting-non-punitive*, and it avoids condemnation of *individuals* with a homosexual orientation, who may and should be treated with compassion. Arguments are advanced, however, which oppose genital expression of homosexual attraction on two grounds. First, homosexual conduct is regarded as a sin against nature because all sexual acts ought to be open to the possibility of procreation. As this argument, attributed to Thomas Aquinas, is no longer accepted generally as applying to heterosexual acts in an overpopulated world, it seems inappropriate to use it to condemn homosexual acts.

A second argument rests on the complementarity of men and women as *together* constituting the image of God; from this viewpoint, to seek personhood in intimate relationship to a person of one's own sex is seen as self-worship or idolatry. For some Christians this second argument has considerable weight, but they can accept homosexuals as persons who think (and feel) differently from themselves. Above all, pastors can and should recognize an obligation to respond to the pastoral needs of gay people – an obligation which has too often been denied in the past.

A third position, which is becoming more common in the West, is *qualified acceptance*. Christians who hold this view affirm that God intends creation to be heterosexual, but they accept that constitutional homosexuality appears to be fixed in childhood and that few people change in adult life. However, they believe that any person who is capable of making such a change is morally obliged to do so. Those who cannot change are advised either to abstain from genital relations or to order their relationships responsibly, meaning for an adult, long-term monogamous commitment. From this viewpoint, homosexual orientation is incomplete and not normative. Although genital acts within a committed relationship are distortions of God's ideal, they are given qualified acceptance because, for some persons, they are the lesser of two evils. This viewpoint asks homosexual people to consider celibacy seriously, as a possible vocation for themselves as well as for heterosexuals.

The final and least common stance amongst Christians is that of *full acceptance*. From this position, homosexual and heterosexual orientations are accepted as morally equivalent and equally part of God's intention in creation, so that homosexual acts and relationships may and should be evaluated by exactly the same standards used for heterosexual behaviour. This view develops a shift in the understanding of human sexuality which began in the seventeenth century, when Protestants elevated the unitive purpose of marriage and sexuality above its procreative purpose, an interpretation of man–woman relationships supported by the oldest account of creation (Gen. 2). Advocates of same-sex relationships contend that such partnerships can fully express God's central purpose for sexuality, which is its unitive aspect. They hold, therefore, that relationships which do not damage but actually serve human fulfilment, and which demonstrate mutual fidelity, ought to be accepted, whether they involve a man and a woman or persons of the same sex.

These different positions depend upon alternative ways of interpreting Scripture and interpreting human behaviour in society, and upon different understandings of the meaning of human sexuality. If, as I shall argue later, the unitive aspect of man–woman relationships contributes to the making-one of all human beings, but is *also* part of the preparation of humanity-made-whole for union with God, then there may be more to add. We worship the Trinity, three persons in one God, different as to person yet united in Godhead. Perhaps the 'difference' between persons which is vital in heterosexual marriage is needed to receive and mirror the image and likeness of the Trinity?

Whichever position individual Christians and Churches choose to uphold, I suggest that all should agree on one basic principle: the unsafe behaviours of vulnerable people ought to be made as safe as possible by the most effective means available, in order to preserve lives and reduce spread of HIV within and beyond vulnerable groups: strategies for action are summarized at the end of this chapter. Another basic principle should be the right of men or women who live celibate lives to privacy: their sexual orientation concerns no-one else but themselves and need not be made public.

INTRAVENOUS DRUG USERS (IVDU)

Yet again, complex links exist between this 'vulnerable behaviour', poverty, sex for sale and educational, social and spiritual deprivation. Drug use is commonest in large cities, and has increased worldwide during the last two decades, most rapidly in the USA, Europe and South America, although drug use is also spreading in Asia and (recently) in Africa. The term 'drug use' is preferred to the more accurate term 'drug abuse', on the grounds that 'abuse' implies an inadmissible value judgement. In this chapter we are not discussing the reasonable use of drugs to promote human welfare, but only their misuse in doses or circumstances which ensure that actual and potential dangers far outweigh benefits. Therefore, I shall use 'misuse' to signify drug taking which has predominantly harmful effects, but adopt the internationally accepted acronym IVDU to refer to the *persons* who misuse drugs. At the end of the twentieth century drug misuse has reached epidemic proportions and is very closely linked to AIDS.

Throughout history human beings have used plant and animal products for pleasure or relief, to make celebrations more joyful and pains more tolerable. In the accounts of creation in Genesis God saw all He had made 'and indeed it was very good' – and God gave the fruit of the garden to His rational creatures for food. There was, however, one prohibition, which was made for the well-being of humankind, according to Irenaeus and Origen, not as a trap. In Genesis 3 human sin is pictured in a story of a simple – even trivial – act of disobedience. However, that trivial act expressed mistrust of God's good intentions towards His creatures, combined with greed for immediate knowledge and power. Mistrust of God's intentions and greed for immediate pleasure still lies at the heart of much human sin and suffering, and are important elements in the complex causation of drug misuse.

Many drugs which can be misused are valuable when used in appropriate doses, for appropriate purposes and at the correct intervals. We need drugs derived from opium and cocaine for relief from severe pain; alcohol helps tired people to relax and shy people to enjoy company; marijuana relieves nausea and helps relaxation, and drugs which alter perception remind us of the large resources of the human brain. But any drugs taken in excess are likely to have undesirable or even lethal consequences, and all drugs which alter mood or perceptions are (at least potentially) able to induce dependence or addiction. In recognition of these dangers, most countries have laws which regulate the use of named 'dangerous drugs', with the consequence that drug misuse is not only physically and mentally hazardous, but also illegal and punishable by imprisonment or large fines. Information about IVDUs is derived mainly from law enforcement agencies, and is therefore biased: a more balanced picture would result if more medical data was available too.

Volatile substances such as *glue and petrol* have no value as drugs, but when sniffed, can make chronically miserable people feel better for a while: glue and petrol are easy to find at low cost and are popular with deprived children, including street kids in developing countries. Both substances are dangerous and cause many sudden deaths of children all over the world. Because not all substances which are used to escape from unhappy feelings or hunger are drugs, the term 'substance abuse' is often used as a general term to cover all addictions: in this phrase 'abuse' appears to be an acceptable word.

Drug-dependency begins when people start to need larger and larger doses of a specific drug in order to achieve the effects they crave. Soon every time the concentration of drug in the blood falls to a critically low level addicts feel acutely ill both physically and mentally (withdrawal symptoms), so they are strongly motivated to find and take further doses.

Unfortunately it is quite easy for someone who tries drugs out of curiosity or under pressure from his peers to be caught in the trap of addiction: episodes of acute pleasure and exhilaration are followed by mental and physical misery, which is relieved by another drug 'fix' – leading to more pleasure but also (inevitably) to more misery. As this process gathers momentum it is common for the dependent person to move on from the less damaging drugs to others which are more likely to induce addiction, for example from marijuana to heroin or cocaine.

At the same time the route by which the drug is taken may change. At first most people are satisfied with the results of smoking, sniffing or swallowing drugs, but as their bodies become accustomed to a drug's effects, higher blood concentrations are needed to induce the sensations they enjoyed at first. At this stage, many addicts are persuaded to try to recapture bliss by intravenous injection of the same, or a more dangerous, drug. Intravenous drug misuse is learned from and supported by the behaviour of other people who have the same habit, but it is supported also by the commercial activities of drug-pushers, who make large profits from selling drugs to desperate people. Drug-pushers naturally want as large a market as possible for their wares, so they encourage young people to experiment with drugs 'for the experience', knowing that some of them will become dependent long-term customers.

Injecting-drug misuse has always been dangerous for many reasons: it is possible to misjudge a dose and inject a lethal quantity of drug (the commonest cause of accidental death for IVDUs); money is spent on drugs rather than food, leading to malnutrition; drug misuse is illegal so it is rewarding for drug-pushers, leading to violence between rival gangs, and addicts ending up in prison for the offence of being in possession of 'dangerous drugs'. Some IVDUs are driven to crime or selling sex for money to buy drugs. Finally, needles and syringes are used by several people without adequate cleaning.

One attraction of injecting drugs is membership of a community of people who accept each other. To confirm that a needle is in the right place, blood is drawn back into the syringe before injecting the drug, so (before AIDS started) this necessary act became a ritual of blood brotherhood to addicts in the West. Often the used needle and syringe ('the works') was handed on to another person in the places where addicts congregate ('shooting galleries') – and sometimes to a series of users. The dangers are obvious: the process passes bacteria or viruses from person to person.

Hepatitis B (a form of jaundice) used to be the commonest and most dangerous infection associated with intravenous drugs, but in the early 1980s many drug-injectors became HIV-infected and later spread HIV into wider society, through their sexual partners. About 80% of persons who inject drugs in Edinburgh were HIV-infected by 1993, and similar or slightly lower infection rates are recorded in other large cities of Europe and the USA.

Wherever injecting drugs is a common behaviour, AIDS control organizations have seen IVDUs as important targets for preventive education and action, for their own sake, because they are so vulnerable to HIV infection, but also because they form a reservoir for infection which overflows into the general population. Moreover, IVDUs need a unique preventive approach, for they must learn to avoid HIV in two quite different sets of circumstances – while injecting drugs and while engaging in sexual intercourse with their partners. The strategies which have been successful in reducing the risks of injecting drugs will be summarized at the end of this chapter.

Christians ought to ponder the conditions of social, economic and spiritual deprivation which combine to make intravenous drug misuse a large and growing problem all over the world. Four sets of factors are interrelated.

Most people, like Adam and Eve, mistrust God and grab at pleasure and power, fearful that they will never have the satisfactions they crave. But some people live in circumstances of such chronic misery and hopelessness that escape seems to be the only option – and drugs offer a quick if temporary escape from misery, at least at first – hence the term 'quick fix'. Many needy people who try this solution live in societies which ignore their problems or even their existence. But this neglect may occur because the societies concerned are themselves sick and economically or spiritually deprived. Many societies are confused and crushed by the complexity of their problems and lack a world view which is large enough to offer a 'way through'. Indeed there seems to be nowhere to get through *to* – beyond the measurable world that 'science' offers, which has already failed them.

In the background, we must not forget poor peasants who get a better price for the raw materials for addictive drugs than for cultivating anything else which will grow on their infertile land – so naturally, to feed their families, they grow opium poppies or coca or marijuana; which brings us back to the deprivations and greed of drug-dealers who buy the raw materials. The behaviour of drug-dealers may be (in part) due to *their* spiritual or material deprivation, because they lack knowledge of their true human vocation, or are in hiding from it. Greed is usually a large element.

In conclusion, Christians need to make some thoughtful investigations in the places where they happen to live, in order to understand the circumstances which combine to make drugs available, and the conditions which drive people to seek comfort from drugs. Precise knowledge and empathetic understanding are needed as a basis for friendship with drug abusers, and to see how to influence the underlying causes of drug misuse.

Many experienced workers believe that the best approach would be to legalize drug *use*, thus reducing the rewards associated with drug-related crime. In 1994 the WHO issued a statement that countries where plant products are widely used as drugs should consider comparing the social effects of legal prohibition with the social effects of legal use of drugs: such studies are needed in many places.

PRISONERS

Most prisons in most countries of the world are overcrowded; many prisons are also dirty and old-fashioned, built decades or even centuries ago, when general standards of living were less comfortable or healthy than they are now. Prisoners are representative of the whole of society in their abilities, advantages and disadvantages, but amongst them there tend to be disproportionately large numbers of people who are mentally ill, addicted to alcohol or drugs, accustomed to receiving and using violence, or lacking experience of sustaining relationships. Many are resentful at being 'caught' breaking the law, because they know others who 'got away with it'. Others are bitter because they think (quite reasonably) that society has a lot to answer for, and that they themselves are the victims of circumstances. Like everyone, prisoners have a share in the bias towards failure and sorrow which we pass on to each other from generation to generation, without meaning to do so. Whether this bias is determined by inheritance or environment or the behaviour of relatives, it is a fact of human existence: theological tradition calls it original sin.

In addition to the common burdens of life, prisoners are deprived of freedom and sexual satisfaction. Many alternative satisfactions are also denied to them, while they are literally locked away into closed societies of unhappy, inadequate or violent people. It is hardly surprising that prisoners try to make their lives more tolerable by misusing intravenous drugs or having sex with each other – or by both activities, either of which may transmit HIV.

The HIV-infection rate of newly admitted prisoners is likely to be the same as, or greater than, the infection rate for the city or town where the prison is located. AIDS therefore poses two sets of problems for prisons: whether and how HIV transmission should be prevented in prisons and how HIV-infected prisoners should be treated.

Unfortunately, the first question asked about AIDS prevention in prison is often: 'Should we even attempt to prevent transmission of HIV through injecting drugs or anal sex, since both activities are illegal and should not be taking place?' The fact is that they *are* taking place; to refuse to admit this, and to neglect to make unsafe acts a little safer, or to provide alternative satisfactions, is equivalent to deciding that HIV infection is an additional punishment which can justifiably be inflicted on prisoners – because infection will be their own fault. In my opinion, Christians ought to be committed to protecting prisoners from the worst risks of their unsafe behaviours, while at the same time offering substitute satisfactions, including the possibility of finding hope and rebirth to life through faith in Christ. Practical implications are summarized at the end of this chapter.

In a large urban prison in a high-incidence country one-third of new prisoners are likely to be HIV-infected. Probably at least half of these will be free of symptoms and unaware of their HIV-infection, but if sentenced for five years or more, most men and women in this category will be ill for HIV-related reasons on several occasions before release, and some will develop AIDS-defining diseases before release – at a rate which may be accelerated by an inadequate diet, TB or other infections.

National AIDS control programmes and prison governors make policies about testing prisoners for HIV, either on admission (whether or not symptoms and signs of disease are found during the initial medical examination), or later when such signs develop. The purposes of testing ought to be quite clear: it should be done for the benefit of individual prisoners, so that they may be treated with justice and humanity. Testing ought not to be done in order to mark them down for elimination: there is evidence that in Latin America HIV-infected inmates of some prisons have been murdered to solve the problem of what to do with them.

It is useful to distinguish between prisoners serving short and long sentences, and between the healthy and those who are already ill. An HIV-infected prisoner who is well and serving a sentence of less than six months needs normal pastoral care, but does not need special privileges. In contrast, a man or woman who already has symptoms or who faces a longer sentence should be entitled to release on medical grounds. Prison chaplains should know prison regulations and be prepared to see that they are applied to the benefit of prisoners, acting as mediators between prisoners and authorities.

It is important to minimize the administrative red-tape surrounding legal decisions: the breakdown of a human immune system occurs a good deal more rapidly than most appeal procedures. This may be an area where Church and legal leaders need to co-operate to examine the legal provisions which could be used to end prison sentences early, and if there are none to campaign to change the law to allow just and humane care responses to HIV-infected prisoners. To be denied the chance to make arrangements for children's welfare or to spend the last weeks of life at home is an unwarranted punishment.

During short sentences heterosexual prisoners in developing countries rarely engage in anal sex, although mutual masturbation may be common, but young prisoners ought to be segregated from long-term inmates, to prevent homosexual rape. A conference on HIV and prisons held in Lusaka in 1990 recommended programmes to educate prisoners about HIV infection, concentrating on the period immediately before release, and ensuring that condoms are supplied as prisoners are discharged into society.

REFUGEES

Refugees share some dangerous circumstances with other vulnerable people, especially prisoners, although they are less likely to have social or psychological disabilities or to be accustomed to risk-taking behaviours. Their vulnerability to HIV is neglected in many national AIDS control plans. The special needs of refugee camps ought to be recognized wherever refugees are in contact with local communities with high HIV-infection rates, especially if refugees come from countries where HIV-infection rates are low, or where government policies prevent mention of AIDS. In circumstances of acute danger an infection which might kill in five years time *is* irrelevant. Women who do know about HIV and who have been raped may be doubly afraid – that they may have been infected with HIV and that if this is discovered, they will be forced to return to the situations of acute danger from which they are trying to escape.

Refugees need general information about HIV and AIDS and about specific risks which affect them, in language which they understand, using images and concepts from their own culture. Pastors who arrange services for refugees, or who befriend refugee pastors, should teach AIDS awareness as part of the pastoral care offered in camps. But information alone is not enough: it is necessary to identify the risk-promoting circumstances to which refugees are exposed and to alter these conditions, too.

STRATEGIES FOR ACTION

Action to reduce spread of HIV is most effective when informed and directed to counteract the specific risks to which specific target groups of people are exposed. Christians need a foundation of accurate knowledge of real situations and real risks: too many endeavours are based on idealized pictures of how people think and behave in society. Based on local knowledge attention should be given to:

1. Identifying and changing social, economic and spiritual conditions which predispose to risk-taking behaviours.

2. Minimizing the danger of intravenous drug use by promoting and supporting needle exchange and drug detoxification programmes.

3. Minimizing the dangers of casual heterosexual or homosexual relations by making condoms available to anyone who may need them; teaching people how to use condoms safely and how to negotiate 'safer sex' with potential partners.

4. Accepting people who take risks with HIV as valuable persons, for whose physical and spiritual well-being we are answerable before God.

Study Suggestions

1. Which groups of vulnerable people are present in (a) your locality? (b) your congregation? How do their circumstances differ from the general account given here? Are other local groups also vulnerable to HIV infection?

2. Select two dis-similar categories of 'vulnerable people' and plan how you would find out why they are vulnerable to HIV infection, in *your* locality. How would you try to gain their co-operation?

CHAPTER 12

Caring for Carers

On one occasion Jesus intended to take his weary disciples away to a lonely place so that they could rest (Mark 6. 30–32). The fact that His plan was interrupted does not alter the importance of the principle Jesus expressed: workers need rest and personal care. If carers distance themselves from the 'others' to whom they minister it is easy to forget that everyone, carer as well as cared-for, needs sleep, food, play, appreciation, and other people to listen attentively to their own stories of grievance and achievement.

Most active people appear 'strong' in their public lives (for example, a doctor appears beyond ill-health to her patients) yet in both public and private life everyone is vulnerable and weak at some point. It is truly said that 'we are all wounded', but many people are not aware of their wounds or refuse healing for them: blindness to their own vulnerability and neediness is a rather common characteristic in professional 'carers' such as clergy, mothers, doctors, and nurses. This denial of need may be due to embarrassment about the triviality of our 'minor' wounds by comparison with the much larger problems of those we care for, or to shame because we know we are partly responsible for our own wounds. Quite often work in a caring profession is chosen because it fulfils an unconscious longing 'to be needed' which the caring persons cannot recognize or acknowledge. In this situation they are likely to deny or misunderstand their own need for love. Yet the capacity to give love and to care for others is directly related to the capacity to *receive* love and care. Anyone whose need for physical, emotional and spiritual nourishment is persistently denied or unmet will become incapable (eventually) of nourishing others: we are *all* emotionally and spiritually hungry.

Often, especially in developing countries, the needs of carers are not considered, or are swept aside as trivial compared with the needs of clients. During a visit to Zambia and Uganda, for example, I travelled in a variety of project vehicles on rural dirt roads and crowded city streets: few vehicles were fitted with safety belts. Such carelessness conveys a hidden message to a worker that 'your safety doesn't matter'.

Identifying and identifying-with carers is an important task for Churches. Carers, too, are part of the flock committed to us and part of the body of Christ. A tired middle-aged mother of a dying woman, her sister who washes soiled sheets day after day, neighbours who go to market for the family and later pray with them, the driver of a Homecare truck and the nurse who gives time, attention and drugs: all of them are 'little ones' for whose well-being we must answer. At the very least, they need to be valued and appreciated as people, not just as workers.

WHO NEEDS CARE?

It is easy to see that primary helpers (professionals or relatives) who provide direct care to sick or bereaved people need support, but it is equally easy to underestimate the number and variety of *other* carers, such as supporting workers, administrators and planners, who deserve attention too. Different groups have different stresses in relation to their professional work, but everyone is likely to have domestic, financial, social or personal problems to add to work-related stress. 'AIDS' as I've said, 'is never the only thing people have to worry about', and it is the *sum total* of things that people worry about (including feelings of insecurity or inadequacy in the face of heavy demands) which can cripple effectiveness at work and at home and lead to 'burnout'.

'Burnout' is a term used to describe physical, emotional and spiritual apathy and tiredness, related to a work or life situation, which is so severe and persistent that sufferers can no longer enjoy their work or do it well. Although the term is comparatively new, the condition is not, and it should be preventable, except in the most extreme circumstances of war or natural disaster.

SUPPORT WORKERS AND PLANNERS

All direct care is supported in some way: drivers take patients to hospitals or nurses to homes, clerks register new arrivals in clinics, neighbours cook extra meals or help with laundry, and men dig graves. Men and women in supporting roles often have to talk with distressed people (for which they need training), while working long hours and sharing the stresses experienced by primary carers, though less intensely. Most carers find that they have to share the stigma attached to AIDS and that some friends disappear – because they don't want to be reminded of their risky life-styles.

People who administer or plan services for HIV-infected persons (and their families) are a hidden and forgotten group of 'carers'. Administrators appear to be shielded from direct contact with AIDS-related distress, but they have their own specific sources of stress. They are summoned to 'urgent' but unplanned meetings at short notice and expected to provide reports and budgets on time – though clerks and secretaries are often absent attending relatives' funerals. Even senior managers may be anxious about their jobs, because they are seconded to their present posts. Very often administrators have to choose between the conflicting priorities and pressures of Government Ministers, civil servants, UN agencies' representatives and donors of much-needed funds – all pursuing their own agendas and expecting instant action. Moreover, administrators' understanding of the large and complex consequences of AIDS contrasts painfully with the smallness of the projects they manage: it is easy to feel defeated and hopeless. The advice to 'Think globally and act locally' is sound, but difficult to live with.

STRESS AND DISTRESS

Challenge and difficulty are normal parts of human life and the right amount of challenge stimulates a healthy person to an enjoyable peak of performance. Stress becomes *dis*tress when the total load exceeds the capacity-to-cope of a particular carer, or touches a vulnerable part of their personality, such as a wound or need, which is hidden from consciousness. Because AIDS concerns sexuality and death, fundamental 'facts of life' with which few people are wholly comfortable, and because carers are surrounded by young people of their own age who are dying, distress is inevitable and should be anticipated in planning.

Distress is communicated through physical symptoms, feelings and behaviour, and may be expressed away from the situation which is provoking it, as well as in the workplace.

Story: A *doctor* who had worked for some years with HIV-infected people lost her dog in a road accident. She was puzzled by the intensity of her grief, which seemed out of proportion to her loss – until she recognized that she was actually mourning for patients who had died, because her 'professional' expectations of herself had denied her the right to mourn naturally at the proper time. Conversely, several years later, the same doctor heard that a woman she had known for a long time and whose marriage she had attended as a friend, had died – but on this occasion she felt nothing and was unable to mourn until she had a long period away from caring for HIV-infected people, which allowed her emotional numbness to heal.

Physical symptoms of distress include tiredness, often made worse by poor sleep; loss of appetite and weight, sometimes alternating with a craving for food; anxiety out of proportion to its apparent causes, and digestive upsets and skin rashes. Sometimes symptoms mimic those which are common amongst sick people the carer sees often.

Sadness and discouragement are easy to understand, but anger may not be recognized, yet anger causes muscle tension (leading to neck or back pain and headache) and overproduction of stomach acid (leading to pain from ulcers) as well as setting the stage for outbursts of wrath. Behaviour alters in ways which may puzzle the carers and their families and colleagues, because the changes seem irrational. Basic characteristics are intensified as control over them is relaxed: a man who tends to overwork becomes incapable of allowing himself (or anyone else!) to rest; a short-tempered woman shouts at her husband or children and later at colleagues – in response to trivial upsets. Even calm people may react to small frustrations with outbursts of anger which frighten everyone. At home a man may drink too much, neglect his family, and lose interest in his hobbies. A woman may be careless over her household duties and her appearance, and the relationships of parents to their children become strained.

At work distressed people arrive late, and go home too early or too late. They put off doing necessary but unwelcome tasks, while wasting time on unimportant details, partly because making decisions is difficult; they lack energy and initiative, make careless mistakes (which may be dangerous if they involve drug dosages or decisions about patient-management) and become difficult to work with. Distressed workers seem too busy to be disturbed and create an atmosphere of anxiety or restlessness in the workplace. Often they find fault with other people's actions or opinions repeatedly, yet seem unaware of defects in their own performance; they are helpless (and unwilling to accept help), hopeless and unable to find enjoyment in either achievement or leisure.

Many of these signs are also signs of pathological depression, which may have physical and physiological causes (such as giving birth or the menopause), as well as being a common response to repeated but unaccepted losses, or to unrecognized anger. Both loss and anger are present in the lives of carers for HIV-infected people and will worsen any physical or learned predisposition to depression.

Distress may lead to misuse of alcohol or drugs, precipitate latent mental illness or lead to compulsive behaviour, including sexual infidelity. Very often, though distress begins with one individual, it quickly spreads to involve family, workmates and friends.

SELECTING CARERS

It may seem that relatives have no choice in the matter, but most families have greater resources for caring than they recognize at first. A family conference may decide that the obvious 'primary carer' is not the only possible choice, and that the tasks (and satisfactions) could be shared between two or three people.

In the case of professional carers or community volunteers, deliberate and careful discernment is needed to match individual gifts and skills, or strengths and weaknesses, to the needs of families. Physical health and stamina are useful – yet many HIV-infected men and women care for relatives or friends, or do professional work success-fully. Reliability is an essential quality, and also endurance, or the capacity to go on and on when discouraged or tired.

Most human beings act from a mixture of selfish and unselfish motives, but it is wise to examine the motives of professionals and volunteers to identify people who are excessively 'needy' themselves, especially if they appear unaware of their own emptiness. A history of mental illness (particularly depression), alcohol abuse or current marriage problems would be good reasons for rejecting a professional applicant for paid work, but might not make a volunteer unsuitable for carefully chosen tasks.

PREVENTING 'BURNOUT': TEAMWORK

What helps professional carers or volunteers to go on working with HIV-affected families for months or years, without strain and with a sense of satisfaction?

HIV-infected or not, all carers need time to *rest* and eat in the middle of the day, duty hours which allow them to plan time with their families, and regular breaks from demanding day-to day routines. Someone who is detached from routines (a teamleader or person working in a similar field) should keep a watchful eye on carers, with gentle reminders that looking after one's own health is not self-indulgence, but good sense: it is a way of loving oneself for God and humbly accepting the 'bodily-ness' of being human.

Good *training for skilled tasks* is the basis for confidence and for the unhurried speed and competence which should develop with experience. Counselling and management are not tasks which anyone of good will can do, but work needing professional skills which must be learned. There is a place for untrained amateurs to 'do their best' in urgent situations, but the AIDS pandemic is not a short-term emergency and it is right to have sufficient and focused training, followed by a refresher course every year or so. *Regular contacts with peers and supervisors* help people to remain self-critical enough to maintain good standards, without needing constant directions from leaders.

AIDS-related work is not for hermits or unsociable people. It is best done by groups of friends who enjoy each other's company and care about each other's welfare. Such teams grow rather than happen accidentally, and their growth can be nurtured by good leadership and planning. Recruitment can be done informally as well as formally, by inviting suitable people who are interested in the work to join the team for a few weeks as part-time volunteers. Those who fit in well ask to continue (often at considerable personal cost) and those who do not, go away.

Good morale has many ingredients, but mutual respect and knowledge of each other as persons (not just workers) are both essential. It takes time, which is not structured by tasks waiting to be done, to achieve this level of mutual knowledge, so it is useful, especially in the early days of team-growing, for members to meet socially, away from their work, with their partners and children, for example at a barbecue or a birthday party.

Training courses and conferences, at home or abroad, help team members to know and like each other, so it is not extravagance, but good sense, to locate these events in pleasant places and to arrange some recreation – a boat trip on a lake or a visit to a game park. Play, too, is a vital part of human living.

Consultations and conferences also allow space for personal growth and provide variety of place and occupation. These are less obvious human needs (often dismissed as luxuries) but both contribute to growth of teams and reduce stress by setting daily work in a larger context.

Story: A *surgeon* headed a busy department in an African medical school for several years. Every three months a professional association of surgeons met in a country town, miles from any capital city, to discuss surgery and medical education. There was always time to relax and to exchange 'big fish' stories of civil wars, air raids, failed coups, food shortages and burglaries. The surgeon never failed to return home refreshed by the knowledge that other people were coping with problems far worse than his!

It is a healthy instinct which leads to self-mocking laughter and irreverent humour. Doctors exchange bawdy stories about sex and death; clergy exchange stories about disasters at funerals. Both groups are acknowledging, in their own ways, that we cannot understand or control the mysteries of our origins and destiny. Kindly humour humbly admits that we are created beings with bodies and that we are not self-sufficient – good preparations for turning to God.

CONFLICT

A group which never experiences conflict is either dead or hiding from its humanity and its vocation. The communities described in the Acts of the Apostles, and the Churches to which Paul wrote, drew thousands of men and women to hazardous belief in the Lordship of Christ, so they were undoubtedly lively and attractive groups of people. But they were also quarrelsome, divided on matters of principle (must believers be made Jews by circumcision before they can share in the new covenant?) and matters of practice. Some believers committed incest or adultery, others were scornful of the poor or of foreigners, and many communities were split into factions by enthusiastic support for popular heroes ('I belong to Paul'; 'I belong to Cephas'. 1 Cor. 1.12). Such conflicts must have caused anger and bitterness for those involved, and Paul's anguish is plain as he responded in letters to the pastoral problems of his sons in the Lord.

But the Church survived and grew. These conflicts drew out from Paul not only sharp reproofs and instructions for dealing with wrong-doers, but also profound explorations of the love of God shown to us in Christ and the implications of incorporation into Christ by baptism. Conflicts over Christology and the doctrine of the Trinity in the second to fifth centuries had a similarly fruitful outcome: a far richer under-standing of the nature of God and of human beings, and a deeper knowledge of God's concern with creation. In our own day controversy over the ordination of women to priesthood is leading to new under-standings of priesthood and diaconate and the way all relationships reflect the community of the Trinity.

So the first response to conflict in a group ought to be a hopeful return to theological principles, not trying to evade pain but acknow-ledging anger and disagreement, while holding to belief that we are all members of the body of Christ. What might this mean, in practical terms?

1. First: to find out whether the conflict actually arises in the group, rather than outside it. Some clashes happen because one person is overtired and worried for external reasons: unexpected expenses, a sick child or a quarrel with a spouse. Informal weekly meetings to discuss day-to-day work give leaders (who are concerned with policies rather than with detail) the chance to know team members well enough to notice changes in mood or behaviour which give clues to external disturbances, so that a tactful, private enquiry can be made and (perhaps) help given.

2. Next, to encourage communication while discouraging judge-mental statements which widen divisions. Many conflicts arise from a failure to check that presuppositions or priorities which seem obvious to some members of a group are shared, in fact not theory, by the rest. Often presuppositions are unrecognized or unexamined, and priorities may not have been agreed within the group, or passed on clearly to newcomers. Communication between NGOs may be faulty, especially if several groups are 'competing' (for clients or services) or possessive about what they see as 'their' territory. Clear communication in an atmosphere of respect and willingness to listen is part of living as one body in Christ, and courtesy is as much a part of the character of God as holiness.

3. In dealing with conflict it is better to make subjective statements

about one's *own* reactions accompanied by an objective statement about a change in behaviour or procedure which the speaker would welcome, instead of making an accusation beginning with the word 'You...'. For example, a worker who constantly leaves a shared office littered with her personal belongings may be resentful and unwilling to reform if she is told: 'You are so untidy *you* make me angry!'. She is more likely to change her behaviour if her co-worker says: 'When I find your things on the floor *I* feel resentful because I have to tidy up before I can start work. Would you use this shelf which I have cleared for you?' Then the other person's actions, but not her identity, are challenged, and a change in behaviour which might be mutually acceptable is suggested.

4. It is useful to distinguish between differences of principle or practice (expressed in different ways of working) and clashes of personality as causes of conflict. Differences of principle are potentially materials for growth in understanding, while personality clashes can lead to personal and community growth.

Differences of principle need to be set in a large enough context, which may require biblical study, re-examination of Christian and cultural traditions (expressed in creeds and rituals), but also analysis of the social situation, in this case the facts about AIDS. Because principles are not always consciously recognized, even though they influence practice, examination of what we actually *do* in meetings, in worship, at meals and in taken-for-granted daily behaviour may illuminate our understanding of faith – and also the reasons for conflict.

5. Some personal clashes are due to one individual's need to dominate and his (or her) wrong assumption that there is only one way of achieving agreed objectives: his way. On other occasions, one team member's behaviour irritates another person because it stirs unconscious memories of an over-critical parent or a harsh teacher. Strong feelings that 'I am superior – or inferior – to the rest of you' disturb a group, and so can rigid systems of thought or feeling in respect of sexuality or death (usually adopted long ago as a defence against harsh experience). Major conflict may require that one or two people withdraw from a team for a time, or even permanently, perhaps by transfer to different work, but sometimes growth towards maturity can be helped forward by counselling or psychotherapy. Minor clashes should be ridden out as couples ride out the small storms of marriage: with humour, patience, and willingness to see a different point of view.

6. No-one should expect a work-group to be a solitary resource for support in coping with multiple losses. Team members should be encouraged to belong to other communities too: isolation from the natural richness of human life is a constant risk for both HIV-infected and affected people.

SUPPORT GROUPS, PEOPLE AND PLACES

This phrase stirs pictures of an earnest collection of men and women meeting once a week for a formal survey of the problems which are bound to have arisen in their work! Some groups are like this caricature-description, and they do more harm than good. Real support comes from shared experience, whether of work, play, prayer or silence. Teams need time for laughter, *and* time for tears, when anger and exhaustion can be acknowledged and expressed.

Formal support groups do have their uses, especially soon after AIDS first appears in a country, when stigma is greatest and informal support is most difficult to find. Later on, as people normally find their sense of identity through membership of several overlapping communities, carers, too, ought to receive and give support in many small communities: families of origin or descent, Church, friends, workingplace, social club, or political party. Such groups vary greatly from culture to culture in their importance and strengths, and in their capacity to give support. In North America and Europe, for example, men with a homosexual orientation have a strong and public sense of group identity, which has been consolidated by the crisis of AIDS. In contrast, men who have sex with men in India or Africa tend to be isolated and unable to acknowledge their sexuality, so it is much more difficult for them to find help if they become HIV-infected.

Everywhere in the world support from their own family of origin becomes more and more important to HIV-infected persons as death approaches, however estranged families may have been in the past. For carers, however, support of indefinite duration cannot come from family alone. This is especially true for relatives of an HIV-infected person, who may themselves be HIV-infected and who foresee, quite realistically, that there will be not one death in the family but many. The needs of distressed families are likely to overstretch the capacity for compassion of conventional Church congregations which are not true communities, though small (or 'basic') Christian Communities (SCC) appear to be less limited in their living-out of the gospel, capable (so far) of enabling families and even districts to live more creatively with AIDS, and allowing their HIV-infected members to give and receive love. But SCCs, too, have limitations, and we consider their lives in more detail in ch. 15.

Support between carers and HIV-infected people is not a one-way exchange: professional carers can and do receive care from their clients, if they are willing to recognize and accept it.

Stories: A *man with AIDS* developed an acute blood cancer. *Peter*, his doctor, explained that this cancer could be treated, though the benefits would be temporary and the side-effects of drugs might be severe. Peter told his patient that, without treatment, he would die in about three weeks, and asked him to decide whether or not he wanted to receive drugs. The man returned later to say that he had decided against treatment; as he spoke he saw the expression of sadness on his doctor's face: 'Peter', he said gently, 'it's not the end of the world!'

Another doctor heard of the death of his own father early one morning and made arrangements to go to his home overseas for the funeral: later in the day he worked in an AIDS clinic, as usual. Throughout the afternoon first one patient, and then another, quietly offered sympathy; the doctor was greatly comforted by this reciprocity of caring.

DETACHMENT OR INVOLVEMENT?

In the Western medical world, until about 30 years ago, relational bonds between patient and doctor were thought to lessen the efficiency of care. This attitude shaped professional behaviour, emphasizing detachment and objectivity at the expense of humanity. At the time few doctors or nurses questioned this authoritarian model of care. Emotions felt by either patient or carer were ignored as though they did not exist, and (at least for carers!) feelings were not *expected* to exist.

Traditional healers in developing countries usually recognize an affective element in human dis-ease, but they, too, work within an authoritarian model of care. Their understanding of the causes of disease emphasizes ill-will (conscious or unconscious) on the part of someone, who is ultimately responsible for the fact that death or misfortune attacks a particular person at a particular point in time, even though other causes, such as an infection or an overloaded truck, are recognized as contributory factors. In either authoritarian model the relationship between carer and cared-for is limited: one person is regarded as 'strong', while the other is thought of as 'weak'. In both traditional systems vulnerability on the part of the carer is seen as dangerous, so emotional detachment is prescribed.

In the West a paternalistic model of care began to be questioned about 25 years ago. Well-educated patients challenged their doctors' decisions, women recognized that they were being treated as second-class citizens, and psychotherapy began to uncover the ill-effects of neglecting human dignity and autonomy. AIDS has accelerated a process of change which had already begun.

In developing and developed nations, the first men and women to contract AIDS were educated and articulate. They questioned practitioners in the medical systems they encountered, and a few professional carers, distressed by the failure of their attempts to help, dropped their defensive detachment and admitted helplessness. An important sign of willingness to be vulnerable was greater use of first names by members of caring teams, who later allowed patients to call doctors and nurses by their first names, too. Patients began to be invited to take part in making decisions about their own treatment. When one London doctor tells a new patient that he is HIV-infected, he holds out his hand to the patient saying: 'Join the team!' Authority and detachment remain necessary, but neither need exclude admission of common humanity, especially when carers are Christians, committed to the view that every human being has equal value as a son or daughter of God.

APPROPRIATE GOALS

A good deal of distress for HIV-affected people and carers results from inappropriate goals or expectations. A man struggling with the news that he is HIV-infected is preoccupied by the short duration of his remaining life and cannot (yet) shift his attention to its quality. When his family learn the news, they, too, need to find realistic goals. A doctor is trained to interpret death as 'failure' and has to consciously shift from a goal of 'cure' to a new goal – to prolong comfortable and active life and then enable his patient to die with dignity, when the time is right. At different stages in the journey of HIV infection different goals are appropriate, taking account of individual vocations. Final responsibility for the choice of a particular path rests with the person who will walk that path, but discernment of vocation may need help from many other people.

SUMMARY: MATURE INTERDEPENDENCE

AIDS is producing millions of sick people who need care and millions of orphaned children and old people who need support. Corresponding armies of 'carers' are forming, and their numbers, too, will grow. Both cared-for and carers share basic needs for food, rest, shelter and safety. Similarly everyone needs respect and self-respect, dignity, love, and the satisfaction of belonging to a human community.

'What is man that you are mindful of him?' asks the psalmist. When emphasis is given to 'mind', the phrase suggests that God is mindful of humankind in the casual sense of someone who has more important preoccupations. An alternative emphasis on 'mind-*full*' conveys a very different picture of God caring for humankind with delighted and undivided attention. Caring for carers should start from and mirror *this* perception of God's care.

There are no short-cuts to mature interdependence, which requires focused training (initial and continuing) for skilled tasks and disciplined attention to the organization of practical detail. No-one is indispensable and teamwork is essential, with 'shadowing' of key roles, delegation of some responsibilities, and willingness to value the complementary skills of men and women. Goals and expectations, for self and others, ought to be realistic. The humility to face one's own frailty, and to respect and tolerate the frailties of other people, ought to lead to a trust in God which is not an escape from responsibility, but an acceptance of creaturehood. Paul told the Colossians: 'You are all one person': in respect of AIDS we are indeed one person.

Study Suggestions For Individuals

1. Recall occasions when you suffered distress (for example bereavement, anxiety over money, theft of property, illness). What *physical* effects did you experience? What *feelings* do you remember? What actions or comments from other people helped you? Were any responses so unhelpful that you still remember them with distaste?

2. Using your answer to question 1, can you recognize areas in your own life where you are 'strong' or 'weak'? Have you discussed these strengths and weaknesses with a spiritual director or pastor?

3. List simple actions you could take to help yourself to cope with distress related to pressure of work, or sadness due to the death of a brother or sister. Talk over your answer to this question with your spouse or a close friend.

For Groups

4. Collect passages from Gospels or Epistles which give advice on recognizing and living with conflict. Discuss the application of these passages to any episode of conflict which has troubled your group in the last six months.

CHAPTER 13

Love Carefully – or Love Faithfully?

We have all experienced the fact that altered circumstances or changing values and priorities lead to spontaneous changes in the ways people behave. Children starting school behave in new ways appropriate to their new environment; moving to a new town requires new routines for doing a new job and for living alongside new neighbours. Adaptation to change is a sign of biological life and unavoidable until our last breath.

Some changes in outlook and behaviour are more dramatic than others: *metanoia* is the term used in the New Testament to describe a change of mind or purpose which results in a redirection of the whole personality towards God, and a profound alteration in behaviour. Repentance has a similar meaning to metanoia, but tends to focus on sorrow for past attitudes and behaviour, rather than on a continuing transformation of life and being in the person who turns.

In the context of AIDS, the term 'behaviour change' has two specific meanings. First (and most often) 'behaviour change' refers to changes in patterns of sexual conduct or intravenous drug use, which are adopted in order to slow or prevent spread of HIV. Second, the term is related to attempts to change attitudes towards HIV-infected or affected people, away from fear and rejection and towards respect and acceptance. Is 'behaviour change', in such limited senses, related to 'metanoia', as used in the New Testament?

This chapter concentrates on changing sexual behaviour to avoid HIV infection, even though knowledge of actual sexual conduct in developing countries is incomplete and anecdotal. What is certain is that present-day sexual behaviour has passed HIV from person to person so rapidly that infection rates have risen from less than 1% in urban adults at the beginning of the 1980s, to 25% to 36% 15 years later.

The objective for changes in behaviour to halt transmission of HIV can be defined precisely: it is necessary to prevent sexual exchange of body fluids between infected and uninfected persons. There are several ways of achieving this objective – with varying degrees of certainty – for example, total sexual abstinence or total fidelity to one uninfected partner (both safe choices), or efficient use of a new condom and a virus-killing lubricant for every sexual act which involves penetration of a body orifice (a slightly less safe choice). The definition may be simple, but the behaviour changes required are not; sexual conduct takes place in the context of social behaviour of other kinds, and it is influenced by many physical, emotional, social and spiritual factors. Around 1986 frightened health educators, in some African countries, plunged into the urgent task of telling whole populations how to avoid infection with HIV – undismayed by their ignorance of what people do together and why they choose to behave in some ways and not others. In their haste, educators forgot that fear is a poor motivating force, so most early campaigns were based on fear, using pictures of hawks labelled 'AIDS' swooping to carry away their victims, or vivid drawings of those victims in terminal illness. Learning through doing in urgent circumstances produces a steep learning curve, but it also leads to many mistakes; most early attempts to educate for prevention were probably counterproductive.

At first it was innocently assumed that once everyone 'knew' how HIV is transmitted and how to avoid infection, then appropriate changes in behaviour would automatically follow. But behaviour is determined by a great deal more than head-knowledge, and hope for positive gain is a far more effective motive for change than avoidance of danger, especially when the danger seems uncertain ('it won't happen to me!'), cannot be imagined because it has never happened before, and is not likely to happen at all for several years.

Translating factual knowledge about HIV transmission into appropriate sexual behaviour requires several stages:

1. Potential listeners must be attracted and persuaded that AIDS is indeed *their* problem.

2. Sexual behaviour has to be viewed objectively, which needs permission from society and willingness on the part of individuals to think and talk about sex, not just to do it or dream dreams about it: both sides of the brain, the left half concerned with reason and analysis, and the right side concerned with synthesis and fantasy, must learn to communicate, both in individual persons and in society.

3. But talk about sex needs a *vocabulary* of words which are clear, yet not offensive to most people in the society; while finding such words it should be possible to learn more about what men and women actually do together, and why they choose to behave in particular ways.

4. Next, we need to think and talk about alternative ways of behaving, to open up unexamined stereotypes about what is 'normal' or pleasurable, and to ask: *'are* there other ways?' Popular ideas about what constitutes normal sexual behaviour, and traditional understandings of what makes a person a person underlie gender roles, and may need to be challenged.

5. And from the start, thought must be given to preparing a community environment in which altered behaviour is possible and can be sustained indefinitely. Poverty, the status of women, unemployment,

leisure facilities (or their absence), standards of housing and of health care have a direct or indirect influence on whether a given society is, or can become, a place where sexual behaviours *could* change, not just in the short term, but for generations to come. An atmosphere of mutual trust and responsibility is indispensable as a basis for such radical change.

6. Finally, something has to happen. People have to decide why and how to change their behaviour (*decision*), actually do it (*action*), see what effects follow (*evaluation*), and decide whether or not they can or will continue in new patterns of conduct (*maintenance*). Later, successful communities may decide whether or not to try to persuade others to follow their examples (*propagation*).

EXAMINING SEXUAL BEHAVIOUR

Let us start with a provisional definition of sexual behaviour: it is any interaction between persons (usually but not always limited to two) which expresses sexual interest or desire between them, even though the interest may be confined to one partner, while the other feels disinterest or even repulsion. Sexual behaviour is not limited to genital acts, for sexuality is such a basic part of every person that it colours all social encounters, even those which do not have an overtly erotic content.

Sexual behaviour is strongly influenced by the culture in which it occurs, and constitutes a language, or system of signs with specific meanings. These meanings may be culturally specific too, which is a hazard for travellers who do not know the sexual or asexual body 'language' of a country they are visiting. For example, uninstructed visitors from Europe, seeing two Zambian men hand-in-hand, tend to assume that they are homosexual lovers, not knowing that a hand-clasp is an expression of friendship between men in Zambian society that has no erotic significance. Interpretation of sexual signs may have a strong personal bias, too, when a man or woman misreads a social gesture as a sexual advance, or vice versa, in accordance with their own desires or fears.

In order to identify behaviours which risk transmitting HIV, it is necessary to know what people do, with whom, how often, when and where (at what age, in which external circumstances) – and what motivates them to behave as they do. What is the background to sexual behaviour, and what functions does it fulfil, besides the obvious functions of procreation and providing sexual pleasure? Earlier three hidden functions were mentioned: Sexual behaviour helps to establish personal identity, it allows powerless people to exercise power over others, and sex is something to do when life is boring, to give meaning to an otherwise meaningless existence.

Sexual behaviour is skilled, learned behaviour that is maintained by sexual appetite, social expectations and habit. Sexual appetite is influenced by health and tiredness, hormone levels and their fluctuations in women, by the presence of erotic stimuli in the social environment, and by mysterious forces of attraction between men and women which probably have chemical, mental and spiritual components. The interplay of some or all of these factors does, or does not, lead to a state of sexual arousal. Whether or not sexual appetite results in arousal and genital activity depends on further influences: opportunity, the potential partners' value systems and their community's expectations.

To a greater extent than many people wish to admit, translation of appetite into activity depends on the physiological state of a man or woman's brain. If judgement is altered by alcohol or drugs or semi-darkness, and conditioned by loud pulsating music or flickering lights (reminders of the rhythm of orgasm), then sexual appetite more easily leads on to actions which may actually contradict a person's chosen value system. Once a real frontier of intact and chosen values has been crossed for the first time, it becomes easier for personal values to be contradicted again, next time they are challenged by circumstances. It is well-said that the brain is the primary sexual organ in human beings.

Sexual expectations are formed through learning, peer influence, cultural norms and opportunities successfully taken, and may be influenced by a need to compensate for inadequacy in another area of life. For example, sexual activity is a common escape from academic or social 'failure', especially for women, and it is a way of taking risks at adolescence, when risk-taking is an important part of making the transition from childhood to adult life. If less dangerous yet socially accepted rites of passage are available, adolescents may not need to take chances with HIV infection or pregnancy. Conversely, AIDS prevention messages which emphasize 'risk' may have exactly the opposite effect from that intended by health educators, by showing people who intend to take risks anyway how to do so enjoyably.

Everywhere in the world, especially in developing countries, cultural norms bias the sexual expectations of men and women rather differently. Most societies expect men to take the initiative, make sexual decisions and have more than one partner. In contrast, most societies expect women to be submissive and do not give them the opportunity or permission to say 'no' to unwanted sexual advances. Skills and habits for both sexes are formed within this framework and much unlearning is necessary if the framework is questioned or changed.

Behaviour and understandings of sexuality in a community can be examined by talking to people individually or in small 'focus groups' of persons who are similar in some relevant way – through age, sex, marital status or religious faith. Interviewers are best chosen from the community to be studied, but need training to use appropriate study materials ('instruments') – which might be pre-tested sets of open-ended questions, topics for group discussions, or outline pictures of the human body for men or women to talk about, while drawing-in their own perceptions of body parts and functions. Drama is useful to stimulate interest and to focus attention on the questions to be asked.

Two Ugandan studies published in 1992 used these methods in a rural area. Words and concepts which investigators had predicted would be culturally forbidden, were readily and positively used by the people interviewed. Outline drawings helped to uncover perceptions of reproductive processes and the body which differed radically from scientific ideas, sometimes explaining the reasons for sexual taboos or resistance to using condoms. Men and women were willing to talk about sex done for pleasure as well as for procreation, and to admit that there are many obstacles to behaviour change through education – some people even suggested new laws and punishments to *force* people to change their sexual behaviour!

OBSTACLES TO CHANGE

The first obstacle to change identified by rural Ugandans was alcohol, partly because people who are drunk forget what they have learnt about AIDS, but also because brewing and selling beer is women's work and often a simultaneous offer of sex is expected. 'You can't be a beer seller and have men fear you . . . as a beer seller you will not refuse them, even if you are married' (a 60-year-old widow). Many Zambians would agree, and in most areas of high-density housing around Lusaka (and other African cities) the only places of recreation are 'bars' – there *are* no other entertainments, much to the distress of thoughtful wives and mothers.

Some Ugandan parents admitted that they do not uphold traditional values in their homes, and fail to discipline their children. 'We parents have failed in our role . . . a child who goes and spends a whole night at a disco is not punished.' The introduction of discos, and all-night wedding or – more commonly in these days – funeral parties, were blamed as occasions for young people to engage in 'careless' sex.

Older people lamented the loss of cultural values which once controlled behaviour but which are no longer taught to children. Behind the helplessness of such statements lie unanswered questions about parents' own conduct: one investigator suggested another question: 'Do you want your kids to behave (sexually) as you do?' He added: 'This question could be a very powerful health education message to parents.'

The importance of peer-group pressures was obvious to most people, but they expected it to have negative effects: 'Peer groups have a bad influence, especially for girls who have been trying to keep their dignity; when they come into contact with girls who have got material gains for their behaviour, then they also fall', and: 'Youths have resisted change in their sexual behaviour because they still have an interest in moving with their friends'. But peer pressure can also operate in the reverse direction, to induce and support safe sexual behaviours; an example of deliberate use of peer pressure to this end is described later.

'Human nature' was regarded as an important obstacle to change. Many people believe in a fatalistic way that it is 'men's nature' to have multiple sexual partners, and that this fact about men drives women 'to seek comfort from another man from the village' if their husbands are travelling, when they will inevitably (it seems) acquire 'in-mates'. An important additional pressure on very young men is their perceived need to practise an essential adult skill, on which a large part of their self-worth is based. In contrast, the skills needed to make and sustain personal relationships strong enough to survive twenty years of raising children are not even considered, so there can be no perceived need to consciously practise them!

An important reason why women may not give up risky behaviour, and why both sexes dislike condoms, is the strong desire to have children. This desire is actually fuelled by the AIDS pandemic, because the prospect of dying without offspring is so real and dreadful to young people who watch their age-mates die. A 21-year-old woman, separated from her husband, said: 'I have never had a child, yet this disease is taking many friends. How can I die without ever having produced?' An older woman said: 'Some fear not having a grandchild for memory, so she gives herself up for birth'. But this longing for children, like peer-group pressure, can be turned round (at least in principle) to encourage *safer* sexual behaviours, but only if men and women can hope that change in behaviour will indeed protect them from HIV infection. Some people believe, however, that HIV is already so common in their communities that no escape from infection is possible, even if behaviour does alter. In these perceived circumstances there is no incentive to change. It cannot be emphasized too strongly that men and women do not alter established and valued behaviours unless they are convinced that their efforts will be rewarded by real benefits for themselves and for their families.

ECONOMIC PRESSURES

Strong economic obstacles to changing present patterns of sexual behaviour were recognized, with resignation or despair, by the people involved. Many women are poor, and therefore at risk: single girls want cash for school fees or for the small luxuries parents cannot afford;

women who are divorced or widowed sell sex to support themselves and their children, and so do married women (without other marketable skills) who cannot feed and clothe their families with what their husbands provide. A 35-year-old married woman said: 'There are some people who do not have enough food and there is a youth who has plenty of food but no wife. So people go to him and give him sex.' Income-generating projects can break into this cycle of need, low self-esteem, greed and despair. Both men and women recognized that women's lack of power and permission to resist male sexual demands is an important barrier to change, to which are added the brutal facts of domestic violence and the traditional view of most cultures (including those of the West until recently) that husbands have the 'right' to beat their wives, just as parents have the 'right' to beat their children.

LINKING SEXUAL BEHAVIOUR TO SOCIAL LIFE

While patterns of sexual behaviour are being explored, there may be opportunities to learn how people view the consequences of different behaviours, and to provide facts about links between STDs and infertility, and early sexual activity and cancer of the neck of the womb (cervix), and to point out the increased risks to mother and child of teenage pregnancies. The records of local courts show how many domestic fights and quarrels were brought to court in the previous six months, and most people will admit that these are often due to sexual infidelity. It may be useful to point out that a fall in the number of 'cases' will be a reliable sign that sexual behaviour is changing for the better in a community. Difficult new patterns of sexual behaviour are more likely to be maintained, and to spread, if it can be shown that change is in fact happening, and if success is celebrated. The ultimate aim is to change *norms* for sexual conduct, so that safer patterns of behaviour are whole-heartedly accepted and supported by the community, becoming (in time) 'the way we live here'.

A link between broken families or quarrelling parents and children's development may be less obvious in traditional cultures, but it should be possible to draw attention to children who failed at school, or who began to steal or use drugs or abscond from home soon after a family broke up, to suggest a connection between these events.

PATTERNS OF SEXUAL BEHAVIOUR

What people do sexually, with whom, when, where and why varies from society to society. Local knowledge, gained by local enquiry, is needed as a basis for attempts to alter behaviour. Here are conjectures about sexual conduct in East and Central Africa, based on a survey of over 1,800 young people in urban and rural Tanzania, supplemented by conversations about their sexual lives with hundreds of adults in Lusaka during the 1980s.

By age 12 almost 15% of boys and 5% of girls in Tanzania have had coitus at least once; thereafter sexual activity increases with increasing age until by age 24 years 85% of men and 91% of women are sexually experienced. Amongst secondary school students the mean age at first intercourse was 14.8 years for boys and 15.9 years for girls. Accurate knowledge of when conception is most likely to occur (mid-cycle) and of contraceptive methods was rare, although induced abortions were common (especially in towns); 75% of pregnancies in women of 20 years and younger were unwanted.

Conversations with adults suggest that some women, but very few men, are still virgins when they begin their first intentionally-permanent sexual partnership. Young people usually have two or three exploratory relationships, which include sexual intercourse, before starting a long-term partnership and having children. If a marriage breaks down both partners usually move on to new relationships quickly, and women may have no alternative if they have children to support.

Within apparently stable marriages which have lasted several years it is common for the man to have one or two regular extra-marital partners, for whom he appears to feel affection and some responsibility. In addition to these regular girl-friends, he may from time to time take casual sexual partners, especially when travelling on business and under perceived pressure from his male friends to 'be a real man' (see, for example, the Federation of Ugandan Employers' comic called 'Ekanya's Guide to Safer Sex' for an account of an urban male's adventures, from his own, not his wife's, perspective). By the age of 30 it is more common than not for most men and many women to admit to five or six different partners since sexual activity started.

A smaller proportion of the population, perhaps 10%, admit to 30 or more lifetime partners, and some men say simply: 'too many to count!' However, few adults admitted to an intermediate number of partners – say ten or 15 – suggesting that there is a qualitative difference between the sexual needs or expectations of the majority of men and women, and those of the most sexually active ('movious') citizens. Clearly the risk of contacting HIV is greatest amongst people with the highest numbers of partners, but these high-risk persons may be included in the casual sexual circles of men and women with far fewer partners, offering a chance for HIV to spread.

The risk of contacting HIV in a second partner whose background is unknown varies with the prevalence of HIV in a society: in Lusaka, for example, the risk was probably less than 1 in 100 in 1981, whereas the risk had risen to one in three in the same city by 1995. When sex is purchased from a casual female partner the risk leaps: four out of five commercial encounters are likely to be with an HIV-infected woman. A similar increase in risk applies to people who have attended a clinic for sexually transmitted diseases in the last year or two, for about half of them are HIV-infected.

ALTERNATIVE SEXUAL CONDUCT

Talk about actual behaviour can lead naturally into talk about alternative ways of behaving, but only when the community definition of what constitutes 'sexual behaviour' enlarges. In Uganda, and probably in other places, men and women generally think that only 'pouring the sperms into the woman' is true sex, and that this release is essential for the physical and emotional health of both partners. In one area of Uganda, for example, it is thought that sperm are produced in a man's brain and pass down his spinal cord to the penis, so that, if sperm are not released regularly, pressure will build up, leading to backache and headache. A similar theory exists for the production of vaginal fluid in women's spines, and that fluid, too, requires regular release through coitus. It is believed that only intravaginal sex provides the appropriate action for the 'real' and healthy release of these pressures for both men and women. Further exploration of such ideas might lead back to unconscious fears of madness or paralysis as a likely consequence of sexual abstinence or blocking the possibility of conception: such fears may contribute to a widespread reluctance to use condoms. No discussion of alternative ways of expressing sexual desire and delight will be pursued seriously until misinformation about sexuality is understood and, as far as possible, corrected.

SEXUAL DESIRE

We thus need to recognize and respect the very wide range of meanings that men and women already give to sexual activity, before different perceptions are offered as a possible basis for change. Sexual desire is not limited to procreation and release of physical tension, but includes a longing for 'singleness of being' with a perfect 'other'. No man or woman is capable of satisfying that longing and restless searching for an ideal sexual partner is doomed to be frustrated – until the searcher encounters the Other for whose sake desire exists.

'Life is for love, and time is only for finding God', said Bernard of Clairvaux. Mary of Egypt, Augustine of Hippo, Charles de Foucauld and many other 'sinners and harlots' turned from disordered sexual lives to creative given-ness to God. It is perverse to dissociate their previous searching and sexual promiscuity from the intensity of their later love for and abandonment to God. Metanoia takes *all* the valid and natural energies of human beings and directs them to their true end in God; it validates the sexual and more-than-sexual desire which is intended to be satisfied, though never satiated.

ALTERNATIVE BEHAVIOURS

Three resources for change are generally available:

1. *A more accurate understanding* of the structure and function of sexual organs, so that people can discard inadequate or harmful theories about sexuality and associated unsafe sexual practices;

2. *A return to traditional conduct*, if its practice would reduce transmission of HIV;

3. *Deliberate decisions to change* a society's norms for sexual conduct.

A society which decides to change its norms for sexual behaviour might choose to:

1. Postpone the start of genital expression of sexual love, both at physical maturity and in developing relationships; the age at first coitus would rise and coitus would not be the opening move in a potential relationship (as tends to happen at present), but an important and much later turning-point in the development of long-term commitment.

2. Accept both pre-marital chastity (or sexual acts which do not involve penetration of a body orifice) *and* mutual faithfulness within marriage as 'normal' behaviour, not as 'unnatural and unrealistic', as at present.

3. Alter criteria for selecting sexual partners, giving greater emphasis to quality than quantity, with concern to find out more about a man or woman's previous way of life than is usual now, before starting a sexual relationship.

4. Make coitus a less frequent expression of sexual love, but more important when it does occur, shifting the emphasis towards increased satisfaction for both partners and restoring an element of seriousness which expresses the loving self-giving of committed persons, rather than impersonal sexual 'play'.

5. Reduce the stimuli to sexual appetite offered in daily life, by approving erotic symbols and messages in the private behaviour of lovers who are committed to each other, but restricting erotic material in films and magazines, advertising, and traditional dancing.

6. Find non-genital rituals to 'free' a widow from her dead husband's spirit and allow her to enter into a new marriage (changing the method, but not the concept of 'cleansing the widow') where this ritual is valued.

7. Restrict coitus to committed relationships or else expect every casual sexual contact to be made safer by correct use of a condom.

8. Shift the emphasis from negative preoccupation with what is

dangerous to creative interest in improving the quality of committed partnerships, by moving from the prevailing quantitative view of sex as a commodity, to a human and biblical view of sex as the loving gift of oneself to another person.

9. Adapt or restore old ceremonies to celebrate virginity, betrothal, reconciliation after a quarrel, or to mark divorce; and apply to marriage the gospel emphasis on forgiveness in order to permit remarriage when Christian marriages break down, as practised already in Eastern Orthodox Churches;

10. Give a positive status and role in society to persons who choose not to marry or who do not have children, in order to accept them as fully human and fully mature people.

PROCESSES: ATTRACTING ATTENTION, INFORMING AND MOTIVATING

A complete inventory of methods for persuading people to change their behaviour is impossible; many methods have been used successfully. In principle, messages are most likely to be effective if they start from the personal experiences and daily lives of hearers, and are given by persons from amongst 'us', with whom hearers can readily identify, especially if the messenger is an attractive role-model. Messages should also:

1. Activate hearers' secret or unconscious wishes.

2. Differ for groups with different interests and needs; for example, primary schoolchildren, mothers of teenagers, women who sell sex, street children, truck drivers, teachers and clergy – all need to be challenged, but each target group has specific needs and interests.

3. Appeal to a large group of peers, so that peer-group pressure will operate positively to support change.

4. Encourage hearers to try new behaviours for positive rewards, rather than condemning present behaviours as unsafe at a stage when change may seem impossible, and negative messages (which evoke fear) could produce despair and an actual *increase* in dangerous conduct.

Teaching strategies may be impersonal (newspaper articles, posters, radio or TV programmes) or personal, involving face-to-face encounters, in street drama, talks or counselling. Both methods can operate at conscious and unconscious levels, if appropriate symbols are used. Educators should know the range of meanings their chosen symbols may have for target groups, for sometimes symbols are used in ignorance of their explosive content, with unexpectedly negative or positive results.

Nowadays citizens in most African towns are surrounded by anti-AIDS messages of varying subtlety – on posters, news-sheets, pamphlets in doctors' waiting rooms and school classrooms, on lapel badges and stickers for cars. Most people probably soon cease to notice messages which had a useful impact when new, if messages convey fear, not hope. A cartoon poster, however, which shows several trendy young men giving their reasons for postponing sex until marriage, might make a youngster of the same age stop to think: 'Maybe I'm *not* the only man who wants to be safe for marriage and a family . . .'.

Cartoon humour which is rooted in day-to-day living is an indirect way to alter unconscious factors that influence behaviour, and so by-pass strong resistances to change. Good cartoons expose the absurdities and inconsistencies in human thinking and behaviour without giving offence – indeed, while giving enjoyment. Laughter releases tensions, heals hurts and allows people to look at beliefs and attitudes in a new light, and to let go of old ideas which are seen, quite suddenly, to be false or useless. The memory of a good joke remains as a long-term defence against reinstatement of discarded ideas. Shared laughter also makes bonds, allowing men and women to talk about subjects they might otherwise avoid, while at the same time subtly communicating support and shared values to each other. Moreover, good humour returns to mind again and again, happily and powerfully reinforcing its hidden messages, so that what might have been painful change may become not only possible, but even enjoyable.

Face-to-face meetings are more valuable than purely visual materials, like films, which allow people to think that messages offered do not apply to them personally.

Story: About a year after radio, television and newspaper education-for-prevention began in Zambia, two *doctors* talked to a group of *parents* about AIDS. At question-time their mood was angry: 'Why,' the parents demanded, 'did no-one *tell* us about this?' We referred, in self-defence, to the media campaign of the past year, but our excuses were brushed aside impatiently: 'No-one *told* us!' That afternoon we discovered that an hour or two of direct personal contact is likely to achieve far more change in knowledge and attitudes than months of radio or television programmes. We also saw that anxiety about the acceptability of sex education in schools was unfounded. We asked: 'Who else needs to know about AIDS?' They answered with a shout: 'Our children!' 'At what age should we begin to teach them?' we asked. 'At 10 years old', they replied, confirming our view that age 13 or 14 is too late.

Face-to-face methods include talks and lectures, but also drama, puppet theatre, and meetings in workplaces – and anywhere else that people congregate naturally: markets, bars, schools, sports clubs, houses where sex is for sale, social centres, and churches.

Who should do the talking? The answer is – anyone who is willing, and who knows enough about HIV transmission to answer straightforward questions accurately, preferably someone from the target group to be addressed (schoolboys, truck drivers, women who sell sex, drug users). Peer-group educators are far more persuasive teachers than strangers, but they need appropriate training, including practice in talking to each other, before they are asked to perform in public. Educators need to be able to say firmly: 'I'm sorry, I can't answer that question but you can find out by asking . . .' naming a help-line or drop-in centre where more experienced counsellors are available. If the speaker is HIV-infected and able and willing to admit that publicly, his or her message gains a hundredfold in effectiveness.

Just as humour helps to overcome embarrassment, so does a senior and confident speaker. To watch a lively and attractive woman, at a public meeting, teaching the deputy Minister of Health how to put a condom onto a banana does more to make talk about sexual behaviour acceptable in one evening than months of newspaper articles!

Drama conveys and repeats information and demands hardly any effort on the part of the audience, who lose themselves in the action and identify strongly with the characters. A good actor can concentrate and convey emotion with an impact which actual events may not achieve. I recall watching a short play about a man who picked up girls in bars, got AIDS and wasted away into terminal illness before our eyes, in an accurate representation of a story I had seen played out in my clinic week after week. But the actor's 'sufferings' on stage projected the misery of terminal illness in a way that real patients did not – just as a painting may be a better representation of the truth of a person than a photograph. Drama allows space for an identification with the 'hero' which would be too threatening in real life.

Drama is also a way to begin to discuss difficult issues, as it encourages the audience to ask themselves, almost involuntarily 'Suppose I was in his/her position, what would I feel? What would I do?' AIDS poses many questions which may not be answerable, but at least difficult questions need to be asked – as in this example:

> **Story**: *Vareka* is an attractive woman of 25 who knows she is HIV-infected. She separated from her husband and picked up a temporary boyfriend. Vareka's husband died and she went, with her two children, to live with her mother in the village, where her sisters and sisters-in-law ignore her, because they fear she will infect their own children if she so much as touches them. Vareka hopes her truck-driver will return, but also knows that other men in the village find her attractive, even though she is an AIDS widow. She is resentful of her dead husband, who was her first sexual partner, as she blames

him for infecting her with HIV. She knows, only too well, that she has no status in the community as a woman on her own. What is Vareka to do now?

'Puppets against AIDS' was founded in South Africa in 1987 as a community-based trust, to expand AIDS education by working through local organizations in vernacular languages and local slang. The puppets have huge heads, grey in colour, carried on the shoulders of performers, who are thus made visible from a distance. The formal heads with stylized features overcome racial, cultural and social barriers which might intrude if live actors' faces were seen. Each open-air performance is followed by a discussion to clarify parts of the show which audiences did not understand, and to answer questions. The group has teams of presenters who tour provinces for a few weeks at a time, holding shows in towns and villages, clinics, schools, bus parks and in the street. Workshops have been held in universities and workplaces, and the project has a documentation centre.

At present 'Puppets against AIDS' deals in 'safer sex' messages, distributes condoms and teaches the crowds how to use them, but there is no reason why larger-than-life puppets should not be used to reach audiences with a wider range of anti-AIDS and community-building messages. Puppets can also be used to stimulate discussion of difficult issues, in the some way as conventional drama.

Anti-AIDS clubs started in Zambia in 1987, when one boy who had watched close relatives die of AIDS (a strong motivating experience) asked a doctor who had given a talk about HIV in his school: 'What can we do to stop AIDS?' Dr Kristina Baker suggested he might start an anti-AIDS club. The first members chose the club promises themselves: no sex before marriage or outside marriage, teach others about HIV and AIDS, and help people who are already infected with the virus. In spite of Western criticism of the clubs' promises and methods as 'unrealistic', anti-AIDS clubs do offer an alternative peer-group pressure to youngsters who want it – and by 1992 there were over 1,000 registered clubs in Zambia, with nearly 38,000 members. Clubs have a strong support organization (helped by NGO funding) which edits and distributes a magazine, answers hundreds of letters from members each month, sells subsidized badges and T-shirts bearing anti-AIDS slogans and also a range of games (such as a modified 'snakes and ladders') to teach AIDS awareness – as well as organizing competitions and World AIDS day events.

Attitudes to casual sex *are* altering; in some circles it has become 'normal' to remain a virgin until marriage. But anti-AIDS clubs have possibilities which have hardly been used, as yet.

Clubs already offer young men and women a chance to meet

members of the opposite sex who are prepared to consider fidelity and monogamy seriously (and who are not likely to expect coitus at the start of a relationship), but the opportunity to offer more deliberate preparation for stable and satisfying marriages has not been taken. Yet young people need support during the years between physical maturity and readiness for marriage, if they are to negotiate exploratory relationships without premature sexual activity in dangerous circumstances – or equally premature parenthood. More training for work, opportunities for community service, discussions on subjects such as 'choosing a life partner', 'avoiding boredom in marriage', 'managing a home when both partners are working', 'managing a budget' or 'spacing births' could be added to senior club activities. With such help, perhaps members would have more stable marriages, and better prospects of rearing healthy families to adulthood.

A CLIMATE FOR CHANGE

No community will promote 'behaviour change' successfully until its members believe that everyone has the capacity to change his or her own behaviour. In 1991 government and NGO agencies held an informal consultation in Senegal, to discuss 'behaviour change' as a strategy for individual and community responses to AIDS. At the end 33 participating bodies drafted a statement, which was endorsed by a further 25 NGOs and national AIDS control programmes or institutions, and distributed by the United Nations Development Programme (UNDP):

Statement: We believe that individuals and whole communities have the inherent capacity to change attitudes and behaviours. The power to fulfil this capacity is often denied or is not exercised.

This power must now be recognized, called forth and supported both from within and without. This will enable people to initiate change and sustain behaviours that promote a healthy state of mind, body, spirit and environment. A critical component in this process is a supportive response to those living with HIV in the community.

We recognize that behaviour change at individual and community level in the present HIV epidemic is a complex and on-going process. It is inextricably linked to such basic human values as care, love, faith, family and friendship, respect for people and cultures, solidarity and support.

The present epidemic affects everyone. Our experience as affected and infected individuals proves that behaviour change is possible. We believe that behaviour change is the most essential strategy in over-coming the HIV epidemic.

In Senegal, delegates analysed their reasons for changing their own sexual behaviour: they learned how HIV is spread, cared for a person who is HIV-infected or discovered that they themselves were infected, or they worked for an AIDS team. Some received support from family, friends or peer groups, or found that a desire to survive, concern for other people or spiritual values helped them to start and sustain changed behaviour.

REDUCING EROTIC STIMULATION
In Zambia a doctor talked recently with 19 college students (who claimed to be Baptists), and heard that 18 of them had watched video films showing sexually explicit scenes; most of the students had felt sexually aroused as a result.

No society has yet (to my knowledge) made a serious attempt to reduce the amount of erotic stimulation to which everyone is exposed, as part of an anti-AIDS programme. Any attempt to change norms would need the co-operation of two generations with differing expec-tations and tastes (parents in their forties and young adults) and almost simultaneous campaigns at national as well as local levels – otherwise societies which want to change might be ridiculed or condemned as out of touch with normal life.

This is a challenge which most societies are still evading, but safer sexual behaviour is unlikely to be achieved and sustained, on a wide enough scale to halt the spread of HIV, until erotic stimulation ceases to be a public phenomenon, and is restored to its proper role – as a private preliminary to love-making between partners who are com-mitted to each other as whole (not just sexual) persons.

New behaviours and new standards need new skills, which have to be learned, and everyone has to learn how to enjoy themselves without the traditional supports of too much alcohol or too much sex.

No-one should be asked to attempt new behaviours which are not openly endorsed as good by society, for few people want to be different from their neighbours, except in limited and stereotyped ways.

Each society should decide for itself which sexual behaviours must change and what the new standards for acceptable behaviour will be, how change will be measured, and who will evaluate the extent of change and the consequences for social life. Signs of favourable change identified by the Senegal consultation were: more sex-education in schools based on the values of family life, bride-price reduced to make it easier for men and women to marry, earlier marriages, fewer assault or adultery cases in the local courts, communities no longer condoning travel for sex, fewer pregnant schoolgirls, and men and women drinking separately rather than together.

Indicators that attitudes towards HIV-infected people have changed were also identified: growth of community support organizations, increasing numbers of counsellors or peer educators trained, HIV-infected persons serving on local AIDS committees or willing to tell their stories, more families willing to care for infected members at home, concern and respect for people living with AIDS shown in the community, numbers of visitors to affected households, care given to surviving elderly parents or children, and numbers of funerals at which it is said openly that the death was due to AIDS. These two sets of 'indicators of change' might provide an initial agenda-for-action for Church and community groups.

'BEHAVIOUR CHANGE' AND METANOIA

What, if anything, does behaviour change in the narrow field of sexual conduct have to do with ideas expressed by the term 'metanoia'? A surprising amount of common ground may exist. If belief and behaviour are interconnected, so that sustained alteration in either tends to produce a corresponding alteration in the other, then efforts to change behaviour, which seem to have quite limited practical objectives, are likely to alter the way their subjects view each other. Conversely, altered beliefs about the nature of their relationships will ultimately be expressed in changing behaviour between men and women.

A serious attempt to take greater responsibility in sexual relationships involves people in new experiences, which often include receiving respectful attention for the first time, while making a critical choice – that is shown to be possible. Similar new experiences confront a man or woman when they learn that they are HIV-infected. If the news is given well, they pass through the shock of diagnosis and become aware of being accepted – and valued – by the man or woman who has grasped responsibility for standing alongside them during the crisis. This experience of acceptance, in a situation of desolation, paradoxically makes taking on new responsibilities and choosing new priorities possible. In the Gospels these were precisely the circumstances in which the 'turning' of metanoia repeatedly took place – and Christian history provides many more examples of repentance, leading to new life, which follow the same basic pattern.

Metanoia is a turning-point into which a person enters voluntarily, though sometimes the 'turning' then happens so swiftly and apparently inevitably that the subjective experience is: 'I was turned'. More often, time is needed, because most men and women fight against being turned.

First of all there has to be encounter with God in Christ, usually indirectly through contact with declared or undeclared disciples. Attraction follows, which may be experienced as such, or as its opposite: repulsion. At this stage an adult or child (for metanoia often, perhaps normally, occurs in childhood) may say 'yes' to God in conscious consent, or there may be a long and painful search for the capacity to respond. Once the choice has been made, then attitudes and behaviour begin to alter to conform to the new direction, a task which goes on until the end of life. It is a work of love: a response of growing joy and desire to God's invitation.

There may be long delays between the successive stages, particularly at the point when a person who is attracted to God in Christ first attempts response. A common reason for delay is divided desire – looking in two directions at once, unable to choose between them. A man as self-aware and honest as Augustine of Hippo may admit as much, as he did in his prayer: 'Lord, make me chaste, but not yet!' Often the person concerned thinks that self-improvement is necessary first, before he can be acceptable to God. Such people may be told that their problem is pride and self-absorption, but this is an unhelpful diagnosis, for someone wounded by early events or relationships may have a sense of unworthiness, and a lack of self-acceptance, so deep and damaging, that it appears to exclude them permanently from acceptance by God.

A related hindrance to metanoia is anger with God, either for 'making me the kind of person I appear to be – which I hate' – or for some event in the past, such as physical or sexual abuse. This is a great block while the anger remains unconscious. Once it is possible to admit and express anger with God, then response to the invitation to 'turn' becomes possible too. Usually these changes happen silently, while my attention is distracted from myself, perhaps by an experience of great sorrow or great joy, such as the shock of learning that I am HIV-infected, or the discovery of artistic gifts I did not know I had.

Sometimes the anger which prevents metanoia is directed against people who I believe have harmed me. The Gospels warn us, solemnly, that deliberately continued anger with a brother makes worship impossible, and that forgiving others is a necessary condition for receiving forgiveness ourselves. Here too, willingness and capacity may appear to be out of step. The *desire* to forgive others is certainly needed as a precondition for metanoia, but the *capacity* to do so often comes later, as a fruit of metanoia. Henri Nouwen points out that we are most wounded by those we love most – so that it is people we love whom we most need to forgive, yet often we only become free to forgive after experiencing the unconditional love of God. 'Once we have heard the voice calling us the Beloved ... and claimed the first unconditional love, we can see easily – with the eyes of a repentant heart – how we have demanded of people a love that only God can give. It is the knowledge of that first love that allows us to forgive those who only have a "second" love to offer.' (31)

My apparent inability to begin to turn is a reminder that what is happening is not under *my* control, but involves relationship with an Other – God – who is utterly well-disposed towards me, but never predictable, so that neither the timing nor the pace at which the relationship develops are mine to choose. God is always a God of surprises.

The beginnings of metanoia do not wait upon capacity, but upon hope and honesty, the hope to be able to say 'yes' one day, and meanwhile the honest admission of my helplessness to do more than hope. However, I must be (or become) willing to allow things to be done for me by others, such as asking other people to help me to find and face the reasons why I cannot respond, and asking for the sacraments of metanoia: baptism, the Lord's Supper and reconciliation – which are signs capable of effecting what they represent. All sacraments focus or concentrate our experience that physical things can be means of communication and communion between God and humankind, which is the argument of ch. 15 below.

But God intends to preserve human freedom, so that at every significant stage on the road to wholeness (or holiness) our willingness to go on is tested once again – so that approach and withdrawal, desire and fear, happen many times – though with increasing certainty of the outcome, and increasing joy as the beloved is drawn further and further into communion with God.

MARY OF MAGDALA

In *The Phenomenon of the New Testatment*, C.F.D. Moule commented on an aspect of the life and character of Jesus 'which seems to have asserted itself in all the traditions, despite an environment to which it seems likely to have been alien. This is Jesus's attitude to women and his relations with them.' Moule pointed out that first-century Jewish attitudes probably did not allow women freedom, nor men companionship with women, outside marriage. How is it, he asks, that 'through all the Gospel traditions without exception, there comes a remarkably firmly-drawn portrait of an attractive young man moving freely about among women of all sorts ... without a trace of sentimentality, unnaturalness or prudery, and yet, at every point, maintaining a simple integrity of character?'(29).

Mary of Magdala is mentioned in Luke 8.1–3 as one of a group of women who went through the cities and villages of Galilee, alongside the male disciples, when Jesus was preaching the good news of the Kingdom of God. These women are described (collectively) as having been healed of evil spirits and infirmities, and whenever Mary is mentioned in the Gospels, she is one 'from whom seven demons had gone out'.

Not only did Mary of Magdala share many experiences with the disciples in Galilee, but she was named as one of the women who watched, from a distance, while Jesus was dying on the cross. After His death, Mary was with the other women who followed the hasty funeral procession to Joseph of Arimathea's tomb.

Mary of Magdala is an example of a person who accepted healing from Jesus and became a disciple, thereafter living a strenuous wandering life, which – by the standards of the time – was probably considered strange for a woman. Her story resembles, in some respects, the stories of twentieth-century people whose search for new life starts with the experience of being HIV-infected or affected.

Such people find themselves in the company of other persons who (like the women travelling round Galilee with Jesus) are outside the usual conventions, and who may be viewed with hostility or fear. They, too, watch while young men or women, whom they love, die a slow painful death, standing helplessly (like Mary) at a place which, when anyone is dying, always feels 'far off'. Like Mary, they may be obliged to hear the cry: 'My God, my God, why have you forsaken me?' and also to watch many burials.

But Mary of Magdala's experience of discipleship did not end when her Lord's dead body was placed in the tomb. Mary was the first person to meet Jesus after He was raised to life, and she – a woman whose statements were not admissible evidence in Jewish law – was the witness sent to the apostles with the instructions: 'Go to my brothers and say to them: I am ascending to my Father and to your Father, to my God and your God'; 'Mary Magdalene went and announced to the disciples, "I have seen the Lord" ' (John 20.1–18).

PART 4
WHAT IS THERE TO HOPE FOR?

CHAPTER 14
Men and Women

'Let us make humankind in our image, according to our likeness.'
(Gen. 1.26).

If humankind is made in the image of God, then it is proper to look to
man–woman relationships for true knowledge of God. But the image is
seen 'darkly' and distorted by our present situation, which has some
features so new that they need special attention.

PRELIMINARIES

1. *Early maturity and delayed economic independence.* Wherever
nutrition has improved, puberty and fertility begin earlier than was the
case 80 years ago. But in industrial societies the age at which young
people reach economic independence has risen by several years, so
there is now a gap of about eight years between puberty (13 to 14 years)
and the age (21 to 23 years) when sexual partnerships may be stable
enough for the welfare of children. As most societies have not adjusted
completely to these changes, different behaviour codes co-exist, which
contribute to conflicts between generations and cultures. Often partnerships which are intended to be permanent start much too soon.

2. *Too many people?* Until this century, human survival required
maximum use of potential fertility, vigorous use of apparently unlim-
ited natural resources, and strong loyalties to family, clan and tribe.
Now the earth is already 'full' and the primary human task should be
shifting away from producing the maximum number of children, to
concentrate instead on living in a 'new creation', where the *quality* of
relationships with others (and with God) is of first importance with just
enough procreation to maintain stable populations).

3. *Language.* The words 'love' and 'sexuality' have many meanings.
'Sexuality' is often used when 'genitality' would be a more appropriate
term. Unless otherwise noted, I do not restrict 'sexuality' to genital
acts, but use it for (some part of) the whole range of physical, emotional, mental, social and spiritual expressions of being male or female.

4. *Sexuality and traditional marriage.* This chapter can offer no more than a 'sketch-map' of present-day sexuality. In using this metaphor, I have in mind maps used by navigators of small aircraft in Africa, which warn users that accuracy is uncertain in respect of the height of hills; I suspect that our present knowledge of human sexuality is equally uncertain – and largely unconcerned – about the God-ward side of relationships between men and women and that the conflict and interaction between ideals and actual behaviours is the situation where we are most likely to encounter God.

Traditional marriages were based on a public covenant or contract between families, ratified by their community. The personal wishes of the partners might or might not be considered, but were of secondary importance. In some cultures a dowry was paid to the man's family as an inducement payment; in other cultures the man's family paid bride-price to the woman's parents, as a sign of the commitment of both families to the relationship. In either case the effect of the payment might be to reduce her status to that of a possession, and reinforce her culturally conditioned perception of herself and her role in marriage: 'Women are born to bear children and to serve their husbands'.

Until this century, the personal side of marriage was subordinate to the social contract, but it has come to dominate relationships now, except in societies where arranged marriages remain normal. But greater emphasis on the personal side of marriage has not resulted in greater stability. Everywhere over the last 25 years, the rate of break-down of partnerships which were intended to be permanent has increased. This has long-term consequences for life in the next century, as careful studies show that divorce or separation usually have adverse effects on the development of children, reducing educational perfor-mance, increasing the risk of delinquency and a later life in crime, and leading to difficulties in forming and sustaining intimate relationships in adult life. Marriage breakdowns tend to be 'visited upon the children unto the third or fourth generation'.

In any case, formal marriage is less and less popular today, partly because life-expectancy is increasing and young people hesitate to commit themselves to partnerships which may last fifty years.

5. *Action – but not discussion.* In many cultures strong taboos inhibit talk about sexual relations, even between married couples. There may be no vocabulary of precise and acceptable words which can be used, so in public or in private language 'about' sexuality is limited to the erotic body-language of traditional dances, and the largely unspoken (and often unconscious) assumptions men and women make about their lives together. Two stories illustrate a few unspoken assumptions, one told from the viewpoint of a man, and the other from that of a woman.

Stories: *Tom* brought his second wife *Mary* to hospital when she was eight months pregnant. She had dark raised patches on the skin of her face and thighs, and swellings in her neck, groins and armpits. Tom's first wife had died two years earlier, and he got to know Mary when she helped him to look after his only child, who was already ill. The child died after a few months, around the time when Tom and Mary decided to marry. Mary had Kaposi's disease and both partners were HIV positive, although Tom's health was still good. Their child was well at birth but soon developed signs of HIV infection. At first Mary's health improved with treatment, but later Kaposi's disease began to affect her lungs. Tom realized that he was about to lose both his second wife and his second child to AIDS, while he remained well. What might Tom think about his future?

Marina, aged 28, was married to *Joe*, an engineer. In 1989 her husband was found to have tuberculosis (TB) and soon their two-year-old daughter was ill too. The child was taken to private doctors, but later admitted to hospital and found to have TB and to be HIV positive. This news did not surprise Marina, for, according to tribal custom, her husband had six wives, of whom she was the last. Joe was tested for HIV at a different hospital. His test, too, was positive, but he would not accept the result. 'They are lying, it is just normal TB', Joe insisted, 'I'm OK, I'm OK.' He died four months later.

Marina gave me permission to use her story. Joe was her second partner, and she already had two healthy children when she married him. Marina became pregnant while still at school and failed her examinations; she and her first partner lived together without a customary marriage, much to the anger of her family. They were faithful to each other, and Marina wanted them to be married in church, but her partner did not agree – so they decided to separate.

Soon Marina's family arranged for her to marry Joe, in a customary marriage with payment of bride-price. Marina knew that Joe's family supported his polygamous behaviour, and she herself found it reasonable enough at the time: 'He was still young; the Tonga have many wives, it is their custom,' she said. Their first child was the daughter who died of HIV-related TB. Their second child was born a year before Joe's death, and he remains healthy.

After Joe's death his family wanted Marina to marry his brother, who already had seven children. This man was well, but Marina did not want to marry him, and her own father supported her decision. She agreed, however, to undergo the customary 'cleansing' intercourse with her brother-in-law. He took advantage of her unwillingness to marry him to take over Joe's substantial property, leaving nothing for Marina – because 'she didn't want to stay with me'. Joe had in fact made a will leaving everything to his children, but although Marina saw a lawyer, only a small amount of money was put into a trust fund for the surviving children.

Marina is now poor; she rents a small house and supports herself and her children by tailoring. When I asked who gives her personal and emotional support, the answer was an angry 'No-one!' She has decided not to marry again and has applied for a job; her own parents live far away and she rarely mentioned them. Marina knows that she herself is HIV positive, but denied that she is either sad or angry: 'I have to accept it'. Her behaviour strongly suggested both anger and grief.

Marina talked about men and marriage: 'Women have no say, the man can do whatever he likes.' During her second marriage she used herbs to dry and tighten her vagina, because men expect the friction of 'dry sex'. Like most Zambian women, Marina accepted the view that men will stray unless this 'need' is supplied – if a woman consults her grandmother for advice about marital problems, the old lady's first question will be about dry sex. When Joe was advised to use condoms during sex with his wives he refused, saying: 'I don't believe in it!'

I asked Marina if she had a message for women, for this book. She said: 'Don't marry in haste and don't re-marry in haste.'

These stories underline the different expectations and wishes of men and women, which may have originated in biological drives to survive in prehistoric times – but the differences are still reinforced by cultural pressures today.

With these stories in mind, this chapter asks three questions:
1. Which is the more basic human need: relationship in general or genital expression of sexuality?
2. What can sexuality, when it is most fully human, teach us about the nature and possible intentions of God?
3. How can we live with the chaos – in thinking and feeling – which complicates interactions between men and women at this time?

1. WHICH IS PRIMARY: RELATIONSHIP OR SEXUAL RELATIONSHIP?

Human beings depend on each other for survival. Children deprived of good early relationships do not thrive: growth slows down, speech and walking are delayed: children in institutions who receive adequate physical care, but no love, lie inert in their cots, like sick animals, and eventually they die.

Temporary separation from the mother also has adverse effects. At first a child shows acute distress, crying and refusing offers of food or comfort, often with anger. When the acute distress subsides he becomes quiet, passively accepting comfort from alternative people. Later he may withdraw from living, refuse food, and pass into a state resembling severe depression in an adult. If the mother returns, this child greets her with hostility or indifference, and it may be weeks or months before their relationship is restored to normal. If the mother is too insecure to understand and cope with her child's hostility, so that she withdraws unconditional love, then the bond may never heal fully.

Difficulties in adult life commonly result from such unseen injuries: lack of trust between people (including marriage partners) and inability to commit oneself to another person may originate in a damaged primary relationship to a mother. Present-day reluctance to enter marriage may be due, not just to changing social circumstances *now*, but also to the effects of social changes twenty or thirty years ago, when education, more travel and migrations in search of work began to separate extended families. Education and travel reduced reliance on 'tradition' and widened generation gaps, so that parents and elders lost confidence in their capacity to guide and support young people, while young people become less willing to accept elders' advice.

Yet young adults still need support, if they are to develop the emotional security and maturity needed to give their own children good parenting. More and more children are reared in a single-parent family, though there is plenty of evidence that children need fathers as well as mothers.

LATER CHILDHOOD

Older children turn to peers for companionship, and information, but relationships remain personal. Sexual exploration is common but occurs in the context of mutual play, not as an end in itself, or for selfish pleasure. From puberty onwards, however, it is increasingly common for people to relate to the many others whom they meet each day in *im*personal ways – although they continue to make friends with a selected few.

At any time after puberty, genitality may come to dominate other aspects of sexuality and relationship, with the result that the bodies of partners meet in sexual 'play', without a corresponding meeting of persons. Sexual play may be pleasurable at the bodily level, but it rarely satisfies the persons who engage in it. Sexuality is not confined to the body, but inseparable from the intellect, emotions and spirit of each human being. Sexual intercourse is potentially capable of expressing meeting at all these levels.

I argue, therefore, that friendly relationships are more important – even to adults – than genital expression of sexuality. Although the sexual act is essential for the survival of our species, it is not essential for the survival of individuals. Quite large numbers of men and women, in every age, have lived for most or all of their adult lives without engaging in genital acts with anyone – and many have been balanced, mature, creative and happy people.

Friendship is a word which has lost some of its beauty as emphasis on genital relations as the only 'normal' adult expression of sexuality has grown – in spite of the obvious fact that even the most sexually active men and women spend most of their lives in non-sexual activities.

Christian tradition has a high regard for holy friendship and historical examples include many instances of loving and fruitful, but celibate, relationships between men and women (Francis and Clare, Teresa of Avila and John of the Cross, Benedict and Scholastica, Francis de Sales and Jeanne de Chantal, to name only the most wellknown).

'*Ubuntu*' is a South African word for the mysterious quality which makes a man or woman a memorable personality. In developing countries it is quite clear that older women with married children and grandchildren *do* have this quality of '*ubuntu*', expressed through their authority and influence on decision-making. It seems questionable whether this degree of personhood is possible for women earlier in life, when they are expected to be submissive to men and older women. Archbishop Desmond Tutu likes to quote a Xhosa saying: 'A person is a person through other persons.' May it be so for *both* men and women.

2. WHAT MIGHT HUMAN SEXUALITY SAY TO US ABOUT GOD?

At the biological level, sexual reproduction indicates a choice for diversity, risk-taking and newness. The re-combination of genetic material from two different persons at conception ensures that the new child is unique, even on the rare occasions when an ovum splits to create identical twins, for twins have the capacity to respond differently to their genetic inheritance.

Randomness operates in the mating of men and women, and again to determine how their genes combine: risk and uncertainty are built into the processes of fertilization. Not only does God seem to play dice, but it appears that God enjoys playing dice!

As the universe evolved, greater complexity allowed greater freedom for animals to respond to each other and to their environment, and encouraged co-operation between individuals in colonies or herds. In a static world (which was all that was visible before men learned to interpret signs of evolution) God was understood as Creator 'in the beginning' of all that existed. In the hugely enlarged universe known to modern people, God appears (if He appears at all) to share His creativity with men and women, through their power to bear and rear children, and their freedom to change the environment to suit their own needs and wishes.

CREATION STORIES

In the earliest biblical account of creation (Gen. 2.4b–25) men and women were seen as companions, not parents. The most ancient Hebrew insight was that: 'It is not good that the man should be alone'. This creation story makes fundamental statements about the 'way things are', as perceived by the traditions which influenced the Yahwist author, which still have authority for modern men and women based on their power to grip and mould the imaginations of peoples of different cultures for about three thousand years. In the Yahwist perspective, man was formed as a non-living body from the earth. Life, not reason, was breathed into his nostrils to make him a living creature: the same term, 'living creature', is used of birds and beasts, emphasizing the continuity of biological life. Immediately after his creation, without any pause for training, man was made a co-worker with God: he was given responsibility for cultivating the garden. In this way human work was declared 'very good'.

Human beings were made for relationship as well as work. In Yahwist thinking human beings stand too far apart from other 'living creatures' to find companionship from them, so God made woman, from the flesh of man – which is seen as the basis for their mutual attraction and union in marriage. The characteristic courtesy of God was shown when He brought the animals and then the woman to man, for his approval. In the Hebrew account of creation there is no hint that physical life is alien to human beings, and no hint of the opposition between mind and matter found in Greek thought. Men and women are physical beings who receive the breath of life from God. In the later (priestly) account of creation, human beings are made 'in the image of God'. Some early Christian writers, influenced by Greek thought, limited the meaning of 'in the image' of God to the intellect and soul of human beings, but the biblical witness implies that the *whole* human person, body as well as spirit, is made in the divine image. It is an important distinction, because upon it depends our view of the reality of God's identification with humankind in Jesus, and our interpretation of redemption – whether as *liberation* from irredeemable flesh, or transformation of body and soul together. 'The body is divinized along with the soul,' said Maximus the Confessor. If Jesus's resurrection and the offer of new life to believers is taken seriously, then what is done in the body between men and women must be taken seriously too, as Paul saw so clearly (1 Cor. 6.14–20).

CREATED CO-CREATORS WITH GOD

In patristic and medieval theology, the primary purpose of marriage was procreation, and other purposes were seen as secondary, even though the creativity of a good marriage actually spreads out to influence people far beyond the immediate or even the extended family. Celibacy does not rule out this second kind of creativity, and may indeed promote it.

> **Story**: In 1970 I attended a Requiem at Westminister Abbey for the celibate Archbishop of Central Africa, who had recently been killed in a road accident in Zambia. The flag of his adopted country flew at half-mast from the tower, and the Abbey was filled with a multi-racial congregation. The service expressed paschal joy and thanks-giving for a loving life given to God and to people. At the end of the service, in the early evening, Abbey officials tried to shepherd the congregation away quickly, so that they could lock the building for the night. But the crowds stayed on, breaking up into groups of friends who were delighted to see each other again and most unwilling to lose this marvellous chance for a reunion. For we were all, in a spiritual yet real sense, children of this celibate man, and our meeting at his Requiem was indeed a family reunion. As the Gospel promised, Archbishop Oliver had been repaid – quite literally – a hundred times over, for choosing to have no wife and no children (Matt. 19.17–29).

LOVE IN MARRIAGE

In the late twentieth century, many people hold inconsistent views of partnerships between men and women. Marriage is idealized as an intimate union of love, where the quality of the relationship is seen as more important than bearing and rearing children, but the idea of marriage as a contract, for the mutual support of the partners and their children, tends to be seen as 'unworthy of true love' or as an unreasonable limitation of human freedom. Realism about the difficulties of long-term relationships, and the need for faithfulness to one another, and to children, often take second place to 'fulfilment' and sexual pleasure.

Since the second Vatican Council, Roman Catholic theology, too, has viewed marriage as an intimate and exclusive love relationship, with procreation as an important aim, but no longer the only value. Despite this convergence with secular views, a fundamental difference remains, for secular society generally regards sexual pleasure as an end in itself. In contrast, Christians understand all human relationships (even those that are exclusively genital) as moving their participants either away from, or towards, union with God – as the love-relationship for which human beings were created. 'You have made us for yourself, and our hearts find no rest until they rest in you', said Augustine of Hippo.

How are we to understand the word 'love', which has both trivial and profound meanings in the English language? Should we project what we think we know about God's love onto the meaning of 'love', and then only use this word to refer to ideal human relationships? Or may we examine actual human experiences of attraction, conflict, effort, meaning and encounter which constitute 'love' in real human partnerships, and ask what our findings suggest about the way God loves us, and even (greatly daring) about the mysterious love within the Trinity?

Probably both approaches are useful, though we may have most to learn from the facts of human love. Popular pictures of how God loves human beings are far too timid, in spite of the rich imagery of the Old and New Testaments, and the testimony of men and women of prayer, who have grasped images of passionate love – and used them to describe their own experience of God.

KINDS OF LOVING

In the Old Testament God's parental love is described as guiding, guarding, correcting and nurturing His people Israel. But Yahweh is also pictured as a tender mother who cannot forget the baby she is breastfeeding (Isa. 49.15) and as a parent holding a baby against his or her cheek, or patiently teaching a tiny child to walk (Hos. 11.3,4). We may find it easier to accept images of a severe, distant paternal figure, than to use Jesus's name for His Father and ours – 'Abba', which is a small child's word – or to consider using Dame Julian's image of 'our kindly Mother, Jesus'.

The Song of Songs celebrates the first extraordinary experience of adult love for another human being, when a man or woman's whole horizon is filled with wonder and humility because a marvellous 'other' person responds with joy to his or her devotion. Onlookers see only an ordinary couple who idealize each other, self-absorbed and blissful. But the man and woman see each other transfigured with beauty and possibility: the woman cries out: 'Your love is more delightful than wine, your name is an oil poured out, . . . how right it is to love you!' (Song 1.2,4) and the man replies: 'How beautiful you are, my love, how beautiful you are!' and: 'I charge you, daughters of Jerusalem, not to stir my love, nor rouse it, until it please to awake' (Song 3.5, JB).

In this love poem the man and woman search for each other, advance, withdraw, dream of the beloved, praise his or her virtues, hope for meeting, fear loss, plan life together, long for physical union, yet long, too, for far more than sexual pleasure. For though sexual attraction is part of the love of which the Song of Songs sings, it is only one element in a far more profound attachment between a man and a woman.

Lovers long for singleness of being, yet simultaneously exult in the 'otherness' of the beloved, and such contradictory longings co-exist with an intensity which no human mate can satisfy. 'Falling in love' arouses hopes which are destined to be disappointed, and it is not a state which can be permanent. What, however, does its existence as a human experience have to tell us about God, if men and women are made 'in the image' of God?

The Song of Songs has been interpreted in three ways: as poetry about ideal human love and marriage, as an allegory of the love-story of God and the people of Israel, or as an allegory of the relationship between Christ and the Church. Elsewhere in both Testaments, marriage has an honoured place as a symbol of divine–human relationship. In the Old Testament marriage was a symbol of the covenant between Yahweh and His people, and unfaithfulness to the covenant on the part of the Israelites was described in terms of infidelity within marriage. In the New Testament marriage is used as a symbol of the relationship between Christ and the Church, especially in Paul's Epistles, but these examples may not exhaust the possible interpretations of human love as a reflection of divine love. I have spoken of human lovers' impossible longing for singleness of being – while at the same time they want to preserve and enjoy the individuality of the beloved. In human terms it *is* an impossible demand, yet it may express what the doctrine of the Trinity is about.

In the Trinity, singleness of Being is perfectly and permanently expressed, while the unique otherness of the three Persons is maintained in a relationship of love and self-giving. This is a love which potentially includes human beings, if we are willing to be 'hidden with Christ in God' (Col. 3.3). Our hunger for what is impossible in human terms may be intended to awaken our hunger to be included in the love of the Trinity, in the relationship for which we were created.

A second transcendent element in human love is worth attention. Lovers see in one another beauties and possibilities to which everyone else is blind. Where does this transfigured view of another human person come from? Is it solely the product of an imagination stimulated by hormones or the chemical messengers released by a contented brain? Or does it have the authenticity and truth which seem so obvious to visionary lovers? There is no 'answer' to such questions, but they are worth asking, for nowadays we are more likely to overlook transcendent elements in human loving than to overemphasize them.

DOMESTIC LOVING

Falling in love either disappears, sometimes with terrible speed, or else in a long-term committed relationship, it develops into a daily caring for one another which offers plenty of material for humour and distress, comfort and endurance – but not much excitement. What is happening between the partners from day to day: is there a God-ward aspect to domestic loving?

Jack Dominian, a Roman Catholic observer of Western couples, sees three purposes for domestic loving: to sustain the partners in their daily lives, to help to heal the weaknesses and wounds that husband and wife bring into their marriage, and to enable both partners to grow towards wholeness. Ordinary time can become significant time – *kairos* – when we encounter God in another human being; such encounters can occur in marriage. What does this mean in practical terms?

SUSTAINING LOVE

Life is a tough journey and we need support on the way. Sustaining love attends to the physical, emotional, spiritual and social well-being of a partner, and receives sustenance from that partner in return. Such love depends upon physical and emotional availability to each other, yet the practical requirements for both are often ignored in modern life. When work or family demands separate husband and wife they need to *plan* enough time together, to share gardening or shopping, or a visit to a child's school, and – it may be necessary to add – time to sleep in the same bed and eat at the same table, avoiding (as far as possible) long separations for study or work. Traditions which expect men to work with men and women to work with women, could be challenged – to encourage marriage partners to work with one another more often. Without physical availability, there is not likely to be much emotional availability either.

Emotional availability requires husband and wife to be in touch with each other's inner worlds, aware of worry or happiness, distress or pleasure – ready to listen if the other wants to talk, but patient if they prefer to keep silent. Sensitivity to each other is natural (but uninformed!) during courtship, but is often lost later, buried under familiarity, guilt, tiredness or the demands of family life.

'Communication' is prescribed often as a remedy for misunderstandings, but men and women do not communicate in the same ways, and may not ponder their differing expectations and needs. Women are usually better at expressing their feelings in words than men, who may see no reason to repeat a feeling-statement, such as 'I love you', until the feeling referred to changes. Many women, on the other hand, need repeated demonstrations of affection – and may not find sexual intercourse without much love-play first a 'good-enough' demonstration. In general, women have a greater need than men for affirmation as persons, for they are more likely to lack self-esteem. But women tend to overestimate the confidence of men and do not see that their self-esteem, too, is fragile, and needs loving support. Habitual criticism naturally distances partners from each other, whereas courtesy and expressions of appreciation strengthen bonds and affirm personhood.

Willingness to face conflict and learn from it is another part of sustaining love. Some couples appear to avoid conflict, but do so at the expense of avoiding real meeting with each other, and with the risk that suppressed conflict will erupt one day in deadly violence. Other couples fight constantly, until one or other partner sees that winning battles is less important than avoiding hurt to the other person next time. It is a matter of experience that when there is mutual willingness to change, couples can learn the skills needed to sustain one another in marriage.

HEALING LOVE

Much conflict in marriage or social life occurs because all human beings are wounded. The pain of these wounds is expressed through malicious behaviour, irrational fears or suspicions, lack of confidence or feelings of worthlessness (often masked by a patronizing manner or over-confidence), by anger or by addictive use of sex, alcohol or drugs. Wounds may start from inherited defects of body or temperament, in the events of childhood, or result from social circumstances in adult life.

'Wounds' are the commonest reason for the unacceptable behaviours which cause marriages to break down, according to Dominian. Yet, paradoxically, marriage is also the human condition where there is potentially a chance for wounds to be healed – for in a committed relationship insecurity may be replaced by security, and insufficient love by unconditional love. It is much less likely that enough security and unconditional love will be given or received in a partnership which is not intended to be permanent.

Growth through adaptive change – or decay – seem to be the only alternative options for living creatures, including married couples. During twenty years or so of rearing a family, wives lose their childbearing capacity, and both partners lose some flexibility of body and mind. Meanwhile, however, the spouses may have become skilled at compensating for one another's weaknesses and using one another's strengths, so that the partners grow from dependence to interdependence and from immaturity to maturity. A main task of marriage is to help each other to grow into wholeness.

SEXUALITY IN MARRIAGE

Apart from the very few acts needed to conceive children, men and women meet sexually for recreation, physical and emotional pleasure, to exercise a personal power-to-be that may have no other outlet and often – but not always – in generous and joyful mutual self-giving.

At the present time, quantity of sexual experience and erotic technique seem to be valued more highly than companionship and loyalty; 'playing sex' is often limited to the skilful meeting of bodies, but is not a loving meeting of persons. Should sexual acts mean more than this? Would a change from 'loving carefully' to 'loving faithfully' mean loss or gain? Is 'loving faithfully' just a rather dull way of stopping spread of HIV and reducing human freedom – or could faithfulness offer much more than safety from HIV infection?

Clearly sexual intercourse can be a form of communication between partners, but the content of the verbal and non-verbal messages which are exchanged is usually less clear. Messages may be commercial, when a schoolgirl agrees to sex with a middle-aged man in exchange for money for school fees, while he congratulates himself on finding a partner who is not (he thinks) likely to be HIV-infected. In contrast, an infertile couple, anxiously copulating on a day that both reckon might be fortunate, aided by whatever medicines their culture supplies, communicate to one another chiefly the importance of the missing child.

Sometimes the messages are hostile: a reluctant woman may convey resentment because unconsciously she suspects she is being used as a 'thing', not valued as a person. Her partner's haste and roughness gives the message: 'You are here to serve me; I am more powerful than you are, and always will be'. When a woman is raped her assailant is usually expressing, in an extreme way, his need to have power over another person, and at the same time how deeply he despises all women. Sexual hunger is reckoned to be a secondary motive.

If however, husband and wife meet freely as loving persons, rather than as hungry bodies, what might they be 'saying' to one another in sexual body-language? A courteous approach, in which the man waits for his wife's slower responses and the woman laughs with her husband at his eagerness and tries to match his mood, says: 'It is you I want to love, in your time, not mine'. Mutual agreement to abandon the tradition of dry sex and to accept the natural anatomical changes of past childbirth and the normal moisture of sexual arousal says: 'I accept you just as you are; *you* are more important to me than physical satisfaction'.

The most valuable message of all is: 'you are the one person I have *chosen*', but this is only given when the relationship is one of trust and mutual faithfulness. When sex goes well, each partner affirms the other's desirability as a man or a woman, and so confirms his or her own sexual identity. If there is hurt in the relationship their meeting is a way of saying silently: 'I am sorry I hurt you' and of offering and receiving forgiveness. The 'being there for me' of a good-enough parent is re-enacted in the attention of loving lovers to one another's needs, and sharing joy together relieves the loneliness of being human, at least for a time. Shared unity, however temporary, is a sign of hope and meaning in daily life, and a sign that it is worth hoping for complete healing of our wounds.

But loving in marriage is not always about reconciliation or healing, important as these aspects are: 'playing sex' is a good verb for sexual relations, for honest play, when adult worries are set aside for a time and the partners simply enjoy each other and relax together, is an important part of loving. But this can only be true within a committed relationship, for sexual play is not honest when it denies the existence of a marriage partner. In those circumstances, the partner who seeks sex outside marriage tends to project his or her guilt onto the partner who is cheated, either directly by accusations of infidelity, or indirectly by finding fault over trivial matters – in order to transfer guilt onto the other person.

Normally sexual meeting should release energy-for-living in husband and wife. Jack Dominian says: 'On each occasion we give each other new life, and occasionally we create *a* new life.' The source of that new life, whether physical or emotional and spiritual, is God, for if husband and wife meet with the whole of themselves, not only as bodies, they encounter God in one another.

Domestic loving may be interpreted as reflecting God's nearness, His immanence. God demonstrates His love daily, gradually, drawing us towards a perfection of beauty and achievement which far exceeds the most optimistic visions lovers have of one another, in the early stages of romantic love. If there was indeed truth in such visions, it was the truth of foreseeing what we might become, as transfigured human beings, not only in relation to another person, but 'hidden with Christ in God' (Col. 3.3).

In the detail of daily lives, God loves us as we are at this particular moment, although we need not stay as we are, but can hope to be transformed into His image, if we consent. In relationship to God, day-to-day domestic loving is the pattern at the *beginning*, whereas single-ness of being with absolute delight in the otherness of the Beloved is the pattern at the end – when: 'knowing the love of Christ, which is beyond all knowledge, you are filled with the utter fullness of God' (Eph. 3.19).

LIVING WITH CHANGE: ARE MEN AND WOMEN EQUALS – OR POLES APART?

We have begun to think about the complementary roles of men and women in marriage, without considering whether 'complementary' is a better term to use than 'equal'. *'Equality'* is a word which has collected negative meanings on the battleground between the sexes of the last thirty years.

Moves towards greater equality of opportunity and status for women are just and necessary, in the many situations where women have been denied human rights which men take for granted. Yet battles for equality have not always led to greater *'ubuntu'* for both sexes, but rather to defensiveness which hinders co-operation and prevents men and women from enjoying their 'otherness'.

Problems arise when women fight for 'rights' aggressively and men retreat, to defend themselves against these unwomanly women, partly because they tend to feel greater anxiety than women about breaking away from their mothers, and partly because at a deep level many men fear being trapped by women. (Earlier we suggested that at present men feel threatened in other areas of traditional male competence, too (p. 114). The ending of a patriarchal view of the world is a crisis for *all* human beings.)

Polarity is a word which emphasizes differences, but does not do justice to the mixture of masculine and feminine characteristics in all human beings. In some cultures certain behaviours are prescribed as correct for women and forbidden to men, while in others the same behaviours are reversed, pointing to the complementary roles which the sexes are expected to take in society, as well as in marriage.

The word *'complementary'* admits and rejoices in differences, and even polarity, but sees that the sexes should be related in an inter-dependent and mutually responsive way. At the present moment, men and women need to get to know one another better, as persons whose thinking, emotions and spiritual lives have complementary strengths and weaknesses.

Before the vote on the ordination of women to priesthood in the Church of England in 1992, a small group of men and women – Anglicans, Roman Catholics, Greek Orthodox and Protestants – met regularly for three years to explore their thoughts and feelings about men and women, priesthood, the doctrines of the Incarnation and the Trinity, considered in the light of the approaching decision about min-isterial priesthood for women. At the end of this time, they wrote a short but hopeful book entitled *A Fearful Symmetry* (3). They did not succeed in finding an 'answer' to their questions about ordination, but they concluded: 'we are only at the beginning of understanding the complementarity of men and women.'

MODEL OR REALITY?

Three words have been used to refer to different views about the natures of men and women and their interdependence. All views and models *are* only models, or representations of a part of reality, made for limited purposes and usually culturally biased. All models are likely to be 'wrong' in some respect, though the defects of the newest ones may not have been noticed yet. 'Polarity', 'equality' and 'complementarity' are useful but not mutually exclusive terms.

Karl Barth's phrase: ' "man" never exists as such, but always as male or female', and Bishop John V. Taylor's vision of the Holy Spirit as the Go-Between God (41) – taken together – suggest another model for man–woman relationships, which attends to the 'and' in 'male *and* female created he them'.

John V. Taylor identified the Holy Spirit as the hidden agent who makes connections in I–thou encounters, including those between men and women. To associate the 'and' between male and female with the work and presence of the Holy Spirit suggests another dimension to the interdependence of men and women, an alternative to 'polarity', 'equality' or even 'complementarity'. Jesus said: 'Where two or three are gathered in my name, there am I in the midst' (Matt. 18.20), but He did not exclude married couples or celibate friends, or limit His presence to times of worship.

Identifying the 'and' between a man and a woman as the Spirit, introducing them to each other, need not deny the reality of their direct relationship. The presence of the Spirit never diminishes the freedom given to creation to be itself – either in non-recognition of God, or in co-operation with Him. We might even see the presence of God in the natural relationships of men and women (whether He is recognized or not), as the source of a transcendent power which is felt, at some point in their lives together, by most ordinary unreligious couples. Sexuality is not *only* a way of maintaining the continuity and increasing the diversity of the human race: it is also one way that divisions between people, caused by their diversity, are bridged, as many 'mixed' partnerships between men and women of different races, cultures or religions testify during the last few years. When a sexual relationship expresses self-forgetful love it becomes open to a wider community than the nuclear or extended family and – whether the man and woman recognize it or not – potentially open to God. Conversely, when the man and woman are (individually and together) open to God, they are likely to be open and creative in their relationship to one another, too. This is the source of the stability of some Christian marriages.

BECOMING AND STAYING MARRIED

If human loving reflects God's love, and marriage is a relationship through which people could – here and now – encounter God in one another, then Christians (at least) ought to approach marriage as truly a sacrament of salvation. In practical terms, the processes of becoming and staying married need a great deal more support than is presently supplied in most societies, Christian or otherwise.

Preparation for marriage starts in the parental home, where a capacity for intimate trusting love is formed, or damaged, by the quality of trust and 'letting-be' between parents and children. In their early lives children learn how to behave in their future roles, and even at the pre-school stage small boys begin to feel superior and small girls sense that they are regarded as slightly less valuable than males. 'Knowledge' acquired so early and so unconsciously is firmly rooted and difficult to alter later.

Preparation for adult sexual roles is absent or haphazard in some cultures, but careful and specific in others. In traditional societies initiation ceremonies prepared young men and women for their future roles in marriage, and as working adult members of the tribe. These roles were usually clearly defined and accepted without question as the will of God and the ancestors; there were no visible alternative ways of behaving. We live in very different societies now, where confidence in tradition is breaking down, there are many different ways of behaving, and old values are questioned or have been discarded. Many societies have lost a coherent sense of the meaning of human life, so it is not surprising that preparation for marriage, as conducted by most societies and Churches, seems out of touch with the realities of their lives to young couples, whether they live in New York, Kampala, Bombay or Bangkok.

In spite of social change, however, traditional preparation for adult roles still goes on in some African tribes, where older women teach girls of 8 or 9 years sexual skills and a submissive and seductive role – and then encourage them to 'practise' with adolescent boys. As a result, both sexes reach puberty with three or four years of genital experience – unlinked to mature love or to mutual responsibility. When producing children (to ensure survival of the tribe) was the main function of marriage, such instruction made sense, but it no longer does so in a time of over-population and HIV infection.

In industrialized countries marriage in church, like the Christmas festival, has become primarily a social event. For most couples it is not a sacrament or a public act of commitment signifying their desire to love each other within the support of a Christian community. Indeed it is becoming less common for *any* formal act to mark the start of a couple's cohabitation. Yet recent research in Britain has shown that marriages preceded by cohabitation are more likely to end in divorce or separation than those which begin with a public ceremony. A return to formality and ceremonial might increase the stability of marriage in general.

A public ceremony need not be expensive. Churches could pioneer a move to simplicity, with dignity, for marriage ceremonies, combined with greater practical support for the couple afterwards. One-third of all marriage breakdowns begin in the first five years, while children are arriving and the partners are gaining maturity.

Societies affected by AIDS could experiment with liturgy, for example, and design an annual celebration to raise the profile of marriage, and provide an occasion for husbands and wives to renew their commitment to one another, express penitence for what has gone wrong between them during the past year, and re-affirm the importance of fidelity and love in their relationship. It could also be a time for laughter and relaxation, feasting and music. At present marriage as a vocation is treated too casually by most Churches, until relationships begin to break down – when it may be too late for guidance or support to be of much use.

In some developing countries, the Roman Catholic Church arranges 'Marriage encounter' weekends for couples to attend together, without their children. The aim is to give the partners space, rest and encouragement to recapture the attention to each other which may have existed during courtship, but has since been lost under the pressures of family life. Some couples who attend these weekends do so reluctantly, not expecting much change in their lives, but many later admit that they did 'encounter' one another again, in a way which revived their marriage, and deepened their love.

Some marriages do break down, however, and, if this happens, both partners need support for their own continued growth, and to minimize damage to their children. Each Church community needs arrangements, therefore, to support various kinds of unmarried people – those who are too young to marry yet, those whose marriages have broken down, and especially single parents. Already one-third of all children are reared in single-parent households; these children are disadvantaged, and Churches should have a particular concern for them.

CELIBACY

Single or celibate life is a valid vocation too, where a significant minority of men and women encounter God. Their lives are made unnecessarily difficult if their situation is idealized, as tends to happen when celibacy is highly valued. Single people need sustaining, healing and support on their journey towards maturity just as much as married couples, but often do not have intimate relationships which provide love of this quality. In societies where genital sexual relations and childbearing are the main criteria for maturity, single women in particular (but also single men) may be regarded as perpetual children. And they are often lonely, because couples see them as threats to their own partnerships, or think it is 'improper' for vowed celibate people, such as priests or religious, to have friends of the opposite sex.

Celibate people need resources for day-to-day sustaining love, company, intimacy of a physical and mental (but non-genital) kind, and practical support, and their creativity needs to be recognized and used. All these needs may be met within a small religious order, but difficult to satisfy in secular society. Single people sometimes limit their lives themselves, by failing to accept celibacy as a permanent or long-term condition – or by idealizing marriage as an effortlessly blissful state, which it is not. Unmarried and childless people sometimes find it difficult to escape from parental control and from a tendency to selfishness, and may need help to achieve mature independence.

As a bridge to the next chapter – on life in communities – here is a true story about young Ugandans who are re-examining sexual conduct in their own society, in the *light* of AIDS.

'YOUTH ALIVE'

Story: In Uganda, in 1993, I talked with young men who are trainers for a behaviour-change programme called 'Education for life'.

These leaders had residential 'training for discipleship' at the Emmaus Centre in Uganda, which accepts men and women who feel a call to service or ministry. In groups of 20, they live together for six months, learning about prayer, the Bible, spirituality, community life and evangelism, and they are trained to give pastoral care to sick or dying persons. They said: 'We received ministry ourselves and we learned to walk with Christ and with one another'. At the end, the group disperse to work with youth or as pastoral counsellors, sometimes living in small groups as lay-communities, or attached to basic Christian Communities.

'Education for life' courses began in Kampala in 1991. They are offered to young adults or school students during vacations. Thirty people (of both sexes) meet all day for four days in a large Church building; a midday meal is provided which leaders and participants eat together; members wear name-labels but there are no introductory rituals or games.

During the first day key facts and figures about AIDS are presented, emphasizing that 50% of all HIV infections happen between the ages of 15 and 25. Self-awareness is emphasized too, so that participants realize that their *own* behaviour is the key issue. With this background, single-sex groups of five persons are formed, each in the care of a trained facilitator. In these groups members reflect about how *they* might think, feel or act in the company of a friend who is HIV-infected, or with a dying person, or if they were *themselves* HIV-infected. Not surprisingly, people find these topics threatening and a few withdraw from the course.

Next day the theme of 'behaviour change' is described as a three-stage process which requires energy, time ('not a one-day thing') and willingness to learn new skills and habits – which is difficult at first. The leader reassures members that change *is* possible and that most people *do* learn to repeat behaviour which is rewarding. In the same small groups (which are maintained all week) and guided by leaders, members use art, role-plays and discussions to ask themselves: 'What is AIDS doing to our society? What is our sexual behaviour like at present?' Using their answers, participants look ahead to the year 2000, and try to imagine what life in Kampala will be like then, if sexual behaviour remains unchanged. Their forecasts are gloomy: young people expect to see many graves and few children. When asked: 'How do husbands and wives behave towards one another?' they are not hopeful about the quality of marriages, either.

Next, young people are invited to create a new and hopeful picture of the future, to answer the questions: 'What do you *want* your lives to be like? What do you *want* to achieve?' Video films such as 'Born in Africa', or 'It is not easy', are shown to stimulate their imaginations. By now embarrassed laughter has stopped, but up to a third of people who started the programme have withdrawn. Those who remain are serious but enthusiastic; talk turns away from death, and sexuality begins to be discussed openly; often the afternoon session develops such momentum that there is no time for the final video!

On the third day, work on the decision-making stage of behaviour change continues. The whole group listens to a detailed and open review of human sexuality, expanding topics which were introduced in outline earlier. Participants learn that some issues particularly concern women – but seem less important to men, while others deeply interest men – but seem strange to women. Pregnancy and contraception, STDs (including AIDS), and the uses and limitations of condoms for preventing STDs or pregnancy, are discussed openly.

Then, in their separate groups, men and women consider different lists of questions, using role-plays to help hidden feelings to emerge. The men discuss why they like to have several female partners; many reasons are given which usually include lack of sexual satisfaction with some women, curiosity about variations in female anatomy, the need for a 'balanced diet' or a matter of 'taste', lack of excitement with the wife, the influence of alcohol, and 'feeling male'. Unmarried men cannot imagine choosing a wife 'who will satisfy me' without a trial of several women. The women discuss their different sexual experiences and expectations. They, too, may not find satisfaction from their partners; some complain about roughness, or express anger at the demands made by drunken men, or describe the pain of being abandoned by their husbands. Some women seek sexual pleasure outside marriage and others sell sex from choice or to earn a living. Unmarried girls may seek or allow casual sex for self-esteem, in order to 'be popular' – and some girls do not know of any other way to spend their leisure time.

Later the groups reassemble to share the insights they have recognized separately, aided by role-plays. At this stage anger may surface, especially when women have the chance to express their perception that 'men use us!' or to report the experience and effects of sexual abuse. Because the pain and anger is shared, there is little personal threat to any one individual, so men and women find it possible to listen to one another (perhaps for the first time) and to consider their different viewpoints. It is important to allow silence and time for people to absorb new experiences, as men watch role-plays which criticize their 'traditional' behaviour. Both sexes may begin to feel compassionate sorrow for the pain they have inflicted unknowingly in the past, and for some groups the day ends in a spirit of reconciliation and peace.

Sister Miriam Duggan described one occasion when this was expressed at a Eucharist, where the celebrant led the men in a simple ceremony of washing the hands of the women, as a sign of their desire for reconciliation. This symbolic act was deeply moving for the women, many of whom wept – before deciding to repeat the hand-washing, in sorrow for *their* lack of understanding and compassion for men in the past. Their mutual joy was sealed in the Eucharist that followed.

The final day continues the theme of reconciliation, now focused on God's loving desire to be reconciled with all His children – because each one is unique and deeply loved. The story of the prodigal son, personal testimonies and drama are used to help members to believe in the reality of God's love and to release their desire and capacity to make choices about their future lives. The Father's welcome for everyone without exception is expressed in Jesus's invitation: 'Come to me' and His promise: 'I am the way', and people are reminded of the power of the Spirit in their lives.

Hindrances to commitment and obstacles to behaviour change are faced realistically but hopefully. Links between alcohol, drug use and sex are pointed out, and members are encouraged to recognize where their own weaknesses and sins lie, and to seek healing and deliverance through prayer and sacrament. One-to-one counselling and prayer with laying-on of hands may be used. It may be necessary to point out that a *choice* is demanded if cultural pressures ('as an African I need sex outside my marriage') and Christian commitment clash. Leaders ask: 'What will the pressures be to go back to old friends? What might prevent you from achieving your goals? Are you prepared to give up that 'something'? Singly or together, how can we resist pressures to return to old habits, and learn new ways to show affection, and to relax and have fun?' Members are encouraged to have more confidence in others' potential goodness and in their own and other people's capacity to change. Above all, they are encouraged to trust in Christ and in the power of the Spirit.

Finally, participants are encouraged to make specific, practical plans for future behaviour and to commit themselves to receiving the Spirit, to a new life and to mutual support. They sing and make music together – 'it is a very beautiful and exciting day'. The programme ends with a party, which demonstrates that enjoyment – even ecstasy – need not depend on physical sex or drugs or alcohol.

Later, 'graduates' become facilitators at future courses (which reinforces their commitment to behaviour change) and some join 'Youth Alive' groups in order to give and find support. The organizers of 'Education for life' are planting seeds of behaviour change outside Kampala too, as they extend courses to other places. They spoke quietly of evidence that behaviour change *does* last, and that women can give up selling sex, because the root causes for it have been overcome.

The Youth Alive movement was launched in Kampala in 1993 with an event designed to gather support, increase awareness of AIDS issues amongst young people and to raise funds for care of HIV-infected persons. In the past, youth were often ignored by official prevention programmes, so they tended not to identify AIDS as 'our problem'. On November 4th: 'We showed that something should be done. We invaded Kampala from its seven hills, singing, spreading the gospel, visiting markets and offices, and drawing other young people to join us.' In the central city square the young people handed over money they had collected to the Director General of the Uganda AIDS commission, which was used later for community care for HIV-infected people. A new song was launched as a 'youth anthem' and sung with enthusiasm by the crowd. Then the organization of local 'Youth Alive' clubs began.

The clubs are Christian in outlook, but welcome young people of any faith or no faith. They aim to provide positive peer-group support to support responsible choices and to encourage an outlook on life which will minimize the risks of HIV infection and increase individual and communal well-being. The clubs plan three kinds of activity – training for work, enjoying leisure and preparation for marriage.

The organizers are well aware of the connections between idleness, lack of self-esteem, unemployment and casual sex, so they offer training for work which requires little or no capital, and they try to restore hope and a sense of purpose to youths who have never been employed, through the discipline of voluntary teamwork to help their own communities, for example by repairing the homes of elderly people.

Many young people have never used their leisure in a productive way or found self-esteem and enjoyment through achievement – so music, drama, sport, and painting or drawing are important activities. Dancing is not avoided, but members are helped to distinguish between dances with a controlled and controllable erotic content, and those which have sexual arousal as their main aim.

Competitions develop creativity and build self-confidence; drawings entered for a World AIDS Day competition on the theme 'action in the face of AIDS' showed the humour and realism needed for AIDS-awareness posters.

In Ugandan law marriage is not legal until both partners are eighteen, but large numbers of young people live together in fragile partnerships, without legal, traditional or religious sanctions. Often neither partner has work and their respective parents cannot give any support. Young married couples who belong to small Christian communities (the *Kabondos* described in ch. 15) are reaching out to youngsters who live together, to help them to understand the meaning of marriage, to offer training for work and support in solving the problems of city and family life. Through these friendships, they hope that couples who are already living in stable partnerships will be encouraged to ask for their unions to be blessed. The blessing is given at a simple ceremony within the Eucharist, either in church or at home, emphasizing the couples' vows to one another. Mature members of the Christian community act as sponsors or 'godparents' at the marriage ceremony, then provide a simple party for the couple and their friends afterwards, and later offer long-term support and interest. Marriage sponsors are likely to be even more necessary, as young people who have lost parents (through AIDS or war) reach maturity, and need support as they establish their families.

For Further Reading see Bibliography, p. 311, (3), (14), (23) and (41).

Study Suggestions:
1. Examine any anti-AIDS youth movement in your locality. Are its aims and methods negative ('you shall not . . .') or positive? Is it well-supported by young people – if so, what policies and attitudes contribute to its success? If the movement does not appeal to youth, in what ways is it out of touch with their concerns?
2. Do marriages need 'godparents' during the early years? Are relatives the right people to provide support (if needed)?
3. Jack Dominian sees three functions for love in marriage: to sustain the partners in daily life, to heal the wounds everyone has, and to support growth into wholeness. Do these ideas also apply to marriage in non-Western societies?
4. Is celibacy an escape from the creation-command to 'be fruitful and multiply' – or a minority vocation which witnesses to the importance of all relationships?

Explain the reasons for your answers to questions 2, 3 and 4.

CHAPTER 15
Community

'How does a society with a history of violence, buckling under the pressure of poverty and land scarcity, react to the news that an unknown third of its members carry the (AIDS) virus?'(1).

In ch. 14 we considered what sexuality might have to teach us about the possibilities of being human and the nature and purposes of God.

This chapter attempts a shift in scale from couples and clans to human communities which are *not* naturally held together by ties of blood, kinship or sexual attraction. The Christian tradition that human beings are adapted to community with God and with each other seems worthy of serious re-examination in societies affected by AIDS.

All definitions agree that a community consists of a group of people: but are they a group through biological kinship, or because they live near each other (a geographical community), or within particular administrative boundaries (parish, civic or national)? Such *structural communities* are thrown together accidentally and arbitrarily, and may be far from peaceful.

Earlier, I offered alternative definitions: a 'community' is 'that to which people wish to belong', or 'a group of people who are interdependent, share interests and values and agree to work together to achieve common goals'. In practice, most people establish themselves in several overlapping groups which satisfy different aspects of their need 'to belong'.

In the West many people who live in structural communities have little experience of true community life. They do not know their neighbours and do not want to know them because they are 'not like us'. This breakdown of community life is spreading all over the world – helped by separation of extended families, migrations of workers or refugees and industrialization.

COMMUNITIES ARE KEY UNITS FOR RESPONSES TO AIDS
Any life-threatening illness happens to one unique person, but affects, and may destabilize, a whole family. A crisis on the scale of AIDS in developing countries is capable of destabilizing entire communities or even regions – yet the same crisis *may* act as the catalyst* which inspires naturally suspicious and separate groups to unite as real communities.

Communities are units where local administrative decisions are made and central political policies are put into effect. They are the ordinary setting for social and intimate relationships and the places where standards for behaviour are consciously (or unconsciously) chosen and enforced. Most communities, however, discriminate against or exclude certain potential members, on grounds of age (youth in the South, old age in the North), gender, origin, or behaviour (sexual, ritual, unemployment). Considered in the abstract, communities are ambiguous: some promote mutual responsibility and caring and choose to be inclusive rather than exclusive, while others harm their own members (and the outsiders with whom they interact) by turning in on themselves and becoming rigid in outlook, uncritical of their own goals and closed off from the surrounding society.

Every community has, and needs to have, agreed boundaries: but dangers arise if a set of boundaries, or a community so defined, becomes an absolute 'good'. Whenever 'we' see ourselves exclusively as over against 'others', rather than alongside them, there is a risk that natural differences will cease to be a source for human delight in variety, and become instead a reason for division or an excuse for hostility.

HOSTILITY AND COMMUNITY BREAKDOWN

In 1992 I attempted, without success, to discuss with AIDS workers in Zambia and Uganda the possibility that stresses might accumulate and lead to community breakdown. These questions were not 'heard', though workers admitted that talk about AIDS may increase rather than reduce stress, and that despairing comments such as 'we will all die' or 'we are facing the end of the world' are heard from time to time, especially at funerals.

Breakdown seems most likely to occur when several sources of stress build up simultaneously in a community – of which AIDS is only one. Unfortunately, in most countries where HIV infection-rates exceed 20%, other problems which threaten community stability already exist.

For example, in a small and poor country with an expanding population and a limited area of land suitable for crops, land-pressure begins to increase the traditional competition and hostility between different ethnic or tribal groups. Add to that situation a long history of outbreaks of violence and lack of trust, and – perhaps fomented by political or religious leaders – a political system which is, or is perceived to be, oppressive towards some citizens, with denial of free speech and human rights. Such a regime is not likely to have the confidence (either in itself or from the population) to acknowledge that HIV infection-rates are high, or that a positive community response is needed, so public discussion of AIDS is inhibited. Soon, however, most families have lost someone to AIDS and many households have no adults left alive – yet people who fear that they are HIV-infected cannot find out the truth or receive help in facing their fears, because testing facilities and counsellors are not available. As elsewhere, HIV infection-rates are particularly high amongst youth and the military, and a survey in a military camp in 1992 finds that 70% of the soldiers are more afraid of HIV/AIDS than of being at war.

The country described is Rwanda, but similar ingredients for disaster exist in other countries too. In 1994, at an AIDS conference in Japan, Stefano Bertozzi (from GPA) said: 'There are two different kinds of response from vulnerable structures. Impact occurs, coping mechanisms cushion impact. Or, impact occurs, coping mechanisms break down, impact ... is magnified. Others have argued that in no country is there evidence of a macroeconomic* impact, to date, from AIDS. But perhaps there is one. Rwanda. It was poor, land-scarce and beset by decades of ethnic tension. AIDS added worsening poverty and thus increasing social inequity. But perhaps more importantly Rwanda had a population HIV prevalence amongst the highest in the world ... The ingredients of the glue that holds the thin veneer of peace on society are unknown. But I suspect that people's concern about their long-term future and that of their children is one important element ... While the relative importance of all the contributing factors will never be understood, surely HIV contributed ... to the breakdown of the country.'

HIV/AIDS is a contribution to disaster which can be combated, *if* the threat of AIDS to stability and development is admitted, open discussion is allowed, and scarce resources are focused on the needs of people who are most vulnerable to HIV infection: youth, single women, soldiers and refugees.

HOSPITALITY AND COMMUNITY GROWTH

Henri Nouwen, in *Reaching Out* (31), contrasted hostility and hospitality as mutually exclusive responses of persons to other persons. Hostility and hospitality are also alternative possibilities for communities who share common space or purposes, but differ markedly in other respects.

'Hospitality' is a fruitful model to explore, because the word presupposes that both hosts and guests have responsibilities towards each other and that they feel mutual respect. Moreover, the roles of host and guest are potentially interchangeable. These presuppositions fit (or should fit) our twentieth-century situation as a global community of very dissimilar peoples, and our Christian vocation to live (however uncomfortably!) as salt or yeast in this dough.

What essential core values are needed, if mutual hospitality is to prove possible? A World Conference of the Religions for Peace, held in Kyoto, Japan in 1970, found that 'the things which unite us are more important than the things which divide us'. Representatives of many faiths shared:

1. 'a conviction of the fundamental unity of the human family, of the equality and dignity of all human beings;
2. a sense of the sacredness of the individual person and his conscience;
3. a sense of the value of the human community;
4. a recognition that might is not right, that human power is not self-sufficient and absolute;
5. a belief that love, compassion, unselfishness and the force of truthfulness and of the spirit have ultimately greater power than hate, enmity and self-interest;
6. a sense of obligation to stand on the side of the poor and the oppressed as against the rich and the oppressors;
7. a profound hope that *good* will finally prevail.' (26)

SAFEGUARDING INTEGRITY

Hospitality presupposes that communities with these core values are distinct and different but complementary, needing each other. Some safeguards to protect people from absolute demands are needed: first the knowledge that each individual can and should 'belong' in several *different* communities. No-one needs to feel limited to the outlook of any single group, which is allowed to define all values and to supply all needs for approval and support. In practical terms *men* need freedom to move between the overlapping but distinct communities of marriage and family, Church, workplace, village or street, sports club and bar – even though the values and demands of some groups are seen as more important and more binding than others. *Women* need a similar freedom to move between *their* different communities. Our responsibility as creatures is to 'let God be God' – which should prevent us from limiting our perception of the presence and activity of the Holy Spirit to any one group of people (including individual Churches) and instead encourage us to enjoy diversity and to look for the unpredictable Spirit in *every* human group. Courtesy, humility and hiddenness are characteristic of God's encounters with human beings.

A second safeguard is that individual communities have and use external points of reference, which are recognized and accepted by its members. A village, for example, is only one unit in a district under the care of a chief and his council; congregations are related to other congregations in the care of a bishop or senior pastor. But the nature of these relationships too, may be healthy or unhealthy, limiting or life-giving.

Another sign of a healthy community is openness to change rather than uncompromising constancy to an original vision. The need for change may be voiced from within, through the prophetic vision of one member: Hebrew prophets and reformers throughout the history of the Church experienced a call to stand over against their companions to proclaim that the community was no longer pleasing to the Lord. From the eighth century BCE onwards, Hebrew prophets understood, too, that the call to return to covenant relationship with God may be mediated indirectly through the hostility of non-believers, who act unknowingly as God's agents (Isa. 8.5–8; 39.5–7; Jer. 1.14–16). If we, in turn, insist on restricting prophecy to people who profess Christian faith, then we may be refusing to 'let God be God' – free to choose believers or unbelievers to recall His people to true relationship with one another and with Him.

Adaptation and growth are signs of biological and of community life; so the evidence that a particular Church is alive includes willingness to listen to and work with other Christian communities (ecumenical exchange) and with people of other faiths (inter-faith dialogue), as well as openness to secular groups and peoples of different cultures.

Any human group that is changing fruitfully may act as yeast, deliberately or unconsciously leavening the surrounding society. But in response to AIDS some communities deliberately set out to change: here we compare two specific responses, one (officially) secular and the other Church-based.

WORKPLACE AND *KABONDO*

A workplace hardly needs definition; it is a business venture which aims to produce goods or services, so as to supply a real (or advertised) need, to the benefit of managers, who make a profit and (hopefully) also of workers, who gain a living wage. '*Kabondo*' is the word used in Kampala to refer to small Christian communities, which exist to *live* the gospel by serving the poor and sick in their own neighbourhoods – regardless of religion, ethnic background or political allegiance.

WORKPLACE PROGRAMMES IN ZIMBABWE

Glen Williams and Sunanda Ray describe workplace-based AIDS programmes in Zimbabwe, in *Work against AIDS, Strategies for Hope* series (45). They saw that 'in a variety of situations such programmes have succeeded in making information about HIV and AIDS widely available, in encouraging informed, supportive attitudes to co-workers infected with HIV, and in promoting changes in sexual attitudes and behaviour'.

Responses *began* as managers learned the facts about AIDS – modes of HIV transmission, and the consequences and rates of HIV infection in their own communities – and linked these facts with their own observations of more sickness in the workforce, and increasing numbers of workers dying in their thirties and forties. The *motivation* for action was fear of the economic and social impact of sickness and death for their businesses, mixed with human concern for the people involved. The *general aims* of individual programmes were to promote changes in sexual behaviour which would reduce spread of HIV, and to minimize the economic and social effects of sickness on business.

The *strategies* chosen varied with circumstances and priorities. First, in a preparatory phase, data about the local impact of AIDS were collected, senior and middle managers made policies and plans based on this local knowledge and committed personnel and funds to the task, peer-educators were trained to talk about HIV infection and, finally, supporting structures (workplace clinic, welfare arrangements) were strengthened. In one company the Health and Safety Committee made the controversial decision to announce the number of AIDS deaths each month on a noticeboard outside the canteen; this helped to raise AIDS awareness in the workforce and to convince people that the matter had to be taken seriously.

The second phase built on the first and on a solid understanding that 'knowledge' about HIV does not lead to sustained changes in sexual behaviour unless norms for behaviour change first, supported by obvious benefits to individual men and women, which can be seen almost immediately, not just in the distant future. It is helpful if the programme starts with a flourish with an official launch and special events, heavily supported by senior staff and attended also by people from local communities. In one company each of over 20 meetings was opened by the Public Relations Manager, who introduced and explained the campaign, and was followed by a presentation of the basic facts about AIDS by the company doctor. Next, an AIDS play was performed 'which moved audiences to both laughter and tears', followed by questions from the audience to the speakers, and finally, distribution of free comic books giving the facts about AIDS. Drama groups which perform both in the workplace, and (by invitation) outside it, help to maintain enthusiasm, and to extend the influence of a workplace community-for-change.

Following the launch, *awareness of AIDS is deepened to knowledge* by talks and discussions about different aspects of HIV infection, held on a regular basis in 'company time', in the canteen or during breaks from work. Condoms are provided, usually in several ways – with pay-packets, at the clinic, free at farm or factory shops – so that it is easy for anyone to obtain supplies without embarrassment. Trained AIDS information officers in every department are continuously available to answer questions informally, and their enthusiasm is maintained by training sessions (with time off work to attend), recognition by their peers and publicity in the company magazine. Peer-educators are not counsellors and do not need lengthy or expensive training, neither do they need to have an impeccable sexual history – some of the best peer-educators are men who have had many partners and women who sell sex, or have done so in the past. One peer-educator said: 'More men are also sticking to their wives now. Take me, for instance. I used to go to the beerhall and have many girlfriends – sometimes six at the same time. But after the course in Mutare I gave up going to the beerhall. If I want some beer I'll just get some and drink it outside my house. Whenever I go out, it's always with my wife.'

Education is not limited to training AIDS information officers, but also includes training workers to do several tasks, so that each one can more readily deputize for a sick colleague or transfer to another team so that production is not held up when workers are absent. Such training increases confidence and competence, and fosters both *'ubuntu'* and community spirit. Some commercial farmers have thought constructively about the special problems of mothers, and now provide opportunities for them to earn an income of their own, through market gardening or crafts, in order to make women less dependent upon the salaries of their partners, and so less likely to need to supplement family income in times of stress by selling sex.

RESULTS

Attitudes and behaviours *do* change in response to such efforts. Workers and managers are less fearful about AIDS and more confident that they will receive help if they need it. HIV-infected people are accepted more readily and they are thankful for support which helps them and their families to cope, expressing their appreciation by greater efforts to stay at work. A few find the courage to tell their workmates about their HIV infection, and usually find that they are respected, not shunned.

Norms for sexual behaviour alter: change is demonstrated by far fewer clinic attendances for STDs (falls of 50% to 75% have been documented) and a corresponding reduction in time off work – which are seen as immediate rewards by both managers and workers. The decrease in STDs appears to be partly due to greater use of condoms for casual sex, but also to a marked reduction in numbers of sexual partners, as workers re-assess priorities and become more aware of their responsibilities to wives and children. Community leaders report fewer rows between husbands and wives because of infidelity and therefore an improvement in the quality of family life. A growing sense of responsibility is shown in one factory where workers set up a fund to assist the orphans of employees who die of AIDS.

Of course there are failures as well as successes, and in many situations the pandemic extends as fast as, or faster, than responses can develop. A frequent problem is that many companies cannot provide enough 'light duties' to keep workers active for as long as they would like to.

Common factors which seem to be crucial to the success of workplace programmes are:

1. Strong backing from senior management who understand that workplaces *can* play a 'frontline role' in the fight against AIDS.
2. Active workforce participation rather than passive exposure to events run by mangers.
3. Continuity over long periods of time.
4. Appropriate messages: 'mutual faithfulness between partners is the best way of preventing spread of HIV' and 'correct use of condoms can provide a high level of protection' – leaving individuals to make informed choices by themselves.
5. Condoms are easily and continuously available.
6. Prevention of HIV infection is linked to control of other STDs, which are widely regarded as a real health problem.
7. Good health care is provided and supportive social policies respect the basic human rights of HIV-infected employees.

Figure 9.   A *Kabondo* or 'caring community' in Uganda.

8. Peer-educators teach informally and understand the concerns, attitudes and problems of their fellow-workers.
9. The work of peer-educators is recognized and appreciated.

CARING COMMUNITIES IN KAMWOKYA, KAMPALA: *KABONDOS*

The small or 'basic' Christian community response to AIDS developed less deliberately in Uganda. It *began* from within a Catholic congregation because their priest was sad to see how little people who came to Mass regularly knew and cared about each other. One Sunday morning he challenged them: 'Do you know your neighbours, their problems, how they live? Do you know if someone is missing from this congregation? When you share the peace at the Mass do you *look* at the person you are greeting?' He talked about the early Christians who met in one another's homes, shared their goods and helped one another – and he challenged people to become 'daily, not just Sunday Christians'.

The *motivation* to form *Kabondos* was not a response to AIDS: but a desire to live the gospel in the same radical way as the earliest Christian communities. The *aim* was – and is – to deepen members' commitment and prayer, and to help them to express their faith through practical ministry to people in need and evangelization. It just so happens that the most needy people in the community seem to be HIV-infected or affected.

The basic *strategy* was to establish stable groups of about a dozen people, meeting regularly once each week. In 1992 I asked the members of one such group: 'How do you care for a young *Kabondo*?' They laughed and told me that the first step is to teach new members that the Church is not a building but themselves; that baptism is not the end but a beginning; that they should not be passive listeners and observers, because 'each person has responsibility in the Church'. 'Next we teach how to share the word of God', so at every meeting the group reads and discusses a passage of Scripture (often the Gospel for the next Sunday), and then decides how to put it into practice: who will cook for an old man on his own, who will wash and dress a woman too weak to care for herself, who will go to market for a family or clean the house where a mother is ill. On the first Sunday of each month an extra collection is taken in church to provide food and clothes for the poorest people. The group concentrates on work which helps people to help themselves: professional teachers run literacy classes for (badly behaved and reluctant!) street boys and girls, and arranges apprenticeships for those who are willing to come off the streets, and they start leisure activities for youngsters. Other members teach women how to give up selling sex – and instead earn a living by baking or tailoring or other work not requiring capital investment.

At meetings of a *Kabondo*, members sit in a circle at the same level, to show that all people are equal; 'No-one is an expert in the word of God' and 'We eat what is there, nothing special'. The attitude is that: 'We are all priests in our own homes, but to serve, not to be served'. Leaders rotate, but are trained for this role and supported by weekly meetings for leaders alone.

FAITH AND SOLIDARITY

At AIDS meetings these two words are used often, but usually without definition. 'Faith', for example, may mean 'we have faith in your community's capacity to cope with the challenges of AIDS' when used by secular speakers, whereas religious groups use the same word to refer to their beliefs, which determine how people behave towards each other and relate to God as the source of their being. If, however, such distinct definitions are received with mutual respect and held together as valid aspects of the same truth, then a basis for dialogue (and change) exists. In the context of AIDS, secular agencies admit that faith *does* influence the capacity of communities to 'cope' with their lives: so perhaps the post-Enlightenment imprisonment of 'faith' in private life is coming to an end.

'Solidarity' is another term which is even less often defined. It includes, but goes far beyond, a simple agreement to pursue certain goals in particular ways. Paul, in his writings to young Churches, described again and again the kind of solidarity he longed to see in their lives: 'be united in your convictions and united in your love, with a common purpose and a common mind' (Phil. 2.2). Paul's characteristic image for the Church community is that together its members form 'the body of Christ', which needs and ought to value the contributions of every limb and organ (Eph. 4.11–16; 1 Cor. 12.12–30). Solidarity, when mature, expresses mutual love.

The maturity of mutual love in a community is a goal, however, not a starting-point. How does community capacity to cope with demands begin and grow into mutual love? The earliest signs of solidarity (as a goal to work towards) are:

1. Members have developed some capacity to deal with conflict within the boundaries of the group;

2. They know, and are comfortable, with the group's chosen values, and

3. feel accountable to each other, not only to an external authority.

4. They also feel confident that their opinions and wishes matter to the group and are significant because they 'make a difference' as individuals and as a community.

CRISIS AND CHANGE

Although disaster may cause human groups to disintegrate, it can be the necessary stimulus which forces an assorted collection of people into integration as a community, and which releases *'ubuntu'* in individual members. Indeed, it is a common experience that human beings need a threat or crisis to jolt them out of sleep. Experience shows that the process of releasing capacity to cope has several stages, which can be helped or hindered.

1. Nothing positive is likely to happen until members of a community *themselves* recognize a threat to its structures or life which is capable of disrupting both, as AIDS does.

2. In this hazardous situation a person or group (from within or outside the community) gives respectful attention to concerns and needs expressed by members of the community, in their own terms – and tries to draw minority groups into the process of defining hopes and fears.

3. Next, members of the community need encouragement to recognize and respect their *existing resources* and skills: this is a critical stage. If self-respect and consciousness of capacity to change *something* in the situation (however small) is achieved, community capacity can begin to grow.

4. At this stage members of the group need to *choose* what to do first, and how to *improve* their resources and skills. When priorities have been chosen by the community – then, an offer of training or demonstration may be useful. For example, helping to care for sick HIV-infected people in the community (towards whom people feel both obligation and guilt) can help to end the inertia associated with guilt and show that help *is* possible – all at the same time.

In contrast, if outsiders or persons with authority within the group merely condemn existing attitudes and behaviours and direct people to do this or that differently, imposing their own ideas without consultation, their 'interventions' are more likely to result in resentment than co-operation and may stifle latent 'capacity to cope'.

RESPECTFUL LISTENING

Adults have many concerns which they do not express because they never have the chance to do so. Some concerns do not even reach consciousness, because people cannot recognize and express painful feelings, and until these are uncovered it is unlikely that hidden hurts and aspirations will be revealed. 'Facilitator' is a present-day term for a person who helps to make possible something which might not otherwise happen: in this case, communication of concerns in a group. Everyone present at a meeting (lowly or great, young or old, female or male, outsider or insider) should have a chance to contribute an idea of their own. A strong chairman, who is well-respected, is needed to ensure that everyone is heard, and an efficient scribe is useful to record the ideas.

The next step is to encourage discussion of these ideas, in an atmosphere of mutual respect, with a view to clarifying hopes and wishes, and later organizing them into a list of priorities. During the process of clarification feelings are expressed, sometimes in words, but more often by tone of voice, posture or gesture, which hint at issues that have not yet been mentioned, which can be drawn out and added to the concerns that have been expressed directly.

Every society has fears and sets up boundaries accordingly, but acceptance of marginal people is likely to increase as the group gains confidence and solidarity; the well-being of a community can be judged by the quality of the respect and care which it gives to disadvantaged minorities.

POWER AND LEADERSHIP

The word 'power' may refer to our capacity, as persons or communities, to 'make a difference' to the societies in which we live. Power is also a vital but ambiguous link between leaders and people who are led. Most traditional power structures in workplaces and Churches assume that a small minority will be leaders, responsible for decisions affecting all the members. At best this system leads to benevolent paternalism, which may be accepted by its objects with gratitude or resentment – or a mixture of both. Hierarchies thrive on stability and submission, but tend to let the potential of a majority of workers or faithful laity remain underdeveloped – for it is not intended that 'they' shall rise to challenge or share leadership. It is a common but fragile system, because it denies the aspirations and ignores the gifts of large numbers of people, who may at any time cease to be submissive and react to their unhopeful situations with violence.

At worst, traditional power structures lead to dictatorship, which tends to spread down through the layers of society, because the natural tendency of oppressed people is to pass on their own discontent and experience of oppression to others who are weaker than themselves. Oppression at work may be a significant factor in maintaining violence in society, because a man who is denied dignity at work may express his anger by beating up a drinking-partner who further offends his pride, or his wife and children, who fail to heal his wounds.

Often traditional leaders are born to privilege and trained for authority in special schools or through secret rituals, which are designed to maintain a gap in knowledge and competence between the élite and the mass of ordinary people. There are few opportunities for outsiders (workers or laity) to break into the system, which tends to maintain authoritarian styles of leadership, and a complementary style of 'being led' which is apathetic or submissive.

Relationships within networks of communities are likely to depend on the views of authority and styles of leadership expressed in the network. It may be useful to examine concepts of 'authority' within a network, to see how it is regarded. Is authority seen as 'imposed', with a fixed form – to which the only acceptable response is obedience? Or is authority understood as a capacity and responsibility-for-living which resides in the community as a whole, even where it is actually exercised by only a few members? Perceptions are important, because the working-out of authority experienced as a burden which limits responses and behaviour in pre-determined ways, will be very different from the working-out of a delegated authority which expresses the living spirit and decisions of the community.

STYLES OF LEADERSHIP

Authoritarian leaders tend to regard rules (especially those relating to external details of dress or protocol) as important, to be rigid in outlook and behaviour, afraid of failure and unwilling to take reasonable risks; they are often people who have not escaped from the influence of internalized and disapproving parents. In contrast, a leader who uses authority easily, to draw energy and co-operation from co-workers, is likely to be flexible, interested primarily in people and secondarily in principles (and then not in particular interpretations), capable of taking risks and intent upon achieving desired aims, rather than afraid of falling short of a predetermined standard of excellence.

JESUS AS LEADER AND TRAINER OF LEADERS

The Gospels describe Jesus of Nazareth as a leader of the second type, a man of authority who was unconcerned about status and the privileges of power. He welcomed and treated with respect everyone who came to Him and rebuked His companions when they tried to keep unimportant, undesirable or importunate people away (Mark 10.14 and 47–49). He rarely seems to have assumed that He knew what a man or woman wanted, but nearly always asked: 'What do you want me to do?' Desperate people appear to have felt safe in His presence and wanted to stay in His company (Mark 5.18–20; 10.52; Luke 8.1–3). He accepted service and affection from such people, and protected them from criticism, even when their attentions were expressed with an extravagance which compromised His own reputation (Luke 7.36–50; Mark 5.25–33; 7.24–30). Jesus Himself expressed the extravagance He attributed to Abba, God, when He fed 5,000 people (Mark 6.30–44) and God's extravagance is a key theme in about a third of His parables

– about a great supper (Luke 14.15–24), a prodigal and a stay-at-home son (Luke 15.11-32), an unmerciful servant (Matt. 18.23-35), a lost sheep (Luke 15.1–10) and a prodigal employer (Matt. 20.1–16).

In speech and in act Jesus of Nazareth identified Himself as the servant or slave of everyone, and He told his followers that they should copy His behaviour – which they report, despite their failures in practice (John 13.1–20). In the Fourth Gospel the story of Jesus washing His disciples' feet is followed by long discourses and a prayer. The status of these passages as straightforward reporting – of what a modern journalist might have tape-recorded – may be doubtful, but their content is consistent with what we know of Jesus from synoptic sources, and the location of the discourses, immediately before Jesus's arrest and trial, shows their significance for the writer's community.

In simple domestic and farming terms, which anyone can understand, Jesus is represented as preparing His disciples for His almost immediate departure, and revealing to them His own relationship to his Father and the extension of that relationship to anyone who genuinely loves Him: 'If anyone loves me he will keep my word, and my Father will love him and we shall come to him and make our home with him' (John 14.23). This indwelling is to be as natural and vigorous as the soundness of a fruitful vine (John 15.1–8); sharing in the life of the vine will be made possible by the future gift of the Holy Spirit (John 14.25–26; 15.26; 16.13–15), whose coming depends upon Jesus's first 'going away' (John 16.6–11).

The long prayer reveals the mutual indwelling of Father, Son and Spirit, which will be shared with 'those you have given me' (John 17.11–13) and Jesus's desire that the love and unity of the Trinity should be expressed in the relations of the disciples with one another (John 17.22-26). Yet the prayer was recorded (if a majority of witnesses are believed) at a time towards the end of the first century CE, when such unity was far from being a reality amongst the Churches. Where does the vision originate, if not with the Lord?

The vision of unity is certainly not confined to the writer of the Fourth Gospel, but appears repeatedly in the Epistles of Paul and Peter. Moule takes 'the extraordinary conception of the Lord Jesus Christ as a corporate, more-than-individual personality' as a second 'phenomenon of the New Testament' which (after the resurrection) cries out for an explanation. 'What remains extraordinary is not the concept of an individual figure summing up a corporate group, but the identification of such an inclusive figure in a known, historical individual ... (These Jews) began to regard the Rabbi, whom some of them had known personally, whom all of them knew of as a recently executed victim of injustice, as the body of which they were limbs.' Moule concludes his argument: 'One cannot, without making nonsense of the whole Gospel story, eliminate from the traditions the sense that where Jesus was, there a titanic battle was always engaged-in with the forces of evil. Both His words and His deeds are blows aimed at the very Kingdom of evil by the Kingdom of God ... the resurrection is not the resuscitation of a mere individual, but victory over death won by New Man' (29).

Jesus of Nazareth preached that the Kingdom of God was very near, so near that everyone had to decide whether to support or fight its coming, and He showed by accepting marginal people, by healings, exorcisms, and other 'mighty works' that the Kingdom of God was indeed present wherever He was. From the start of Jesus's public ministry, but with greater intensity towards its end, He trained a group of men and women for the kind of community life required in the Kingdom. By story-telling, direct instruction and most of all by example, Jesus described and demonstrated what their new life was to be like. Kingdom-life will start in hidden, undramatic ways, as invisible at first as seeds hidden in soil. The Father's Kingdom will grow slowly – like a crop springing up in a field or like yeast working in dough, and its demands will be governed by relationships, not by regulations. Jesus's disciples are to relate to each other with mutual respect and forbearance. Perfection is certainly not expected, for Jesus assumes that there will be plenty of occasions when forgiveness is needed for real or imagined injuries. He teaches that mutual forgiveness must go on and on, a long way beyond even extravagant limits. His disciples are to serve each other, to the extent of denying their own needs, and service (not pomp) is to be the hallmark of their leaders, just as it is characteristic of Jesus. It is to be a willing, unassuming, hospitable service, equally ready to share joy or sorrow, marked by generosity rather than moderation. Mutual love is to be a willed attention to the true well-being of others – and warm enjoyment of their 'otherness'. Indeed the community will exist only *for* those others, 'that the world may believe'.

This mutual love is to become universal, no longer (reasonably) limited to family or tribe, but extended to all human beings, because they *are* human beings, to the utterly extravagant limit of loving and forgiving even enemies, 'those who persecute you'. Jesus did what He prescribed for others, as the account of His arrest, trial and execution records.

The demand that mutual love should be universal, not limited, is a critical demand of the gospel, seen by most people as 'impossible!' – if the demand is made concrete and applied to enemies who are known, not distant. Both Donders and Donovan, writing about their understanding of African traditional theology and their experience of evangelism, identify the requirement for universal love as the crucial testing point for Christian faith. It is also, in our present day, the crucial testing point for the survival of humankind, as Kung and many others see so clearly (15), (16) and (26).

How can mutual love, to these absurd limits, become possible? The answer offered in the Fourth Gospel is: through God living in men, women and children. Jesus speaks familiarly to the Father and asks: 'With me in them and you in me, may they be so completely one that the world will realize that it was you who sent me and that I have loved them as much as you loved me' (John 17.23).

How *can* God live in human beings? The answer, in the actual experience of first century believers, was: through the coming of the Holy Spirit of God, a coming which began at a particular place and time, a few weeks after Jesus's death and rising to life – but which has continued ever since. Often the Holy Spirit comes to human beings, as individuals and also in communities, anonymously and without (apparently) enquiring first whether they hold – or do not hold – particular sets of beliefs. But the Spirit always courteously asks permission to enter the secret place of their '*ubuntu*', where He is at home.

The characteristic activity of the Holy Spirit in communities is to bring hope, to liberate their members from fears and restrictions, and to introduce them to each other across barriers which previously seemed insurmountable – in order to make *koinonia*, communion between them. The word '*koinonia*' is derived from the Greek verb for 'to share in with (someone)'. In the New Testament it is used infrequently in practical exhortations to share one's possessions with people in need (Rom. 12.13) or to avoid sharing in someone else's wrongdoing (1 Tim. 5.22). But it is also used to speak of the fellowship believers have with one another and with God (1 John 1.3,6) and of the union of believers with the Lord, and with one another, at the Lord's supper. 'The cup of blessing that we bless, is it not *koinonia* in the blood of Christ? The bread that we break, is it not *koinonia* in the body of Christ?' The reference to 'one loaf' implies that we form a single body because of our share in the 'one loaf' of the Eucharist (1 Cor. 10.16).

Koinonia is also the word used to emphasize that Jesus Christ shared human physicality: 'Since all children share the same blood and flesh, he too shared equally in it, so that by his death he could take away all the power of the devil, who had power over death, and set free all those who had been held in slavery all their lives by the fear of death' (Heb. 2.14,15).

This *koinonia* is characteristic of the Holy Spirit when God is named as Trinity in the New Testament: 'the grace of the Lord Jesus Christ and the love of God and the *koinonia* of the Holy Spirit be with you all' (2 Cor. 13.13). Much later, during the fourth century CE, Christians around the Mediterranean Basin were working out the implications of speaking about God in this way. In their debates (often pursued in an atmosphere of fierce dispute!), the word *koinonia* was chosen as one which could be used of the relationship between three Persons in one God, for 'there is no division, but only a continual and inseparable communion between them' (Gregory of Nyssa).

A contemporary of Gregory of Nyssa, Gregory Nazianzen, expressed a sense of the unfolding self-revelation of God, seen in and through the controversies of his time: 'the Old Testament preached the Father clearly, but the Son only in an obscure manner. The New Testament revealed the Son, but did no more than hint at the godhead of the Holy Spirit. Today the Spirit dwells among us, manifesting himself to us more and more clearly. For it was not safe, when the divinity of the Father had not yet been acknowledged, plainly to proclaim the Son; nor, when that of the Son had not yet been accepted, to burden us further – if I may use a somewhat bold expression – with the Holy Spirit. So, by gradual additions and ascents, advancing from glory to glory, the splendour of the Holy Trinity shines upon the more enlightened. You see illuminations breaking upon us gradually; while the order of theology, which it is better for us to observe, prevents us both from proclaiming everything at once and from keeping it all hidden to the end.'

In the early history of the Church the first barrier to koinonia which had to be overcome was the enmity between Jew and Gentile, and the New Testament bears witness to many triumphs and setbacks in a process of reconciliation and growing-together which is still far from complete. Later the barriers to reconciliation shifted: as people confronted seemingly unbridgeable gulfs between the civilized world and 'barbarian' conquerors, and nearer to our own time, between slave-owners and slaves.

In the last fifty years koinonia is beginning to appear in new places, as persons and communities begin to cross divisions between races, cultures, Christian denominations, ancient religions, 'haves and have-nots' and – a basic and previously invisible gulf – between women and men.

A modern Orthodox writer, Paul Florensky, has expressed our baffling experiences of the Spirit's anonymity, and his own understanding (shared with others), that we are only at the beginning of seeing the activity of the Holy Spirit, towards whom: 'our characteristic attitude . . . it seems to me, is precisely one of expectation, of hope; a gentle and reconciling hope'. He continues: 'People hardly know the Holy Spirit as a person, and then only in an incomplete, dim and confused fashion. It cannot be otherwise. For a full knowledge of the Holy Spirit would make all created being entirely spirit-bearing, entirely deified . . . Then history would be ended; then the fullness of time would be at hand, and all waiting would be over; there would indeed be no more time. . . . knowledge of the Spirit has always been a pledge or a reward – at special moments and with exceptional people; and this is how it will be until "all is fulfilled". That is why, when reading the Church's writings, we cannot fail to be struck by something that seems strange at first . . . that all the holy fathers and mystical philosophers speak of the importance of the idea of the Spirit in the Christian worldview, but hardly any of them explains himself precisely and exactly. It is evident that the holy fathers know *something*, but what is even clearer is that this knowledge is so intimate, so hidden, without echo, ineffable, that they lack the power to express it in precise language. . . . But the closer we draw to the end of history, the more do new, hitherto invisible roseate rays of the coming Day without evening appear on the domes of the holy Church.' (19)

I do not think we need confine our sightings of the 'rays of the coming Day' to the domes of the Church, for they light up some of the very imperfect secular people and structures of our own time. I have in mind several unpredicted and hopeful new beginnings in political and social systems, often in – although not confined to – the developing world.

For example, resources for 'coping' with AIDS are very unevenly deployed around the world; there are fierce disputes about priorities and some (apparently) wilful neglect of disadvantaged minorities by the international organizations concerned about AIDS. But the fact remains that there *is* true concern, now reaching a global scale, and koinonia *is* being expressed – of a warmth and generosity which astonishes many HIV-infected people and their families, who are potentially divided by differences of background, sexuality, behaviour and religious belief – yet find that they are not (for most of the time) actually divided.

Or consider the ending of years of civil war in Mozambique, or Ulster Unionists' expression of public sorrow for their part in 25 years of violence in Northern Ireland, or the 'celebration of the century' after the elections in South Africa in 1994. Community exhaustion and revulsion from violence, coupled with political expediency, played a part in these surprising developments – but something or someone more was and is active: these events are not simply reducible to the predictable working out of ordinary political principles.

If these examples show koinonia beginning to grow visibly, it is at the price of immense suffering. It is not accidental that a final use of the word koinonia, in the New Testament, refers to ordinary human suffering as potentially a sharing in Christ's suffering. 'My dear people, you must not think it unaccountable that you should be tested by fire. There is nothing extraordinary in what has happened to you. If you can have some *koinonia* in the sufferings of Christ, be glad, because you will enjoy a much greater gladness when His glory is revealed (1 Pet. 4.12.13).

For Further Reading see Bibliography, p. 311, (1), (15), (16), (18), (19), (41), (45) and (46).

Study Suggestions *For Groups*

1. Can you identify additional factors, other than those mentioned on pp. 236–7, which may lead to community breakdown in developing countries where there is a high prevalence of HIV infection? How do you rate the vulnerability of your *own* community? (If serious concerns about the future stability of a civic or national community emerge in discussion, the group may want to write a well-referenced letter to the Editor of a new journal *Medicine and Global Survival*, Jennifer Leaning, MD, Medical Director, Health Services Division, Harvard Community Health Plan, 10 Brookline Place West, Brookline, MA 02146, USA).

2. If interfaith dialogue is permissible for Christians, is it actually obligatory? Discuss.

3. Is 'political spirituality' (Charles Elliott (18)) a distortion of the gospel or essential in Christian responses to AIDS?

CHAPTER 16
Loss and Death

'All discussions of the world's sorrow are to some extent distortions. Sorrow is at most only one half of reality.' (6)

'And what the dead had no speech for, when living,
They can tell you, being dead: the communication
Of the dead is tongued with fire beyond the language of the living.'
(17)

'And the last of the enemies to be destroyed is death.' 1 Cor. 15.26.

The apostle Peter wrote to an unidentified group of people: 'There is nothing extraordinary in what has happened to you'. But there *is* justification for the view that in countries where a third of urban adults are HIV-infected, something 'extraordinary' *is* happening. In these countries or regions, the cumulative losses and deaths due to AIDS occur on the scale of disasters such as famine or civil war, not on the scale of ordinary lifetime bereavements which happen to everyone.

At first there are no dramatic signs that anything extraordinary is happening: individual people suffer losses due to AIDS over two or three years, occurring rather early in their lives. Soon, however, their distress no longer stands out as unusual in a generally happy society, but is experienced to some degree by most families. Later, it is slowly understood that this crisis will not end in the foreseeable future, nor be 'followed' by a programme of reconstruction which will restore normal conditions.

Most men and women facing disaster, ask a similar set of questions: 'Why did this happen to *me*?' or 'Why does God let my child or husband or brother suffer so much?' Then: 'What does this suffering mean?' and 'How can I escape?' Behind these questions lies a basic fear: 'Does this disaster mean that I am rejected by God?' It is a fear fuelled by the rejection many HIV-infected men and women actually experience from family or friends, if the nature of their illness is suspected.

Questions about meaning are crucial. Human beings have a strong sense of justice (as applied to themselves) and a horror of waste: only transcendent 'meaning' might be capable of making sense of severe suffering. But questions about meaning are difficult to face for religious people (including Christians), who make certain critical assumptions about human life and the nature of God. Often religious people are not aware of assuming that:

1. Suffering only happens to guilty people (as Job's friends thought), also
2. Suffering is probably inflicted by God as deserved punishment.
3. An all-powerful and all-loving God 'ought' to intervene to prevent suffering, but
4. As God does *not* intervene He must be either un-loving or powerless.
5. Suffering is always destructive so a creative outcome is impossible.

Many people do not notice that these assumptions are mutually inconsistent.

'WHY SHOULD THIS HAPPEN TO ME?' – CONSISTENCY OR CHANCE

In the context of specific suffering, there may be useful intermediate answers to the question 'Why me?', which relate to my choice (or bad luck) to be in a particular place at a particular time, either doing or not doing certain things; but the basic answer to the question is still 'because the world is the way it is'. We can add either: 'quite arbitrarily, it seems', or 'because that is the way it was made'.

We observe both consistency and chance in events. Consistency appears to be a necessary condition for human beings to be able to learn about themselves and the world, and to be able to plan their actions. If there were no consistent patterns in the way matter behaves, we would be unable to use natural resources for farming or forestry, and unable to develop technologies for building, metalwork, or transport. It would be impossible to plan purposeful acts to yield desired results, so we would not be free, in any real sense, to choose between alternative futures. But it is difficult to see how 'alternative futures' could arise, if chance did not operate to mould events, as well as consistency.

If consistency and chance yielded only 'good' events with 'favourable' outcomes (from a human perspective), many values which we regard as positive would be lost. For example, no-one could experience the satisfaction of triumphing over adversity if no adversity ever arose; and courage, compassion and justice could never be expressed, because there would be no negative events to call forth those virtues. Freedom, truth, justice and compassion appear to depend upon both the order *and* the randomness in the world, which together produce an unpredictable mixture of good and bad. (6)

This is a rational (Western) approach to thinking about choice and freedom, which visualizes 'things' (including human beings) influencing each other in a logical but rather mechanical way. In many developing countries a different way of thinking about consistency and chance stands alongside this model, replacing the emphasis on 'things' interacting with a vision of people and God in interlocking relationships. In cultures which set a high value on kinship, people may give different answers to the question: 'Why me?'

WITCHCRAFT

If a society believes firmly in the essential goodness of Creator and creation, an alternative explanation for things going wrong is found in disordered relationships. From this viewpoint misfortune is attributed to human revenge (begging the question of where the impulse to revenge came from), or to the malice of evil spirits operating through human agents (begging the question of the origin of those evil spirits).

The reason, therefore, why *my* child, not my neighbour's, suffers fits (due to malaria) includes the existence of malaria parasites and the failure of the city council to prevent mosquitoes from breeding, but is thought to be determined by the ill-will of another human being. This person is thought to be the agent who locks together the 'natural causes' of a disaster and directs them to me. Sometimes the ill-will is reckoned to originate in resentment for an injury which I inflicted, whether intentionally or not, years ago. Now my victim or my victim's family avenges the wrong, by exacting 'an eye for an eye and a tooth for a tooth'. Premature death in youth or early adult life is particularly likely to need an explanation of this kind.

Sometimes the forces of evil are thought to be directly involved, through the malice of evil spirits operating in someone who is named as a 'witch'. The 'witch' need not necessarily consent to this malice or even be aware of being used for evil purposes – until the evil is unmasked by a witch-finder. The witch's essential innocence may be confirmed by their willingness to undergo unpleasant treatment in order to be freed from an invading spirit. A deep experience of personal forgiveness, which results in willingness to forgive other people who have injured *us*, combined with trust in the superior power of the Holy Spirit, is needed to release men and women from fear of witchcraft.

'WHY DOES GOD ALLOW SUFFERING'

This question wrestles with the assumptions about the meaning of suffering referred to earlier, asking whether the Being we name 'God' is actually in charge of all events and their consequences. If this is the case, then is God *also* all-loving?

The 'problem of evil' hinges on the answer given to the last question. If God is *not* all-loving there is no reason to feel outraged by the existence of evil. On the other hand, if we are convinced, on good evidence, that God *is* all-loving, then we can legitimately ask if He is indeed all-powerful too? In the world we know, is it possible to regard God as infinitely loving *and* infinitely powerful – both at the same time?

We may overlook an important difference between potential power and power which is used. Human beings have powers which they can choose not to use, in order to give other people freedom to exercise their different powers. The only way a Creator can give creatures real freedom is to *choose* to limit the exercise of His own freedom to act. Absolute power and delegated freedom do not coexist: free choices can only be made in 'space' which is at least partially uncontrolled. Some theologians argue that the creation of anything at all, whether or not creatures are given freedom, required self-limitation on the part of God. From this perspective, God's *kenosis** (self-emptying) began with creation, not with the incarnation of the Word.

John Austin Baker reminds us that: 'the ways in which mankind finds or makes its pleasures are far more varied than its pains', and reverses the question about the origin of evil, to ask: 'Where does *good* originate, and why does good exist at all?'. (6)

WHAT IS THE ORIGIN OF SUFFERING AND EVIL?

Most people begin by attributing suffering and evil to three sources:

1. Disorder in the *natural* world (illness, flood, drought, earthquake), related to the freedom and consistency of its structures;

2. Disordered human *moral* choices (cruelty, injustice, oppression);

3. *Metaphysical* disorder – death, which (seemingly) mocks and destroys all that is good and beautiful in human lives.

The suffering of pandemic AIDS arises partly in the natural order and partly through moral choices made by women and men (irresponsible social or sexual behaviour), but the greatest problems arise from the apparent wastefulness of the deaths of young children, and of adults in their most productive years.

Some philosophers and theologians think that human beings do not have the resources to answer questions about the origin of evil. Others believe that questions about the origins of suffering and evil *are* admissible. Here, in outline, are several approaches to the problem.

1. *Pantheists* view God and the universe as identical, and hold that opposites such as good and evil must either both exist together in God (the Hindu view) or else evil must be illusory ('less than real').

2. *Dualists* believe that evil is indeed real, eternal, and perpetually at war with good, but they cannot satisfactorily explain how evil originated.

3. *Theists* may choose to challenge the supposition that evil is a 'something' and suggest that it is actually a 'nothing' or lack of good (Augustine of Hippo). (Traditional *theists* have difficulties because they can neither deny the reality of evil, nor allow that evil is a force which

exists independently of the Creator – dualism – nor admit to any limitation of the power of God – not even the voluntary kenotic limitation suggested earlier. On the other hand, the theory that evil is only a 'lack of good' is difficult to reconcile with experience of the power and energy of evil in the Jewish Holocaust, or in more recent attempts at genocide).

4. Philosophers and theologians who regard *human freedom as the supreme value* argue that evil is 'necessary' if human beings are to be able to freely choose either to love *or to reject* God. If, they argue, the operations of chance and consistency resulted only in alternative 'good' outcomes, then it would be impossible to actively *reject* 'good'. Chance and consistency must, therefore, allow for the possibility of 'bad' outcomes, if human beings are to be truly free to reject the 'good' — and (ultimately) relationship with God. (In lecture rooms and tutorials Western philosophers defend this *free-will* argument with passion: it is less easy to defend in a casualty department or a prison cell, faced with the passionate grief of a mother who has just lost a child, or the fear of a man about to be tortured.)

5. A different approach is not to attempt to explain the origin of evil at all, but simply to accept the presence of a *mystery*: that *good and evil are inextricably bound up together*, so that where evil is most intense, there, too, must be the greatest potential good. This theory is supported by some people with practical experience of severe suffering, who came to see that they were 'privileged to take part in an *act of redemption*' (9).

I find this last approach to suffering and evil to be the only one that matches the facts of my own and others' experience of pandemic AIDS. It is the approach to the problem of evil presupposed throughout this book, and by the Yahwist authors of Genesis. The tree of knowledge in the Garden of Eden 'was a delight to the eyes, and the tree was to be desired to make one wise' (Gen. 3.1–7), but the fruit gave knowledge of good *and* evil.

GOOD AND EVIL ARE 'INEXTRICABLY BOUND TOGETHER'

In times of mass disaster it may be necessary to dig a large grave with bulldozers and to shovel hundreds of dead bodies into it, almost unmourned. It is equally necessary that later the dead should be named and honoured, not just to acknowledge *their* dignity, but also for the well-being of survivors: John Donne said: 'Every man's death diminishes me, because I am a part of the whole.'

But all the disasters recorded in history have not eliminated from human thought a link between hope to be delivered from suffering, and hope for entry into a completely new world. Edward Schillebeeckx wrote: 'in the spontaneous experience of every people there is invariably assigned to each ... experience of disaster ... a religious dimension. *It is felt instinctively that ... the ill is not to be contained within a merely human reference.* And so where men have looked for salvation, their hope has received a religious name. Reaching above and beyond themselves, men learned to expect that this good must come "from God". *They look for mercy and compassion at the very heart of reality, despite every contrary experience.*' (My italics). (38).

In a similar vein, John V. Taylor wrote: ' ... tragedy does more than arouse our pity or our horror. The protagonist's cry of anguish, outrage or despair moves us to identify ourselves with him or her at an emotional level below consciousness ... we are persuaded to recognize in these shattered representatives of our race a greatness that soars above the catastrophe, and even the evil flaw that brought it about. Achieving such surpassing stature at the very moment of their fall, they revive in us, through our identification with them, our own mysterious transcendence.' (40).

This 'mysterious transcendence' is reinforced when we experience the ambiguity of suffering and death. Often enough the effects of suffering appear purely destructive, but some outcomes of disaster are visibly creative. In retrospect, it may even seem unlikely that a great good would have come to pass, if death or evil had not been suffered first. The deaths of Martin Luther King and Steve Biko catalysed* change in the status of black people and in attitudes to racism, not just in their own countries but on a far wider scale, and the long imprisonment of Nelson Mandela has had similar effects.

The pattern of new-life-through-death is not confined to the death and resurrection of Jesus, but appears repeatedly as a basic pattern for re-creation in the physical and social orders. 'We can believe that God has an end in view which is never abandoned, but no predetermined route for getting there. There is no grieving over what might have been ... God's action within the cosmic process resembles the habitual response that we have seen demonstrated on the human scale in the career of Jesus. It is always *ad hoc*: "Where shall we go from here? What shall we make of this?" ' (40). The strategy God is using to 'defeat' evil appears to use consistency and chance (and even deliberately chosen evil) as the raw material for re-creation. The 'end in view' is a freely-chosen sharing by all rational creatures in the life of the Trinity. How should we attempt to respond to God's actions, as we cope with the losses and deaths of AIDS?

POSSESSION, LOSS AND MOURNING

When a young child discovers that his mother is not part of himself he soon learns that other comforting or disturbing experiences are not parts of himself either. A little later, he begins to appropriate desirable persons and objects as 'mine!' – one of his earliest words. We have an instinctive need to 'possess' or control: to have a thing or person at our own disposal. Loss of 'control' is painful (seen in a child's anger and anguish when his mother leaves him alone), so relationships are both satisfying and threatening because the otherness of another person prevents control; vulnerability is inevitable.

Growth to maturity passes through three long overlapping stages: children learn independence, to accept some imposed limitations, to exercise control over things and to co-operate with people – in some degree at least. Adolescents and adults work at becoming persons through relationships with other persons. The final stage normally begins about halfway through life, when a man or woman recognizes that there is not enough time left to satisfy all the hopes and dreams of youth. The work of maturity aims to fulfil some possibilities and to 'let go' of other powers, hopes and relationships.

On this journey progress is marked by transitions, which rehearse the kenosis or letting-go of death, because it is necessary to 'let go' of roles and capabilities which belonged to an earlier stage – in a necessary preparation for gifts and tasks belonging to the next stage. No-one can receive a new gift while their hands remain clamped around something old.

MOURNING

Letting-go in order to receive new life is the essence of mourning, which is a normal response to loss of a valued person, task, attribute, or hope, at any age. In early life it is primarily a process of *de*tachment in preparation for a new *at*tachment. In later life a more definitive mourning is demanded for relationships, strength and independence which will not be regained in another form; this mourning is likely to be most intense when these losses occur prematurely, due to illness (like AIDS) in the prime of life. People who know that mourning can be a reconstructive process are not let off doing it, or excused from feeling the same grief as everyone else. The comedian's comment: 'I don't mind dying, but I just don't want to be around while it's happening!' is a healthy and normal reaction. We do well to remember that dying happens to people who are still alive.

Normal mourning allows people to acknowledge the goodness and value of what they have lost, but to detach themselves from the past and reinvest their energies in what lies ahead. Whether the loss has already occurred (bereavement, job-loss, robbery) or is still potential (knowledge of terminal illness for self or relative) – the stages of mourning follow a similar pattern of denial, anger, pining or bargaining, depression and acceptance. Grieving requires physical and emotional energy, so it is normal for a mourner to feel empty, hungry and exhausted. Some cultures (for example North American Indians) recognize the effort and energy needed to mourn well, by relieving bereaved persons of responsibilities, and even the small tasks of self-care, for several months, marking the stages of recovery by rituals which help mourners to express sorrow and turn slowly but firmly towards new life. In these societies mourning may end with a celebration which expresses a return to life and joy.

One adverse effect of frequent deaths due to AIDS is that healthy mourning rituals are cut short and often dropped for practical reasons, rather than adapted to new circumstances – which include the probability that several deaths will occur in the same family.

LOSS OF CONTROL: ARE DEMENTED PEOPLE STILL HUMAN?

A key issue in the cumulative losses of HIV infection is loss of *control* of events, work and health. Physical dependence, loss of dignity and loss of self-respect are feared because if we lose these, we fear that we shall no longer be human. The question: 'What is a human person?' is particularly acute when dementia leads to loss of skills and memory and seems to destroy a familiar personality. Is this shadow of the person we once knew still loved and redeemed by God? Is there a human spirit left in whom God might dwell? Where is God?

The links between human mind and human brain are mysterious. The more scientists learn about thinking and remembering, the less possible it becomes to give a reductionist, mechanical account of these processes – and faced with the problems of dementia it is not helpful to try to do so.

All young creatures are helpless in varying degrees, but human babies are more helpless than most. They cannot communicate anything more complicated than general distress – or even survive without care. While babies are full of potential for the future they have no utility in the present, yet they are human beings. The Gospels insist that Jesus of Nazareth was born as helpless and vulnerable as all babies, and that He grew slowly, in the same way as other children. Paul wrote to the Philippians (2.6–8) 'His state was divine, yet He did not cling to His equality with God but emptied Himself to assume the condition of a slave, and became as men are; and being as all men are, He was humbler yet, even to accepting death, death on a cross.' The helplessness and inability to communicate of Jesus, the God-Man, in babyhood and in death, is our guarantee that no possible degree of helplessness or dementia could remove our status as human beings. The losses of dementia can be interpreted as a premature beginning to the more general letting-go of death: the dignity of the human person remains and ought to be respected. 'Nothing, therefore, can come between us and the love of Christ, even if we are troubled or worried, or being persecuted or lacking food or clothes, or being threatened or even attacked ... For I am certain that neither death nor life, no angel, no prince, nothing that exists, nothing still to come [not AIDS or dementia], not any power, or height or depth, nor any created thing can ever come between us and the love of God made visible in Christ Jesus our Lord' (Rom. 8.35, 37–39).

Just as we need to allow children to *be* children, and not to burden them with adult responsibilities too soon, so that they lack 'space' to experiment and play, so it is equally necessary to allow ageing or dying people 'space' for the letting-go which is the work proper to their stage of life. A Russian Orthodox monk, Seraphim of Sarov (who had many demands on his time), said: 'At the extremes of life, everything that happens is of the utmost consequence, in the middle time a man or woman has nothing to do except to learn detachment from achievement and distress': Seraphim therefore gave priority to seeing the very young and the very old. Perhaps we should do the same.

DIFFERING PERSPECTIVES ON LOSS AND DEATH

The impacts of loss and death on HIV-infected and affected people are not the same. Although the losses experienced by an HIV-infected man or woman (when adequately mourned) often lead to new life and new possibilities, these small 'resurrections' occur during the approach to death. In contrast, the HIV-affected person's experience of loss takes place in the context of a good deal more living still to be done, and with the possibility of replacing something of what is about to be lost, as Job did after his experience of desolation (Job 42.10–17). Pastoral responses to both groups should take note of their different viewpoints.

HIV-affected persons are troubled by a multitude of practical concerns which interrupt mourning and distract attention from the dying person, thus increasing guilt. It is difficult to cope with disturbed nights, repeatedly soiled clothes and bedding, irrational demands and the sorrow of watching a beloved person change and waste away. Children in the family are unhappy and confused, there may not be enough money for food, neighbours are distant or unkind, it is disappointing when medical treatments fail, and boring to be housebound. Carers are anxious about how and when death will happen and how to move the dead body to a mortuary and meet funeral expenses. They look ahead to further anxiety about who will support surviving children, to loss of property and home and perhaps to uncertainty about the need to undergo – or avoid – traditional ceremonies such as 'cleansing the widow'. It is not surprising that carers are exhausted and angry, even if they are not also HIV-infected, as is often the case. Pastoral planning which removes even one or two anxieties lightens the burdens of caring and makes it more possible to cope.

The dying person shares these concerns, but is increasingly unable to solve practical problems, as scope for action narrows. His perspective differs from that of observers, for whom his expected death is a future loss, but with life to be lived on the far side of loss. For the dying person death is a present mystery, with no certain information about anything at all on the far side. He too, mourns, for he dreads separation from those he loves and feels increasingly separated, already, from their daily lives. He may fear what follows death, but more often he fears the process of dying; no-one else can do his dying for him and there is no turning back. Often he or she has to face this loneliness without even the comfort of talking about what is happening, because no-one will allow mention of death. Friends and family evade the subject out of concern for the sick person and because speaking of death makes its approach more real. Only people who have begun to face their own deaths are able to talk comfortably about death with others.

PASTORAL CARE: LAST WEEKS

Medical and nursing care should be good, so that the dying person is physically as comfortable as possible. This requires listening to what he has to say about his symptoms, and accepting his priorities. In the last weeks of life the dying person and his doctor should decide *together* when treatment is appropriate, having first agreed about goals: maximum duration of life, or the best possible quality of life, or a judicious mix between the two, for example to allow him to take part in a daughter's wedding, or to see his son return from study overseas. Although treatment decisions belong to the patient and his doctor or nurses, a pastor may need to remind both parties that this is so, and should encourage the dying person to express his wishes.

Dying people and carers need not be defined by their roles. To emphasize this, and to avoid repeatedly writing: 'the dying person', in the pages that follow I shall use names, Tom or Naomi. As living persons, Tom and Naomi are entitled to feelings, including 'unacceptable' feelings such as anger. Until negative emotions are admitted it is difficult to see death's more positive face.

Dying is often boring and usually exhausting; a balance needs to be found between enough visitors to provide company and a sense of still being part of the community, and so many visitors that there is no time for rest or for reconciliation and continuing growth in relationships. Some Western hospices help patients and families by having one day each week when (apart from emergencies) no visitors are received, so that relatives feel freed from the obligation to visit, and patients can rest, weep, reflect, be silent or pray. In a developing country Naomi and Tom are likely to be cared for at home, where a complete break from visitors may be impractical – but it is worth remembering the old tradition that conversation is not necessary after greetings have been exchanged. It is good to sit in silence, quietly present to each other, speaking occasionally in words which do not need a reply. An old man's description of prayer – 'I look at God and he looks at me' – can be applied to human conversation too.

HOMECARE TEAMS

When Naomi is nursed at home, support may be needed from a visiting team, to make terminal care easier. Many such teams already exist, linked to government hospitals, NGOs, or associations for Church-related hospitals. In areas without a Homecare team local medical services or NGOs should be encouraged to start one, with support from the community – which Christians can help to mobilize. If a service exists, it may or may not have a spiritual component, and Churches can offer to provide pastoral care (alongside the team's other activities), using trained lay volunteers and ordained ministers.

MAKING – AND IMPLEMENTING – A WILL

Often Tom has not made a Will, either because he assumes that this is not necessary, as his relatives will 'do what is right', or because the act of making a Will forces him to admit that death is near. Naomi worries constantly about who will care for her children, but does not realize that a Will would make it more likely that her wishes will be respected: at least her wishes will be *known* so lawyers will be in a position to obey them. Tom or Naomi should be reminded of the Christian duty to provide for their families. Homecare teams or organizations such as the Society for Women and AIDS in Africa (SWAA) usually have access to lawyers who are willing to help, for a nominal charge.

Pastors ought to know how much or how little protection the law gives to the dependents of men or women who die without leaving a Will. It may be necessary to support – or even to start – a campaign to improve laws which give inadequate protection to widows and orphans. In Zambia, for example, the law of inheritance was altered in 1989 to give a widow and her children the right to all household property, the family home and 70% of outside assets – yet in 1994 this law was mostly disregarded because women fear that they will be beaten or bewitched by their in-laws, if they try to take legal action.

It may be necessary also, to change the law relating to death certification to allow the doctor who has treated Tom or Naomi to certify death when this takes place at home. At present people are often taken to hospital a day or so before death, to die in great loneliness in an overcrowded and understaffed emergency ward – sometimes almost untended because treatable patients absorb the time and energies of staff. These tragic ends happen for two reasons: death at home must be reported to the police (to obtain a death certificate) and there are no local mortuaries. While it is difficult and expensive to transport a dead body to a central (and overcrowded) mortuary, taking a dying person to a central hospital is an everyday occurrence in large cities. By 1992 the teaching hospital in Lusaka had acquired a nickname: it was called 'Heathrow' by citizens, in half-cynical, half-humorous recognition that it had become a place for departures from life.

The image of an airport is not out of place for a hospital or hospice – if the sense of adventure and expectancy found in airports is remembered too. Expectancy, humour and festivity are still appropriate, even when people are dying. A pastor may be the person best placed to help Tom or Naomi to express a sometimes unrecognized longing for a little normality and fun, which a pastor can help to keep alive by watching for natural opportunities for small celebrations. Morris Maddocks, in *Healing Ministries*, described the last days of a woman who had loved giving and receiving hospitality. She received sacramental anointing with oil when she appeared to be dying, but she unexpectedly regained strength, sat up in bed and arranged small parties for her friends at her bedside – which she much enjoyed – before dying a week later. (27)

One celebration which Tom or Naomi may wish to plan is the funeral. The prayers, readings, hymns, music, instruments, choice of preacher, whether or not the family should spend money on flowers, even the style of the coffin – these are all matters about which Tom is entitled to express an opinion. A pastor may be able to help to prevent family quarrels after death or during the funeral, by asking Tom who might make trouble later, and offering to act as a mediator to help resolve conflicts while there is time for reconciliation. 'While there is time' is an important phrase, because over half of HIV-infected people who do not receive anti-viral drugs suffer some loss of memory and mental agility in their last weeks. It is necessary, therefore, that tasks needing average mental powers (making a Will, decisions about the care of children, resolving conflicts and planning the funeral) are tackled early rather than late, while death is weeks or months away.

PASTORAL CARE: DYING

Most people fear being treated as dead before they are actually dead, a fear based on repeated experiences of being ignored or patronized. Naomi's family and pastor should know where she wants to die, and who she wants to be with her. The pastor needs to listen with sensitivity to hear about unfinished tasks with which Naomi would like help, and to detect fears about death which may seem too small – or much too large – to mention. With the co-operation of doctors or nurses it should be possible to give realistic reassurance that physical symptoms will be controlled. Strong reassurance can be given about the actual moment of death, which – if the person is not already unconscious – is usually painless or even joyful. This statement is based on numerous reports from persons who have been at the point of death, on the observations of doctors and nurses and on the last words of dying people (5). Men and women who have been resuscitated after their hearts had stopped beating consistently say how unwilling they were to 'come back' from the joyful threshold of death, and afterwards they lose all fear of dying.

Fear of judgement may persist, if Tom is oppressed by actual sins, wasted opportunities, broken relationships or unfinished work, and if he thinks of God as a stern tyrant who is more anxious to condemn than to save. This distorted image of God deserves to be replaced with a Christlike image: 'God is Christlike, and in Him is no un-Christlikeness at all'. Confession of sins to a priest allows individual absolution to be given, joy *is* released when the burden of sin falls away – and it may suddenly become possible to forgive others too. For a prodigal son or daughter, already embraced and washed clean, dying may be faced more lightly and even with humour.

> **Story**: *Faith* died of cancer complicated by HIV infection. Near the end of her life she repented, returned to belief in God and felt herself to be lovingly received as a prodigal daughter. Faith spent her last weeks in hospital because the cancer disfigured her face and made self-care difficult, but she walked out of the ward on good days, to sit in the sun and talk to whoever was around. She was relaxed, at peace with herself and with God, so she was good company. One evening I went to Faith's bedside, before I left to go home. We talked for a few minutes and Faith said, with a smile: 'When I get out of this place, I'm going to take you out on the town!' 'I shall hold you to that promise!' I replied, kissed her and went away. Faith died that night. In her locker we found a letter for her father, apologizing for dying before he arrived to see her.

Farewells are difficult, particularly as it is so rarely clear when a last meeting is actually taking place. Death, like the onset of labour, may have several false starts. It is reported that Steve Biko, who knew that his political protest put his life at risk, used to say farewell to his friends with a quick touch 'which was between a flick and a caress' and the words: 'See you some more!'

Family and friends may wish to take part in the sacrament of anointing, laying their hands with other ministers on Tom or Naomi's head – in silence, leaving the Spirit, who understands our beseeching, to express what we cannot express. When priest or catechist or parent or child brings the sacrament of the Lord's Body and Blood for Tom or Naomi to receive for the last time, it is good for family members to share this 'food for the journey'; they too have a journey to make, through grief to new life.

At the end, the dying person may no longer be able to speak to those around him, who have no means of knowing whether or not he is conscious. It is best to assume that Tom or Naomi still hears and feels what is going on, because consciousness comes and goes, and touch and hearing are the last senses to be lost. (Julian of Norwich, writing about the revelations she received, described her sensations while she and her friends thought she was dying. She was aware of people around her and grateful for their ministrations, but unable to speak, and her body felt 'dead from the middle downwards'. 'After this my sight began to fail. It grew dark around me in the room as if it had been night.' (25).

Short familiar prayers, singing a verse of a favourite hymn or psalm, greetings or farewells spoken slowly and distinctly with the reassurance: 'I know you can't answer me . . .', a hand held, a kiss – these signs show that a loving person is still there.

A few people show a remarkable capacity to hold on to life in order to complete an important task, such as caring for someone else through a crisis, or finding reconciliation with a relative. My experience as a doctor suggests that the day of death is more often within the choice of a dying person than we recognize, providing that they feel secure enough to die and have permission to do so.

Story: *Grace*, aged 35, was dying of cancer at home in the care of her husband *Robert* and their teenage children, with visits from a nurse and a doctor. She had severe difficulty in breathing but she struggled on, waiting for her brother, whom she had not seen for years, to arrive from overseas. On the day he did so, she spent several hours talking with him, then she called the rest of her family into the room to say goodbye. For a while Grace fell into restless sleep. When her doctor arrived later in the day, Robert asked, in great distress: 'How much longer will this struggle go on?'

Robert and the doctor agreed together that Grace needed permission to die, and that the time had come to offer her that permission to 'let go'. In her room they found Grace awake, struggling to breathe, conscious of her surroundings but no longer able to speak. Robert sat beside his wife, holding her hand in his; the doctor took her other hand and asked 'Can you hear us clearly?' Grace nodded at once. The doctor said quietly: 'Grace, if you want to, you could say the words, now, that Jesus said on the cross: "Father, into your hands I commend my spirit" – would you like us to say those words for you?' Grace nodded firmly. Robert took his wife's face between his hands and began to cover it with kisses, while the doctor slowly spoke the words of abandonment to God; before the words were finished Grace had died, gently and peacefully. The next day the doctor called to see the family; Robert and his children brought out an album of photographs taken on holiday the previous year and for an hour or so everyone talked naturally and happily about Grace, and the fun they had shared together. She had gone, quietly and in control of her departure, but she was still part of her family and joy was mixed with their sorrow.

IMMEDIATE CARE FOR THE DEAD BODY

The dead body is 'empty', no longer part of a living person, and this fact has to be grasped by relatives and friends, even if death was expected for a long time. Preparation of the body for burial is an act of respect for the person who has died and helps mourners to accept the reality of death. Whoever washes the body should wear plastic gloves, to protect their hands from secretions which may contain HIV or other infectious agents. Clothing, sheets and cloths used for washing the dead body are laundered in the usual way and hard surfaces (bed, bowls, floor) ought to be cleaned by wiping with diluted bleach. Some health services provide a strong plastic bag to cover the body as a shroud, before it is placed in a coffin. If death takes place in hospital these tasks will be done by nurses, but relatives ought to be allowed to help if they so wish, or to recite psalms or prayers.

When the law demands that the body is taken to a hospital before a death certificate is issued, the family face extra expense and their distress may be exploited by 'businessmen' with trucks. It would be a service to bereaved families for parishes to arrange for two or three fair-minded men, who own suitable trucks, to be available on a rota basis to take dead bodies to hospital, for a fair fee. An alternative solution is to encourage Homecare teams to include use of a mortuary van amongst their services, and also to campaign for small mortuaries (large enough to hold three or four bodies) to be built alongside selected urban or rural health centres. As with other suggestions, the words: 'encourage and campaign' actually mean: 'support campaigns to acquire land and obtain official permission to build, raise funds to buy mortuary freezers, recruit men and women with building experience to clear the site and then construct a professionally designed building, using appropriately simple technology and supervised local labour'!

Making dying at home easier, and providing local mortuaries, would relieve much distress and reduce the costs of funerals. Other sick people and hospitals would benefit too, because emergency wards would no longer be crowded with dying men and women who would have preferred to end their lives at home.

BEREAVEMENT

Bereavement involves carers as well as family, and each fresh bereavement adds to cumulative grief, if deaths are frequent. In severely affected countries people say: 'There is too much grief', and normal mourning is often cut short by the next death, or prevented by emotional numbness, so that abnormal responses to grief are becoming more common.

Prolonged *denial* that death has occurred is unlikely when the final illness is long, as in AIDS. The next stage of mourning – anger – may appear very quickly, and be directed at anyone, including the dead person and professional carers. It seems unacceptable to be angry with a dead person, so this *normal anger* is often hidden, but usually needs to be acknowledged, if mourning is to proceed successfully. The next stage is *pining* (a craving for the presence of the dead person), often made more painful by self-blame, expressing a psychological guilt which has no basis in moral guilt. A pastor can help to relieve psychological guilt by gently questioning the mourner, to draw out the facts and to comment positively upon them, and by assurances that no-one else reproaches him or her for neglect. It is useful to refer publicly to the quality of care key people gave to the dead person, for example at the funeral.

Sometimes relatives and friends arrive after the death and are distressed because they had no chance to say farewell or mend a broken relationship. In these circumstances it may be helpful for the mourner to say aloud, in the presence of the body, what might have been said, if the meeting had occurred earlier. The pastor can ask: 'What do you think Tom would say to you, if he was still alive?' Reconciliation is indeed possible beyond death, as many mourners testify.

After a death professional carers, too, feel angry, lost and intensely aware of their own vulnerable humanity, but afraid to express it. There is nothing left to do, yet staying around for a while to share the helplessness of others shows concern, and helps everyone.

BEFORE THE FUNERAL

The time between death and funeral seems like a continuation of life with the dead person. Ritual wailing, visits to mourners' homes and viewing the body help relatives to grasp the reality of death, and provide time to start the work of mourning. Cultures which have lost their healthy customs need to relearn the value of talking about a dead person, viewing the body to see the stillness of death, and touching one another as reassurance: 'You are real, you are still alive, and we matter to each other'. Tears are natural for both men and women, and noisy weeping often occurs in outbursts which are difficult to watch: there is nothing to do, except stay with the weeping man or woman, with a hand ready to grasp theirs (if it is wanted), silently showing 'We are here with you'.

Loss of fluid and salt through weeping, coupled with lack of attention to meals, may lead to dehydration, so offering tea or fruit juice serves several useful purposes – providing an excuse for company, replacing lost fluids, and involving mourners in everyday comforting routines for a short while. Pastoral time spent with a family early in the mourning process helps to prevent illness, as well as showing sympathy. In the West one-third of all psychiatric illnesses are related to unresolved grief, and it is likely that unsatisfactory mourning contributes to mental and emotional illness on a similar scale in developing countries, too.

In non-industrial countries bereaved families rarely lack support (as they may in the West) but instead receive so many visitors that no-one can rest or be silent, so that preparations for the funeral may become a nightmare of sleeplessness and anxiety about feeding everyone.

Unfortunately not all guests have charitable motives: in Zambia it is said that a widow can cry with one eye only, for the other eye must keep watch over her in-laws, who may strip her of home and property. Most widows are too upset, and too uncertain of their rights in law (especially when changes in the law are recent and unpopular), to challenge tradition, particularly in towns. Churches and women's organizations should be prepared to tell widows about their legal rights and to give practical help in claiming the protection already offered by the law.

Children tend to be forgotten as mourners. It is easier to assume that they do not understand what is happening, or 'do not grieve like adults' than to take their needs seriously and to include them – appropriately – in family mourning. It ought to be someone's special task to attend to their needs. Children need to know what plans for their future are being made, a familiar and trusted person to talk to or cuddle up to (according to age), regular food and bathing, somewhere quiet and undisturbed to sleep, and a quick return to the comforting routines of school and contact with friends of their own age. If there is no older sibling or other relative able to give acute care to bereaved children, it is a suitable task for volunteer mothers. Churches or voluntary organizations could provide training and give volunteers support, in order to define realistic boundaries for the extent and duration of their help.

FUNERALS
Except in Hindu societies, burial remains the normal way of disposing of dead bodies in most developing countries, where cremation is diffi-

cult to arrange, and is outside tradition. Communal burial grounds are important as places to visit, for prayer and continuing contact with the 'living dead'. However, in countries which are already short of agricultural land it will soon be urgently necessary to challenge burial traditions and to learn to cremate bodies – and bury ashes.

In places where funerals are now very frequent traditional practices have already changed – for example, fewer mats are used to wrap the body, and fewer mourners contribute food for the funeral feast, which is much simpler than before. Alterations in the time-scale for mourning are far more important than material changes. In one society, for example, burial used to take place two or three days after death, and a widow was expected to mourn for a year. At the year's end, the dead man's son was named as his heir, property was shared out, decisions made about the long-term care of children and 'widowship' formally ended. Now, in the same society, burial takes place on the day of death or next day, and rites previously performed after a year are completed in a day or two more.

Elders admit that in these circumstances widows can no longer mourn properly, because they lose custody of their children, their property and their status as widows so quickly, and no longer receive the material gifts which used to be their privilege. Nowadays, immediately after the death of a father, senior members of the clan decide who will be responsible for his children: usually the children's opinions are not thought worth hearing and often siblings are separated. The ritual for 'cleansing the widow' (by sexual contact with a male relative of her late husband) may be planned at this time too, when the woman concerned is too upset to know or assert her own wishes.

QUESTIONING FUNERAL CUSTOMS

Christians could contribute, by way of the arrangements made for their own funerals, to community decisions about how traditional burial customs should change (as they must) in response to the crisis of AIDS. Should Christians disregard customs which are primarily opportunities to display status or wealth? Could distant relatives pay their respects at the time of the funeral by a telephone call, timing a later visit to the family to coincide with an anniversary, so helping to extend the period of mourning in a healthy way? Are trucks used to carry mourners safe, or is an accident likely to occur because the lorry or van is overloaded, or driven by a man who drank too much alcohol at the funeral feast? (As a doctor I cared for many people who were seriously injured or died as a result of accidents affecting funeral vehicles.)

Is an ornate coffin necessary, or would it be better to buy a cheap coffin and use the money saved for schoolbooks and shoes? Is it safe to provide beer for the funeral feast, or would road accidents and casual sexual encounters be less likely if soft drinks and tea wre offered instead? May burials take place on any convenient day, or should Fridays and weekends become the accepted days for funerals, so that normal work is disturbed as little as possible? In societies with fragile economies and frequent deaths the avoidable loss of productivity caused by funerals adds significantly to *unavoidable* economic losses due to early deaths.

In some cities it is now necessary to protect the grave from robbers, who re-open new graves to remove the coffins, which are sold to unsuspecting mourners. As funerals may be watched by potential robbers, a very plain coffin may offer some protection, but leaving guards by the grave would probably be a dangerous and unsuccessful remedy. In Lusaka, families who can afford the additional expense arrange for a load of gravel, cement and water to follow the funeral procession, so that a slab of concrete is laid over the coffin, before the grave is filled with earth. Cremation would stop this trade in used coffins.

There never will be enough professional pastors to cope with all the demands of AIDS deaths. Ministers share in the cumulative sorrows of their communities and ought to be able to share with lay people the work of visiting, conducting funerals and bereavement support. Volunteers need training, support from clergy and one another, and regular 'holidays' from death and funerals, to prevent them from being overwhelmed by sadness. In these days *everyone* needs to be reminded of the 'other half of reality' where 'mankind finds or makes its pleasures' (6) – which is a vital function for the arts.

One function of a funeral is to express this 'other half of reality' and to prepare mourners to continue life in the future. Healing begins when burial rituals undo or reverse the ugly circumstances of dying: the dignity of the dead person is restored through graveclothes, coffin and lying in state; the marks of suffering are replaced by cleanliness and beauty; disbelief and numbness are ended by healthy weeping; sudden departure is regretted and time given to unhurried farewells; the silence of death is broken by lamentation; the private act of dying is given public recognition; a person withdrawn from normal life by lengthy sickness is named and their place in society celebrated. Even when 'there are too many funerals', each one commemorates and celebrates the existence of one unique person who cannot be replaced.

Ritual, music, drama, and painting exist not just to give pleasure, but also to express a human longing for ordinary life – and death – to be transfigured into entirely new life.

Community and individual sorrows and hopes should be expressed in many ways – through religious ceremonies certainly, but also through traditional customs, music and art (at every level of popularity or formality), buildings, gardens and planting fruit or forest trees. 'World AIDS week' meetings and services offer a stimulus to create new art, and opportunities to celebrate the spiritual dimensions of human life to which art points.

'WHAT IS DEATH?'

Two questions recur in this book: 'What is death?' and 'Where is God?' At death, is a unique person destroyed for ever? Or is death actually a gateway out of one stage of life into the next, analogous to the birth of a baby, which (from a baby's perspective) must feel like death?

Christians believe that death is overcome in the raising to life from death of Jesus of Nazareth. That event is not an 'explanation' which gives self-evident answers to our questions: 'What is death?' and 'Where is God?' – but human freedom to *dis*believe would be destroyed by certain answers to such fundamental questions. Instead of a reasoned defence of God to explain the facts of suffering and death (theodicy), human beings are actually offered *encounter* with God, or theophany.

ENCOUNTER WITH GOD

The theme of encounter with God appears repeatedly in the Old Testament in moments of disaster or despair. An infertile couple, Sarah and Abraham, were visited by three strangers who represent Yahweh; Abraham offered a feast to the strangers, who asked after Sarah and predicted that she would bear a son, although she was well past child-bearing age – and a year later she gave birth to Isaac (Gen 18.1–15). Jacob, Isaac's son, approaching a critical meeting with his brother Esau, made a camp for his family in the desert, but he himself spent the night in the open, alone and afraid. In the darkness a man appeared who wrestled with Jacob all night long and injured him. The stranger disappeared at daybreak, but he gave Jacob a new name – Israel – which means 'He has been strong against God'. Jacob limped away from the lonely place saying: 'I have seen God face to face, and I have survived' (Gen. 32.4–32).

Elijah presented his tribe with a choice between local nature gods and Yahweh the God of history, in a dramatic confrontation with the priests of Baal at Mount Carmel. Soon afterwards his exultation at success ended abruptly (as exultation is apt to end!) and was replaced by exhaustion and fear for his own life. Elijah went into the southern desert and prayed for death – but he was given food and sent on to Horeb, the mountain of God, where Yahweh appeared to him, not in a mighty wind, or in an earthquake which tore the mountain apart, nor in fire which followed the earthquake, but in 'a sound of sheer silence' (1 Kings 18.20–46; 19.1–14).

THE STORY OF JOB

The book of Job was written after the Exile, to recount the disasters which befell a virtuous man. In his misery, Job was advised by three friends who offered explanations for his suffering, in the tradition of Wisdom literature. Job rejected their conventional wisdom and maintained his innocence of any offence, crying out for a just hearing (Job 29, 30, 31). A. S. Peake wrote: '(Job) charges God outright with immorality, yet he feels that fellowship with Him is the highest good ... (Job) holds together incompatible conceptions of God ... that his present experience of God does not reflect God's inmost character' (32). In the end Job states his great belief: 'For I know that my Redeemer lives, and that at the last he will stand upon the earth; and after my skin has been thus destroyed, then in my flesh I shall see God, whom I shall see on my side, and my eyes shall behold, and not another.' (Job 19.24–27).

From the tempest of suffering God gave Job his answer, but it was neither an explanation of Job's individual suffering nor of the general problem of human suffering. 'Job, while he has spoken of God's power as displayed in the world, is quite unable to explain its phenomena. One by one God makes him ponder them: if each is an inscrutable mystery, what must be the mystery of that universe, whose government Job has so confidently condemned? ... thus man comes to a humbler view of his own importance, and learns that he must transcend his self-centred attitude, if he is to judge the ways of God aright' (32). Job learns 'that it is not for him to lay down the terms on which God must meet him'. In this encounter (still with no answer to his question 'Why?') Job, humbled but trustful, cast himself upon God, and found that God's 'wisdom and omnipotence no longer crush, but uphold and uplift him'.

Job's encounter with a God who says: 'Brace yourself like a fighter, now it is my turn to ask questions and yours to inform me' (Job 40.2) revived trust; it is a profound response to the insoluble problem of our own or others' pain. 'Job does not know now, any more than before, why he suffers. But his ignorance no longer tortures him, he does not wish to know. For he has escaped into a region where such problems exist no longer. He has attained peace and knows that all is well, though he does not know, or care to know, how it is possible' (32).

In the story of Job, God was present alongside the sufferer, to hear his complaints with respect and to defend His own righteousness. But God was not a participant in Job's suffering.

ENCOUNTER WITH GOD IN CHRIST

The first members of the early Church believed that God *is* a participant in human suffering. Their assessment of Jesus of Nazareth and the effects of His life, death and resurrection in their own lives led them to insist that '*God* was in Christ, reconciling the world to himself'. Separation between suffering humanity and God disappeared: even in the shameful circumstances of death by crucifixion it was *God* who suffered, *God* who died. This interpretation of the death of Jesus was expressed repeatedly by the early Christian Fathers. For example, Melito of Sardis, in an Easter homily, wrote:

'He who suspended earth is suspended,
He who fastened the heavens is fastened,
He who fixed the universe is fixed to wood,
God has been murdered . . . '

Jesus of Nazareth was betrayed by a man He loved, He sweated with fear as He waited to be arrested, He was condemned in a flawed trial and hastily executed in public. In fact Jesus suffered and died as other people suffer and die – whether they happen to be HIV-infected, trapped by informers while trying to change an unjust social system or just caught accidently in the wrong place at the wrong time. Mark's early Gospel gives the least edited and harshest account of the crucifixion, which the Church retained to express the conviction that, in dying, Jesus shared 'all men's lostness, when all worldly . . . supports have failed, and God himself seems to have gone. And yet in Christ's case, He will not let God go, but dares to cling to Him and to name Him still "My God, my God" ' (4).

Paul's epistles and the early Christian Fathers interpreted the death of Jesus of Nazareth in terms of the conquest of death by a new Adam, reversing the bondage to death which was the result of the Fall. Patristic thought offered alternative interpretations of the 'fall' of Adam (Gen. 3). For some theologians this story expressed the idea that human beings lost, through disobedience, a virtue and a harmony with each other and the rest of creation which they once possessed. Other Church Fathers, however, saw the first state of human beings as one of only *potential* perfection – which would be realized through a long process of growing-up in faith and loving trust in God. From their perspective, the 'fall' was humankind's attempt to take a short cut to maturity and the always-intended goal of 'being like gods, knowing good and evil' (Gen. 3.5) by means of an 'extension of human existence beyond the limits set for it by God at creation' (G. von Rad, *Genesis* (36).

From this point of view, God barred human beings from 'the tree of life' so that they would not live for ever in a state of falsehood and self-idolatry: death marks a limit to the evil consequences of their disobedience. Gregory Nazianzen said that Adam 'gained us death . . . so that evil should *not* be immortal'. Death is a remedy for sin 'since it makes humanity aware of its finiteness, and lays it open to grace' (11). Certainly death often has this aspect of 'laying open to grace' in the lives of HIV-infected persons.

Julian of Norwich learned that there is a mystery in death and evil which men and women are not ready to have unveiled, and should not seek to grasp, in the course of the Revelations she received in May 1373. Julian lived in a time of corruption, war, dangerous epidemic disease and religious uncertainty, like our own. She received a vision of Jesus in which she heard Him promise that 'all shall be well'. For twenty years she pondered these words and 'it was simply not clear to her how "all shall be well", or how the sin and misery of this world could be turned "to good account with none of it wasted or unnecessary" ' (24). In the end, although Julian still did not see the purpose of the world's pain any more clearly than we do, she was assured that this will not always be the case: 'I saw hidden in God an exalted and wonderful mystery, which He will make plain and we shall know in heaven. In this knowledge we shall truly see the cause why He allowed sin to come, and in this sight we shall rejoice forever.' (24). Julian looked forward to a new deed at the end of time, through which 'all shall be made well'.

A 'great deed' *was* accomplished, *in* time, when Jesus Christ was raised to life from death. Although Jesus shared death with all human beings, He was raised from death 'as the first fruits of many brothers', a theme which the Apostles and Fathers return to again and again.

A vital question remains: is liberation from evil and death through Christ's death and resurrection, which the early Church proclaimed so joyfully, a benefit restricted to 'us' Christians or is it offered to all human beings everywhere?

In the New Testament and Church tradition two opinions exist side by side. The parables of judgement in the Gospels support claims that a conscious decision for Christ is necessary for salvation. This viewpoint has had the greatest publicity, particularly in times of persecution, when victims like to see themselves as 'over against' the rest of humankind. But there has always been an alternative point of view, which interpreted the resurrection of Jesus Christ as the first action in a drama of re-creation involving the whole universe.

'He has let us know the mystery of his purpose, the hidden plan He so kindly made in Christ from the beginning to act upon when the times had run their course to the end: that He would bring everything together under Christ, as head, everything in the heavens and everything on earth' (Eph. 1.9–10 JB). From this perspective, liberation from death is offered to the whole human race without exception, a view more forcefully expressed in the early Church than it is in our own day. Olivier Clement writes: 'For the early Church salvation is not at all reserved to the baptized. We repeat: those who receive baptism undertake to work for the salvation of all. The Word has never ceased and never will cease to be present to humanity in all cultures, all religions, and all irreligions. The incarnation and resurrection are not exclusive but inclusive of the manifold forms of this presence.' (11).

In the second century CE, Irenaeus of Lyons wrote: 'Christ did not come only for those who, since the time of the Emperor Tiberius, have believed in Him, nor has the Father exercised His providence only in favour of people now living, but in favour of all without exception, right from the beginning, who have feared God and loved Him and practised justice and kindness towards their neighbours and desired to see Christ and hear His voice, in accordance with their abilities and the age in which they were living.'

It appears necessary to deliberately *refuse* the Kingdom of God, if one does not want to be included in the new humanity begun in Christ.

For Further Reading see Bibliography, p. 311, (5), (6), (11), (24), (40).

Study Suggestions
1. Compare the 'rational' and 'relational' approaches to 'the problem of evil' What is gained by *combining* their insights?
2. What practical steps have proved useful, in your own experience, when helping men and women to cope with fears of witchcraft?
3. 'God created the *fact* of freedom, man performs the *acts* of freedom. God made evil possible; creatures make it actual.' (*New Dictionary of Theology*, p. 242.) Discuss this statement.
4. What traditions exist in your own community for care of people who are about to die? In what ways have Churches altered and adapted tradition?
5. What changes in funeral customs have been made already in your Church or locality, in response to increasing numbers of funerals? What effects have these changes had on social life and mental health?
6. Discuss the special needs of mourning children.
7. Is encounter with God (theophany) an adequate substitute for an explanation of God's responsibility for evil (theodicy) in the book of Job – and in your own experience of suffering?
8. Learn about the Law relating to inheritance in the case of

persons dying without a Will, in your own country. Listen to the opinions men and women express about this Law, first in separate single-sex groups, and then in a mixed group. Do men and women 'hear' each other's points of view? (It may be useful to role-play the scene at a house where there is a funeral, with a *man* taking the role of the widow, and a *woman* playing the part of the widow's brother-in-law.)

9. Discuss arguments for and against cremation of dead bodies. To what extent are these arguments based on theology, different views of the nature of death, or emotion?

CHAPTER 17

Attention and Celebration in Worship

'The true way to approach the mystery is in the first place celebration, celebration by the whole cosmos.' (11).
'Those who love me . . . the Father will love, and we will come and make our home with them' (John 14.23).

In ch. 1 I invited readers to 'question the questions' posed by AIDS, and to consider the meaning of 'redemption' and whether it is possible for HIV-infected persons to live in the light of the resurrection, as well as in the shadow of death. By describing the main consequences of HIV infection and exploring the challenges faced by societies where a quarter, or more, of adults are HIV-infected, the questions have (I hope) been clarified, but only very partially answered.

In chs. 15 and 16 I explored three themes:

1. Our present day need to develop communities capable of living with and transcending differences, in the *koinonia* which is made possible by the indwelling Spirit of God.

2. Evil, suffering and death are mysteries, not explicable in terms which satisfy reason or emotion; however, good and evil are 'bound up together', so that where evil is most intense, there, too, is the greatest good.

3. Encounter with God is the redemptive 'answer' to suffering and death offered in biblical and Christian experience; this encounter makes it possible for people (including HIV-infected and affected people) to live in the light of the resurrection, as well as in the shadow of death.

So far, this book has concentrated mainly on ways of tackling the practical tasks of caring, so as to minimize the personal and social suffering caused by HIV infection, and to make possible a mutual encounter with God through service. People who offer friendship or service should see Christ in the sick or hungry brothers or sisters they try to help, and the servants who know that they are wounded and needy too offer caring which reveals God's courtesy and love: 'Truly I tell you, just as you did it to the least of these who are members of my family, you did it to me.' (Matt. 25.31–46).

Christians should not, however, be so concerned with practical responses to acute problems that they neglect to attend directly to God and to celebrate the life, death and resurrection of Jesus Christ. Service is not the only, nor indeed a sufficient, way of encountering God, expressing koinonia, or finding the good hidden in suffering and death. Worship is needed too.

Worship has been defined as 'a human response to knowledge of God', but – more fundamentally – it is the response of human love to Christ's love, which allows the Father to answer His Son's prayer: 'I ask . . . that they may all be one. As you, Father, are in me and I am in you, may they also be in us, so that the world may believe that you have sent me.' (John 17.20,21).

Worship has two aspects, which reflect experience: we are invited to attend to God who is close (*immanent*) in the natural world, and also to God *transcending* what can be seen or touched. When believers attend to God, they do so not just for themselves, but also on behalf of everyone (of any faith or none) who searches for meaning in suffering. Worship is not intended to be separate from the rest of life, but rather to be located at its central point, 'standing in the place where two worlds meet' (21), and at 'the intersection of the timeless with time' (17). Christian liturgy re-enacts 'real historical events involving ordinary people' – events through which human beings pass between one world and the other.

Those 'real historical events' are the life, death and resurrection of Jesus of Nazareth, the Christ.

'God has clothed himself in humanity,
For me a sufferer he has suffered;
For one condemned he has been judged;
For one buried he has been buried;
But he is risen from the dead
And he cries:
Who will plead against me? I have delivered the one who was
    condemned,
I have given back life to him who was dead,
I have raised up one who was buried.
Who will dispute my cause?
I have abolished death,
I have crushed hell,
I have raised humanity to the highest heavens,
Yes, I the Christ . . . '
Melito of Sardis *Easter Homily*, (11).

From this resurrection-perspective, worship approaches the mystery of death, and expresses and develops koinonia, the mutual love that is capable of transcending diversity and hostility. We *need* salvation, to be able to return 'home', to find the meaning, beauty and joy which we know is proper to ourselves and the whole universe.

This chapter considers four aspects of worship, to see how they contribute to building community, setting the light of the resurrection alongside the shadow of death, and opening the door to encounter with God. These are: *baptism*, the *Eucharist, reconciliation* and corporate and personal *prayer*.

THE WORLD AS SACRAMENT

The Judeo-Christian vision sees the whole natural world as given to human beings as means of communion with God, not only through an appreciative and right use of things needed for survival and festivity, but also through representative acts, which are understood to concentrate and draw out the hidden meanings already present in material things or everyday events. In these symbolic acts, ordinary things are allowed to become extra-ordinary and so to convey 'more than' they would naturally signify: water signifies more than physical washing, a shared meal becomes a means of sharing the life sacrificed to provide the feast. The *whole* of physical life is potentially sacramental, but this dignity is focused in particular sacraments which are part of the living tradition of the Christian community.

Attention to God in and through the natural world is balanced by attention to God transcendent: which is less easy to describe – except in terms of 'not this, not that'. Such prayer is like a mother gazing with attention and love at her child. The baby gazes back equally intently, at last smiling in response to her mother's smile – so entering a dialogue of love which sustains her growth into personhood. In the same way, a man or woman turned to God in prayer comes under the 'creative eye of Holy love' and is slowly and hiddenly transformed by that gaze. True prayer progressively allows God to take possession of us, drawing us into the life of the Trinity, to share in God's koinonia and creativity (8). Both corporate prayer and sacrament *and* solitary attention to the gaze of God contribute both to '*ubuntu*' and to making community between people who, in the natural order, would be separated, not united, by their diversity.

The whole of human life, in all cultures, is potentially opportunity for encounter with God, as Pope Gregory knew when he sent Augustine to evangelize the people of Britain with instructions to adapt and use the Angles' existing shrines and forms of worship – and as Donovan practised in our own day, in his work with Masai people. AIDS should encourage Churches to rediscover old forms of Christian worship (Syrian, Coptic, Celtic, Greek Orthodox) and to explore unfamiliar forms used by African traditional religion and other faiths (Buddhist, Hindu, Muslim, American Indian). Although worship uses words and texts it is primarily *activity*, something *done* by the people of God.

REBIRTH: ENTRY INTO NEW LIFE

Nicodemus asked: 'Can a person enter a second time into his mother's womb and be born again?' to which Jesus replied: 'Amen, amen, I say to you, except a person be born of water and the spirit, he cannot enter the Kingdom of God' (John 3.4,5.)

The Church, which is not identical with any visible body that calls itself a Church (nor yet with the sum of all such bodies), is the place where new birth in water and Spirit is possible. 'In its deepest understanding the Church is nothing other than the world in the course of transfiguration, the world that in Christ reflects the light of paradise. The paradise of his presence is in truth Christ Himself, who could say to the thief full of faith who was crucified beside Him, "Today you will be with me in paradise" (Luke 23.43)'. ((11) p.95). Christ's offer still extends to every penitent person crucified alongside Him, whether or not their sufferings are judged 'innocent' by the watching crowd.

Rebirth takes place in a rite of initiation, Baptism. In 1982 the major denominations defined the essential elements of initiation thus: 'The proclamation of scripture referring to baptism; an invocation of the Holy Spirit; a renunciation of evil; a profession of faith in Christ and the Holy Trinity; the use of water; a declaration that the persons baptized have acquired a new identity as sons and daughters of God, and as members of the Church, called to be witnesses to the Gospel. Some Churches consider that Christian initiation is not complete without the sealing of the baptized with the gift of the Holy Spirit and participation in Holy Communion.'

Baptism itself is a once-for-all rite which cannot, and does not need to be, repeated; other rituals are provided to deal with the wounds caused by post-baptismal sin and to nourish the community from day-to-day. But the brief acts which are essential to Christian initiation are rich with a symbolism which could be emphasized through teaching and ceremonial. What could the experience of baptism now, or remembrance of baptism in the past, mean to an HIV-infected or affected man or woman?

In *Christianity Rediscovered* Donovan wrote: 'There was no need to explain to the Masai the symbolism of living, life-giving water. It was sacred to them long before I got there. Their word for God means rain – it being the most beautiful description of God they can think of.' (16). What does water, this rain, do for us?

Water washes away our sin: all the acts and words we regret and want to put away *are* put away in the water of baptism, which begins to heal the effects of habits of wrong-doing – which is why it may be appropriate for adults to confess their sins in the presence of a priest (1 Cor. 6.11) before baptism. The water of baptism also begins to heal wounds we have *received* – in physical or sexual abuse, denial of dignity or opportunities, through discrimination or through mockery.

Baptism makes us daughters and sons of God, introducing us into God's family where new loyalties (which are much larger than traditional loyalties to blood relatives, clan and tribe) ought to take over (1 Cor. 12.13; Eph. 2.13–19). We become age-mates of Christ and of the saints and martyrs, from Janani Luwum, Bernard Mizeki and Kizito, right back to Paul of Tarsus, Peter the fisherman and Mary the mother of Jesus. These people become, collectively and really, our immediate relatives. *Now* we are obliged to listen to Jesus as He looks round a circle of people and says: '*Here* are my mother, and my brothers!' (Mark 3.31–35). We begin to learn that in Christ there are no longer any barriers of race, or status, or education or gender (Gal. 3.26–28), even for an HIV-infected man or woman.

According to Harry Sawyerr, African society is held together through two life-lines (37). The vertical line runs through parents, grandparents and more remote ancestors, to connect each individual to God as the giver of life, and it must run on into the future through children and grandchildren, who are ancestors yet to be born. If this life-line is broken through failure to bear children, then the connection to God appears to be broken too. The second life-line runs horizontally, from person to person across a group who undergo initiation together as age-mates. Donders (15) likened these two life-lines to the warp and woof of a piece of cloth, and saw the great strength of a traditional society in which both threads were securely woven together. But in modern times this traditional strength is being undermined as initiation ceremonies are abandoned, so that horizontal links between age-mates are no longer made. AIDS comes as another threat to the stability of African society, because for many men and women it severs the vertical life-line too, as they do not leave living children to connect them to God.

As we have already seen, the creation-command to 'be fruitful and multiply' and 'to fill the earth' is called into question today by over-population and its consequences. Energetic reproduction needs to be replaced by long-term voluntary restriction on the number of children born, in most countries of the world. This is a difficult turning-point for peoples who find their link to God through child-bearing – for them, the crisis is aggravated by the appearance of AIDS.

In this situation the gospel message *is* 'good news' for men and women who were afraid to die without children, because through baptism they are initiated into the life of Jesus Christ, and they become mature human beings, whether or not they are able to bear children.

The gospel is also 'good news' for people who know that they will soon die. Although each individual still has to pass through the 'narrow gate' of physical death, the possibility of losing personhood and identity is past, dealt with in the death and resurrection of Christ (Col. 2.11–13).

Baptism is also the sacrament of entry into the royal priesthood of the people of God. When sealed with the Holy Spirit, each person receives unique gifts which are to be used in the ministry of the whole family of God (1 Cor. 12.4–30). The Masai people understood, with a clarity which startled their evangelist Donovan, that 'Baptism is indeed everything; that the reception of baptism is the acceptance of the total responsibility and the full, active sacramental power of the Church, the Eucharistic community with a mission.'(16).

In order to 'remind' Christians of their baptism, its symbols – water and light – should play a greater part in their lives. If the HIV-infected person's baptismal candle is taken home, to be lit again on the anniversary of initiation – and finally as physical death approaches, this is a reminder that he will rise with Christ who is even then carrying him to the Father (John 14.1–4; 2 Cor. 5.1,2).

BEING AND BECOMING: ONE LOAF

Baptism is a once-only event, like physical birth, yet it is obvious that healing and holiness are not completed at once, either in individuals or communities. How is the healing begun in baptism continued and how is growth in holiness supported and maintained after baptism? How is new life in Christ and in the Spirit renewed, when damaged by sin, and how is the fellowship (koinonia) of the family of God expressed from day to day? The answer given by tradition and verified in the experience of Christians is: through eating the bread of heaven and drinking the cup of salvation as they share in the Lord's Supper, and so feeding on the new life which He gives.

Jesus startled and antagonized the people of Galilee and many of his disciples when he said: 'I am the living bread ... if anyone eats this bread, he will live for ever; and the bread which I shall give for the life of the world is my flesh ... Amen, amen, I say to you, unless you eat the flesh of the Son of man and drink his blood, you have no life in you' (John 6.51–54). When Jesus's followers in the twentieth century obey this command, they believe (like their predecessors) that they are living the new life of their Baptism, and becoming one loaf broken for everyone, outsiders included. Irenaeus said: 'The Son of God was made man so that man might become son of God' and 'the Word was made flesh ... to destroy death and give life.' (11).

Yet it may be difficult to maintain the vision of a group of believers as *together* forming the body of Christ, and together being the family of God, when fear of AIDS and of HIV-infected people is at work amongst them. People who feel guilt or shame may quietly leave the congregation to avoid exposure, or vigorously oppose anti-AIDS teaching for youth groups on 'moral' grounds. Frightened people avoid the chalice. What is the remedy?

The Eucharist has to become (once again) something that the members of a congregation *do* together – which may require changing the scale, or the place, or the style of the celebration, so that people re-experience the Eucharist as new. A request to bless a house, or to take communion to a sick person, might be seized as an opportunity to celebrate the Eucharist in someone's home, with the family gathered round a table, using an ordinary bread roll, with the priest wearing everyday clothes, the children included (not excluded), and everyone taking part.

Communities may need to develop a new vision of priesthood, along the lines of the model Donovan suggested: 'a man taken from among men, to stand for them, to signify and focus for them the meaning of the life of the people of God in community.' This understanding of priesthood was implied by his Masai friends' choice of a name for a priest: 'These new African Christians do not conceive of the priest as preacher, prophet, pray-er or sacramentalist . . . they think rather of the priest as the one (seemingly the *only* one) who can bring a community into existence, call it together, hold it together, enable the community to function as a community, and enable each member to carry out his or her Christian task in the community. Without this *helper* the Christian community can neither exist nor function. With him it becomes a eucharistic community with a mission.' The name for a priest which several groups of Masai chose, quite independently of each other, came from a recognized role in Masai culture, that of a servant or helper of all, 'who was interested in all the flocks and every phase of the life of the community, a man to whom anyone could turn in difficulty.' (16). A renewed sense that every member has 'their own Christian task' illuminates St Paul's saying: 'This bread that we break, is it not the koinonia (fellowship) of the body and blood of Christ?'

In far too many Churches people are excluded from Holy Communion, the koinonia, through sickness, because they are too weak to get to church, because they are reckoned to be 'too young to understand', or as an expression of an ecclesiastical discipline which makes failure in marriage an unforgivable sin.

In the early centuries of persecution, daily Communion was usual, and the petition 'give us this day our daily bread' was interpreted by Cyprian of Carthage (252 CE) as applying to the Eucharist as well as to ordinary food. It was normal, and remained normal for several centuries, for Christians to take home (from the community Eucharist on a Sunday) a supply of consecrated Bread, so that they and members of their families might receive the Bread of life every day – and especially if death threatened.

This practice of taking home the consecrated bread from the Sunday Eucharist might well be revived, to reintegrate housebound sick people into the community week by week – especially at the time of death, when the parish priest may be far away. The Bread of life should not be received in a casual or magical way, but reverently, with other members of the family, who postpone their own communion until it can be shared with the sick person at home.

It may also be appropriate that baptized children, especially those who have lost a parent, or who are sick or dying themselves, should be full members of the Eucharistic community, not excluded from communion on the grounds of age alone. In Churches where children come to the altar with their parents, to be blessed, the priest sees how often and how expectantly small children watch as their parents receive the Body of Christ, and how hurt they are to be excluded from receiving what they see as a precious gift.

SACRIFICE AND CELEBRATION:
DEATH AND RESURRECTION

The Eucharist is an act of remembrance which does more than recall past events. It involves those who take part in the death and resurrection of Jesus in Jerusalem nearly 2,000 years ago. From the point of view of someone who is overwhelmed by suffering, the Eucharist is a chance to hand over to God their misery and despair, all the fears and experiences which feel intolerable, and yet have to be lived with. 'Nothing is lost, nothing is wasted, all is gathered into the offering' which Jesus made in His mocked and mutilated flesh, that is now 'remembered' or made present in the lives of His twentieth-century brothers and sisters, as they, too, are ground into flour for his Bread.

As Ignatius of Antioch was travelling to Italy to die in the arena, he sent a letter ahead to the Christians living in Rome. He wrote: 'Let me be the food of beasts thanks to which I shall be able to find God. I am God's wheat and I am being ground by the teeth of wild beasts in order to become Christ's pure bread.' Suffering does 'grind' those who experience it – and no Christian should dare say that one kind of suffering is acceptably 'holy' and another kind is not.

The Eucharist is realistic about the destructiveness of suffering, but it is also truthful about the reality of rescue and rebirth, even though both can only be foreseen by faith. Ignatius begged his Roman brothers not to attempt to protect him from death: 'My new birth is close at hand. Forgive me, brethren, do not hinder me from living. Let me come into the pure light.When I reach that point I shall be a man. Allow me to reproduce the passion of my God.' (11).

But the food of the Eucharist is not only torn flesh and shed blood, but also the bread and wine of God's feast. Every Eucharist should remind us of the great homecoming, when 'Yahweh Sabaoth will prepare for all peoples a banquet of rich food, a banquet of fine wines (Isa. 25.6). Each Eucharist should hold in tension the present acceptance and offering of all suffering – with a light-hearted anticipation of homecoming, when there will be an abundance of food and joy, more than enough for everyone.

Some Eucharists therefore, should be quite literally celebrations, sung and danced with all the splendour, colour, rhythm and joy of which we are capable: occasions when *everyone* (HIV-infected or not, well or ill, woman or man, stranger or relative, widow or orphan, confused or intellectual, child or elder) is greeted with dignity and joy as a first-born child come home. If a gathered Church family numbers so many thousands of people that no building is large enough, then the reality that *we* are the living temple of God can be acted out in the open air, worshipping under trees or arches of flowers, branches and balloons. Most likely the celebration will go on for several hours and end with a shared meal, to which many people have contributed their 'five loaves and two fish' (Mark 6.38).

EUCHARIST: SETTING FOR UNDERTAKING AND CELEBRATING VOCATION

Because the Eucharist is the act which takes us into the Kingdom and makes us a community in Christ, it is the proper setting for most of the particular acts (of baptism, marriage, anointing, blessing for different states in life, acceptance of disability) which concern the life of the community as a whole – and very little that happens to an individual man or woman should be considered purely private.

Donovan described a Masai community for whom the Eucharist did indeed celebrate the whole of life:

'We had tried to teach these people that it was not easy to achieve the eucharist. It was not an act of magic accomplished with the saying of a few words in the right order. One wonders how often we really do achieve the eucharist in our lives. If the eucharist was not an offering of their whole life – the family raising, the herding, the milking and working and singing – it was hardly the eucharist ... if the life of the village had been less than human or holy, then there was no Mass. At other times the will was there to override the weaknesses in the community, the will to ask the Spirit to come on this community to change it into the Body of Christ, so that we could say together, "This – not just the bread and wine, but the whole life of the village, its work, play, joy, sorrow, the homes, the grazing fields, the flocks, the people – all this in my Body." The leaders made the decision, and asked me to say again the words of institution. And we took and ate. And we sent some of the blessed bread to the sick in bed ... I stood up and said, "May God the

Father, his son Jesus, and his Spirit bless you. Go and sleep in peace. In your homes tonight, in your work tomorrow, in your contact with other villages and other people, this Mass is continuing ... may your Mass never end.' (16)

RECONCILIATION

Turning from failure, disorder and evil in the past, and starting again, is repeatedly necessary in the lives of all communities and all individuals. Breaking bread together is one expression of reconciliation and the Masai community rightly recognized that they could not make eucharist together if selfishness and lack of forgiveness persisted amongst them. In Masai culture a tuft of grass, 'offered by one Masai and accepted by the second, was an assurance that no violence would erupt because of the differences and arguments. No Masai would violate that sacred sign of peace offered, because it was not only a *sign* of peace; it *was* peace. Just as spittle was forgiveness.' (16)

Reconciliation and forgiveness are bound together, and both are concerned with freeing people and communities from fear and bondage to the past, and from the continuing influence of past habits, attitudes or events. In addition to baptism and the eucharist, the Christian rites of exorcism and penitence offer liberation from past sins and strength for the future. The purpose of penitence is not to destroy our passions, but to redirect and release all our energies and potentialities. Forgiveness, healing, joy and freedom are closely connected.

In the early Church the final preparations for initiation lasted forty days. During this period of intense preparation the candidates submitted to symbolic actions, ending with a solemn exorcism when each candidate recited the creed for the first time, in the presence of the bishop and the faithful. The anthropology of the time assumed the existence of an Evil One 'who holds your spirit in bondage', and though this world-view will not commend itself to all present-day Christians, it may still be a useful image.

For example, exorcism in preparation for adult baptism, or as part of a rite of individual penitence, might help to set free a man or woman who repents of his or her responsibility for *consenting* to witchcraft, (or addictive use of sex or drugs), yet who is 'held' by the 'powers' of habit and peer pressure. In such a case, there may still be a place for a solemn public exorcism, following careful private preparation – which should emphasize that the candidate seeks release from the power of old habits and the influence of old companions, rather than freedom from external demons. Yet external help *is* needed to 'renounce evil' and a public ceremony has value – added to short-term support from a group of other people who are making similar transitions from bondage into freedom.

PENITENCE

Bonhoeffer noticed, in the seminary where he ministered, that the breakthrough to community happens when a congregation 'ceases to be a fellowship of the devout and becomes instead a fellowship of the undevout, holding each other as forgiven sinners.' (10) When Church people begin to accept that they are *not* whole but wounded (although in the process of being made whole), then it becomes possible for them to truly welcome damaged outsiders, people who know full well that *they* are wounded.

'Sharing the peace' at the Eucharist each week can acknowledge that we are a fellowship of the undevout, if people have the courage and humility to seek out someone with whom they have quarrelled, or a neighbour who has said something hurtful, in order to make peace. Many parables concern repeated mutual forgiveness, for 'I do not say to you (forgive) seven times, but seventy times seven' (Matt. 18.21–22). Making up a quarrel takes precedence over the duty of worship: 'when you are offering your gift at the altar, if you remember your brother or sister has something against you ... go; first be reconciled to your brother or sister ... then come and offer your gift.' (Matt. 5.23,24).

Litanies of penitence and liturgies for communal reconciliation are often not enough for men and women imprisoned by guilt, or held by habits of wrongdoing and seemingly unable to 'move on'. Yet true repentance *does* bring transfiguration and a release into joy and freedom. Gerard Hughes, in *God of Surprises*, contrasts the marks of true and false repentance: 'True repentance frees from self-preoccupation because our trust is in God's goodness working in us. In his light we see our darkness. True repentance brings joy and inner freedom ... can welcome criticism and learn from it ... true repentance brings understanding, tolerance and hope ... compassion and therefore a sharpened sensitivity to all forms of injustice. True repentance shares God's laughter and frees the mind to see the humour of all situations. In true repentance a person feels drawn to God.' (50) But how is true repentance found when formal public rites fail?

The Church offers reconciliation through private confession of sin, out loud in the presence of a priest who has authority through the Church, to pronounce God's forgiveness. The place, time and method may be formal or informal, deliberate or unpremeditated, providing only that there is privacy and freedom from interruptions. Sometimes confession of sin comes out, painfully and unexpectedly, in the course of a pastoral visit or interview.

A premeditated first confession requires determination, courage, and willingness to give time to reflective preparation, and some people need instruction on how to go about self-examination. The priest listens with total attention, sometimes asking one or two discreet questions to clarify the extent of responsibility, gives advice (if asked to do so) – and offers encouragement and a 'penance', a simple act to show willingness to 'make satisfaction' for sin. Then the priest pronounces God's forgiveness. It may then be appropriate to pray for the Holy Spirit to enter the person 'swept clean' by penitence (Luke 11.24–26), or to recall the parable of the two sons, and the joy of the father preparing a welcome-home banquet. In the book of Revelation God said: 'See, I am making all things new' (Rev. 21.5). Absolution is a beginning of that 'making new' and sometimes it feels like it – even when suffering continues and physical death is approaching.

CELEBRATING COMMON PRAYER

Set forms of prayer (the daily office) provide a bridge between communal, sacramental forms of worship, which attend to God in creation and events, and silent prayer which attends to God who is also transcendent. This helps to sustain awareness of God throughout the week and to orientate individual worshippers to life in the Kingdom. From the earliest days the daily prayer of Christian communities centred on praise and intercession, expressed through psalms and canticles taken from Scripture. Later, short Bible readings, hymns and collected prayers were added. But a short office can be prayer for *all* God's people, equally suitable for solitary use or family worship – whether the family is one of blood or of choice.

Psalms were the prayers of Jesus and His contemporaries and they are important for us because of their scope and honesty: their subject matter is all of human life. HIV-infected people will find that many psalms anticipate, in quite extraordinary detail, their own painful situations (Psalms 6, 31, 32, 35, 38, 39, 41, 51, 55, 57, 64, 69, 70, 73, 82, 86, 88, 90, 102, 109, 123, 130, 140, 142, 143). But most of the remaining 125 psalms express hope, trust in God, thanksgiving or joy. If we use the psalms set for each day in a modern lectionary then we shall not be too selective in our worship, but able to share in the sorrows of people who suffer (when we happen to be comfortable) and to sing for joy, when joy seems far away. Local prayer is never 'private', for we pray and praise in the Church with all creation, adoring the Father, through Jesus, in the power of the Holy Spirit.

To prepare the heart for prayer and to link local celebrations to sacramental and communal worship, some Christians use signs and symbols, such as: lighting a candle to mark the start of common prayer; making the sign of the cross on oneself or each other (perhaps using blessed water); burning incense; decorating the place of prayer with flowers or a picture to mark a festival, or sharing the recitation of psalms and prayers, so that everyone has a part.

A place for prayer at home is helpful, within sight of any sick person in the house, marked by a shelf on the wall or a small table, where there is always something to act as a reminder of God's love: an open Bible, an icon, a crucifix, a candle and a few flowers, a stone as a reminder that God is our rock.

BECOMING PRAYER

Many people are afraid to pray without support from a set form of words, waiting for God in silence. What if nothing happens – or what if God should speak? Why pray at all, if we do not ask for anything in particular, or do not know what to ask for? Dare we say, with Mary, 'let what you have said be done to me' (Luke 1.38)? Is silent prayer selfish or an evasion of responsibility, as some Christians think?

'Waiting on God' is especially suited to people who (in any case) do a good deal of waiting because they are ill. But this form of prayer is equally suited to the lives of busy people who are torn between demands on their time and energies; many energetic and productive leaders and reformers in the Church (and the world) were men and women of prayer. Paul of Tarsus, Augustine of Hippo, Francis of Assisi and Teresa of Avila are well-known examples from the past, and in our own times, Martin Luther King, Dag Hammarskjold, Helder Camara and Desmond Tutu.

Gregory the Great, thinking about the work of an abbot, wrote: 'when he is preoccupied with exterior matters he must not lessen his solicitude for the interior. Nor when he is preoccupied with the interior may he relax his watch on the exterior.' Similar principles and priorities apply to parish priests and bishops, civil servants and surgeons, and leaders of Homecare teams or fund-raisers for NGOs.

MOODS AND EXPERIENCES AT TIMES OF PRAYER

Sometimes nothing appears to happen and the time of prayer seems wasted – though changes in us and our behaviour may be seen by other people, when we notice nothing. Sometimes people who pray feel caught up in a storm of anger, or resentment, or longing or sadness – which may be a sign of opening up to God's healing work in the depths of our hearts and minds – and so a sign of hope. At other times, waiting silently, we feel held in God's mercy, like a child in his mother's arms – and we want to reach out and draw our brothers and sisters 'under the shadow of His wing', too. At those times we *know* that silent or solitary prayer is not just for ourselves, but for the whole of creation.

Sayings of the Desert Fathers and Mothers, of the third and fourth centuries, show the humour and simplicity of people who wait on God and who learn not to judge their neighbours: 'A goat is someone such as I am, but as for the sheep, well, only God knows!' and 'A dog is better than I am because it also has love, but it does not pass judgement.'

This same non-judgemental openness is the appropriate Christian response to unfamiliar ways of attending to God, whether encountered in a different Christian tradition, or in the customs of people of another faith.

DEATH: GATEWAY TO LIFE

'The true way to approach the mystery is in the first place celebration'. Death is a mystery, like worship, where two worlds meet. As death approaches, there is no time left for pretence or hiding. Family and friends can accompany the dying person up to the gateway, but no-one else can go through. The journey appears lonely and unprotected, but in reality it is a moment of meeting: 'doubtless Christ has to wait about through years of hardening and spiritual insensitivity before He can rediscover the vulnerable and astonished child' in us at the moment of death. And what is prayer, if not a rehearsal for this moment of astonished vulnerability? (11)

'For your faithful people life is change, not taken away, and when our mortal flesh is laid aside an everlasting dwelling place is made ready for us in heaven'. This is the Christian hope.

For Further Reading see Bibliography, p. 311, (11), (16), (21), (29), (39), (48) and (49).

Study Suggestions

1. Should an 'Occasional Office' be provided to dedicate sexual maturity? If so, what form might the service take?
2. Do you agree that baptized children who may die should become communicants? What about other children?
3. Can people who are too ill to come to church continue as members of the Eucharistic community in *your* town or village? If not, suggest what arrangements should be made for them.
4. In what ways, if any, could the Eucharist be celebrated more joyfully, in your Church, so that it is experienced as 'a foretaste of the heavenly banquet'?
5. Is attentive waiting on God recognized as prayer by your congregation? If so, how can people, who are at different points in their journey of faith, be helped to grow in prayer?
6. Should exorcism be reintroduced before baptism, or to rites of reconciliation? If so, what theological teaching should be given beforehand, to interpret its meaning?

CHAPTER 18
Hope: a new Heaven and a new Earth

'Man has been defined as "the animal who can think about what is not there" '. Hope looks to the future expecting good things. Sometimes we hope for the return of benefits enjoyed in the past (such as a satisfactory rainy season or heavy crops), but often we long for imagined goods which we have never yet had. At the natural level, hope depends on the consistency of experience and it is supported by seasonal and human cycles: part of the meaning of children lies in our hope that they will fulfil potentialities we ourselves have lost.

At this human level hope is an extraordinarily robust and persistent attitude, which can survive in extreme circumstances, and without it human beings do not themselves survive. In the early days of the AIDS pandemic an unknown official in the Zambian Ministry of Health returned a manuscript about the impact of AIDS on African societies to its author with a question: 'What is there to hope for?' At about the same time, in Britain, an NGO employed a journalist to research and write a series of booklets about creative responses to AIDS, under the title: *Strategies for Hope*. Hope is necessary for survival: we search for hope, plan strategies through which to grasp it and work to make hope happen. The opposite of hope is despair which, unrelieved, removes all will to live and leads to death.

HOPE IN CHRISTIAN PERSPECTIVE

For Christian faith, hope is both a gift to be received *and* a virtue to be lived. Paul wrote to Corinthian Christians that other gifts of the Spirit are temporary, but hope will abide for ever – with faith and love, though the greatest of these is love (1 Cor. 13.13). In apostolic times the content of hope, the thing hoped-for, was the return of Christ (at the *parousia*) with all its consequences: resurrection for believers and the total fulfilment of creation in the established Kingdom of God. Meanwhile hope was to shape the daily living of all believers, during a short period of waiting for this near – but still future – event.

As time passed, and the apostolic era ended without the return of Christ, Christians had to live with disappointment and questioning: was the content of their hope wrong? The focus of their interest shifted gradually from corporate expectation of a fast-approaching *parousia*, to the fate of individual believers after death. And there, for the most part, orthodox emphasis has rested ever since.

Although hope for the second coming of Christ is recalled each year in the Advent liturgies of mainstream Churches, the hope expressed is formal or symbolic, and lacks the warmth, eagerness and practical effects of a real looking-forward to an actual event. From time to time during the last 2,000 years groups of people (who were usually on the margins of orthodox belief) interpreted the signs of their own age and announced that the second coming of the Lord was near at hand, and sometimes they dared to suggest a date. As none of these predictions were fulfilled, and as these groups were often unorthodox in their other beliefs, real expectation of Christ's second coming became a suspect activity and ceased to influence daily living.

For a time, individuality was hidden in the corporate Body of Christ, although leaders stood out amongst the faithful. Later the personal responsibility of individual believers for their own lives began to be emphasized, during the Middle Ages and at the Reformation. This shift of concern, from the body to the individual, strengthened interest in the outcome of judgement for each person, but weakened corporate hope for Christ's second coming. Later still, the Enlightenment led to a gradual reduction of the content of reality to things which can be observed and measured. At about the same time, the Enlightenment removed religious belief and practice from public life to the realm of private behaviour. As a result, belief in the second coming of Christ came to be seen as an unworthy relic of primitive Church life, in need of restating in a demythologized form. In practice, in most present-day Churches, hope does not centre around the second coming of the Lord but has a smaller and more humanly-determined content, which is rather similar to the content of 'hope' in surrounding societies.

DIMENSIONS OF HOPE

What is the content of 'hope' at this present time, and what are the assumptions hidden behind an attitude of hope?

Hope assumes that things could, and *should*, be different; it expresses dissatisfaction with the way things are. If a choice between happiness and meaning is necessary, then hope prefers significant meaning, even in distress, to meaningless happiness. Hope wants people to have ultimate significance; it demands that, despite the size of present-day cities and societies – and even of the universe – human beings should be seen to matter.

Next, hope assumes that change is possible. In its Judeo-Christian form it also assumes that history has a goal – that history is not an endlessly cyclic process, but that its crises occur in a series which will end. Although belief in a goal to history (determined by God) has faded from Western thought, the idea of 'progress' as a force driving humankind towards greater achievement remained influential until the second decade of this century. Since then 'progress' has ceased to seem inevitable, although the habit of hoping for progress persists.

Most people hope for change over a range of scales, from hope for a trivial but pleasant event today or tomorrow, through hope for social or political change which will provide a better arena for living, to hope for cosmic transformation, particularly when circumstances are tough. At the intermediate scale, human beings hope for justice, peace, and for fulfilment of their capacities for creativity and relationship; they hope to find meaning in events, and to be valued for themselves, by significant people in a sheltering home and by society at large. Often these fundamental hopes seem to be too large, so they are hidden under a host of smaller hopes for more material (and apparently accessible) substitutes – clothes or cars or casual sex or status, which do not (in fact) satisfy those who hope for them. Knowledge of HIV infection often strips away all these inadequate hopes instantly, leaving the person concerned face to face with a real but painfully unattainable hope – for healthy children and time to rear them. This stripping of false hopes is a dark experience.

It might be expected that popular 'hope' would be limited to what seems possible from our present understanding of the physical world, so eliminating the cosmic dimension of hope referred to earlier. But in practice human thinking is not consistent, so hope for escape from final limitations is very persistent.

At least since records began, men and women have hoped for a transformation of the very conditions of existence (as we know them) in order to overcome the ultimate limitation of death. We cannot imagine ceasing to exist ourselves, and we desperately want the people we love to continue to *be*, in all their exasperating but beautiful individuality. The finality of death seems to deny meaning to human lives, and to destroy personalities which were built up with great effort and pain. When life is easy hope may seem to sleep, but societies living with AIDS ask: 'What is there to hope for?' and demand answers, at all three levels of expectation.

FANTASY AND HOPE

Normally we distinguish fantasy (an ungrounded work of the imagination which we do not expect to see come true) from hope, which, by contrast, looks for things at present unseen, but nevertheless potentially real and capable of fulfilment. Fantasy seeks escape from reality, whereas hope asks that reality should be transformed.

If it is not to be fantasy, hope needs foundations: it needs to be built on and projected forwards from past events in an orderly and consistent world. At one end of the spectrum, it merges with prediction (especially in popular usage) and as prediction, it can and should be criticized: as in ch. 5 we criticized the hope that a vaccine against HIV might allow men and women to avoid HIV without permanently changing their sexual behaviour.

True hope must be grounded in reality, not in a reality which is restricted to a predetermined and limited range of measurable physical phenomena, but in a reality which is wide enough to include the whole unmeasurable range of actual human experience. For example, joy at the birth of a longed-for child, the power of simple words spoken between people who love one another, humour shared without speech, music, delight in natural wonders or human artefacts, the new meanings found in memories with the passage of time, art, poetry and prayer – all need to be included. The full reality of these experiences cannot be expressed in the language of mathematics, yet they are part of human life. If all non-physical 'knowing' is dismissed – as a work of the imagination which does not correspond in a consistent way to external reality – then the basis for accepting other people as 'real' disappears too, and so does the basis for community living.

Usually Western readers need to enlarge the foundation of 'experience' on which they build their hopes, which tends to be limited by their exaggerated reverence for 'science', while people from developing countries may need to re-examine some parts of *their* 'experience' more critically, to discard fantasy.

THE FOUNDATIONS OF CHRISTIAN HOPE

Christians do not limit their expectations about God's future activity to clock-time. They interpret the qualitative difference, which everyone has experienced, between clock-time (*chronos*) and significant time (*kairos*), as a sign of God's activity, and as evidence for their hope that God's plans for humanity extend beyond time into a new dimension.

Christian hope is grounded in the character of God, as Christians believe it has been revealed in the history of the ancient Jewish people, in the character and actions of Jesus of Nazareth, and in the survival and growth of the Church in the last 2,000 years.

In searching for authentic hope for a world living with AIDS, we might begin by looking for a pattern which resembles the pattern (if there is one) in the history of the Jewish people and in the life of Jesus of Nazareth. The historical events, on which his argument is based, are well-supported by evidence (documents, inscriptions, comments by Greek and Roman writers) outside and additional to the evidence found in the Old and New Testaments. The Christian interpretation of these events deserves serious comparison with alternative explanations.

BIBLICAL EVIDENCE

In the earlier books of the Old Testament, both judgement and salvation were expected to occur in history, and there was no hope for life beyond death; indeed death was seen as ending relationship with God. Later, prophets began to hope for a final resolution to history which would lead into a permanent age of peace and justice in a transcendent world. During the development of these ideas about a transcendent Kingdom, God was experienced as active and personal, unpredictable yet consistent, above all as living Being who was intimately interested in the lives and actions of the covenant people. God was not quiet or remote, dependant for publicity upon the writings of philosophers, but Being, terrible or tender, who erupted into the lives of people who would often (as in the cases of Moses or Jeremiah) have preferred a much quieter existence.

At first God's interest was thought to be limited to patriarchs, kings and prophets, but later it was seen to extend, in a very detailed way, to the lives of ordinary citizens. Although God's actions as they unfolded showed continuity with His past activity, and although the prophets claimed to receive revelations about God's plans for the future, God's interventions, when they actually occurred, were shocking or even catastrophic. How could the Holy One of Israel allow His people to be taken into exile or permit Jerusalem to be destroyed?

In the Gospel accounts, Jesus took over the theme of the future Kingdom of God – but announced that it is already dawning. The nearness of the Kingdom was the chief theme of His early preaching, and the tension He introduced between 'here, at the very door' and 'yet to come' continued in the experience and writing of the early Church. John and Paul insisted in the plainest language that in Jesus of Nazareth God is already with us and has acted decisively to change the status of human beings, even though the fulfilment of this altered status awaits a new and future event. Meanwhile human beings are 'in Christ' and the Spirit of God lives 'in them', as a sign of the new life they are entering.

Modern people are apt to underestimate the value, as evidence, of the mere existence of such language, used in relation to a man who died only about twenty years before the documents were written, and whose actions and character hundreds of individuals could remember.

The interpretations recorded and explained in Letters and Gospels (a new form of writing) were based on related events: the life, death and resurrection of Jesus and the visible actions of the Spirit in the community of believers. Searching these accounts of events attributed by believers to the activity of God, can we find qualities which, taken together, form a characteristic signature? Many commentators have attempted answers to this question; here are my suggestions:

1. The events are credible and dramatic, implying that history has direction and that the plot is not predetermined but develops in the interplay between God's actions and human beings' responses.

2. New episodes in the drama are always congruent with what has happened earlier, but in spite of this consistency each new act is also

3. surprising or even outrageous, often contradicting commonsense piety and straining the goodwill of believers (who do not *want* to believe in a God who acts like this).

4. Part of the outrage is due to a reversal of human standards and part relates to the indignity, scale, severity and apparent pointlessness of the human suffering involved.

5. Adding to the outrage, ordinary lives are seen to change dramatically for the better, but change happens to the 'wrong' people – to outsiders, the underclass, even to criminals and sex workers.

6. The event which is central to the evidence, the resurrection of Jesus to life, is 'impossible' yet it fits into a series of 'impossible' interventions which brought life out of darkness to Jewish patriarchs, and to disabled people who sought Jesus's help; nobody at the time seriously expected these events, any more than we would.

7. The gifts given to people who are hopeless enough or helpless enough to receive them are magnificently generous, always much more than human beings can 'hope or desire'.

8. This generosity is not 'reasonable' but foolish; but for those who will accept such foolishness there is much to celebrate.

9. The tension between present and future, actual and potential, 'here' and 'still to come' is not resolved, but simply accepted as part of the human condition, to be lived with.

10. The evidence never compels a certain interpretation but is ambiguous enough to give any person responding to it real freedom of choice and action.

11. A tension between individual and corporate needs is not resolved either, but persists, perhaps as a reminder that both are vital to the life of the Kingdom.

12. A pattern of crisis (darkness and death) as the precondition for new life is normal, *not* steady development without conflict.

LIVING IN HOPE

A provisional theology of hope for a world with AIDS will have to be lived concretely, or it will not be credible to those who need it. But any attempt to live a theology of hope will expose and judge the inadequacies of that theology, and should serve to stretch or challenge theory and to develop practice. How shall we begin? What should be our perspectives?

It seems essential to maintain the tension between 'here, at the very gate' and 'not yet', so that we plan and work constantly for concrete expressions of hope in present time (*chronos*), yet sit lightly to all success (or failure) because we know that we are pilgrims and the fullness of the Kingdom lies ahead. So in planning to work for hope, it is useful to keep three scales in mind:

1. The immediate present where individual persons need something to hope for today and next week.

2. The near and further future (on this side of death) where we want structures, both personal and communal, to be transformed to give ourselves and our children prospects for a better life.

3. Hope for life beyond death, where humankind 'shall stand forgiven before the Father's throne' at the beginning of the first glorious day of a new heaven and a new earth.

Another basic attitude is to admit that our present perspective, from the early years of the pandemic, is too close to events for clear vision, or to see the meaning of what is happening. Also, the essential perspective is not ours, but God's, and we cannot force disclosure, but must wait for understanding in His time (*kairos*).

TODAY AND NEXT WEEK

When politicians or administrators are accused of 'moving the goal-posts' the phrase is usually intended as criticism. However, moving the goalposts to more realistic positions is often necessary, if we are to express hope today and tomorrow to someone who is living with HIV. It is a strategy practised by every parent as his or her child grows, and it is equally appropriate for people coping with the diminishments of old age or terminal illness. But before moving the goalposts we need to listen attentively to fears and wishes, and not to assume that we know (already) what is best for the persons we want to help. Their greatest hope may be to have someone's total attention paid to them, just as they are, to reassure them that they are still alive and that they still matter.

The desires and fears which may be expressed have been described in detail earlier: most people want to go on contributing to the life of their family and society and they want some light-hearted enjoyment (even now). Human beings hope for dignity up to and through the moment of death, freedom from loneliness and continuing significance. The resources needed have been explored already, and they, too, are not complicated: concerned people with time to listen and 'be there', imagination and motivation to solve practical problems, willingness to share food and shelter, leadership and some simple community organization (not organizations). Some countries may not be able to afford anti-viral drugs for every HIV-infected person, but no-one should spend hours alone in a room with a leaking roof, hoping that someone will bring a mug of tea or a bowl of porridge before night; no-one should have to lie in their own excrement, humiliated by weakness and dependence on others; no person should listen to neighbours returning from Sunday worship and remain uncomforted by the sacraments – examples drawn from recent experience in Zambia and Uganda. Our communities need to learn to be 'opportunists' on behalf of God.

Celebrations, or something to look forward to, are as important to people living with HIV as they are to anyone else, and an event to antici-pate not only adds quality to living, but often extends its duration too. However, a time will come for everyone when the goalposts should shift to achieving two aims: maintaining control of symptoms and 'dying well'. Both subjects have been explored earlier, but the art of dying has been neglected so consistently by present-day societies that it deserves emphasis: to pass through the 'gate of death' well is worth hoping for, and worth planning. Festivals and sacraments are ways of linking together small hopes for today and next week with transcendent hopes for fulfilment in the Kingdom, focusing and demonstrating the truth that the whole earth is given to humankind as communion with God.

In Christian belief the Eucharist constitutes the Church both in present clock-time and in the *kairos* of the Kingdom. Each eucharist is an event which 'takes place' simultaneously in particular physical sur-roundings (a warehouse-like church in Kampala, or a thatched shelter in eastern Zambia, or a medieval cathedral in France, or a hospital side-ward in New York) and *also* in the Kingdom, in the presence of those forgotten millions of believers, the Church triumphant and the Church expectant; together with the whole company of heaven. The eucharist is the most authentic point of 'intersection of the timeless with time' ((17), see ch. 17), which we have.

The Eucharist is also a foretaste of the heavenly banquet and it is sad that it so rarely has the qualities of a good party.

Experience: I recall a Eucharist in Lusaka which took place in unpromising surroundings – a school gymnasium in need of cleaning and redecoration. The priests who were to concelebrate unpacked their crumpled vestments from bags and briefcases and put a plain table onto a platform. There were readings, two sermons, singing in English, Chewa and in tongues, followed by more readings. Exchanging the peace had the character both of liturgy and of a country dance: women and men who looked as though no-one had noticed them for months were greeted and hugged, then handed on graciously to the next dancer. I lost count of time for three hours – until the shared Meal was over and I realized that the celebration was about to end – but I did not want it to end. I thought 'What a splendid party this is! If the heavenly banquet is like this, but better, then there really is something to look forward to!' Celebrations of such quality may not happen often but should be within everyone's actual experience.

We have seen that rituals for the end of life fulfil many functions, but amongst these, celebration as well as solemnity has a place. Death is common, physical, sometimes undignified, out of our control and (except that it is rarely painful) remarkably like birth, and it probably has a similar significance. As the moment for a child's delivery approaches, a woman has little control over the birth-process and she is conscious of hardly anything beyond her own painful labouring body. Her whole being is focused on the physical effort of expelling her child and on gathering strength for the beginning of her next contraction. When at last the child slides out, cries, breathes, and is put into her arms, the mother's horizon expands instantly to vast distances. Those who watch see even the plainest woman transfigured to beauty by her unselfconscious joy. Death is another birth, and there is enough evidence from accounts of the deaths of people (saints and otherwise), and from the experiences of persons who have been resuscitated after their hearts had stopped beating, to suggest that physical death, like birth, leads to an experience of great joy, of which a small part is sometimes shared with those who watch. Jesus of Nazareth told us to weep with those who weep and to rejoice with those who rejoice; every person's death not only diminishes me because I am a part of the whole, but potentially opens a window into eternity.

If the element of celebration is consistently missing from death rituals, especially for men and women who die young, then repeated mourning tends to blunt emotion or lead to a settled mood of sadness which rejects hope. In either case grieving may not be completed and bereaved persons may not move on to reinvest their energies in life. It is too easy, in the context of yet another funeral for another member of a community, each week, to slip into responses to death which conform to secular values. We do not mourn as 'those who are without hope', but as those who believe that 'Jesus died and rose again, and that it will be the same for those who have died in Jesus: God will bring them with Him' (1 Thess. 4.14). Mourning which expresses the new values of the Kingdom needs support from a living and trusting community.

INTERMEDIATE HOPE: LIVING IN COMMUNITIES

We need transformed communities, if we and our children are to have hope for a better temporal future. But they will be communities in the plural, for most human beings 'belong' in more than one family, and both human richness and diversity and the activities of the Spirit of God require pluralism of community life. If the unity (as well as the diversity) of humankind is to be lived adequately, links between communities are necessary. The most creative links, however, may not be constitutions, central planning or hierarchical structures, but the natural movements of people from one group to another, and the largely anonymous activities of the Spirit, so truly named as the Go-between-God.

A proper perspective keeps the tension between 'now, at the very gate' and 'still to come', and tries to balance the needs of individual persons and of the communities to which they belong, grasping opportunities for different Christian congregations and peoples of different faiths to work together. Whatever the reasons for common action (and despite the difficulties of living alongside others who are 'not like us'), common action undertaken because little people and their sufferings matter is action directed towards the Kingdom of God. In 1992, in Malawi, Roman Catholic bishops, Muslims, members of the Law Society and of the Chamber of Commerce, leaders of the Christian Council and ex-Cabinet ministers joined together to form a Public Affairs Committee, which challenged the government, with the result that a referendum was held, and free elections have now taken place. Christ is for all peoples, whether or not they akcnowledge His lordship yet.

Another essential perspective is that of pilgrims who build a temporary village but do not expect to be here for ever. It is a difficult balance to maintain. We must not neglect present misery and promise bliss which is entirely in the future, but neither should we expect to build a perfect society in our present circumstances, however correct we suppose our current ideology to be. Pilgrims who are genuinely moving should often find that their maps are no longer the right maps for the new roads on which they are travelling.

Although Paul's Epistles, and the Gospels, which were written later, forbid speculation about the actual date of the *parousia*, they do encourage watchfulness and authorize increased expectation when signs of end-time appear. Some observers argue that we may reasonably interpret the events of our own age as signs of end-time. But are we living in end-time as individuals facing premature death from AIDS, or in the end-time of our industry-based civilization or in final end-time for the whole of humanity? It is an unanswerable question, and one which biblical wisdom discourages. However, if we are indeed living through end-time of one or other kind, it may be worthwhile to rediscover the skills and attitudes our predecessors found useful when they lived through end-time in the past, or to examine the strategies of reconciliation and community building which are being used, in our own days, in societies which were recently split by racial or political rivalry.

In Mozambique a Conference for Reconciliation was held in September 1994, shortly before the election. The president of the Commission for Peace and Reconciliation and of the Christian Council in Mozambique, Bishop Dinis Sengulane, defined reconciliation as an effort to eliminate enmity, not enemies, and to protect the lives of all. He then outlined concrete proposals for the conduct of the elections, and for living with the results of voting later. He advocated dialogue, saying: 'What brought peace in Mozambique was a dialogue' – but few people know better than he does that peace was brought through effort, innumerable meetings, much travelling, many disappointments, prayer and fasting, too. At the end of the Conference Bishop Dinis preached, and like his Master, he picked up a child and used her to show that true greatness lies in being small. The same emphasis on secret, humble action, and the same willingness to be 'small' will be needed to change structures so that everyone, HIV-infected or not, can live and die with dignity in our communities.

A NEW HEAVEN AND A NEW EARTH

There are at least six common present-day theories about what follows death: nothing except personal extinction or the end of conscious existence (Western materialism); reincarnation in a new physical life as a different human being or as an animal (Hinduism and Buddhism); sad half-existence in a spirit world which may reflect events in this world (Spiritualism); a more lively but still partial place in community life as 'living dead' (African culture); escape from the cycle of birth and death into an event-less but peaceful state of being (Buddhist nirvana); and entry into a new sphere of life which fulfils and expands the potentials in human living which are frustrated in the physical world we know. There are several versions of this last theory, of which the Christian version is the only one to claim empirical supporting evidence in history. In this respect it competes with the first theory.

The first possibility builds on our experiences of efficient anaesthesia or of deep unconsciousness. It is the authorized version of end-time 'hope' for men and women who deny the reality of anything which is not accessible to their senses and who deny the reality of the event which 'rips a great hole in history' – as the resurrection of Jesus of Nazareth does (29).

It is difficult to write about 'a new heaven and a new earth'. For a start, prose is not adequate. A new creation demands the languages of poetry and myth; the symbolism of liturgy, of epic stories and of paradise-dreams; the public discourse of community celebrations and the private languages of lovers and parents with their children; the embodied visions of painting or sculpture; the mysterious sensual and spiritual language of music, and the presence-filled silences of prayer. If these non-mathematical languages are discounted in advance, then there can be no talk of a new heaven and a new earth.

But many people find that such non-mathematical languages actually gain credibility and power as they wrestle with the realities of living in a world with AIDS. At the Amsterdam Conference in 1992, when a group of HIV-infected and affected people from many different cultures came together to reflect on how they 'cope' with multiple losses, what emerged was a common experience of death and resurrection to new life, expressed through different cultural and faith-languages, in symbols, stories and music. It is because these symbols and stories have such positive power to influence present living and to move it forwards, that we dare to claim that they correspond to truth. In scientific thinking, only hypotheses which correspond to reality (however partially) move understanding forward; we ask for equal respect for the theory that a new heaven and a new earth lie beyond death.

Christians claim, however, that the crucial evidence for a new creation, which defeats evil and transcends death, already exists: Jesus was raised to new life after His well-attested death by crucifixion. The best explanation for the strange stories of the resurrection, and for the existence of Christianity apart from Judaism in the first century of our era, is that the resurrection actually happened. All alternative explanations fail at some point.

As we have little direct evidence for what a new heaven and a new earth might be like, is it right to attempt to 'describe' the fulfilment of life in the Kingdom? Yes, because hope needs content, and unguided human imagination constructs very strange fantasies! Neither Scripture nor tradition forbid attempts to anticipate our future state, using metaphor and pictorial language, providing we recognize that our pictures bear about the same relationship to the reality that awaits us as a child's first drawings of his parents bear to *their* reality. The Gospels report that Jesus constantly used metaphor when He talked about the Kingdom – 'the kingdom is like ... ' using concrete and homely examples. Scientists may reflect that they, too, make use of metaphor as a tool when they are developing hypotheses about the way things are.

Christian Scripture and tradition provide rich resources of vision and metaphor to direct imaginative anticipation, and there are neglected treasures in our own experiences of *kairos* and ecstasy. For brevity, I shall use 'Kingdom' to stand for 'a new heaven and a new earth'. I write (necessarily) within the limitations of Western culture and what I have experienced of present-day African culture: others must add their own symbols and visions drawn from other cultures.

DIMENSIONS OF HOPE

The most basic characteristics of the Kingdom, gleaned from the Gospels, seem to be surprise, an absurd generosity, reversal of most of our prudent human standards, healing and release from all limitations, growth, and the primacy of intimate relationship with God and relationships with other human beings. The atmosphere is one of homecoming and joyful celebration in the setting of a meal; the Gospels are full of stories about eating together and compelling outsiders to come in. There is no explicit mention of laughter but joy in the restoration of wholeness and beauty, and delight in human meeting, shine behind all the stories of healing and table-fellowship. There is nothing abstract about the Kingdom, as depicted in the Gospels; it is concrete, physical, earthy. When John the Baptist sent for reassurance that the Kingdom he had preached was indeed dawning the answer sent back was: 'The blind receive their sight . . . the lepers are cleansed' (Matt. 11.5).

The generosity of welcome into the Kingdom in the Gospels, and Jesus's explicit statements about it, forbid limitation of the Kingdom to dimensions which we can imagine now. God will give more than we deserve but also far more than we are capable of imagining and desiring, so we can hope that potentialities of which we are at present ignorant will unfold for us, and that *chronos*, clock-time, will become *kairos*, significant time. The meaning of events unfolds for us throughout our lives, as new experiences alter our memories and alter us. We may expect that in the Kingdom these different layers of meaning will not only provide a richer understanding of what we have experienced, but (perhaps) restore experience, purged of evil and suffering. A pagan writer suggested 'everything, all at once' as a description of heaven. Poetry is less limited than prose as a way of expressing the many levels of knowing and being.

'See, now they vanish,
The faces and places, with the self which, as it could, loved them,
To become renewed, transfigured, in another pattern.'(17).

John's vision of the apocalypse emphasizes the social character of the Kingdom, and repeats the Gospel themes of feasting, marriage, worship and celebration. Isolation and loneliness are emphatically temporary and this-worldly states: there everyone will 'belong' in the fullest possible way to the community of the Kingdom. Yet individuality will not be lost. In the apocalypse the dead are 'varied, both great and small'; they are judged individually, in accordance with what they have done before death; they are named (and in biblical culture, as

Figure 10. Hope assumes that change is possible, and as we saw (p. 253) there *is* true concern, now reaching a global scale, with unpredicted and hopeful beginnings in political and social systems, often in the developing world. Koinonia *is* being expressed, as in 1994 by the 'celebration of the century' in South Africa, and by this poster in a Maputo street to celebrate the first year of peace – 'Let us preserve it for ever!' – after a long civil war in Mozambique. And the same emphasis is needed, even at the price of suffering, so that everyone, HIV-infected or not, can live and die with dignity in our communities.

in many others, a name is not merely a label, but an expression of the nature of the person who bears it). Finally, to each one it is said: 'I will be his God and he a son to me' (Rev. 21.7,8). What we have been will be valued, so we shall not suffer the diminishment of having our past (and what our past has made us) either discounted or wasted.

We hope that injustice and suffering will end: 'there will be no more death, and no more mourning and sadness' (Rev. 21.4). An end to mourning implies that, from the perspective of the Kingdom, all the pain and suffering we have experienced here (including experience of AIDS) will no longer seem senseless, but will be discovered to have profound meaning – otherwise we should continue to mourn lost potential and opportunities. Many voices in tradition add that it is only as this shadow side of experience is finally integrated that human beings become whole, healed. Julian of Norwich goes even further when she sees our wounds turned into honours rather than eliminated, but she has the authority of the Gospels to support her vision, for we are told that the body of the risen Lord still bore the marks of His crucifixion.

'Now I am making the whole of creation new' and the totality of 'whole' is emphasized in the phrase 'a new heaven and a new earth'. We are to hope for cosmic re-creation. But the old is not scrapped, so we should hope for continuity and fulfilment of possibilities we have only half-seen here. Two common human experiences illustrate what those possibilities might be.

Music is – simultaneously – a sensual and a spiritual language; it stirs emotions, enhances sensual pleasures, expresses solidarity and builds community, especially for young people. But sometimes music seems to open a door between this world (of sense) and a more real reality which is at once familiar – and not yet known. Is this experience an illusion or due to the effects of complex chemicals (endorphins) released from the human brain in certain circumstances? Let us leave this question (like others) unanswered, and examine the experience itself more closely. When first heard, music often does not attract more than passing attention, but with repetition or deliberate study, patterns emerge and there comes a moment when it is 'heard' for the first time, and known at some deep level to be significant to the listener: 'this will be important to me'. As the patterns of a particular piece of music become familiar, the listener commonly anticipates a climax which the music seems to promise, but which is never (quite) reached, even when the experience is one of communion with 'music heard so deeply that it is not heard at all, but you are the music while the music lasts' (17). I suggest that the promise of 'more that we can desire' implies a fulfilment of this-world experiences which will be analogous to hearing at last the music we have loved reach its anticipated climax and move on to new peaks. For it is part of tradition to hope that we shall never have had enough of the joys of the Kingdom; they will not grow stale and we shall never reach the sadness of satiety. 'I will make all things new' is not a promise for a single event, but a promise that the new creation will have a dynamic perfection.

The picture of passive listening to music is less satisfactory than the related metaphor of *making* music, a metaphor used in Scripture and throughout tradition to express the corporate creativity of the Kingdom, where voices and instruments (no doubt expanding the range we know, and singing or playing with perfected talent), will each contribute to the whole, making new and joyful music to the glory of God.

Music is one form of communication, but all communication with one another in this sense-world is, at best, disappointingly incomplete and transient. We do make contact, but only for a limited time and in a limited way, for we can never convey the whole of what we mean in feeling or in thought. So often we are misunderstood, or our moods and ideas are mis-matched. Even in the closest friendships and in the best of marriages there are areas where we do not meet, for we cannot escape from our separateness and wholly indwell each other.

But tradition authorizes us to hope that the experience of one person will become the experience of all, so that the losses and diminishments of present life will no longer matter. It will no longer matter that one woman did not have children while others did, or that one man's life was short. The Gospel expects us to weep with those who weep, but when there are no longer any sorrows to share, all that will be left to share will be joy, and we shall have a perfected capacity to share that. In the words of Steve Biko, we shall indeed 'see you some more'.

Perhaps our present preoccupation with the complementarity of men and women, and our fear of each other's otherness is a sign that we are living in end-time. Certainly an 'end to mourning' will require healing of hostility and mistrust between men and women and restoration of joyful appreciation of each other. Meanwhile women hope that in the Kingdom their part in the image of God will be known at last, and that both feminine and masculine in humanity will be fully satisfied or transcended. 'God is not masculine. Neither is God feminine. God is the source of masculinity and femininity ... God's nature is reflected in the balance and interaction between them' (Lambeth Conference Resolution 1978).

In spite of present-day difficulties over relationships between men and women, the metaphor for life in the Kingdom which has the strongest support from Scripture, from tradition, and from experience remains that of the marriage relationship. In this metaphor we are authorized by tradition to include the courtship imagery of the Song of Songs, celebrating the first delighted recognition (now at last justified) of the Beloved's perfection, combined with passionate but tender (and therefore fully human) anticipation of sexual consummation. Now, however, this imagery is applied to the relationship between Christ and the Church, which is to be Christ's bride. If the promise of 'more than we can desire' is to be fulfilled, then we can hope that the joy and fruit-fulness of marriage between God and humankind in the Kingdom will exceed the greatest ecstasy human sexual and parental intimacy has to offer, and also exceed the (comparable) ecstasy of relationship with God in prayer.

But wedding ceremony and sexual consummation are only the beginning of a human marriage, which has many later significant moments. Alongside music as a metaphor for life in the Kingdom, the metaphor of relationship offers hope that the joy of consummation and of welcoming a longed-for first child, the delights of reunion after separation, all the festivals of a growing family and the silent unconsidered living in each other of maturity – will come together, in a multi-dimensional whole. Even the remembered sorrow of bereavement may be transfigured into joy, if mourning was the occasion when husband or wife was truly valued for the first time.

It may be rare for a married couple to so grow together, and so lovingly to heal each other's wounds, that their physical union is (even nearly) matched by mental and spiritual communion. Yet this is the goal of marriage and of human community: one new humanity, a separateness-in-unity and fruitfulness which mirror, in human scope, the relationship and creativity of the Trinity. Paul told Corinthian believers: 'You are all one person'. If this is potentially true for everyone and for all time, then together we are the Person created and redeemed for life with God, not in any external form of companion-ship, but 'hidden with Christ in God' in the Trinity.

Appendices

A. Bibliography and Further Reading

(1) *AIDS Analysis Africa*, Editorials Vol. 4 Nos 2, 4, 5, 6 1994; Vol. 5 No 1 1995.
(2) *AIDS Analysis Asia*, Editorials Vol. 1 Nos 1 and 2 1995.
(3) A. M. Allchin, S. Figess, Kallistos of Diokleia, W. Robinson, G. Rowell, S. Verney, R. Wickremasinghe, L. Woodhead, G. Woolfenden, *A Fearful Symmetry*. SPCK 1992.
(4) Hugh Anderson, *The Gospel of Mark*. Marshall, Morgan and Scott 1976.
(5) Norman Autton, *Pastoral Care of the Dying*. SPCK 1966.
(6) John Austin Baker, *The Foolishness of God*. Darton, Longman and Todd 1970.
(7) Tony Barnett and Piers Blaikie, *AIDS in Africa*. Belhaven Press 1992.
(8) Wendy Beckett, *The Gaze of Love*. Marshall Pickering 1993.
(9) Iulia de Beausobre, *Creative Suffering*. Fairacres Publication No 88, 1984 (first published Dacre Press 1940).
(10) Dietrich Bonhoeffer, *Life Together*. SCM Press 1954.
(11) Olivier Clement, *The Roots of Christian Mysticism*, New City London 1993.
(12) Werasit Sittitrai and Glen Williams, *Candles of Hope*, the AIDS programme of the Thai Red Cross Society. *Strategies for Hope* Booklet 9 1994.
(13) Current Science, *AIDS 1991 A Year in Review* 1992 and *AIDS 1993 A Year in Review* 1993.
(14) Jack Dominian, *Passionate and Compassionate Love*. Darton, Longman and Todd 1991.
(15) Joseph G. Donders, *Non-Bourgeois Theology*. Orbis 1986.
(16) Vincent Donovan, *Christianity Rediscovered*. SCM Press 1982.
(17) T. S. Eliot, *Four Quartets*. Faber & Faber 1944.
(18) Charles Elliott, *Praying the Kingdom*. Darton, Longman and Todd 1985.
(19) Paul Florensky, in *Seasons of the Spirit*, ed. G. Every, R. Harries, K. Ware. Triangle SPCK 1984.
(20) Nicholas Lash, *Why Theology?* Concilium 1994–6. SCM Press and Orbis 1994.
(21) G. Guiver, *Company of Voices*. SPCK 1988.
(22) Alan Haworth, *A study of the effects of AIDS upon the children of 112 Zambian families.*

(23) Edmund Hill, *Being Human*. Geoffrey Chapman 1984.
(24) Grace Jantzen, *Julian of Norwich*. SPCK 1987.
(25) Julian of Norwich, *Revelations of divine Love*, ed. Edmund Colledge and James Walsh. Paulist Press New York 1978.
(26) Hans Kung, *Global Responsibility*. SCM Press 1991.
(27) Morris Maddocks, *The Christian Healing Ministry*, SPCK 1981.
(28) Hugh Montefiore, ed. *The Gospel and Contemporary Culture*. Mowbray 1992.
(29) C. D. F. Moule, *The Phenomenon of the New Testament*. SCM Press 1967.
(30) National Society/Church House Publishing, *How Faith Grows*. 1992.
(31) Henri Nouwen, *Reaching Out*. Collins 1976, Fount Paperback 1980.
(32) A. S. Peake, *Commentary on the Bible*. Nelson 1962.
(33) John Polkinghorne, *Science and Christian Belief*. SPCK 1994.
(34) A. M. Ramsey, *God, Christ and the World*. SCM Press 1969.
(35) John Robinson, *The Human Face of God*. Xpress Reprints 1994.
(36) G. von Rad, *Genesis*. SCM Press 1961, 1972.
(37) Harry Sawyerr, *Creative Evangelism*. Lutterworth 1968.
(38) Edward Schillebeeckx, *Jesus*. Collins London 1974, Fount Paperback 1983.
(39) K. Stevenson and B. Spinks, *The Identity of Anglican Worship*. Mowbray 1991.
(40) John V. Taylor, *The Christlike God*. SCM Press 1992.
(41) John V. Taylor, *The Go-Between God*. SCM Press 1972.
(42) UNICEF, *The State of the World's Children 1992*. Oxford University Press 1992.
(43) UNICEF, *The State of the World's Children 1995*. Oxford University Press 1995.
(44) WHO, *Global Programme on AIDS*: 6-monthly bulletins on the global situation of the AIDS pandemic.
(45) Glen Williams and Sunanda Ray, *Work against AIDS. Strategies for Hope*. Booklet 8, 1993.
(46) Glen Williams and Nassali Tamale, *The Caring Community. Strategies for Hope*. Booklet 6, 1991.
(47) *AIDS in Subsaharan Africa* in *World Development* 1990.
(48) Society of St Francis, *Celebrating Common Prayer*. Mowbray 1992.
(49) *Lent, Holy Week and Easter, Services and Prayers*. Church House Publishing/Cambridge University Press 1984.
(50) Gerard Hughes, *God of Surprises*. Darton, Longman and Todd.
(51) Lesslie Newbigin, *The Other Side of 1984*. WCC 1984.

(52) *AIDS Prevention Research in the Developing World.* Vol. 9, Supplements 1–5, July 1995.

(53) J. W. Carswell, *Impact of AIDS in the Developing World*, in *AIDS and HIV Infection – the Wider Perspective*, eds A. J. Pinching, R. A. Weiss, D. Miller. *British Medical Bulletin.* Vol. 44, Churchill Livingstone 1988.

B. Glossary and Abbreviations

ACRONYM: standard abbreviation used to represent a longer name or phrase.

ANTHROPOMORPHIC: shaped like or modelled on human beings.

ANTIBODY: a specific protein produced in lymph tissue as part of body-defences against an antigen.

ANTIGEN: a substance (usually a protein) which is recognized as 'foreign' by the body's defences.

BACTERIA: simple one-cell organisms capable of independent life; some bacteria cause disease.

BISEXUAL: sexually attracted to both sexes.

BLUEPRINT: an outline drawing or plan from which a tool or building is constructed or a process of work carried out.

CATALYST: a thing or person whose presence causes or promotes change.

DEMOGRAPHIC ENTRAPMENT: describes the situation which exists when a population has outgrown its food supply.

DIAGRAM: a line drawing which represents an object or illustrates relationships.

ENDEMIC: a disease which occurs regularly in a given population or place.

ENLIGHTENMENT: a historical turning point in the 17th and 18th centuries when the 'rule of reason' and the idea of human autonomy introduced the age of science and democracy.

EPIDEMIC: frequent occurrence of one disease in a given population, with spread to more than one other person from each sufferer.

EPIDEMIOLOGY: a study of epidemics.

EXPONENTIAL: a quantity which grows more and more rapidly as it enlarges. For example a group of HIV-infected people grows faster and faster as the group enlarges and more and more people pass on HIV to their sexual partners.

FOETUS: an animal developing in the womb – in humans so-called after the 8th week of pregnancy when the main features and organs have formed.

FUNGUS (pl.–I): organisms with many cells which live in colonies usually on dead or dying plant or animal tissues some fungi cause disease.

GENE (n), GENETIC (adj.): genes carry the information needed to form a particular living creature and to control its physical functions.

HAEMOPHILIA: an inherited failure of blood to clot normally.

HETEROGENEOUS: mixed, differing in kind.

HETEROSEXUAL: sexually attracted to the opposite sex.

HOMOGENEOUS: the same or having the same nature.

HOMOSEXUAL: attracted to the same sex ('gay' if male, 'lesbian' if female).

IMMUNE: protected against a particular infection.

IMMUNODEﬁCIENCY: an inadequate body defence system.

INCIDENCE: how often an event or abnormality occurs in a specified *period of time* in a defined population.

INTRAVENOUS: in or injected into a vein.

KENOSIS: self-emptying.

LYMPH: a tissue fluid found outside blood vessels.

LYMPH NODE: sponge-like tissue which filters lymph and produces antibodies and defence-cells.

MACROECONOMIC: large-scale economics.

MICRO-ORGANISM: living organisms too small to be seen without a microscope.

MONOGAMOUS: married to only one partner of the opposite sex.

OPPORTUNISTIC: taking advantage of (a weak immune system, in the case of AIDS).

OVUM (pl.–A): an unfertilized egg-cell in a female.

PANDEMIC: simultaneous epidemics of the same disease in many countries or regions.

PATHOGENIC: capable of causing disease.

PER CAPITA: per head or per person.

POLYGAMOUS: married to more than one partner of the opposite sex.

PREVALENCE: how often an event or characteristic can be counted at a stated *point in time and space*, expressed as a rate within a given population.

RETROVIRUSES: a family of viruses which use RNA not DNA to carry genetic information; they depend upon host cells in order to multiply.

SCARIFICATION: scratching or cutting skin as part of traditional treatment of disease.

SCREENING: simple tests to seek hidden disease in people who appear well.

SENSITIVITY: capacity (of a test) to demonstrate a characteristic accurately and sensitively.

SERUM: fluid part of blood which separates from a clot.

SEROLOGY: any test performed using blood serum.

SERONEGATIVE: a negative result to a test done on serum.

SEROPOSITIVE: a positive result to a test done on serum.

SIGN (medical): a sign – usually of disease – detected by physical examination.

SYMPTOMS: unpleasant sensations reported by a sick person.

SYNDROME: a collection of symptoms and signs which do not add up to a single diagnosis.

SOCIETAL (adj.): belonging to society.

SPECIFIC, SPECIFICITY: confined to a single event or set of circumstances.

THEODICY: the attempt to defend the goodness of God, even though evil is mixed with good in the world we claim that God has created.

THEOPHANY: encounter with God.

TUMOUR: literally 'swelling'; usually refers to a cancer, or uncontrolled growth of new tissue that has no useful purpose, leading (if untreated) to death.

VIRULENCE: dangerous capacity to cause disease.

VIRUS: a simple organism, very small, survives only in the cells of a 'host'; some viruses cause disease.

ABBREVIATIONS

AIDS/SIDA: Acquired immune deficiency syndrome.

ARC: AIDS-related complex; early HIV-related disease.

AZT: Azidothymidine, the most widely tested and used drug to slow down the effects of HIV infection.

BCE: Before Christian or Common Era (same as BC).

BMB: British Medical Bulletin.

CE: Christian or Common Era (same as AD).

ddC and ddI: Drugs which slow down the effects of HIV infection, used less often than AZT.

DNA: The complex molecule which carries genetic information in the cells of most living creatures.

FAO: Food and Agriculture Organization.

GPA: Global Programme on AIDS, based at WHO from 1987.

GPCA: Global Policy Coalition on AIDS, in Boston, USA.

GNP: Gross National Product.

HCW: Health Care Worker.
HIV: Human immunodeficiency virus.
IMF: International Monetary Fund.
INAH: Isoniazid, cheap and effective oral drug for TB.
NACO (India): National AIDS Control Organization.
NGO: Non-governmental organization.
PCP: Pneumocystic carinii pneumonia, a common chest infection in HIV-infected Western patients.
RNA: The messenger molecule which is related to DNA.
STD: Sexually transmitted disease.
TB: Tuberculosis (illness) and also the bacteria causing TB.
UN: United Nations.
UNICEF: United Nations Children's Fund.
WB: World Bank.
WHO: World Health Organization.

C. Resources

This list suggests *sources* for educational materials, and for reliable new information about AIDS and related issues which is combined with responsible comment. The *organizations* and *publications* named are concerned with the impact of AIDS in developing countries and throughout the world. The material covers a wide range of topics, and much of it is supplied free or at low prices.

Continuing study of the situation will help concerned people to keep up to date as understanding of AIDS develops, see their local problems in a wider context, and learn about other people's successes (to stimulate hope) and also their failures (to avoid waste of time and effort). Accurate information and knowledge of what has been done elsewhere are essential for effective campaigns to change public opinion locally, and – where necessary – to change laws or government policies which maintain social conditions that promote spread of HIV, or worsen the impact of AIDS.

Sources are grouped under the following headings, with book, journal, film and video titles shown in italics:
1. International secular agencies;
2. International Church sources;
3. Regional agencies;

4. Programmes concerned with special groups: women, youth, refugees, street children, men who have sex with men, commercial sex workers;
5. Films, videos and media;
6. Directories and overviews.

1. INTERNATIONAL SECULAR AGENCIES

UNAIDS, the new Joint and Co-sponsored Programme on AIDS/HIV of the UN will use the present address of WHO.

WHO, World Health Organization, CH 1211 Geneva 27 Switzerland. Telex Unisante Geneva 415416, Fax 41 22 791 0317. Publishes *Living with AIDS in the Community*, an illustrated handbook, FREE, which can be copied or reproduced to meet local needs.

UNICEF, United Nations Children's Fund, UNICEF House, 3 UN Plaza, New York NY 10017 USA. For regional offices see local telephone directories.

UNDP, United Nations Development Programme, AIDS Programme, 1 UN Plaza, New York NY 10017 USA, Fax 1–212 906 5365. Publishes *Community Responses to HIV and AIDS*, experiences from India and Thailand, FREE, reproducible.

PANOS, The Panos Institute, Panos Publications Ltd, 9 White Lion Street, London N1 9PD UK, Fax 0171 278 0345. Dossiers on AIDS issues include: No 4. *Triple Jeopardy, Women and AIDS* 1990; No 6. *The Hidden Cost of AIDS, the Challenge of AIDS to Development* 1992, demographic impact, health and social costs, labour, food and agriculture; *WORLD AIDS*, a bi-monthly news magazine with global coverage, FREE to developing-world subscribers.

UK NGO AIDS Consortium for the Third World, Fenner Brockway House, 37/39 Great Guildford Street, London SE1 OES UK, Fax 0171 4012 2124, E-mail ukaidscon@gn.apc.org. Information about regional networks of NGOs.

AIDS Analysis Africa and *AIDS Analysis Asia*, **Suite 71, Ludgate House, 107–111 Fleet Street, London EC4A 2AB UK**, Fax 0107 353 1516, E-mail (Geonet) MCRI: Africa-Analysis and Asia-Analysis. Bi-monthly bulletins @ US$100 or £60 each a year (or £90 for both). Concise, accurate on political, economic, employment and social impacts and responses.

Current Science, **34 Cleveland Street, London W1P 5PB UK**, Fax 0171 580 1938. *AIDS 1991 A Year in Review* and *AIDS 1992 A Year in Review.*

Arid Lands Information Network, Casier Postal 3, Dakar-Fann, Senegal. Accurate cartoon-style educational booklets.

The Population Council, 1 Dag Hammarskjold Plaza, New York NY 10017. For Nairobi office see Regional list below.

SidAlerte Internationale, 7 rue du Lac, 69003 Lyon France. A network of community organizations and NGOs. Publishes *SidAlerte*, monthly journal in French about AIDS in tropics and sub-tropics, and *TB & HIV*, quarterly journal in English.

AHRTAG, Appropriate Health Resources & Technologies Action Group, Farringdon Point, 29–35 Farrington Road, London EC1M 3JB, Fax 0171-242 0041. Supports and provides information on a network of sex-industry related projects. Publishes *AIDS Action* quarterly, FREE, in English, French, Portuguese (for Africa and Brazil) and Spanish; also *Essential AIDS Information Resources* 1994 listing books, training materials, teaching tools, videos, catalogues, newsletters and resource guides; and *Practical Issues in HIV Testing* 1944 a briefing paper, both FREE to developing countries.

Child-to-Child Trust, Worldwide Health Education Charity, 20 Bedford Way, London WC1H OAP UK, Publishes *Children for Health* and booklets/packs to involve children as peer-educators (play, street and camp life, disability, disaster, AIDS readers and activities). TALC (see below) will supply list.

Save the Children Fun, HIV technical Adviser, 17 Grove Land, Camberwell, London SE1 8RD UK, Fax 0171 703 2278.

TALC, Teaching Aids at Low Cost, PO Box 49, St Albans, Herts AL1 4AX UK, Fax 01727 846852. Distributes *Strategies for Hope* booklets (10 in print in 1995) and videos in English and French. See Videos and Media list (below), Bibliography and Further Reading section for some individual titles.

Action Aid, Hamlyn House, MacDonald Road, London N19 5PG UK, Fax 0171-263 7599. Supports development Projects.

IPPF, International Planned Parenthood Federation, The AIDS Prevention Unit, PO Box 759, Inner Circle, Regents Park, London NW1 4NS UK. Publishes *Preventing a Crisis, AIDS and Family Planning* 1989.

OXFAM, Health Policy Adviser, 274 Banbury Road, Oxford OX2 7DZ UK. Fax 01865 312600.

Daniels Publishing, Barton, Cambridge CB3 7BB UK, Fax 01223 264888. PHOTOCOPY FREE Educational Resources: 6 different AIDS packs, sample sheets available on request.

CAB International, Wallingford, Oxon OX10 8DE UK, Fax 01491 883508. Publishes *AIDS Newsletter* every 3 weeks @ £99 a year: summarizes global reports in media and technical press, with medical/social bias.

ICASO, International Council of AIDS Services Organizations, Central Secretariat, c\o Canadian AIDS Society, 701 Sparks Street, Ottawa, Ontario, Canada K1P 5B7. An international network of community-based organizations for AIDS prevention and the care

and treatment of people living with HIV/AIDS. Secretariats in Europe and North America, and: **Latin America and the Caribbean Secretariat, c/o Colectivo Sol, Apartado Postal 13–320 Mexico DF, 03500 Mexico.**
African Regional Secretariat, c/o Enda TM 4, rue Kieber, BP 3370 Dakar, Senegal.
Asia/Pacific Regional Secretariat, Kabalikat Ng Pamilyang Pilipino, Unit 104, First Midland Condominium, Gamboa Street, Legaspi Village, Makati, Metro Manila, Philippines.
Global AIDS Policy Coalition, Harvard School of Public Health, 677 Huntington Avenue, Boston, MA 12110 USA, Fax 1–617 432 4310. An independent network of professionals promoting socially committed prevention and control programmes.
RISCT, Research Institute for the Study of Conflict and Terrorism, 136 Baker Street, London W1M 1FH UK,

2. INTERNATIONAL CHURCH SOURCES

World Council of Churches, 150 Route de Ferney, PO Box 2100, CH 1211 Geneva 2, Switzerland. Publications: *Making Connections, Facing AIDS*, FREE HIV/AIDS resource book published by YouthTeam of WCC; *Living in Covenant with God and One Another*, a study guide on sexuality and human relations 1990, suitable for study groups.
CAFOD, Catholic Fund for Overseas Development, AIDS Section, 2 Romero Close, Stockwell Road, London SW9 9TY UK, Fax 0171 274 9630. Publishes information and *AIDS and Development* pack.
Caritas Internationalis, contact through **CAFOD**. Roman Catholic organization concerned about development issues, including AIDS. See also Directories list below.
ICAN, International Christian AIDS/HIV Network, c/o The Basement, 178 Lancaster Road, London W11 1QU UK.
London Churches HIV/AIDS Unit, St Paul's Church, Lorrimore Square, London SE17 3QU UK. Networking in London.
Institute for the Study of Christianity and Sexuality, Oxford House, Derbyshire Street, E2 6HG UK. Mainly Western preoccupations, but good resources.
USPG, United Society for the Propagation of the Gospel, 157 Waterloo Road, London SE1 8XA UK, Fax 0171 928 2371.
HIV/AIDS Ministries Network. United Methodist Church, Room 350, 475 Riverside Drive, New York NY 10115 USA. Internet aidsmin@gbgm-umc.org. Focus papers (with a USA bias) are published by Health and Welfare Ministries Program Development, General Board of Global Ministries.

Christian Aid, PO Box 100, Interchurch House, 35–41 Lower Marsh, London SE1 7RT UK.

Africa Christian Press, PO Box 30, Achimota, Ghana. Publishes *AIDS, Sex and Family Planning, a Christian View*, for individuals or small groups, upper primary level.

SJ Mission Press, PO Box 71581, Ndola, Zambia. Publishes *Calming the Storm* by Robert Kelly, short, pastoral, easy to read but profound.

TASO, The Aids Service Organization, PO Box 10443, Kampala, Uganda and WASN Book Project, PO Box 1554, Harare, Zimbabwe (Attention Sunanda Ray), distribute *We Miss You All* by Noerine Kaleeba, written from a Christian standpoint.

3. REGIONAL AGENCIES AND NGO CONSORTIA

SANASO, PO Box 6690, Harare, Zimbabwe, Fax 263 4 720 801. A network of AIDS service NGOs in Southern Africa.

TASO, address as above in Church Sources list, Fax 256 41 244642. Information and training.

AMREF, African Medical and Research Foundation, AIDS Control Programme, Wilson Airport, PO Box 30125, Nairobi, Kenya. Publications and information.

AREPP, African Research and Educational Puppetry Programme, PO Box 51022, Radene, 2124 Johannesburg, South Africa, Fax 27–1 483 1786. AIDS education through puppets.

The Population Council, PO Box 17643, Nairobi, Kenya. Publishes information and case studies on community-based AIDS prevention and care in Africa.

4. PROGRAMMES CONCERNED WITH SPECIAL GROUPS

Women

Harper Collins, 77–85 Fulham Palace Road, London W6 8JB Fax 0181-307 4440, distributes *Women and AIDS* ISBN 0-04-440876-5 (1st pub. by Pandora Press). Handbook listing comprehensive international resources.

SWAA, Society for Women and AIDS in Africa. Contact **Dr Nkandu Luo, Secretary, University Teaching Hospital, PO Box 50110, Lusaka, Zambia** or local offices. A network of national organizations devoted to education and support for African women affected by AIDS, changing social norms that increase women's risk of infection.

Mothers' Union Overseas Department, 24 Tufton Street, London SW1P 3RB UK, Fax 0171 222 1591.

Youth

Child-to-Child Trust, address as above in International Secular list, or contact UNICEF or TALC in that list.

Anti-AIDS Clubs (Zambia), Anti-AIDS project, Private Bag RW 75 X, 15102 Ridgeway, Lusaka, Zambia. Information, magazines, support for primary and secondary-aged groups in schools or in the community.

Youth Alive (Uganda), c/o Kamwokya Community, PO Box 555, Kampala, Uganda. Information, training for prevention.

Street Children

AHRTAG, address as in International Secular list above. Publishes *Resource Pack on Sexual Health and AIDS Prevention for Socially Apart Youth* 1993, ISBN 0–907320–24–4. FREE to groups concerned with street children in developing countries, otherwise £5 sterling or US$10. Any part can be reproduced without permission provided distribution is free or at low cost and source is acknowledged. Lists newsletters, training materials, games, posters, comics, videos, books and articles (with samples). Addresses and brief descriptions of 300 organizations worldwide concerned with 'socially apart youth', region by region, from a larger database held by AHRTAG and the Brazilian Center for the Defence of the Rights of Children and Adolescents; index identifies resources that are free, specific to AIDS or to developing countries. Also obtainable from **Centro Brasileiro de Defesa dos Direitos da Crianca e do Adolescente (SOS Crianca), Caixa Postal 4884, Ag. Central, CEP 20 100, Rio de Janeiro, RJ Brazil**.

Men who have Sex with Men

Terrence Higgins Trust, 52 Gray's Inn Road, London WC1X 8JU UK, Fax 242 0121. Information, publications, library.

Commercial Sex-workers

AHRTAG, address as in International Secular list above. Network of Sex-work Related HIV/AIDS Projects.

Refugees

UK NGO AIDS Consortium, address as in International Secular list above. Contact Sue Lucas for material in preparation.

5. FILMS, VIDEOS AND MEDIA

Media for Development International, PO Box 281, Columbia MD 21045 USA, Fax 410 730–8322. Promotes development through communications, mobile film and video units. Film *Children Under Stress*, on needs or orphans; Video *The Faces of AIDS*.

TASO, address as in Regional Agencies list above. Videos (Strategies for Hope) *Living Positively with AIDS* and *The Orphan Generation*.

DSR Inc., 9650 Santiago Road £10, Columbia MD 21045 USA. Distributes Video *"It is not easy . . .".*

Folens Publishers, Albert House, Apex Business Centre, Boscombe Road, Dunstable LU5 4RL UK, Fax 01582 472575. Issues Information Pack with Video *Your Choice or Mine? HIV Education for Young People*, price £39.99 p.&p.

Health Education Authority, Marston Book Services Ltd, PO Box 87 Oxford OX2 0DT UK, Fax 01865 791927. Issues, with Merchant Navy Welfare Board, Video and Leaflet *HIV and AIDS Information for Seafarers*, versions in English, Polish, Portuguese, Spanish and Tagalog, price £15 p.&p. to purchasers outside UK.

6. DIRECTORIES AND OVERVIEWS

UK NGO AIDS Consortium, address as in International Secular list above. *Directory of European Funders of HIV/AIDS Projects* 2nd edition 1993, FREE to developing countries.

General Secretariat, Palazzo San Caisto, V-00120 Citta del Vaticano, Rome, Italy, cable address: Intercaritas, Rome. *Caritas Internationalis* lists staff and addresses for Africa, Asia/Oceania, Europe, Latin America, Middle East/North Africa and North America.

Bistandsinformation/FOI, Hornsgatan 54, S-117 21 Stockholm, Sweden publishes *Swedish NGOs in Development and Solidarity* 1988, single copies FREE, specify Language.

National Committee on AIDS Control, Poldeweg 92, NL-1093 KP Amsterdam, The Netherlands Distributes *AIDS and Mobility* 1993 ISBN 90–73177–31–6. Material about AIDS for ethnic minorities and migrant communities, in English.

WHO, UNAIDS or UK NGO AIDS Consortium, addresses in International Secular list above, distribute *Inventory of Nongovernmental Organizations working on AIDS in countries that receive development co-operation or assistance* 1991.

Overviews

UNICEF, address as in International Secular list above, issues *Action for Children affected by AIDS* ISBN 92 806 3149 7. Global perspective and detail from 7 countries, text of Lusaka Declaration of 1994.

WHO Office of Publications, address as in International Secular list above, *AIDS, Images of the Epidemic*, 1994 ISBN 92 4–156163–7.

Index

This combined index lists proper names of persons and places, as well as main references to the wide range of topics relating to the HIV/ AIDS pandemic, and to its social, economic and theological implications, which are discussed in the book.